M000307571

THE KINGS
BEFORE THE
NORMAN
CONQUEST

WILLIAM OF MALMESBURY

THE KINGS BEFORE
THE NORMAN CONQUEST

Translated from Latin
by Joseph Stephenson

First published by Seeleys of London.
Facsimile reprint from the series
The Church Historians of England
published in 1989 by **Llanerch Enterprises**
ISBN 0947992 32 4

MALMESBURY'S

HISTORY OF THE KINGS.

THE AUTHOR'S EPISTLE[1] TO ROBERT EARL OF GLOUCESTER, SON OF KING HENRY THE FIRST.[2]

To my respected lord, the renowned earl Robert, son of the king, greeting; and, if aught they may avail, his prayers, from William, monk of Malmesbury.

The virtue of celebrated men holds forth as its greatest excellence, its tendency to excite the love of persons even far removed from it: hence the lower classes make the virtues of their superiors their own, by venerating those great actions to the practice of which they themselves cannot aspire. Moreover it redounds altogether to the glory of exalted characters, both that they do good, and that they gain the affection of their inferiors. To you therefore, princes, it is owing that we act well; to you, indeed, that we compose anything worthy of remembrance : your exertions incite us to make you live for ever in our writings, in return for the dangers which you undergo to secure our tranquillity. For this reason I have deemed it proper to dedicate the History of the Kings of England, which I have lately published, more especially to you, my respected and truly amiable lord. None surely can be a more suitable patron of the liberal arts than yourself, in whom combine the magnanimity of your grandfather, the munificence of your uncle,[3] the circumspection of your father ; more especially as you add to the qualities of these men, whom while you equal in industry, you resemble in person, this characteristic peculiarly your own, a devotion to learning. Nor is this all : you even condescend to honour with your notice, those literary characters who are kept in obscurity either by the malevolence of fame, or the slenderness of their fortune. And as our nature inclines us not to condemn in others what we approve in ourselves, therefore men of learning find in you manners which are congenial to their own ; for, without

---

[1] In two MSS. (D.E.) this dedication occurs at the end of the third book; in two others (C.K.) it appears at the commencement of the work; but in others (A.G. H.L.) it is not found at all.

[2] Robert earl of Gloucester was one of the natural children of Henry I. He married Maud, or Mabell as she is sometimes called, the eldest co-heir of Robert Fitz-Hamon, and in her right had the honour of Gloucester. He died on the 31st of October, 1147. Dugd. Baron. i. 534.

[3] An allusion probably to Robert duke of Normandy, to whose munificence Malmesbury more than once alludes in this work.

4

the slightest indication of moroseness, you regard them with kindness, admit them with complacency, and dismiss them with regret.[1] Indeed, the greatness of your fortune has made no difference in you, except that your beneficence can now almost keep pace with your inclination.

Accept then, most illustrious sir, a work in which you may contemplate yourself as in a glass, where your highness's sagacity will discover that you have imitated the actions of the most exalted characters, even before you could have heard their names. The preface to the first book declares the contents of the work; on deigning to peruse which, you will briefly collect the whole subject-matter. Thus much I must request from your excellency, that no blame may attach to me because my narrative often wanders wide from the limits of England, since I design this as a compendium of many histories, although, with reference to the larger portion of it, I have entitled it an "History of the Kings of England."

PREFACE.

Here begins the Prologue of William, Monk of Malmesbury, to the First Book of the History of the Kings of England.

THE history of the English, from their arrival in Britain to his own times, has been written by Beda, a man of singular learning and modesty, in a clear and captivating style.[2] After him you will not, in my opinion, easily find any person who has attempted to compose the history of this people in Latin. Let others declare if their researches in this respect have been, or are likely to be, fortunate: mine, though diligent in the extreme, have down to this period been without reward. There are indeed some notices of antiquity, written in the vernacular tongue after the manner of a chronicle,[3] and arranged according to the years of our Lord. By means of these, the times succeeding this man have escaped the canker of oblivion: for of Elward,[4] a noble and illustrious character, who attempted to arrange these chronicles in Latin, and whose intention I could applaud if his language did not disgust me, it were better to be silent. It has not escaped my knowledge that there is also a work of Edmer,[5] written with a chastened elegance

---

[1] V. R. "with presents."

[2] Venerable Beda, who died in A.D. 735, wrote, besides a great number of other works, "The Ecclesiastical History of the English," which is here referred to, and of which a translation has already been given.

[3] Reference is here made to the Saxon Chronicle, a translation of which has been given in the second volume of this Collection of Historians.

[4] Elward, or, as he is more commonly designated, Ethelwerd, was descended from Ethelred, the brother of king Alfred. His work, consisting of an abridged translation into Latin of the Saxon Chronicle, merits the censure pronounced upon it by Malmesbury. Yet it is too important to be passed over, and accordingly a translation of it has already been given in the present series of writers, ii. 405.

[5] Eadmer, a monk and precentor of Canterbury, wrote a history of his own times, extending to the year 1122. It will be found in its proper place in our series.

of style; in which, beginning from king Edgar, he hastily glances at the times down to William the First; and thence, taking a freer range, gives a narrative, copious, and of great utility to the studious, until the death of archbishop Anselm.[1] Thus, from the time of Beda, there is a period of two hundred and twenty-three years left unnoticed in his history; so that the regular series of time, unsupported by written evidence, halts in the middle. This circumstance has induced me, as well out of love to my country as respect for the authority of those who have enjoined me the undertaking, to fill up the chasm, and to season the crude materials with Roman art; and that the work may proceed with greater regularity, I shall cull somewhat from Beda, whom I must often quote, glancing at a few facts, but omitting more.

The first book, therefore, contains a succinct account of the English, from the time of their descent on Britain till that of king Egbert, who obtained the monarchy of almost the whole island; its former potentates having been dispatched by various fates.

But as among the English arose four very powerful kingdoms, that is to say, those of Kent, of the West Saxons, of the Northumbrians, and of the Mercians, of which I purpose severally to treat, if I have leisure, I shall begin with that which attained the earliest maturity, and was also the first to decay. This I shall do more clearly, if I place the kingdoms of the East Angles and of the East Saxons after the others, as not meriting either my labours, or the regard of posterity.

The second book will contain the history of the kings till the coming of the Normans.

The three following books will be employed upon the history of three successive kings, with the addition of whatever in their times happened elsewhere, which from its celebrity may demand a more particular notice.

This then is what I purpose, if the Divine favour shall smile on my undertaking, and carry me safely by those rocks of rugged diction, on which Elward, in his search after sounding and far-fetched phrases, so unhappily suffered shipwreck. "Should any one, however," to use the poet's expression,

"Peruse this work with sensible delight,"[2]

I deem it necessary to acquaint him, that I vouch nothing for the truth of long past transactions, but the consonance of the period: the veracity of the relation itself must rest with its authors. Whatever I have recorded of later times, I have either myself seen, or heard from credible authority. Moreover in either part, I pay but little respect to the judgment of my contemporaries, trusting that I shall gain with posterity, when love and hatred shall be no more, if not the reputation of eloquence, at least the credit of industry.

[1] Here some MSS. (C.K.) read "Ralph;" others, as in the text, "Anselm." (A. D.E.F.G.H.L.M.) Eadmer's first edition of his history ended with the death of Anselm; but, on a second revision of the work, he continued it as far as the death of Ralph, in 1122.   [2] Virg. Eclog. vi. 10.

THE HISTORY, &c.

BOOK I.

§ 1. In the year of the incarnation of our Lord four hundred and forty-nine,[1] came the Angles and Saxons into Britain; and although the cause of their arrival be universally known, it may not be improper here to subjoin it: and, that the design of my work may be the more manifest, I shall begin even from an earlier period. That Britain, compelled by Julius Cæsar to submit to the Roman power, was held in high estimation by that people, may be collected from their history, and be seen also in the ruins of their ancient buildings. Even their emperors, sovereigns of almost all the world, eagerly embraced opportunities of sailing hither, and of spending their days here. Finally, Severus and Constantius, two of their greatest princes, died[2] upon the island, and were there interred with the highest pomp. The former, to defend this province from the incursion of the barbarians, built his celebrated and well-known wall from sea to sea. The latter, a man, as they report, of courteous manners, left Constantine,[3] his son by Helena, a tender of cattle,[4] a youth of great promise, his heir. Constantine, greeted emperor by the army, led away, in an expedition destined to the continent, a numerous force of British soldiers, by whose exertions, the war succeeding to his wishes, he gained in a short time the summit of power. For these deserving veterans, when their toil was over, he founded a colony on the western coast of Gaul, where to this day their descendants, somewhat differing in language and manners from their parent stock, remain with wonderful increase.[5]

§ 2. In succeeding times, in this island, Maximus,[6] a man well fitted for command, had he not aspired to power in defiance of his oath, assumed the purple, as though compelled by the army, and preparing immediately for his passage over into Gaul, he despoiled the province of almost all its military force. Not long after, also, one Constantine,[7] who had been elected emperor there on account of his name, drained its whole remaining warlike strength; but

---

[1] Some MSS. (A.D.L.M.) read 469.

[2] Severus died 4th Feb. A.D. 211, at York, where also died Constantius, 25th July, 306.　　　　　[3] Constantine the Great.

[4] "Ex Helena stabularia." Helena's origin has been much contested: Gibbon decides that she was daughter of an innkeeper. The word "stabularia" literally implies an Ostler-wench; and it has been conjectured that it was applied to her, by the Jews and heathen, on account of her building a church on the spot where stood the stable in which our Lord was born. On this question see Ussher, Brit. Eccl. Antiq. p. 97, ed. fol. Lond. 1687.

[5] According to Gildas and Beda, Britain owed its first ruin to Maximus, who carried with him into Gaul the youthful and military population of the country. Archbishop Ussher, who has diligently collected the continental legends respecting our island, states, (Antiq. Brit. Eccles. pp. 107, 108,) that the whole emigration consisted of thirty thousand soldiers, and one hundred thousand plebeians, who settled in Bretagne. Various periods, however, have been assigned for the British settlement there, and great obscurity still prevails on the subject.

[6] Ussher, id. pp. 309, 310.　　　　　　　　　　[7] Id. p. 308.

both being slain, the one by Theodosius, the other by Honorius, they became examples of the instability of human greatness. Of the forces which followed them, part shared the fate of their leaders; the rest fled to the continental Britons.[1] Thus, when these ambitious men had left none but half-savages in the country, and, in the towns, those only who were given up to luxury, Britain, despoiled of the support of its youthful[2] population, and bereft of every useful art, became for a long time subject to the rapacity of neighbouring nations.

not migration

§ 3. For immediately, by an incursion of the Scots and Picts, numbers of the people were slain, their villages burnt, their towns destroyed, and everything laid waste by fire and sword. Of the harassed islanders, who thought anything more advisable than contending in battle, some fled for safety to the mountains; others, burying their treasures in the earth, many of which are dug up in these present times, proceeded to Rome to ask assistance. The Romans touched with pity, and deeming nothing more important than yielding succour[3] to the faltering condition of their allies, twice extended their aid, and defeated the enemy. But at length, wearied with the distant voyage, they decline returning in future; exhorting them not to degenerate from the martial energy of their ancestors, but to learn to defend their country with spirit and with arms. They accompany their advice with the plan of a wall, to be built for their defence; the mode of keeping watch on the ramparts; of sallying out against an enemy, should it be necessary; together with other duties of military discipline. After giving these admonitions, they depart,[4] accompanied by the tears of the miserable inhabitants; and favouring fortune, smiling on their progress, restored them to their country. The Scots, learning the improbability of their return, immediately began to make fresh and more than usual irruptions against the Britons, to level their wall, to kill the few opponents they met with, and to carry off considerable booty; while those who escaped flew to the royal residence, imploring the protection of their sovereign.

§ 4. At this time Vortigern was king of Britain; a man calculated neither for the field nor the council, but wholly given up to the lusts of the flesh, the slave of every vice, a character of insatiable avarice, ungovernable pride, unquenchable lust. To complete the picture, as we read in the History of the Britons,[5] he had defiled his own daughter, who was lured to the participation of such a crime by the hope of sharing his kingdom, and she had borne him a son. Regardless of treasure at this dreadful juncture, and wasting the resources of the kingdom in riotous living, he was awake only to the blandishments of abandoned women. Roused at length, however, by the clamours of the people, he summons a

[1] "ad superiores Britannos."—Orig.

[2] Instead of "youthful," C. and S. read "military."

[3] On these embassies to Rome for assistance, and their results, see Ussher, id. pp. 335, 594, 595.

[4] The precise time when the Romans finally quitted Britain is still involved in the greatest obscurity.

[5] Malmesbury here alludes to the History of Nennius, § 39.

council, to take the sense of his nobility on the state of public
affairs. To be brief, it was unanimously resolved to invite[1] over
from Germany the Angles and Saxons, nations powerful in arms,
but of a roving life. It was conceived that this would be for their
mutual advantage: by their skill in war, it was said these people
would easily subdue their enemies; and, having no certain habitation, would in return gladly accept even an unproductive soil,
provided it afforded them a stationary residence; moreover, that
they could not be suspected of ever entertaining a design against
the country, since the remembrance of this kindness would soften
their native ferocity. This counsel was adopted, and ambassadors,
men of rank, and worthy to represent the country, were sent into
Germany.

§ 5. The Germans, hearing that very thing voluntarily offered,
which they had long anxiously desired, readily accepted the invitation; their joy quickening their haste. Bidding adieu therefore to
their native fields, and renouncing the ties of kindred, they spread
their sails to fortune, and, with a favouring breeze, arrive[2] in Britain
in three of those long vessels which they call "ceols."[3] At this
and other times, came over a mixed multitude from three[4] of
the German nations; that is to say, Angles, Saxons, and Jutes.[5]
Indeed, almost all the country lying to the north of the British
ocean, though divided into many provinces, is justly denominated
Germany, from its germinating so many men. And as the pruner
cuts off the more luxuriant branches of the tree to impart a livelier
vigour to the remainder, so the inhabitants of this country assist
their common parent by the expulsion of a part of their members,
lest she should perish by giving sustenance to too numerous an
offspring; but, in order to obviate discontent, they cast lots who
shall be compelled to migrate. Hence the men of this country
have made a virtue of necessity, and, when driven from their native
soil, have gained foreign settlements by force of arms: as did the
Vandals, for instance, who formerly overran Africa; the Goths,
who made themselves masters of Spain; the Lombards, who, even
at the present time, are settled in Italy; and the Normans, who
have given their own name to that part of Gaul which they subdued. From Germany, then, came at first into Britain an incon-

---

[1] This invitation is supposed by Pagi (Critica in Baronium) to have been given
in the year 447. From the testimony of Nennius, it might be inferred that the
arrival of Hors and Hengist was more by accident than design; "Interea venerunt
tres ciulæ a Germannia expulsæ in exilio, in quibus erant Hors et Hengist" (§ 31);
but it is probable that the lot of exile had fallen upon them according to the
custom of emigration among the Germans, as narrated by Malmesbury, § 5.

[2] The year 449 is that which is usually assigned for the first arrival of the
Saxons in England under Hengist and Hors; but this date must be accepted
with much caution, as there is very strong evidence to show that they had gained
a footing in this island many years before this date.

[3] This term is still retained as the name for the vessels used in the coal trade
on the Tyne and Wear.

[4] Concerning the tide of immigration into England generally, and these three
nations in particular, see the investigations of Dr. Latham, in his work on "The
English Language," E. H. § 15, ed. Lond. 1850.

[5] One MS. (Claud. c. ix.) reads "Wichtis," a variation, the importance of which
will be seen by reference to the work last quoted, § 16. The same reading is
repeated at the end of this paragraph.

siderable number indeed, but well able by their courage to make up for their paucity. They were under the conduct of Hengist and Hors, two brothers of suitable disposition, and of noble race in their own country. They were great-grandsons of that most celebrated Woden, from whom almost all the royal families of these barbarous nations deduce their origin, and to whom the nations of the Angles, fondly deifying him, have consecrated by immemorial superstition the fourth day of the week, as they have the sixth to his wife Frea. Beda[1] has related in what particular parts of Britain the Angles, Saxons, and Jutes fixed their habitations: my design, however, is not to dilate, though there be abundance of materials for the purpose, but to touch only on what is necessary.

§ 6. The Angles were eagerly met on all sides upon their arrival:[2] from the king they received thanks, from the people expressions of good-will. Faith was plighted on either side, and the Isle of Thanet was appropriated for their residence. It was agreed, moreover, that they should exert their invincible prowess in arms for the service of the country; and should, in return, receive soldiers' pay from the people whose safety they watched over. Ere long the Angles make an attack upon the Scots, who were advancing upon them, and as usual secure, as they supposed, of a great booty with very little difficulty. However, scarcely had they engaged before they were put to flight, the cavalry pursuing and destroying the fugitives. Contests of this kind were frequent; and, victory constantly siding with the Angles, it happened, as is customary in human affairs, that while success inflamed the courage of one party, dread increased the cowardice of the other, and so the Scots in the end avoided nothing so cautiously as an engagement with the Angles.

§ 7. In the meantime Hengist, not less keen in perception than ardent in the field, (Vortigern not objecting,) sends back some of his followers to his own country, for the purpose of representing the indolence of the king and people, the opulence of the island, and the prospect of advantage which it afforded to new adventurers. Having executed their commission adroitly, in a short time they return with sixteen ships, bringing with them the daughter[3] of Hengist, a maiden (as we have heard) who might justly be called the master-piece of nature, and the admiration of mankind. At an entertainment provided for them on their return, Hengist commanded his daughter to assume the office of cup-bearer, that she might gratify the eyes of the king as he sat at table. Nor was the design unsuccessful; for he, ever neighing after female beauty, deeply smitten with the gracefulness of her form and the elegance of her carriage, instantly conceived a vehement desire for the possession of her person, and immediately proposed marriage to her father; urging him to a measure to which he was already more

[1] Eccl. Hist. i. 25.

[2] The current tradition is, that they landed at Ebbsfleet, in the island of Thanet.

[3] Geoffrey of Monmouth is the first writer who gives her name; he calls her Ronwen, vi. xii.

than sufficiently inclined. Hengist, at first, kept up the artifice by a refusal, stating that so humble a connexion was disgraceful to a king; but at last, appearing to consent with reluctance, he gave way to his importunities, and accepted, as a reward, the whole of Kent, where all justice had long since declined under the administration of a "Gorong,"[1] who, like the other potentates of the island, was subject to the monarchy of Vortigern. Not satisfied with this liberality, but abusing the imprudence of the king, the barbarian persuaded him to send for his brother and son,[2] men of warlike talents, from Germany, pretending that he would defend the province on the east, while they might curb the Scots on the northern frontier. The king assenting, they arrived at the Orkney Isles; after sailing round Britain, and involving those people, together with the Picts and Scots, in equal calamity, at this and after times, they settled in the northern part of the island, now called Northumbria. Still no one there assumed the royal title or ornaments till the time of Ida, from whom sprang the regal line of the Northumbrians; but of this hereafter. Now to the present labour.

Concerning Wortemer, the Son of Vortigern; and of Arthur.

§ 8. Wortemer, the son of Vortigern, thinking it unnecessary longer to dissemble that he saw himself and his Britons circumvented by the craft of the Angles, turned his thoughts to their expulsion, and stimulated his father to make the attempt. At his suggestion, the truce was broken seven years after their arrival; and during the ensuing twenty, they had frequent skirmishes,[3] and, as the Chronicle[4] relates, four general actions. From the first conflict they retired on equal terms: one party deeply lamenting the loss of Hors,[5] the brother of Hengist; the other, that of Katigis,[6] another of Vortigern's sons. The Angles having the advantage in all succeeding encounters, peace was concluded; Wortemer, the instigator of the war, being taken off by an untimely fate; he, far differing from the indolence of his father, would have

---

[1] Hardy remarks that "this word has been frequently mistaken for a proper name, and that Camden defines a Guorong to be a viceroy or freeman. See Camd. Brit. col. 187, edit. Gibson. Lond. 1695."

[2] Ebusa and Otha were the names of Hengist's brother and son. See § 8, ad fin.; and § 44, ad init.

[3] For an account of his battles, and the subsequent treachery of the Saxons, see Nennius, § 43, 44, 45; and compare Matth. Westm. an. 460, et seq., who has incorporated the British accounts into his Chronicle.

[4] Malmesbury alludes to the Saxon Chronicle, which gives these dates of the battles: at Æglesford (Aylesford, on the Medway), A. D. 455; at Crecanford (Crayford), in 457; at Wyppedesfleote (Ebbsfleet, in the Isle of Thanet, near Stonar), in 465; and the fourth in the year 473, the place not mentioned. Nennius, § 44, describes the battles as having been fought, "super flumen Derevent" (Darent, in Kent, probably at the spot where it is joined by the Cray), at Episford, or Rit Hergabail, supposed to be Aylesford, and "in campo juxta Lapidem tituli" (Stonar, in the Isle of Thanet; by some, Folkstone, in Kent).

[5] Hors was slain at the battle of Aylesford in 455, and is supposed to have been buried at Horsted, in Kent. See Beda, § 35. Nennius calls the battle Episford.

[6] Called by Nennius Categirn, and mentioned as the second son of Wyrtgeorne.

governed the kingdom in a noble manner, had God permitted. When this man died, the British strength decayed; their hopes, becoming diminished, fled; and they would have soon perished altogether, had not Ambrosius,[1] the sole survivor of the Romans, who became monarch after Vortigern, quelled the presumptuous barbarians by the powerful aid of warlike Arthur. This is that Arthur,[2] of whom the Britons fondly fable[3] even to the present day; a man worthy to be celebrated, not by idle fictions, but in authentic history. He, indeed, for a long time upheld the sinking state, and roused the broken spirit of his countrymen to war. Finally, at the siege[4] of Mount Badon,[5] relying on an image[6] of the Virgin which he had affixed to his armour, he engaged nine hundred of the enemy single-handed, and dispersed them with incredible slaughter. On the other side, the Angles, although they underwent great vicissitudes of fortune, filled up their wavering battalions with fresh supplies of their countrymen; rushed with greater courage to the conflict, and extended themselves by degrees, as the natives retreated, over the whole island; the counsels of God, in whose hand is every change of empire, not opposing their career. But this was effected in process of time; for while Vortigern lived, no new attempt was made against them. About this time, Hengist, from that bad quality of the human heart, of always grasping after more, the more it possesses, with a treacherous design, invited his son-in-law and three hundred of his followers to an entertainment; and when, by more than usual compotations, he had made them ready for strife, he began, purposely, to taunt them severally with sarcastic raillery: this had the effect of making them first quarrel, and then come to blows. Thus the Britons,

---

[1] Of Ambrosius Aurelianus, or the time when he lived, nothing certain is known: § 43. He has been confounded with Natan-leod, of the Saxon Chronicle, who lost his life, with five thousand of his subjects, in a battle fought in the year 508, against Cerdic the West Saxon. See further on this subject, Ussher, Primord. p. 1116, and Carte's Hist. Engl. vol. i. pp. 197—205.

[2] He was the hereditary prince of the Silures, in South Wales. Malmesbury here observes of him, that he was a man worthy to be celebrated, not by idle fictions, but by authentic history. It has by some been doubted whether he ever existed, because Gildas, a coeval historian, makes no mention of such a person. Higden, the author of the Polychronicon, appears to have been the first writer who doubted whether such a king as Arthur ever reigned in Britain. The following is a translation of his words:—"Concerning Arthur, whom Geoffrey, alone of chronologers, extols, many wonder how the things which are related of him can be true; because if Arthur, as Geoffrey relates, acquired thirty kingdoms, subdued the king of France, killed Lucius, governor of the republic of Italy, why have all historians, Roman, French, Saxon, and British, omitted so many great acts of such a man, when they have related so many deeds of inferior men?" Geoffrey of Monmouth first collected, from the bards of Wales and Armorica, the traditions of his exploits, and translated them into Latin. Concerning Arthur, see Nennius, § 56.

[3] Concerning these fables, see the Preface to the History of William of Newborough, which will be given in a subsequent volume of this Collection.

[4] Beda, misunderstanding Gildas, incorrectly assigns the year 493 to the siege of Bannesdon: according to the Annales Cambriæ, it was fought A.D. 516.

[5] Said to be Caer-Badon, the hill of Bannesdon, near Bath. Gildas places it near the mouth of the Severn. See note to Gildas, § 26.

[6] Upon this subject, see Ussher, Primord. p. 639, and the Annales Cambriæ, A.D. 516. Nennius describes the circumstance as having taken place in the battle "in Castello Guinnion;" but the slaughter of nine hundred and sixty men in one day, by the hand of Arthur, he assigns to the battle in Monte Badonis, § 56.

basely murdered to a man, breathed their last amid their cups. The
king himself having been made captive, purchased his liberty at the
price of three provinces.   In the thirty-ninth year after his arrival
died Hengist, a man who, urging his success not less by artifice
than courage, and giving free scope to his natural ferocity, preferred
effecting his purpose by cruelty rather than by kindness.   He left
a son named Eisc, who, more intent on defending than enlarging
his dominions, never exceeded his paternal bounds.   At the expiration of twenty-four years, he had for his successors his son Oth,
and Oth's son, Yrmenric, who, in their manners, resembled him,
rather than their grandfather and great-grandfather.   To the times
of both, the Chronicles [1] assign fifty-three years ; but whether they
reigned singly or together does not appear.

Concerning King Ethelberht, and of the coming of S. Augustine.

§ 9. After them Ethelbert, the son of Yrmenric, reigned fifty-
three [2] years according to the Chronicles ; fifty-six according to
Beda. [3]   Let the reader see for himself how this difference is to be
reconciled ; as I think it sufficient to have apprised him of it, I
shall let the matter rest.   In the infancy of his reign, he was so
much an object of contempt to the neighbouring kings, that, being
defeated in two battles, he could scarcely defend his frontier ; but
afterwards, when to his riper years he had added a more discreet
knowledge of war, by successive victories, he subjugated every kingdom of the Angles, with the exception of the Northumbrians.
And, in order to obtain foreign connexions, he entered into affinity
with the king of France, [4] by marrying his daughter.   Then, indeed,
by its association with the Franks, the nation, hitherto savage and
wedded to its own customs, began daily to divest itself of its rustic
propensities, and incline to gentler manners.   To this was added
the very exemplary life of bishop Letard, [5] who had come over with
the queen, by which, though silently, he allured the king to the
knowledge of Christ our Lord.   Hence it arose that his mind,
already softened, easily yielded to the preaching of the blessed
Augustine ; [6] and, first of all his race, he renounced the errors of
paganism, that he might obscure by the glory of his faith those
whom he surpassed in power.   This, indeed, is spotless nobility ;
this, exalted virtue ; to excel in worth those whom you exceed in
rank.   Besides extending his concern to posterity, he enacted
laws, [7] in his native tongue, in which he appointed rewards for the

---

[1] The copies of the Saxon Chronicle now extant do not contain this information.
[2] The contradictory statements here alluded to by Malmesbury still remain
unexplained.   The entries of the Saxon Chronicle are irreconcilable with each
other.   It is there stated that Ethelbert succeeded to the throne in 565, and
reigned fifty-three years ; and again, under 616, he is said to have then died after a
reign of fifty-six years. Wheloc fixes the commencement of his reign in 560, but
on what authority does not appear.   [3] E. H. ii. 5, § 101.
[4] Bertha, daughter of Charibert, king of Paris, by Ingoberga. See Anderson's
Geneol. Tables, No. 373, p. 614.   [5] See E. H. § 54.
[6] It may be enough to state here, once for all, that it is assumed that the
reader will consult the parallel passages contained in the Ecclesiastical History of
Beda.
[7] These laws are extant, and have been frequently printed.

meritorious, and opposed severer restraints to the abandoned, leaving nothing doubtful for the future.

§ 10. Ethelbert died[1] in the twenty-first year after he had embraced the faith, leaving his diadem to his son Edbald. He, as soon as he was freed from the restraints of paternal awe, rejecting Christianity, overcame the virtue of his stepmother[2] also. But the severity of the Divine mercy opposed a barrier to his utter destruction; for immediately the princes, whom his father had subjugated, rebelling, he lost a part of his dominions, and being perpetually haunted by an evil spirit, he paid the penalty of his obstinate unbelief. While Laurence,[3] the successor of Augustine, offended at these transactions, after having sent away his companions, was meditating his own departure out of the country, he was induced by the chastisement of God to change his resolution.[4] The king conversing with him on the subject, and finding his assertions confirmed by his stripes, became, they say, easily converted, accepted the grace of Christianity, and broke off his incestuous intercourse. But, that posterity might be impressed with the singular punishment due to apostasy, it was with difficulty he could maintain his hereditary dominions, much less rival the eminence of his father. For the remainder of his life, his faith was sound, and he did nothing to sully his reputation. The monastery also, which his father had founded without the walls of Canterbury,[5] he enriched with large estates, and most sumptuous presents. The praises and merits of both these men ought ever to be proclaimed, and had in honour by the English, because they allowed the christian faith to acquire strength in England, by calm assent and dispassionate belief. For who can contemplate, without satisfaction, the just and amiable answer which Beda relates king Ethelbert to have given to the first preaching of Augustine?—"That he could not thus early embrace a new doctrine and leave the worship which he had always practised in common with the whole English nation; but still it was his opinion, that persons who had undertaken so long a journey for the purpose of kindly communicating to the Angles what they deemed an inestimable benefit, far from meeting with ill-treatment, ought rather to be allowed full liberty to preach, and also to receive the amplest maintenance." He fully kept his promise; and at length the truth of Christianity becoming apparent by degrees, he and his subjects were admitted into the number of the faithful. And what did the other? Though led away at first, more by the lusts of the flesh than perverseness of heart, yet did he not pay great respect to the virtuous conduct of the prelates, although he neglected their faith? And lastly, as I have related, being easily converted through the sufferings of Laurence, he became of infinite service to the

[1] Aethelberht died on the 24th Feb. A.D. 616: the twenty-one years must, therefore, be reckoned from the mission of Augustine, and not from Aethelberht's conversion. Compare Beda's statements, § 100, 101, which are at variance.

[2] After the death of Bertha, Aethelberht married another French princess; but her name is not mentioned by historians, probably on account of her incest with Eadbald. See Beda, E. H. § 102, and Saxon Chron. A.D. 616.

[3] There is considerable doubt as to the exact date of the death of Augustine, and the accession of his successor Laurence. See E. H. § 96.

[4] See id. § 104   [5] St. Augustine's, Canterbury.

propagation of Christianity. Both, then, were laudable ; nay, both deserving higher encomiums : for the good work, so nobly begun by the one, was as kindly fostered by the other.

§ 11. To him,[1] after a reign of twenty-four years, succeeded Ercombircht his son, by Emma,[2] daughter of a king of France. He reigned an equal number of years with his father, but under happier auspices ; alike remarkable fôr piety towards God, and love to his country. For his grandfather and father, indeed, adopted our faith, but neglected to destroy their idols ; whilst he, thinking it derogatory to his royal zeal not to take the readiest mode of annihilating openly what they only secretly condemned,[3] levelled every temple of their gods to the ground, that not a trace of their paganism might be handed down to posterity. This was nobly done, because the mass of the people would be reminded of their fanatic superstition, so long as they could see the altars of their deities.   In order, also, that he might teach his subjects, too much given to sensual indulgence, to accustom themselves to temperance, he enjoined the solemn fast of Lent[4] to be observed throughout his dominions. This was an extraordinary act for the king to attempt in those times ; but he was a man whom no blandishments of luxury could enervate, no cares of empire seduce from the worship of God. Wherefore, protected by the favour of the Almighty, and everything at home and abroad succeeding to his wishes, he grew old in uninterrupted tranquillity.   His daughter Ercongota,[5] a child worthy such a parent, and emulating her father in virtuous qualities, became a shining light in the monastery of Cala in Gaul.[6]

§ 12. His son Egbert, retaining his father's throne for nine years,[7] did nothing memorable in so short a reign ; unless, indeed, it be ascribed to the glory of this period, that now arrived Theodore the archbishop, and Adrian the abbot, two scholars who were thoroughly versed in all branches of learning.   Were not the subject already trite, I should willingly record what light they shed upon the British hemisphere ; how on one side the Greeks, and on the other the Latins, emulously contributing their knowledge to the public stock, made this island, once the nurse of tyrants, the constant residence of philosophy.[8]

§ 13. To Egbert succeeeded his brother Lothaire, who began his reign with unpropitious omens. For being harassed during eleven years[9] by Edric, the son of Egbert, and engaged in many civil conflicts which terminated with various success, he was ultimately pierced through the body with a dart, and died while they were applying remedies to the wound. Some say that both the brothers perished by a premature death, as a just return for their cruelty,

---

[1] Eadbald died 20th Jan. 640.
[2] Emma was the daughter of Theodberht, king of Austria. See Pagi, ad an. 640, § 7.   [3] See E. H. iii. 8, § 172.   [4] Ibid.   [5] Ibid.
[6] Ibid.   [7] Namely, from 664 to 673. See id. iv. 5 and 26.
[8] Saville's text and two MSS. (D.M.) add, "but this and every other merit of the times of Egbert is clouded by the crime of his having destroyed, or calmly suffered to be destroyed, his cousins Elbert and Egelbrict." Three other MSS. (A.E.L.) omit the whole passage.   [9] From July 673, to 6th Feb. 685.

because Egbert murdered the innocent children of his uncle;[1] and Lothaire ridiculed the notion of holding them up as martyrs, although the former had bewailed the action, and had granted a part of the Isle of Thanet to the mother of his nephews, for the purpose of building a monastery.

§ 14. Nor could Edric long boast the prosperous state of his government; for within two years, being despoiled both of kingdom and of life, he left his country to be torn in pieces by its enemies. For immediately Kedwalla with his brother Moll, in other respects a good and able man, breathing an inextinguishable hatred against the people of Kent, made vigorous attempts upon the province; supposing it must easily surrender to his views, as it had lately been in the enjoyment of long continued peace, but at that time was torn with intestine war. But he found the inhabitants by no means unprepared or void of courage, as he had expected: for, after many losses sustained in the towns and villages, at length they rushed with spirit to the conflict. Superior in the contest, they put Kedwalla to flight, and driving his brother into a little cottage, they set it on fire. Thus, wanting courage to sally out against the enemy, and the fire gaining uncontrolled power, Moll perished in the flames.[2] Nevertheless Kedwalla ceased not his efforts, nor retired from the province; but soothing his sufferings at the repeated expense of the inhabitants, he left the avenging of this injury to Ina, his successor, as will be related in its place.[3]

§ 15. In this desperate state of the affairs of Kent, there was a void of about six years in the royal succession. In the seventh,[4] Wihtred, the son of Egbert, having repressed the malevolence of his countrymen by his activity, and purchased a peace from his enemies by money, was chosen king[5] by the inhabitants, who entertained great and well-founded hopes of him. For, an admirable ruler at home, and invincible in war, he was a truly holy follower of the christian faith, extending its power to the utmost;[6] and, to complete his felicity, after thirty-three years[7] reign, he died in extreme old age, which mortals reckon most happy, leaving his three children his heirs. Of these, Edbert for twenty-three, Edelbert for eleven,[8] and

---

[1] Malmesbury, in another place, enters more fully into an account of this murder. See § 209.

[2] This narrative is founded upon the statement of the Saxon Chronicle, A.D. 686, 687.   [3] See § 35.

[4] This interregnum in Kent appears to be overstated, if it be meant to extend from the deposition of Eadric, in 686, to the accession of Wihtraed, in 690. But possibly Malmesbury intended that it should be calculated from the death of Lothaire, early in 685, to the accession of Wihtraed, late in 690, in which case it might, in round numbers, be calculated at seven years.

[5] Wihtraed began his reign at the end of the year 690. It appears by the Saxon Chronicle that at this time, A.D. 692, there were two kings in Kent, Wihtraed and Suaebhard. See also Florence of Worcester, an. 691, and Beda, § 375.

[6] One MS. (A.) here adds, "He it was who built the monastery of S. Martin at Dover;" and the same statement is made in the genealogy of the kings of Kent, appended to Florence, ii. 393. As to his donations, see the Saxon Charters, numbers 37, 39, 41—44, 47, and 996.

[7] One MS. (C.) reads, "thirty years." See Beda, E. H. § 447.

[8] Malmesbury's meaning respecting the sons of Wihtraed is rather obscure. He probably intends to express that Acthelberht reigned eleven years after the

Alric[1] for thirty-four years, regarding the ordinances of their father, conducted the government in a similar manner; except that Edelbert, by the casual burning of the city, and Alric, by an unsuccessful battle with the Mercians, considerably obscured the glory of their times. Thus, if anything disgraceful occurs, it is not concealed, if anything fortunate, it is not sufficiently noticed in the Chronicles; whether it be done designedly, or whether it arise from that bad quality of the human mind, which makes the regard for what is good transient, whereas the recollection of evil remains for ever. After these men the noble stock of kings began to wither, the royal blood to flow cold. Then every daring adventurer, who had acquired riches by his eloquence, or whom faction had made formidable, aspired to the kingdom, and disgraced the ensigns of royalty. Of these Edelbert, otherwise called Pren,[2] after having governed Kent two years, overrating his power in a war with the Mercians, was taken by them, fettered, and put in prison; but being soon afterwards set at liberty by his enemies, though not received by his own subjects, it is uncertain by what end he perished. Cuthred, heir to the same faction and calamity, reigned, in name only, for eight years. Next Baldred, the abortion of royal dignity, after having for eighteen years possessed[3] the kingdom of Kent, went into exile, on his defeat by Egbert, king of the West Saxons. Thus the kingdom of Kent, which, from the year of the incarnation of our Lord four hundred and forty-nine,[4] had continued three hundred and seventy-five years, became annexed to another.[5] And since, by briefly tracing the royal line of the first kingdom which arose among the Angles, I have elicited a spark, as it were, from the embers of antiquity, I shall now endeavour to throw light on the kingdom of the West Saxons, which, though after a considerable lapse of time, next sprung up. This, with an extensive territory, while the others wasted away neglected, flourished with unconquerable vigour, even to the coming of the Normans; and, if I may be permitted the expression, with greedy jaws swallowed up the rest. Wherefore, after tracing this kingdom in detail down to Egbert, I shall, avoiding prolixity for fear of disgust, subjoin some notices of the two remaining; which finding a suitable termination in the first book, the second will embrace the West Saxons alone.

Of the Kingdom of the West Saxons.

§ 16. The kingdom of the West Saxons,—and one more magnificent or lasting Britain never beheld, springing from one Cerdic,—

death of Eâdberht (with whom he had previously conjointly reigned twenty-three years), and that Alric reigned thirty-four years after the death of Aethelberht. This would be quite consistent with other authorities, which state that upon the death of Wihtraed, his sons Eâdberht and Aethelberht jointly succeeded. The former died in the year 748, and the latter reigned alone until the year 761; he was succeeded by Alric, who died in the year 794.

[1] Alric died in the year 794, and with him ended the race of Hengist. He is generally considered the last of the Kentish kings.

[2] Concerning this individual, see further, § 95.

[3] C. reads, "possessed rather than governed." [4] V. R. 444, 446.

[5] Namely, in A. D. 823, under which year see the Saxon Chronicle.

soon increased to great importance.   He was a German by nation, of noblest race, being the tenth from Woden ;[1] and having nurtured his ambition in domestic broils, determined to depart from his native land, and extend his fame by the sword.   Having formed this daring resolution, he communicated his design to Cenric his son, and on his assenting, (for he closely followed his father's track to glory,) he transported his forces into Britain in five ceols.[2] This took place in the year of our Saviour's incarnation four hundred and ninety-five, and the eighth after the death of Hengist. Coming into action with the Britons on the very day of his arrival, this experienced soldier soon defeated an undisciplined multitude, and compelled them to fly.   By this success he obtained perfect security in future for himself, as well as peace for the inhabitants of those parts ; for never daring after that day to attack him, they voluntarily submitted to his dominion.   Nevertheless he did not waste his time in indolence, but, on the contrary, extending his conquests on all sides, by the time he had been twenty-four years[3] upon the island, he had obtained the supremacy of the western part of it, called West Sex.   He died after enjoying it fifteen years,[4] and his whole kingdom, with the exception of the Isle of Wight, descended to his son.   This, by the royal munificence, became subject to his nephew, Wihtgar ;[5] who, as dear to his uncle by the ties of kindred[6] as by his skill in war, formed a noble principality in the island, where he was afterwards splendidly interred.[7]   Cenric moreover, as illustrious as his father, after twenty-six years,[8] bequeathed the kingdom, somewhat enlarged, to his son Ceaulin.

Concerning Ceaulin.

§ 17.   The Chronicles extol the singular valour of this man in battle, so as to excite a degree of envious admiration ; for he was the astonishment of the Angles, the detestation of the Britons, and the destruction of both.   I shall briefly subjoin some extracts from them.   Attacking Ethelbirth, king of Kent,[9]—a man in other respects laudable, but at that time endeavouring, from consciousness of his family's dignity, to gain the ascendancy, and, on this account, making too eager incursions on the territories of his neighbours,— he routed his troops, and forced him to retreat.   The Britons, who, in the times of his father and grandfather, had escaped destruction either by a show of submission, or by the strength of their fortifications at Gloucester, Cirencester, and Bath, he now pursued with

---

[1] On the genealogy from Woden to Cerdic, see the Saxon Chronicle, A.D. 552 and 597.

[2] According to the Saxon Chronicle (from which authority nearly the whole of Malmesbury's present details are borrowed), they landed at a place called Cerdices-ora.

[3] Namely, in 519, under which year see the Saxon Chronicle.

[4] One MS. (C.), adopted by Saville, reads, sixteen years.

[5] See the Saxon Chronicle, under the year 530.

[6] Some MSS. here add, " for he was his sister's son."

[7] See the same authority, A.D. 544.

[8] Four MSS. (A.D.L.M.) here read, twenty-four, unsupported by any copy of the Saxon Chronicle.   [9] A.D. 568.   Sax. Chron.

ceaseless rancour;[1] ejected them from their cities, and chased them
into mountainous and woody districts, as at the present day.   But
about this time, as some unlucky throw of the dice in the table of
human life perpetually disappoints mankind, his military successes
were clouded by domestic calamity.   His brother Cuda[2] met an
untimely death, and he had a son of the same name cut off in
battle; both young men of great expectation, whose loss frequently
caused him to bewail his diminished felicity.   Finally, in his latter
days, he himself, banished from his kingdom, presented a spectacle
pitiable even to his enemies; for having sounded, as it were, the
trumpet of his own detestation on all sides, the Angles as well as
the Britons conspired against him, and his forces being destroyed
at Wodensdik,[3] he lost his kingdom thirty-one years after he had
assumed it,[4] went into exile, and shortly after died.   The floating
reins of government were then directed by his nephews, the sons of
Cuda, that is to say, Celric[5] during five,[6] Ceolwulf[7] during fourteen years: of these the inferior with respect to age, but the more
excellent in spirit, passed all his days in war, nor ever neglected
for a moment the protection and extension of his empire.

§ 18.   After him, the sons[8] of Celric, Cinegisl and Quicelm,
jointly put on the ensigns of royalty; both active, both contending
with each other only in mutual offices of kindness, insomuch that,
to their contemporaries, they were a miracle of concord very unusual amongst princes, and to posterity an example worthy of
imitation.   It is difficult to say whether their courage or their
moderation exceeded, in the numberless contests in which they
engaged both against the Britons,[9] and against Penda,[10] king of the
Mercians, a man, as will be related in its place, wonderfully
expert in the subtleties of war, and who, overpassing the limits of
his own territory, in an attempt to add Cirencester to his possessions, being unable to withstand the power of these united kings,
escaped with a few followers.   A considerable degree of guilt,
indeed, attaches to Quicelm, for attempting to cut off, by the hands
of an assassin, Edwin,[11] king of the Northumbrians, a man of
acknowledged prudence.   Yet, if the heathen maxim,[12]—

" Who asks if fraud or force avail'd the foe ?"

be considered, he will be readily excused, as having done nothing
uncommon in wishing to get rid, by whatever means, of an en-
croaching rival on his power; for he had formerly lopped off
much from the West-Saxon empire, and now receiving fresh

[1] A.D. 577. Sax. Chron.   [2] A.D. 584. Id.
[3] Florence of Worcester, following the existing copies of the Saxon Chronicle,
calls this place Wodnesbeorh. The reading of Wodnesdic is peculiar to Malmesbury. The locality is uncertain. Wemborough in Wiltshire (see Camd. Brit.
col. 101) is probably the place intended.
[4] One MS. (C.) assigns him a reign of only twenty-one years.
[5] Ceol, or Ceolric, reigned from 591 to 597. See Sax. Chron. 590.
[6] "During six" is the reading of one MS. (C.), which corresponds herein with
the Laud copy of the Saxon Chronicle.   [7] From 597 to 611.
[8] Cynegils and Cwichelm were the son and grandson of Ceolric, and not his
sons, as Malmesbury here states. See Sax. Chron. A.D. 611.
[9] Id. A.D. 614.   [10] Id. A.D. 628.
[11] Beda, E. H. § 113.   [12] Virg. Æn. ii. 389.

ground of offence, and his ancient enmity reviving, he inflicted heavy calamities on the people. The kings, however, escaped, and were, not long after, enlightened with the heavenly doctrine, by the means of Birinus[1] the bishop, in the twenty-fifth year of their reign, and the fortieth after the coming of the blessed Augustine. Cinegisl,[2] vailing his princely pride, received immediately and willingly the rite of baptism : Quicelm[3] resisted for a time, but warned, by the sickness of his body, not to endanger the salvation of his soul, he became a sharer in his brother's piety, and died the same year. Cinegisl died six years afterwards, in the thirty-first year of his reign, enjoying the happiness of a long-extended peace.

§ 19. Kenwalk[4] his son succeeded : in the beginning of his reign, to be compared only to the worst of princes ; but in the succeeding and latter periods, a rival of the best. The moment the young man became possessed of power, wantoning in regal luxury, and disregarding the acts of his father, he abjured Christianity and legitimate marriage : but being attacked and defeated by Penda, king of Mercia, whose sister he had repudiated, he fled to the king of the East Angles.[5] Here, by a sense of his own calamities and by the perseverance of his host, he was once more brought back to the Christian faith ;[6] and after three years, recovering his strength and resuming his kingdom, he exhibited to his subjects the joyful miracle of his reformation; and so valiant was he, that he who formerly was unable to defend his own territories, now extended his dominion on every side. He totally defeated in two actions the Britons, furious with the recollection of their ancient liberty, and in consequence perpetually meditating resistance ; first, at a place called Wirtgernesburg,[7] and then at a mountain named Pene ;[8] and again, avenging the injury of his father on Wulfer, the son of Penda, he deprived him of the greatest part of his kingdom. Moreover, so religious was he, that, first of all his race, he built, for those times, a most beautiful church at Winchester, on which site afterwards was founded the episcopal seat, with more skilful magnificence.

[9]But since we have arrived at the times of Kenewalch, and the proper place occurs for mentioning the monastery of Glastonbury, I shall trace, from its very origin, the rise and progress of that church, as far as I am able to discover it from the mass of evidences. It is related in annals of good credit, that Lucius, king of the Britons, sent to pope Eleutherius, thirteenth in succession from St. Peter, to entreat that he would dispel the darkness of Britain by the light of Christian instruction. This surely was the

---

[1] Beda, E. H. § 167.   [2] Id. § 168.   [3] Sax. Chron. A.D. 636.

[4] See Saxon Chronicle, A.D. 643. The MSS., however, fluctuate between that year and 641 and 642, in marking the beginning of his reign.

[5] Beda, E. H. § 169 ; Sax. Chron. A.D. 645.   [6] Sax. Chron. A.D. 647.

[7] The Saxon Chronicle does not mention this place (the site of which is unknown), but it states under the year 652, that he defeated the Britons at Bradford by the Avon.

[8] See Sax. Chron. A.D. 658. Pen, in Somersetshire, Camd. Brit. col. 107.

[9] The text from "But since," to "Now I shall return in order to Kenwalk," in § 29, is omitted in some MSS. Malmesbury wrote a history of the Church of Glastonbury, from which he has extracted this account. The work has been printed in Gale's Collection, i 291, and by Hearne.

commendable deed of a magnanimous prince, eagerly to seek that
faith, the mention of which had barely reached him, at a time when
it was an object of persecution by almost every king and people to
whom it was offered.   In consequence, preachers, sent by Eleutherius, came into Britain, the effects of whose labours will remain
for ever, although the rust of antiquity may have obliterated their
names.[1]   By these was built the ancient church of St. Mary of
Glastonbury, as faithful tradition has handed down through decaying
time.   Moreover, there are documents of no small credit, which
have been discovered in certain places, to the following effect :—
" No other hands than those of the disciples of Christ erected the
church of Glastonbury."   Nor is it inconsistent with probability :
for if Philip the apostle preached to the Gauls, as Freculfus[2]
relates in the fourth chapter of his second book, it may be believed
that he also planted the Word on the hither side of the channel.
But that I may not seem to disappoint my readers' expectation by
vain imaginations, leaving all doubtful matter, I shall proceed to the
relation of substantial truths.

Of the Church of Glastonbury.

§ 20. The church of which we are speaking, from its antiquity
called by the Angles, by way of distinction, " Ealde Chirche,"
that is, the Old Church, of wattle-work at first, savoured somewhat of heavenly sanctity, even from its very foundation, and
exhaled it over the whole country ; claiming superior reverence,
though the structure was mean.   Hence, here arrived whole tribes
of the lower orders, thronging every path ; hence assembled the
opulent, divested of their pomp ; hence it became the crowded
residence of the religious and the literary.   For, as we have heard
from men of elder time, here Gildas,[3] an historian neither un-
learned nor inelegant, to whom the Britons are indebted for whatever notice they obtain amid other nations, captivated by the
sanctity of the place, took up his abode for a series of years.   This
church, then, is certainly the oldest I am acquainted with in England, and from this circumstance derives its name.   In it are
preserved the mortal remains of many saints, some of whom we
shall notice in our progress; nor is any corner of the church destitute of the ashes of the holy.   The very floor, inlaid with polished
stone, and the sides of the altar, and even the altar itself above and
beneath are laden with the multitude of relics.   Moreover, in the
pavement may be remarked on every side stones designedly inter-
laid in triangles and squares, and sealed with lead, under which if
I believe some sacred mystery to be contained, I do no injustice to
religion.   The antiquity, and multitude of its saints, have endued

---

[1] Their names are said to have been Faganus and Duvianus. See Ussher,
Antiq. p. 29.
[2] Freculfus, bishop of Lisieux, wrote a chronicle extending from the creation to
the time of Boniface, the successor of Gregory the Great. See Cave, Hist. Lit. ii. 18.
He died before A.D. 853.
[3] The history of this writer forms a portion of the first volume of this collection
of Historians.

the place with so much sanctity, that at night scarcely any one presumes to keep vigil there, or during the day to void the spittle which may arise : he who is conscious of pollution shudders throughout his whole frame : no one ever brought hawk or horses within the confines of the neighbouring cemetery, who did not depart injured, either in them or in himself. Those persons who, about to undergo the ordeal of fire or water, did there put up their petitions, have in every instance that can be now recollected, except one, exulted in their escape. If any person erected a build-ing in its vicinity, which by its shade obstructed the light of the church, it forthwith became a ruin. And it is sufficiently evident, that the men of that province had no oath more frequent, or more sacred, than to swear by the Old Church, and from fear of swift vengeance avoided nothing so much as perjury in this respect. The truth of what I have asserted, if it be dubious, will be sup-ported by testimony in the book which I have written on the anti-quity of the said church, according to the series of years.

§ 21. In the meantime it is clear that the depository of so many saints may be deservedly styled an heavenly sanctuary upon earth. There are numbers of documents,—though I abstain from mentioning them for fear of causing weariness,—which prove how extremely venerable this place was held by the chief persons of the country, who there more especially chose to await the day of resurrection under the protection of the mother of God. Willingly would I explain, could I but ascertain the truth, a thing which is almost incomprehensible to all, and that is, the meaning of those pyramids which, situated some few feet from the church, border on the ceme-tery of the monks. That which is the loftiest and nearest the church, is twenty-eight feet high, and has five stories : this, though threatening ruin from its extreme age, possesses nevertheless some traces of antiquity which may be clearly read, though not perfectly understood. In the highest story is an image, in a pontifical habit. In the next, a statue of regal dignity, and the letters, Her Sexi, and Bliswerh. In the third, too, are the names, Wencrest, Bantomp, Winethegn. In the fourth, Bate, Wulfred, and Eanfled. In the fifth, which is the lowest, there is an image, and the words as follow : Logor, Weaslieas, and Bregden, Swelwes, Hiwingendes Bearn. The other pyramid is twenty-six feet high, and has four stories, in which are read, Centwine,[1] Hedde[2] the bishop, and Bre-gored and Beorward. The meaning of these I do not hastily decide, but I shrewdly conjecture that within, in stone coffins, are con-tained the bones of those persons whose names are inscribed without.[3] At least Logor is said to imply the person from whom Logweresberh formerly took its name, which is now called Mon-tacute ; Bregden, from whom is derived Brentacnol and Brente-meirs ; Bregored and Beorward were abbots of that place in the

---

[1] King of Wessex, died 685.   [2] Bishop of Winchester, died 705.
[3] Pyramids were occasionally used by the Saxons for interment. See Anglia Sacra, ii. 110. The names here mentioned were probably intended for those of the twelve monks who are said to have been established at Glastonbury on St. Patrick's arrival there.

time of the Britons; of whom and of others which occur, I shall henceforward speak more circumstantially. For my history will now proceed to disclose the succession of abbots, and what was bestowed on each monastery, and by what particular king.

§ 22. And first, I shall briefly mention Saint Patrick, with whom the series of our records dawns. While the Saxons were disturbing the peace of the Britons, and the Pelagians assaulting their faith, Saint Germanus of Auxerre[1] assisted them against both; routing the one by the chorus of Halleluiah,[2] and hurling down the other by the thunder of the Evangelists and Apostles. Thence, returning to his own country, he summoned Patrick to become his associate, and after a few years, sent him, at the instance of pope Celestin, to preach to the Irish. Whence it is written in the Chronicles, "In the year of our Lord's incarnation four hundred and twenty-five,[3] Saint Patrick is ordained to Ireland by pope Celestin." Also, "In the year four hundred and thirty-three Ireland is converted to the faith of Christ by the preaching of St. Patrick, accompanied by many miracles." He executed his appointed office with diligence, and in his latter days returning to his own country, he landed in Cornwall, from his altar,[4] which even to this time is held in high veneration by the inhabitants for its sanctity and efficacy in healing the infirm. Proceeding to Glastonbury,[5] and there becoming monk, and abbot, after some years he paid the debt of nature. All doubt of the truth of this assertion is removed by the vision of a certain brother, who after the saint's death, when it had frequently become a question, through decay of evidence, whether he really was monk and abbot there, had the fact confirmed by the following oracle. When asleep he seemed to hear some person reading, after many of his miracles, the words which follow: —"This man then was adorned by the sanctity of the metropolitan pall, but afterward was here made monk and abbot." He added, moreover, as the brother did not give implicit credit to him, that he could show what he had said inscribed in golden letters. Patrick died in the year of his age one hundred and eleven, of our Lord's incarnation four hundred and seventy-two, being the forty-seventh year after he was sent into Ireland. He lies on the right side of the altar in the old church, within a stone pyramid which the care of posterity has cased in silver. Hence the Irish have an ancient usage of frequenting the place to kiss the relics of their patron.

§ 23. Wherefore the report is extremely prevalent, that both

---

[1] See Beda, E. H. i. 17—21.   [2] Id. § 45.

[3] The history of Patrick is exceedingly obscure; this, however, is no place to enter upon an examination of the difficulties which attend it. Malmesbury wrote a life of Patrick in three books, the first and second of which Leland had seen, and from which a few extracts are embodied in his Collectanea, iii. 273, ed. 1770.

[4] Patrick is said to have floated over, from Ireland, on this altar, and to have landed near Padstow in Cornwall. Gough's Camden, i. 19. See further, Dugd. Monast. i. 11, ed. 1655.

[5] This statement is opposed by Ussher, who maintains that Patrick of Ireland is distinct from the Patrick who resided at Glastonbury. See the question examined at considerable length in the Prolegomena to his Life, § 72. Acta SS. Bolland. mens. Mart. ii. 530, seq. On the other hand, see Alford, Annal. D.A. 472, § 1, seq.

St. Indract[1] and St. Brigid, no mean inhabitants of Ireland, formerly came over to this spot. Whether Brigid returned home or died at Glastonbury, is not sufficiently ascertained, though she left here some of her ornaments; that is to say, her necklace, scrip, and implements for embroidering, which are yet shown in memory of her sanctity, and are efficacious in curing various diseases. In the course of my narrative it will appear, that Saint Indract, with seven companions, was martyred near Glastonbury, and afterwards interred in the old church.

§ 24. Benignus[2] succeeded Patrick in the office of abbot, but for how long remains in doubt. Who he was, and how called in the vernacular tongue, the verses of his epitaph at Ferramere express, not inaptly:—

> "Beneath this marble Beonna's ashes lie,
> Once rev'rend abbot of this monastery;
> Saint Patrick's servant, as the Irish frame
> The tale, who call him Beon from his name."

The wonderful works both of his former life, and since his recent translation into the greater church, proclaim the singular grace of God which he anciently possessed, and which he still retains.

§ 25. The esteem in which the great David, archbishop of Menevia, held this place, is too notorious to require repetition. He established the antiquity and sanctity of the church by a divine oracle; for, purposing to dedicate it, he came to the spot with his seven suffragan bishops, and everything being prepared for the due celebration of the solemnity, on the night, as he purposed, preceding it, he gave way to profound repose. When all his senses were steeped in rest, he beheld the Lord Jesus standing near, and mildly inquiring the cause of his arrival; and on his immediately disclosing it, the Lord diverted him from his purpose by saying, that the church had been already dedicated by Himself in honour of his mother, and that the ceremony was not to be profaned by human repetition. With these words He seemed to bore the palm of his hand with his finger, adding, that this was a sign for him not to reiterate what Himself had done before; but that, since his design savoured more of piety than of temerity, his punishment should not be prolonged; and lastly, that on the following morning, when he should repeat the words of the mass, " With Him, and by Him, and in Him," his health should return to him undiminished. The prelate, awakened by these terrific appearances, as at the moment he grew pale at the sight of the purulent matter, so afterwards he hailed the truth of the prediction. But that he might not appear to have done nothing, he quickly built and dedicated another church. Of this celebrated and incomparable man, I am at a loss to decide, whether he closed his life in this place, or at his

---

[1] Malmesbury also wrote a life of this Indractus, which has not yet been printed; a translation of it forms a part of the first volume of this collection of Historians.

[2] Malmesbury further employed himself in writing an account of the miracles of this Benignus, which may be seen in an abbreviated form in the Nova Legenda of Capgrave, fol. xxxvi.

own cathedral. For they affirm that he is with St. Patrick ; and the Welsh, both by the frequency of their prayers to him and by various reports, without doubt confirm and establish this opinion ; openly alleging that bishop Bernard[1] sought for him more than once, notwithstanding much opposition, but was not able to find him. But let thus much suffice of St. David.

§ 26. After a long lapse of time St. Augustine, at the instance of St. Gregory, came into Britain in the year of our Lord's incarnation five hundred and ninety-six, and the tradition of our ancestors has handed down, that the companion of his labours, Paulinus, who was bishop of Rochester after being archbishop of York, covered the church,—built, as we have before observed, with wattlework,—with a casing of boards. The dexterity of this celebrated man so artfully managed, that nothing of its sanctity should be lost, though much should accrue to its beauty: and certainly the more magnificent the ornaments of churches are, the more they incline the brute mind to prayer, and bend the stubborn to supplication.

§ 27. In the year of our Lord's incarnation six hundred and one, that is, the fifth after the arrival of St. Augustine, the king of Donnonia,[2] on the petition of abbot Worgrez, granted to the old church which is there situated the land called Ineswitrin, containing five cassates.[3] " I, Maworn, bishop, wrote this grant. I, Worgrez, abbot of the place, signed it."

§ 28. Who this king might be, the antiquity of the instrument prevents our knowing. But that he was a Briton cannot be doubted, because he called Glastonbury Ineswitrin, in his vernacular tongue; and that in the British it is so called, is well known. Moreover it is proper to remark the extreme antiquity of a church, which, even then, was called the " old church." In addition to Worgrez, Lademund and Bregored, whose very names imply British barbarism, were abbots of this place. The periods of their presiding are uncertain, but their names and dignities are indicated by a painting in the larger church, near the altar. Blessed, therefore, are the inhabitants of this place, allured to uprightness of life by reverence for such a sanctuary. I cannot suppose that any of these, when dead, can fail of winning heaven, when assisted by the virtues and intercession of so many patrons.

§ 29. In the year of our Lord's incarnation six hundred and seventy, and the twenty-ninth of his reign, Ceonwalh gave[4] to Bertwald, abbot of Glastonbury, two hides of land, at the request of archbishop Theodore. The same Bertwald, against the will of the king and of the bishop of the diocese, relinquishing Glastonbury, went to govern the monastery of Reculver. In consequence, Bertwald, equally renowned for piety and high birth, (being son of a brother of Ethelred, king of the Mercians,)

---

[1] In his Antiquities of the Church of Glastonbury (Gale, i. 299), Malmesbury speaks of this Bernard as "episcopus Rosinæ vallis," i.e. of St. David's. See Godwin, de Præsul. p. 576.

[2] A king of the name of Dero, D. M.;—king of Devonshire.

[3] That is, five hides, or about five hundred acres.

[4] See Kemble's Saxon Charters, No. 7. A forged document.

and residing in the vicinity of Canterbury, on the demise of archbishop Theodore, succeeded[1] to his see. This may be sufficient for
me to have inserted on the antiquity of the church of Glastonbury.[2] Now I shall return in course to Kenewalch, who was so
munificent, that he denied no part of his patrimony to his relations,
and with noble generosity conferred nearly the third part of his
kingdom on his brother's son.[3] These princely qualities were
stimulated by the admonitions of those holy bishops of his province,
Angilbert, of whom you will find many commendable things in the
History of the Angles,[4] and his nephew Leutherius, who after him
was for seven years bishop of the West Saxons: this circumstance
I have thought proper to mention, because Beda has left no
account of the duration of his episcopate,[5] and to disguise a fact
which I learn from the Chronicles,[6] would be against my conscience; besides, it affords an opportunity which ought to be
embraced, of making mention of a distinguished man, who by a
clear and divinely inspired mind advanced the monastery of
Malmesbury, where I carry on my earthly warfare, to the highest
pitch. This monastery was so slenderly endowed by Meildulf,[7] a
Scot, as they say, by nation, a philosopher by erudition, a monk
by profession, that its members could scarcely procure their daily
subsistence; but Leutherius, after long and due deliberation, gave
it to Aldelm, a monk of the same place, to be by him governed
with the authority then possessed by bishops. Of which matter,
that my relation may obviate every doubt, I shall subjoin his own
words.

§ 30. "I, Leutherius, by divine permission bishop supreme of
the Saxon see,[8] am requested by the abbots who, within the jurisdiction of our diocese, preside over the conventual assemblies of
monks with pastoral anxiety, to give and to grant that portion of
land called Meildulfesburh[9] to Aldelm the priest, for the purpose
of leading a life according to strict rule: in which place, indeed,
from his earliest infancy and first initiation in the study of learning,
he has been instructed in the liberal arts, and passed his days,
nurtured in the bosom of the holy mother church; and on which
account fraternal love appears principally to have conceived this
request: wherefore assenting to the petition of the aforesaid abbots,
I willingly grant that place to him and his successors, who shall
sedulously follow the laws of the holy institution. Done publicly
near the river Bladon,[10] this seventh of the kalends of September,
in the year of our Lord's incarnation six hundred and seventy-
two." [11]

§ 31. But when the industry of the abbot was superadded to
the kindness of the bishop, then the affairs of the monastery began

---

[1] Elected 1st July, 692.
[2] The preceding account of Glastonbury is abridged from Malmesbury's own
History, De Antiq. Glaston. Eccl., written subsequently to the year 1129. It
occurs in four of the best MSS. which have been consulted, viz. D. E. F. M.
[3] See Sax. Chron. A.D. 648.   [4] See E. H. iii. 25 and 28.
[5] Id. iv. 12, § 286.   [6] See Sax. Chron. A.D 670.
[7] See, concerning this Irish Maidulf, the Annals of Alford, A.D. 648 and 675.
[8] "West Saxon," D. M.   [9] Maidulfsbury, or Malmesbury.
[10] Probably the river Avon.   [11] V. R. 675 and 671.

to flourish exceedingly; then monks assembled on all sides; there was a general concourse to Aldelm; some admiring the sanctity of his life, others the depth of his learning. For he was a man as unsophisticated in religion as multifarious in knowledge; whose piety surpassed even his reputation: and he had so fully imbibed the liberal arts, that he was wonderful in each of them, and unrivalled in all. I greatly err, if his works written on the subject of Virginity,[1] than which, in my opinion, nothing can be more pleasing or more splendid, are not proofs of his immortal genius: although, such is the slothfulness of our times, they may excite disgust in some persons, not duly considering how modes of expression differ according to the customs of nations. The Greeks, for instance, express themselves involvedly, the Romans clearly, the Gauls gorgeously, the Angles turgidly. And truly, as it is pleasant to dwell on the graces of our ancestors and to animate our minds by their example, I would here, most willingly, unfold what painful labours this holy man encountered for the privileges of our church, and with what miracles he signalized his life, did not my avocations lead me elsewhere; and his noble acts appear clearer even to the eye of the purblind, than they can possibly be sketched by my pencil.[2] The innumerable miracles which at this time take place at his tomb manifest to the present race the sanctity of the life he passed. He has therefore his proper praise; he has the fame acquired by his merits: my history pursues its course.

§ 32. After thirty-one years, Kenwalk dying,[3] bequeathed the administration of the government to his wife Sexburga; nor did this woman want spirit for discharging the duties of the station; she levied new forces, preserved the old in their duty; ruled her subjects with moderation, and overawed her enemies: in short, she conducted all things in such a manner, that no difference was discoverable except that of sex: but breathing more than female spirit, she died, having scarcely reigned a year.

§ 33. Escuin[4] passed the next two years in the government; a near relation of the royal family, being grand-nephew to Cinegisl, by his brother Cuthgisl; at whose death, either natural or violent, (for I cannot exactly find which,) Chentwin,[5] the son of Chinegisl, filled the vacant throne in legitimate succession. Both were men of noted experience in war; as the one routed the Mercians,[6] the other the Britons,[7] with dreadful slaughter: but they were to be

---

[1] Concerning these treatises, see Beda, § 410. The prose version is printed by Wharton, 4to, 1693; and the verse in Canisii Thesaurus Monumentorum, i. 709, ed. Basnage, Antverpiæ, 1725, folio; and at Paris, 1676, 8vo.

[2] Malmesbury wrote a life of St. Aldhelm, which forms the fifth book De Gestis Pontificum; it has been published by Gale, and by Wharton in the Anglia Sacra, part ii. p. 1. It forms part of the present collection of Historians. Aldhelm died on the 25th of May, A.D. 709.

[3] Cynewealh died without issue, A.D. 673; his widow, Sexburh, reigned one year after him, and died in the beginning of the year 675.

[4] Aescwin succeeded Sexburh in the beginning of the year 675, and died at the end of the year 676. Instead of two years, as in the text, one MS. (C.) reads three years.

[5] Centwin succeeded to the throne in 676, and died A.D. 685.

[6] Aescwin fought at Beadan-head (Bedwin) in 675. Sax. Chron.

[7] A.D. 682, Centwin drove the Britons to the sea. Sax. Chron.

pitied for the shortness of their career; the reign of the latter not extending beyond nine, nor of the former more than two years, as I have already related. This is on the credit of the Chronicles: however, Beda [1] records that they did not reign successively, but divided the kingdom between them.

§ 34. Next sprang forth a noble branch of the royal stock, Kedwalla,[2] grand-nephew of Cheaulin, by his brother Cuda; a youth of unbounded promise, who allowed no opportunity of exercising his valour to escape him. He, having long before, by his active exertions, excited the animosity of the princes of his country, was, by a conspiracy, driven into exile.[3] Taking advantage of this outrage, as the means of depriving the province of its warlike force, he led away all the military population with him; for whether out of pity to his broken fortunes, or regard for his valour, the whole of the youth accompanied him into exile. Edelwalch,[4] king of the South Saxons, hazarding an engagement with him, felt the first effect of his fury: for being routed with all the forces which he had collected, he, too late, repented his rash design. The spirits of his followers being thus elated, Chedwalla, by a sudden and unexpected return, drove the rivals of his power from the kingdom. Enjoying his government for the space of two years, he performed many signal exploits: hostile towards the South Saxons with inextinguishable hatred, he totally destroyed Edric, the successor of Edelwalch, who opposed him with renewed boldness. He all but depopulated the Isle of Wight, which had rebelled in confederacy with the Mercians. He also attacked the people of Kent and gained repeated victories over them. Finally, as is observed above,[5] he retired from that province, on the death of his brother, compensating his loss by the blood of many of its inhabitants. It is difficult to relate how extremely pious he was even before his baptism, insomuch that he dedicated to God the tenth of all the spoils which he had acquired in war. In which, though we approve the intention, we condemn the example; according to the saying :[6] "He who offers sacrifice from the substance of a poor man, is like him who immolates the son in the sight of the father." That he went to Rome to be baptized[7] by pope Sergius, and was called Peter, and that he yielded joyfully to the will of heaven, while yet in his white baptismal robes,[8] are matters too well known to require our illustration.

§ 35. After his departure to Rome, the government was assumed by Ina,[9] grand-nephew of Chinegisl by his brother Cuthbald, who ascended the throne, more from the innate activity of his spirit, than by any legitimate right of succession; he was a rare example

---

[1] E. H. iv. 12, § 286.
[2] Caedwalla began to reign A.D. 685. Sax. Chron.
[3] See Beda, E. H. iv. 14.   [4] Id. iv. 15, § 297.
[5] See § 14.   [6] Ecclus. xxxiv. 24.
[7] Caedwalla abdicated, and went to Rome, A.D. 688. He was baptized by pope Sergius on the Saturday before Easter Sunday, A.D. 689, and died a few days afterwards (20th April). Beda, E. H. § 372.
[8] The catechumen was generally baptized the Saturday immediately before Easter Sunday, and wore a white robe until the first Sunday after Easter; hence the term "Dominica in albis."   [9] Ine came to the throne A.D. 688. Sax. Chron.

of fortitude; a mirror of prudence; unequalled in piety: thus
regulating his life, he gained favour at home, and respect abroad.
Safe from any apprehensions of treachery, he grew old in the
discharge of his duties for thirty-eight years,[1] the pious conciliator
of the public esteem.   His first expedition was against the people
of Kent, as the indignation at their burning Mollo[2] had not yet
subsided.   The inhabitants resisted awhile; but soon finding all
their attempts and endeavours fail, and seeing nothing in the disposition of Ina which could lead them to suppose he would remit
his exertions, they were induced, by the consideration of their
losses, to treat of a surrender: they tempt the royal mind with
presents, lure him with promises, and bargain for a peace for thirty
thousand mancas[3] of gold, that, softened by so high a price, he
should put an end to the war, and, being thus bound in golden
chains, sound a retreat.   Accepting the money, as a sufficient
atonement for their offence, he returned into his kingdom.   And
not only the people of Kent, but the East Angles also, felt the
effects of his hereditary anger; all their nobility being first expelled,
and afterwards routed in battle.   But let the relation of his military
successes here find a termination.   Moreover how sedulous he was
in religious matters, the laws[4] he enacted to reform the manners
of the people are proof sufficient; in which the image of his purity
is reflected even upon the present times.   Another proof are the
monasteries nobly founded at the king's expense,[5] more especially

[1] According to Saville's text he reigned fifty-eight years.   [2] See § 14.

[3] The manca and the ancient marca are by some thought to be synonymous,
and to be money, either gold or silver, which was paid in weight. The value of
the manca of gold is not exactly known; it is believed to be eight to the pound.
The manca of silver in the time of Henry I. was estimated at six shillings, five
pence to the shilling; and in the reign of Edward III. at only thirty pence of the
money of that period. According to the Saxon Chronicle, Ine received thirty
thousand pounds from the Kentishmen, because they had formerly burned Mull.
This payment seems excessive; but it was probably the legal compensation for
the death of Mull. Ethelward says it was "30,000 solidi per singulos constanti
numero sexdecim nummis;" and Florence of Worcester, three thousand seven
hundred and fifty pounds.

[4] The laws of Ine may be seen in Thorpe's edition, i. 102.

[5] After "expense" A. L. G. and some other MSS. with slight variations read,
"More especially that at Glastonbury, most celebrated in our days, which he
erected, in a certain washy corner, in order that the monks might more eagerly
thirst after heavenly, in proportion as they were less affected by earthly things.
Father Aldelm assisted the design, whose precepts, in this respect, he heard with
humility, nobly adopted, and joyfully carried into effect. Lastly, he readily confirmed the privilege which Aldelm had obtained from pope Sergius, for the
immunity of his monasteries; gave much to the servants of God by his advice,
and finally honoured him (though he constantly refused it) with a bishopric;
but an early death malignantly cut off this great man from the world, for scarcely
had he discharged the offices of his bishopric four years, ere he made his soul an
offering to heaven, in the year of our Lord's incarnation 709 [on the vigil of St.
Augustine the apostle of the Angles, the 8th of the kalends of June (25th May).]
Some say that he was the nephew of the king, by his brother Kenten; but I do
not choose to assert for truth anything which savours rather of vague opinion,
than of historic credibility; especially as I can find no ancient record of it, and
the Chronicle clearly declares, that Ina had no other brother than Inigeld, who
died some few years before him. Aldelm needs no support from fiction; such
great things are there concerning him of indisputable truth, so many which are
beyond the reach of doubt. The sisters indeed of Ina, were Cuthburga and
Quenburga: Cuthburga was given in marriage to Alfrid, king of the Northumbrians, but the contract being soon after dissolved, she led a life dedicated to

Glastonbury, whither he ordered to be conveyed the bodies of the
blessed martyr Indract and of his associates, after having taken
them from the place of their martyrdom. The body of St. Indract
he deposited in the stone pyramid on the left side of the altar,
where the zeal of posterity afterwards also placed the blessed
Hilda :[1] the others he distributed beneath the pavement as chance
directed or regard might suggest. Here, too, he erected a church,
dedicated to the holy apostles, as an appendage to the ancient
church of which we are speaking ; enriched it with vast possessions, and granted it a privilege in these words :—

§ 36. "In the name of our Lord Jesus Christ ; I, Ina, supported in my royal dignity by God, with the advice of my queen
Sexburga, and the permission of Beortwald archbishop of Canterbury, and of all his suffragans ; and also at the instance of the
princes Baldred and Adelard, to the ancient church, situate in the
place called Glastonbury (which church the great High Priest and
chiefest Minister formerly through his own ministry, and that of
angels, sanctified by many and unheard-of miracles to Himself and
the ever-virgin Mary, as was formerly revealed [3] to St. David,) do
grant out of those places which I possess by paternal inheritance,

God, first at Berking, under the abbess Hildelida, and afterwards, as superior of
the convent at Wimburn ; now a mean village, but formerly celebrated for containing a full company of virgins, who, dead to earthly desires, breathed only
heavenly affections. She embraced the profession of holy celibacy from the
perusal of Aldelm's books on Virginity, dedicated indeed to the sisterhood of
Berking, but profitable to all who aspire to that state. Ina's queen was Ethelburga, a woman of royal race and disposition ; who perpetually urging the necessity of bidding adieu to earthly things, at least in the close of life, and the king
as constantly deferring the execution of her advice, at last she endeavoured to overcome him by a stratagem. For on a certain occasion, when they had been revel-
ling at a country seat with riot and luxury, the next day, after their departure,
an attendant, with the privity of the queen, defiled the palace in every possible
manner, both with the excrement of cattle and heaps of filth ; and lastly he put
a sow, which had recently farrowed, in the very bed where they had lain. They
had hardly proceeded a mile, ere she attacked her husband with the fondest
conjugal endearments, entreating that they might immediately return thither,
whence they had departed, saying, that his denial would be attended with
dangerous consequences. Her petition being readily granted, the king was
astonished at seeing a place which yesterday might have vied with the luxury of
Sardanapalus, now filthily disgusting and desolate ; and silently pondering on
the sight, his eyes at length turned upon the queen. Seizing the opportunity,
and pleasantly smiling, ' Where, my noble spouse,' said she, ' are the revellings of
yesterday ? Where the tapestries dipped in Sidonian dyes ? Where the ceaseless
impertinence of parasites ? Where the sculptured vessels, overwhelming the
very tables with their weight of gold ? Where are the delicacies so anxiously
sought throughout sea and land, to pamper the appetite ? Are not all these
things smoke and vapour ? Have they not all passed away ? Woe be to those
who attach themselves to such, for they in like manner shall consume away. Are
not all these like a rapid river hastening to the sea ? And woe to those who are
attached to them, for they shall be carried away by the current. Reflect, I entreat you, how wretchedly will these bodies decay, which are now pampered with
luxury. Must not we, who gorge so constantly, become more disgustingly putrid ?
The mighty must undergo mightier torments, and a severer trial awaits the strong.'
Without saying more, by this striking example, she gained over her husband to
those sentiments, which she had in vain attempted for years by persuasion."

[1] Abbess of Streaneshalch [Whitby], born in 614, and died 17th Nov. 680.
She was the daughter of Hereric, son of Eadfrith, son of king Eadwin.

[2] The charter of Ine of Wessex, A. D. 725, is not considered genuine. See it
printed in the Cod. Dip. Ævi Sax. i. 85, No. lxxiii.   [3] See ante, § 25.

and hold in my demesne, they being adjacent and fitting for the purpose, for the maintenance of the monastic institution, and the use of the monks, Brente ten hides, Seweie ten hides, Piltun twenty hides, Dulting twenty hides, Bledanhide one hide, together with whatever my predecessors have contributed to the same church : to wit, Chenewalch,[1] who, at the instance of archbishop Theodore, gave Ferremere, Bregereie, Coneneie, Matineseie, Ederedseie ; Chentwin, who used to call Glastonbury ' the mother of saints,' and liberated it from every secular and ecclesiastical service, and granted it this dignified privilege, that the brethren of that place should have the power of electing and appointing their ruler, according to the rule of St. Benedict : Hedde[2] the bishop, (who, with permission of Chedwalla, though an heathen, confirmed it with his own hand, gave Lantocai ; Baldred, who gave Pennard, six hides; Adelard, who contributed Poelt,[3] sixty hides; I permitting and confirming it. To the piety and affectionate entreaty of these people I assent, and I guard by the security of my royal grant against the designs of malignant men and snarling curs, in order that the church of our Lord Jesus Christ and the ever-virgin Mary, as it is the first in the kingdom of Britain, and the source and fountain of all religion, may obtain surpassing dignity and privilege, and, as she rules over choirs of angels in heaven, so it may never pay servile obedience to men on earth. Wherefore the chief pontiff Gregory[4] assenting, and taking the mother of his Lord, and me (however unworthy) together with her, into the bosom and protection of the holy Roman church ; and all the kings, archbishops, bishops, dukes, and abbots of Britain consenting, I appoint and establish, that all lands, places and possessions of St. Mary of Glastonbury be and remain free, quiet, and undisturbed, from all royal taxes and works, which are wont to be appointed, that is to say, expeditions, the building of bridges and forts, and from the edicts and molestations of all archbishops and bishops, as is found to be confirmed and granted by my predecessors, Chenewalch, Chentwin, Chedwalla, and Baltred, in the ancient charters of the same church. And whatsoever questions shall arise, whether of homicide, sacrilege, poison, theft, rapine, the disposal and limits of churches, the ordination of clerks, ecclesiastical synods, and all judicial inquiries, they shall be determined by the decision of the abbot and convent, without the interference of any person whatsoever. Moreover I command all princes, archbishops, bishops, dukes, and governors of my kingdom, as they regard their own honour and my esteem, and all dependants, mine as well as theirs, as they value their personal safety, never to dare to enter the island of our Lord Jesus Christ and of the ever-virgin Mary, at Glastonbury, nor the possessions of the said church, for the purpose of holding courts, making inquiry, or seizing, or doing anything whatever to the offence of the servants

---

[1] See ante, § 29.
[2] Bishop of Winchester. See note to § 21.   [3] Woelt, D. M.
[4] Gregory the Second was ordained pope 19th May, A.D. 715 ; died 10th Feb. A.D. 731.

of God there residing.   Moreover I particularly inhibit by the curse of Almighty God, of the ever-virgin Mary, and of the holy apostles Peter and Paul, and of the rest of the saints, any bishop on any account whatever from presuming to take his episcopal seat, or to celebrate divine service, or consecrate altars, or dedicate churches, or ordain, or do anything whatsoever, either in the church of Glastonbury itself, or its dependent churches, that is to say, Soweie, Brente, Merlinch, Sapwic, Stret, Budecalech, Piltun, or in their chapels, or in the islands, unless he be specially invited by the abbot or brethren of that place.   But if he come upon such invitation, he shall take nothing to himself of the things of the church, nor of the offerings ; knowing that he has two mansions appointed him in two several places out of this church's possessions, one in Piltun,[1] the other in the vill called Poelt,[2] that, when coming or going, he may have a place of entertainment.   Nor even shall it be lawful for him to pass the night here unless he shall be detained by stress of weather or bodily sickness, or invited by the abbot or monks, and then with not more than three or four clerks.   Moreover let the aforesaid bishop be mindful every year, with his clerks that are at Wells,[3] to acknowledge his mother church of Glastonbury with litanies on the second day after our Lord's Ascension.   And should he haughtily defer so doing, or fail in the things which are above recited and confirmed, he shall forfeit his mansions above mentioned.   The abbot or monks shall direct whom they please, so that he celebrate Easter canonically, to perform service in the church of Glastonbury, its dependent churches, and in their chapels.   Whosoever, be he of what dignity, profession, or degree he may, shall hereafter on any occasion whatsoever attempt to pervert or nullify this instrument, the witness of my munificence and liberality, let him be aware that, with the traitor Judas, he shall perish, to his eternal confusion, in the devouring flames of unspeakable torments.

"The charter of this donation was written in the year of our Lord's incarnation seven hundred and twenty-five,[4] the fourth of the indiction, in the presence of king Ina, and of Beortwald, archbishop of Canterbury."

§ 37.   For[5] after his triumphal spoils in war, after many successive degrees in virtue, he aspired to the highest perfection, and went to Rome[6] in the year of our Lord's incarnation seven hundred and twenty-six.   There, not to make the glory of his conversion public, he

---

[1] Wiltune, D.M.   [2] Woelt, D.M.   [3] "Cum clericis suis qui Fontineto sunt."
[4] Two copies, D.M., give A.D. 715 as the date of this charter.
[5] The account of the foundation of Glastonbury, and of the measures adopted by queen Ethelburga to induce her husband to undertake the pilgrimage to Rome, printed in note [5], § 35, is omitted in D.E.F.M., and Ine's charter to Glastonbury is inserted instead.
[6] The exact time of Ine's abdication and journey to Rome is not by any means certain.   Several of the MSS. entirely omit the date.   In two MSS. (D.M.) however, the year 720 is assigned for it, incorrectly as it seems.   Beda writes, that Ine had reigned thirty-seven years when he left his kingdom ; and, according to this computation, his abdication must have taken place at the end of the year 725, or in the beginning of 726 ; but, according to the Saxon Chronicle and Florence of Worcester, it occurred in 728.   A.D. 726 would seem to be the correct date.

was shorn in secret, and, clad in homely garb, that he might be acceptable in the sight of God alone, grew old in privacy. Nor did his queen, the author of this noble deed, desert him, but as she had before incited him to undertake it, so, afterwards, she made it her constant care to soothe his sorrows by her conversation, to stimulate him when wavering by her example ; in short, to omit nothing that could be conducive to his salvation. Thus united in mutual affection, in due time they trod the common path of all mankind. This was attended, as we have heard, with singular miracles, such as God often deigns to bestow on the virtues of happy couples.

§ 38. To the government succeeded Edelard,[1] the kinsman of Ina ; though Oswald,[2] a youth of royal extraction, often obscured his opening prospects. Exciting his countrymen to rebellion, he attempted to make war on the king, but soon after perishing by some unhappy doom, Edelard kept quiet possession of the kingdom for fourteen years, and then left it to his kinsman Cudred, who for an equal space of time, and with similar courage, was ever actively employed. He conferred many benefits on the church of Glastonbury, and gave it a charter in these words :—

§ 39. "[3] In the name of our Lord Jesus Christ. All the possessions granted by former kings, to wit, Chentwin, Baldred, Chedwalla, Ine, Ethelard, and Ethbald king of the Mercians, in vills, streets, fields, farms, and manors, I Cudred, king of the West Saxons, do by this instrument marked with my own hand with the sign of the cross confirm, in the same manner as the ancient city was confirmed to Glastonbury : and do decree that the said grants of preceding kings shall remain fast and lasting as long as the revolving pole shall in its steady course turn the heavens round sea and land. But if any one swollen with tyrannical insolence shall at any time attempt to diminish or make void this my grant, may he, when dead, at the judgment be winnowed away from the congregation of the saints, and, mixed with the herd of the spoilers, for ever pay the penalty of his wicked rashness. But whoever with kind intent shall endeavour to advance, strengthen, and uphold it, may he obtain his desires, and hear for ever the glories of the Most High, in the joyful company of angels and all saints.

"This charter was made and delivered in the aforesaid monastery in the presence of Cuthred the king, who laid it with his princely hand on the altar, in the wooden church in which the brethren of abbot Hemgisl are buried, in the year[4] of our Lord's incarnation seven hundred and forty-five."

§ 40. The said Cuthred exerted himself greatly against, and after frequent efforts he obtained victories over, Athelbald,[5] king of

---

[1] Aethelheard succeeded to the government upon the abdication of Ine, A. D. 726 : according to the Saxon Chronicle, he died A. D. 741.

[2] In the Saxon Chronicle called Oswald the Atheling ; he was the son of Aethelbald.

[3] A charter of Cuthred, king of Wessex, dated A. D. 744, is printed in Cod. Dip. Ævi Sax. i. 112, No. xciii. The language differs in some respects from that in the text. Kemble does not consider it a genuine charter.

[4] "On the day before the kalends of May, A. D. 745." D. M.

[5] See the Saxon Chronicle, A. D. 752, 753.

the Mercians, and over the Britons, and after fourteen years he laid down the reins of government.

§ 41. Sigebert[1] then seized on the kingdom ; a man of inhuman cruelty among his own subjects, and noted for excessive cowardice abroad ; but the common detestation of all men conspiring against him, he was driven from the throne in a twelvemonth, and gave place to one more worthy than himself. Yet, as commonly happens in similar cases, the severity of his misfortunes brought back some persons to embrace his cause, and the province which is called Hamtunscire [Hampshire] was by their exertions retained in subjection to him. Still, however, unable to quit his former habits, and exciting the enmity of all against him by the murder of one Cumbrand, who had adhered to him with unshaken fidelity, he fled to the recesses of wild beasts, where, misfortune still attending him, he was stabbed to death by a swineherd.[2] Thus the cruelty of a king, which had almost desolated the higher ranks, was put an end to by a man of the lowest condition.[3]

§ 42. Kinuulf[4] next undertook the guidance of the state. Illustrious for the exact regulation of his conduct, and his deeds in arms, but suffering extremely from the loss of a single battle, in the twenty-fourth year of his reign, against Offa king of the Mercians, near Bensigitune,[5] he was also finally doomed to a disgraceful death. For after he had reigned thirty-one years,[6] neither indolently nor oppressively, becoming either elated with success, because he imagined nothing could oppose him, or alarmed for his posterity, from the increasing power of Kineard, the brother of Sigebert, he compelled him to quit the kingdom. Kineard, deeming it necessary to yield to the emergency of the times, departed as if voluntarily; but soon after, when by secret meetings he had assembled a desperate band of wretches, watching when the king might be alone (for he had gone into the country for the sake of recreation), he followed him thither with his party, and learning that he was there giving loose to improper amours, he beset the house on all sides. The king, struck with his perilous situation, and holding a conference with the persons present, shut fast the doors, expecting either to appease the robbers by fair language, or to terrify them by threats. When neither plan succeeded, he rushed furiously on Kineard, and had nearly killed him ; but, surrounded by the multitude, and thinking it derogatory to his courage to give way, he fell, while nobly avenging his death. Some few of his attendants, who, instead of yielding, attempted to take vengeance for the loss of their lord, were slain. The report of this dreadful outrage soon reached the ears of the nobles, who were waiting near

---

[1] A.D. 755.   [2] A.D. 756.   [3] See Juv. Sat. iv. 153.   [4] He came to the throne A.D. 756.

[5] Bensington, in Oxfordshire. The battle was fought in 777. (Sax. Chron.) This could not, however, have been the twenty-fourth year of Cynewulf's reign, as stated by Malmesbury.

[6] Some authorities assign thirty-one years to the reign of Cynewulf. He commenced his reign at the end of the year 756, and was slain in 785 ; consequently he reigned only twenty-nine years. It is possible that Malmesbury wrote "uno de triginta annis," (not "uno et triginta," as it stands in the original,) as he uses a similar expression when writing of the reign of Caedwalla, § 35, "annis duobus de quadraginta."

at hand. Of these Osric, the chief in age and prudence, exhorting
the rest not to leave unrevenged the death of their sovereign to
their own signal and eternal ignominy, rushed with drawn sword
upon the conspirators. At first Kineard attempted to argue his
case, to make tempting offers, to hold forth their relationship; but
when this availed nothing, he stimulated his party to resistance.
Doubtful was the conflict, where one side contended with all its
powers for life, the other for glory; at length victory, wavering for
a long time, decided for the juster cause. Thus, fruitlessly valiant,
this unhappy man lost his life, unable long to boast the success of
his treachery. The king's body was buried at Winchester, and the
prince's at Respendun,[1] at that time a noble monastery, but at
present, as I have heard, with few or scarcely any inmates.

§ 43. After him, for sixteen years, reigned Brictric;[2] more
studious of peace than of war, skilful in conciliating friendship,
affable with foreigners, and giving great allowance to his subjects
in those matters at least which could not impair the strength of the
government. To acquire still greater estimation with his neighbours, he married[3] the daughter of Offa king of Mercia, at that
time all-powerful, by whom, as far as I am acquainted, he had no
issue. Supported by this alliance he compelled Egbirt, the sole
survivor of the royal stock, and whom he feared as the most
effectual obstacle to his power, to fly into France. In fact Brictric
himself, and the other kings after Ina, though glorying in the
splendour of their parentage, as deriving their origin from Cerdic,
had considerably deviated from the direct line of the royal race.
On Egbirt's expulsion, then, he had already begun to indulge in
indolent security, when a piratical tribe of Danes,[4] accustomed to
live by plunder, clandestinely arriving in three ships, disturbed the
tranquillity of the kingdom. This band came over expressly to
ascertain the fruitfulness of the soil, and the courage of the inhabitants, as was afterwards discovered by the arrival of that multitude which overran almost the whole of Britain. Landing then,
unexpectedly, when the kingdom was in a state of profound peace,
they seized upon a royal vill which was nearest them, and killed
the steward, who had advanced with succours; but losing their
booty through fear of the people, who hastened to attack them,
they retired to their ships. After Brictric,[5] who was buried at
Werram, Egbert ascended the throne of his ancestors; justly to
be preferred to all the kings who preceded him. Thus having
brought down our narrative to his times, we must, as we have
promised, next give our attention to the Northumbrians.

[1] Repton in Derbyshire. Concerning this outrage, see the Saxon Chronicle,
A. D. 755.
[2] Beorhtric obtained the throne in 785, and died in 802; consequently he
reigned seventeen years : this agrees with the period assigned to his reign by
Simeon of Durham.
[3] Beorhtric married Eadburh, king Offa's daughter, in 787. See the Saxon
Chronicle, and Florence of Worcester, A. D. 787.
[4] See the authorities last quoted.
[5] According to the Saxon Chronicle and Florence of Worcester, Beorhtric died
in 800; but Simeon of Durham (apparently with greater accuracy) states that he
died A. D. 802, having reigned seventeen years.

Of the Kingdom of the Northumbrians.

§ 44. We have before related briefly,[1] and now necessarily repeat, that Hengest, having settled his own government in Kent, had sent his brother Ohta and his son Ebusa, men of activity and tried experience, to seize on the northern parts of Britain. Sedulous in executing the command, affairs succeeded to their wishes : for frequently coming into action with the inhabitants, and dispersing those who attempted resistance, they conciliated with uninterrupted quiet such as submitted. Thus though, through their own address and the good-will of their followers, they had established a certain degree of power, yet never entertaining an idea of assuming the royal title, they left an example of similar moderation to their immediate posterity. For during the space of ninety-nine years,[2] the Northumbrian leaders, contented with subordinate power, lived in subjection to the kings of Kent. Afterwards, however, this forbearance ceased, either because the human mind is ever prone to degeneracy, or because that race of people was naturally ambitious. In the year, therefore, of our Lord's incarnation five hundred and forty-seven, the sixtieth after Hengest's death, the principality was converted into a kingdom, and the most noble Ida,[3] in the full vigour of life and of strength, first reigned there. But whether he himself seized the chief authority, or received it by the consent of others, I by no means venture to determine, because the truth is unrevealed : however, it is sufficiently evident, that, sprung from a great and ancient lineage, he reflected much splendour on his illustrious descent by his pure and unsullied manners. Unconquered in war, at home he tempered his kingly power with peculiar affability. Of this man, and of others in their respective places, I could lineally trace the descent, were it not that the very names, of uncouth sound, would be less agreeable to my readers than I could wish. It may, however, be proper to remark, that Woden had three sons : Weldeg, Wiltheg, and Beldeg. From the first, the kings of Kent derived their origin ; from the second, the kings of Mercia ; and from the third, the kings of the West Saxons and Northumbrians, with the exception of the two whom I am going to particularise. This Ida, then, the ninth from Beldeg, and the tenth from Woden, as I find positively declared, continued in the government fourteen years.[4]

---

[1] See § 7.   [2] Malmesbury's authority for this statement cannot be traced.

[3] Prior to the accession of Ida, the Saxon Chronicle contains no notice of Northumbria. That authority, however, and Beda, (E. H. § 452,) both consider Ida the founder of this kingdom in 547. It seems doubtful whether Ida was king of both the provinces of Bernicia and Deira, or of the former only. Upon his death in 559, he was succeeded in Bernicia by his sons, who reigned successively till the year 588, when Aethelric, upon the death of Alla, king of Bernicia, and the expulsion of his son Edwin, obtained the government of both kingdoms, which he held for five years, until his death in 593. Compare the statements of Florence of Worcester, A.D. 559, and the Appendix to that writer, p. 397, with the statements of Simeon of Durham upon this subject.

[4] There is some little uncertainty as to the duration of the reign of Ida. The Saxon Chronicle and Florence of Worcester (A. D. 547) assign him a reign of twelve years, herein following Beda, (E. H. § 452,) but Simeon of Durham says he reigned eleven.

§ 45. His successor Alla,[1] originating from the same stock, but
descending from Woden by a different branch, conducted the
government, extended by his exertions considerably beyond its
former bounds, for thirty years.   In his time youths from Northumbria were exposed to sale, after the common and almost native
custom of this people ;[2] so that even, as our days have witnessed,
they would make no scruple of separating the nearest ties of relationship through the temptation of the slightest advantage.   Some
of these youths, then, carried from England[3] for sale to Rome,
became the means of salvation to all their countrymen ; for exciting
the attention of that city by the beauty of their countenances and
the elegance of their features, it happened that, among others, the
most blessed Gregory, at that time archdeacon of the apostolical
see, was present, who, admiring such an assemblage of grace in
mortals, and at the same time pitying their abject condition as
captives, asked the by-standers, " Of what race are these ? whence
come they?"   He was answered, " By birth they are Angles ; by
country, Deiri[4] (Deira being a province of Northumbria); they are
subjects of king Alla, and are Pagans."   Their concluding characteristic he accompanied with heartfelt sighs ; to the others he elegantly alluded, saying that " these Angles, *angel*-like, should be
delivered from *ire*, and taught to sing *Alleluia*."   Obtaining permission without delay from pope Benedict,[5] the industry of this
excellent man was all alive to enter on the journey to convert
them ; and certainly his zeal would have completed this intended
labour, had not the mutinous love of his fellow-citizens recalled
him when he was already on his progress.   He was a man as celebrated for his virtues as beloved by his countrymen ; for by his
matchless worth he had even exceeded the expectations which they
had formed of him from his youth.   His good intention, though
frustrated at this time, received afterwards, during his pontificate,[6] an honourable termination, as the reader will find in its
proper place.   I have made this insertion with pleasure, that my
readers might not lose this notice of Alla, mention of whom is
slightly made in the life of pope Gregory ; for although this king
was the primary cause of introducing Christianity among the Angles,
yet either by the counsel of God, or some mischance, was never
himself permitted to know it.   The calling, indeed, descended to
his son.

[1] He was king of Deira, and ascended the throne A. D. 560. (Sax. Chron.) It
does not appear from any other authority that Alla ever reigned over Bernicia,
though he is here described as the successor of Ida, whose sons at this time were
successively kings of that province.
[2] This custom of selling their children and near relatives to foreign merchants
was probably most frequent in Northumbria.
[3] Compare this story with Beda (E. H. ii. 1, § 89), who relates it as merely tra-
ditional.
[4] Britain, north of the Humber, was composed of two great regions, Deira and
Bernicia. Deira extended from the Humber to the Tyne, and Bernicia from the
Tyne to the Frith of Forth. Each province at first had its independent sovereign.
[5] Benedict presided from 3d June, A. D. 574, till 31st July, A. D. 578.
[6] Gregory the Great presided from 3d Sept. A. D. 590, to 12th March, A. D.
604.

§ 46. On the death of Alla,[1] Ethelric[2] the son of Ida, advanced to extreme old age, after a life consumed in penury, obtained the kingdom, and after five years was taken off by a sudden death. He was a pitiable prince, whom fame would have hidden in obscurity, had not the conspicuous energy of the son lifted up the father into notice.

§ 47. When therefore, by a long old age, he had satisfied the desire of life, Ethelfrid,[3] the elder of his sons, ascended the throne, and compensated the greenness of his years by the maturity of his conduct. His transactions have been so displayed by graceful composition, that they want no assistance of mine, except as far as order is concerned. So eagerly has Beda[4] dwelt on the praises of this man and his successors, and has dilated on his neighbours the Northumbrians at greater length, being better acquainted with them because of their proximity; our history, therefore, will select and compile from his relation. In order, however, that no one may blame me for contracting so diffuse a narrative, I must tell him that I have done it purposely, that they who have been nauseated with such high-seasoned delicacies, may find breathing space for a little while on these humble remnants; for it is a trite saying, and venerable for its age, that "The meats which cloy the least, are eaten with keenest appetite." Ethelfrid then, as I was relating, having obtained the kingdom, began at first vigorously to defend his own territories; afterwards, eagerly to invade those of his neighbours, and to seek occasion for signalizing himself on all sides. Many wars were begun by him with foresight, and terminated with success; as he was neither restrained from duty by indolence, nor precipitated into rashness by courage. An evidence of these things is Degstan,[5] a noted place in those parts, where Edan, king of the Scots, envying Ethelfrid's successes, had constrained him, though averse, to give battle; but being overcome, he took to flight, though the triumph was not obtained without considerable hazard to the victor: for Tetbald, the brother of Ethelfrid, opposing himself to the most imminent dangers, that he might display his zeal in his brother's cause, left a mournful victory indeed, being cut off with his whole party. Another proof of his success is afforded by the city of Caerleon,[6] now simply called Chester, which till that period, possessed by the Britons, fostered the pride of a people hostile to the king. When he bent his exertions to subdue this city, the townsmen preferring any extremity to a siege, and at the same time confiding in their numbers, rushed out in multitudes to battle; but deceived by a stratagem, they were overcome and put to flight; his fury being first[7] vented on the monks, who came out in numbers to pray for the safety of the army.[8] That their number was

---

[1] Alla died A.D. 588. (Sax. Chron.)

[2] Aethelric reigned over both of the provinces of Bernicia and Deira. He succeeded to the former A.D. 586, and obtained the latter in 588: he died in the year 593. See note [3], at § 44.

[3] Aethelfrith succeeded to the kingdom of the Northumbrians A.D. 593. (Sax. Chron.)

[4] See Beda, E. H. ii. 2 and 12.   [5] See Beda, E. H. § 80.

[6] "Legionum civitas." See Beda, E. H. § 94.   [7] C. here reads "afterwards."

[8] Beda (E. H. § 94) states that twelve hundred priests were slain, who went

incredible to these times, is apparent from so many half-destroyed walls of churches in the neighbouring monastery ; so many winding porticoes ; such masses of ruins as can scarcely be seen elsewhere. The place is called Bangor, at that day a noted monastery, but now changed into a cathedral.[1] Ethelfrid thus, while circumstances proceeded to his wishes abroad, being desirous of warding off domestic apprehensions and intestine danger, banished Edwin,[2] the son of Alla, a youth of no mean worth, from his kingdom and country. He, wandering for a long time without any settled habitation, found many of his former friends more inclined to his enemy than to the observance of their engagements ; for as it is said,[3]

> "So long as fortune smiles, thy friends abound :
> Change but the season, and alone thou'rt found."

At last he came to Redwald, king of the East Angles, and bewailing his misfortunes, was received into his protection. Shortly after there came messengers from Ethelfrid, either demanding the surrender of the fugitive, or denouncing hostilities. Determined by the advice of his wife not to violate, through intimidation of any one, the faith which he had pledged to his friend, Redwald collected a body of troops, rushed against Ethelfrid,[4] and attacked him suddenly, while suspecting nothing less than an assault. He availed himself of the only remedy that courage, thus taken by surprise, could suggest, there being no time to escape. Wherefore, though almost totally unarmed, though beset with fearful danger on every side, he fell not till he had avenged his own death by the destruction of Reiner, the son of Redwald. Such an end had Ethelfrid, after a reign of twenty-four years ;[5] a man second to none in martial experience, but entirely ignorant of the holy faith. He had two sons[6] by Acca, the daughter of Alla, sister of Edwin ; Oswald, aged twelve, and Oswiu, four years ; who, on the death of their father, fled, through the management of those who had the charge of them, and escaped into Scotland.

---

thither to pray for the Welsh army. The exact date of this massacre is not known. There is no date assigned to this event in Beda. Florence places it in the year 603 ; the Annales Cambriæ in 613 ; the Saxon Chronicle in 607. Ussher, following the Ulster Annals, refers it to the year 613.

[1] Malmesbury here confounds the ancient monastery of Banchor, near Chester, with the more modern see of Bangor, in Caernarvonshire. See also Tyrrell, vol. i. book iv. p. 164. There was likewise a monastery at Bangor, in Ulster. See Smith's note to Beda, E. H. ii. 2.

[2] Upon the death of Alla, King of Deira, his son Edwin, being only three years old, was driven from the succession by Aethelric, king of Bernicia, who thereupon united the government of the two provinces. Aethelric died in 593, and was succeeded by his son Aethelfrith ; who still continuing his persecution, Edwin sought the protection of Redwald, king of East Anglia.

[3] Ovid. Trist. ix. 5.

[4] Aethelfrith was slain A. D. 617, in a battle with Redwald, near Retford, on the river Idle, in Nottinghamshire. (Sax. Chronicle, A. D. 617 ; Flor. of Worcester, A. D. 616 ; and Henry of Huntingdon.)

[5] Simeon of Durham, incorrectly as it seems, assigns twenty-eight years to the reign of Aethelfrith.

[6] Oswald and Oswiu had an elder brother, Eanfrith, who afterwards became king of Bernicia. See afterwards, § 49.

Concerning Edwin, the King of the Northumbrians.

§ 48. In this manner, all his rivals being slain or banished, Edwin,[1] trained by many adversities, ascended, not meanly qualified, the summit of power. When the haughtiness of the Northumbrians had bent to his dominion, his felicity was crowned by the timely death of Redwald, whose subjects, during Edwin's exile among them, having formerly experienced his ready courage and ardent disposition, now willingly swore obedience to him. Granting to the son of Redwald the empty title of king, he himself managed all things as he thought fit. At this juncture, the hopes and the resources of the Angles were centered in him ; nor was there a single province of Britain which did not regard his will, and prepare to obey it, except Kent alone : for he had left these people free from his incursions, because he had long meditated a marriage with Ethelburga,[2] the sister of their king Edbald. When she was granted to him, after a courtship long protracted,—to the intent that he should not despise that woman when possessed, whom he so ardently desired when withheld,—these two kingdoms became so united by the ties of kindred, that there was no rivalry in their powers, no difference in their manners. Moreover, on this occasion the faith of Christ our Lord, introduced into those parts by the preaching of Paulinus,[3] reached first the king himself ;[4] the queen, among other proofs of conjugal affection, perpetually instructing him in it ; nor was the admonition of the bishop wanting in its own place. For a long time he was wavering and doubtful ; but once received, he thoroughly imbibed it. Then he invited neighbouring kings to the faith ; then he erected churches; and neglected nothing that might aid its propagation. In the meanwhile, the merciful grace of God smiled on the devotion of the king, insomuch that not only the nations of Britain, that is to say, the Angles, Scots, and Picts, but even the Orkney isles and the isles of Mevania, which they now call Anglesey, that is, islands of the Angles, both feared his arms and venerated his power. At that time there was no public robber, no domestic thief; the tempter of conjugal fidelity was far distant, the plunderer of another man's inheritance was in exile ; a state of things redounding to his praise, and worthy of celebration in our times. In short, such was the increase of his power, that righteousness and peace willingly met and kissed each other, imparting mutual acts of kindness. And now, indeed, would the government of the Angles have held a prosperous course, had not an untimely death, the stepmother of all earthly felicity, by a lamentable turn of fortune, snatched this man from his country ; for in the forty-eighth year of his age, and the seventeenth of his

---

[1] He succeeded to the kingdom of Northumbria on the death of Aethelfrith, in the beginning of the year 617.

[2] Edwin's marriage with Ethelburga, also called Tatae, daughter of Aethelberht, king of Kent, took place A. D. 625. (Beda, E. H. § 111.)

[3] Paulinus was ordained bishop of York, 21st July, A. D. 625.

[4] Edwin was baptized on Easter Sunday, (12th April,) A. D. 627, in the eleventh year of his reign. (Beda, E. H. § 132.)

reign, being killed, together with his son,[1] by the princes whom he
had formerly subjugated, Chedwalla of the Britons and Penda of
the Mercians, rising up against him, he became a melancholy
example of human vicissitude.   He was inferior to none in prudence : for he would not embrace even the Christian faith till he
had examined it most carefully; but when once adopted, he esteemed
nothing worthy to be compared to it.

Concerning S. Oswdld the King.

§ 49. Edwin thus slain, the sons of Ethelfrid, who were also the
nephews of Edwin,[2] Oswald and Oswiu, now grown up, and in the
budding prime of youth, resought their country, together with
Eanfrid,[3] their elder brother, whom I forgot before to mention.
The kingdom therefore was now divided into two.   Indeed Northumbria, long since separated into two provinces, had produced
Alla, king of the Deirans, and Ida, of the Bernicians.   Wherefore
Osric, the cousin of Eadwin, succeeding to Deira, and Eanfrid, the
son of Ethelfrid, to Bernicia,[4] they exulted in the recovery of their
hereditary right. They had both been baptized in Scotland, though
scarcely were they settled in their authority, ere they renounced
their faith : but shortly after they suffered the just penalty of their
apostasy through the hostility of Chedwalla.[5]   The space of a year
passed in these transactions improved Oswald,[6] a young man of
great hope, in the science of government.   Armed rather by his
faith (for he had been admitted to baptism while in exile with
many nobles among the Scots) than by his military preparations,
at the first onset he drove Chedwalla, a man elated with the recollection of his former deeds, and, as he used himself to say, born for
the extermination of the Angles, from his camp, and afterwards
destroyed him with all his forces.[7]   For when he had collected the
little army which he was able to muster, he excited them to the
conflict by saying that, laying aside all thought of flight, they must
determine either to conquer or die together, and that it must be
a circumstance highly disgraceful for the Angles to meet the
Britons on such unequal terms, as to fight against those persons
for safety, whom they had been used voluntarily to attack for
glory only; that, therefore, they should maintain their liberty with
dauntless courage and the most strenuous exertions; but that of

---

[1] Edwin, with his son Osfrid, was slain at the battle of Hatfield Moor on the
12th October, A. D. 633.   (Beda, E. H. § 146; Sax. Chron. A. D. 633; and Flor. of
Worcester, A. D. 633.) The day of his celebration in the English Martyrology is the
4th of October.
[2] They were sons of Aethelfrith by Acca, sister of Edwin. See before, § 47.
[3] See Beda, E. H. § 150.
[4] See Saxon Chron. A. D. 634, and Beda, E. H. § 150. Osric was the son of Aelfric,
brother of Alla, and cousin of Edwin.
[5] Osric and Eanfrith were both slain by Ceadwalla, king of the Britons ; Osric
in the summer of 634, and Eanfrith shortly afterwards. During this period, the
government of the two provinces was usurped by Ceadwalla.
[6] Osuuald obtained the kingdom of Northumbria in 634. Concerning him, see
Beda, E. H. iii. 2, 3, 6.
[7] Ceadwalla was slain at Dilston, near Hexham, in Northumberland. (Beda,
E. H. § 151.) See also Smith's Appendix, No. xiii.

the impulse to flight no feeling whatever should be indulged.   In consequence, they met with such fury on both sides that it may be truly said no day was ever more disastrous for the Britons, or more joyful for the Angles : so completely was one party routed with all its forces, as never to have hope of again recovering ; so exceedingly powerful did the other become, through the effects of faith and the accompanying courage of the king.   From this time, the worship of idols fell prostrate in the dust; and he governed the kingdom, extended beyond Edwin's boundaries, for eight years,[1] peaceably and without the loss of any of his people.   History[2] sets forth the praises of this king in a high style of panegyric, of which I shall extract such portions as may be necessary, by way of conclusion.   With what fervent faith his breast was inspired, may easily be learnt from the circumstance, that when at any time bishop Aidan[3] addressed his auditors on the subject of their duty, in the Scottish tongue, and no interpreter was present, the king himself directly, though habited in the royal robe, glittering with gold or glowing with Tyrian purple, would graciously assume that office, and explain the foreign idiom in his native language.   It is well known, too, that frequently at entertainments, when the guests had whetted their appetites and bent their inclinations on the feast, he would forego his own gratification, procuring by his abstinence comfort for the poor.[4]   So that I think the truth of that heavenly sentence was fulfilled even on earth, where the celestial oracle hath said, " He hath dispersed abroad, he hath given to the poor, his righteousness remaineth for ever."[5]   And moreover, what the hearer must wonder at and cannot deny, that identical royal right hand, the dispenser of so many alms, remains to this day perfect, with the arm, the skin, and nerves, though the remainder of the body, with the exception of the bones, mouldering into dust, has not escaped the common lot of mortality.   It is true there are the corporeal remains of some saints unconscious altogether of decay. Wherefore let others determine by what standard they will fix their judgment; I pronounce this still more gracious and divine, on account of its singular manifestation, because matters however precious degenerate by frequency, and things are valued in proportion to their rarity.   I should, indeed, be thought prolix, were I to relate how diligent he was to address his prayers on high, and to fill the heavens with supplications.   This virtue of Oswald is too well known to require the support of our narrative.   For at what time would that man neglect his supplications, who, in the insurrection excited by Penda, king of the Mercians,[6] when his guards are put to flight, and himself actually carrying a forest of darts in his breast, could not be prevented, by the pain of his wounds or the

---

[1] According to Beda, Oswald reigned nine years, inclusive of the year of Ceadwalla's usurpation.   Two copies of Malmesbury, D. and M., limit the duration of his reign to seven years.   [2] See Beda, E. H. iii. 2—6.
  [3] Concerning the life of Aidan, bishop of Lindisfarne, see Beda, E. H. § 162, and Acta Sanctorum, August. tom. vi. p. 688.
  [4] See Beda, E. H. § 166.   [5] Psalm cxii. 9.
  [6] Oswald was slain by Penda at Maserfelth, (now Oswestry,) 5th Aug. A.D. 642, in the thirty-eighth year of his age.   (Beda, E. H. § 175, and Sax. Chron.)

approach of death, from praying to God for the souls of his faithful companions?   In such manner this personage, of surpassing celebrity in this world, and highly in favour with God, ending a valuable life, transmitted his memory to posterity by a frequency of miracles; and that indeed deservedly.   For it is not common, but even " more rare than a white crow,"[1] for men to abound in riches, and not to give indulgence to their vices.   When he was slain, his arms with the hands and his head were cut off by the insatiable rage of his conqueror, and fixed on a stake.   The trunk indeed, as I have mentioned, being laid to rest in the calm bosom of the earth, returned to its native dust; but the arms and hands, through the power of God, remain, according to the testimony of an author[2] of veracity, without corruption.   These being placed by his brother Oswy in a shrine, at Bebbanburg[3] (for so the Angles call the city), and shown for a miracle, bear testimony to the fact.   Whether they remain in that place at the present day, I venture not rashly to affirm, because I waver in my opinion.   If other historians have precipitately recorded any matter, let them be accountable : I hold common report at a cheaper rate, and affirm nothing but what is deserving of entire credit.   The head was then buried by his before-mentioned brother[4] at Lindisfarn; but it is said now to be preserved at Durham, in the arms of the blessed Cuthbert.[5]   When queen Ostdritha,[6] the wife of Ethelred king of the Mercians, and daughter of king Oswi, through regard to her uncle, was anxious to take the bones of the trunk to her monastery of Bardney, which is in the country of the Mercians, not far from the city of Lincoln, the monks refused her request for a short time at first ; denying repose even to the bones of that man when dead, whom they had hated whilst living, because he had obtained their country by right of arms : but at midnight, being taught by a miraculous light from heaven shining on the reliques, to abate their haughty pride, they became converts to reason, and even intreated as a favour what before they had rejected.   Miracles from on high became frequent in this place : every sick person who implored this most excellent martyr's assistance immediately received it.   The withering turf grew greener from his blood; it restored a horse to health;[7] and some of it being hung up against a post, the devouring flames fled from it in their turn.   Some small portion of dust, moistened from his reliques, was equally efficacious in restoring a lunatic to his proper senses.   The washings of the stake which had imbibed the blood fresh streaming from his head, restored health to one despairing of recovery.   For a long time this monastery, possessing so great a treasure, flourished in the sanctity of its members and the abundance of its friends; more especially after king Ethelred received the crown of monastic tonsure there, where also his tomb is seen even to the present day.   After many years, indeed, when the

---

[1] Juvenal, Sat. vii. 202.   [2] Beda, E. H. iii. 6.
[3] Bamborough in Northumberland.
[4] C. here incorrectly reads, "a beato Germano."
[5] St. Cuthbert is represented in illuminations and sculptures as holding the head of Oswald in his arms.   [6] E. H. §§ 180, 181.
[7] See Beda, E. H. iii. 9, 10, and for the other stories, to c. 13.

barbarians infested these parts, the bones of the most holy Oswald were removed to Gloucester.   This place, at that period inhabited by canons,[1] contains but few inmates.   Oswald, therefore, was the man who yielded the first-fruits of saintliness to his nation, since no Angle before him, to my knowledge, was celebrated for miracles : for after a life spent in sanctity, in liberally giving alms, in frequent watchings and prayer, and lastly, in waging war with a heathen through zeal for the church of God, he poured out his spirit, according to his wishes, before he could behold what was his greatest object of apprehension, the decline of Christianity.   Nor indeed shall he be denied the praise of the martyrs, who first aspiring after a holy life, and next opposing his body to a glorious death, trod in their steps : in a manner he deserves higher commendation, since they consecrated themselves alone to God, but Oswald, not only himself, but all the Northumbrians with him.

Concerning Oswiu, the Brother of S. Oswald.

§ 50.   On his removal from this world, Oswiu, his brother, assumed the dominion over the Bernicians, as did Oswin, the son of Osric, whom I have before mentioned,[2] over the Deiri ; and after meeting temperately at first on the subject of the division of the provinces, under a doubtful truce, they each retired peaceably to their territories.   But not long after, by means of persons who delighted in sowing the seeds of discord, the peace, often mocked by ambiguous treaties, was finally broken, and vanished into air. Horrid crime ! that there should be men who could envy these kings their friendly intimacy, nor abstain from using their utmost efforts to precipitate them into battle.   Here, then, fortune, who had before so frequently caressed Oswin with her blandishments, now wounded him with scorpion sting : for thinking it prudent to abstain from fighting, on account of the smallness of his force, he had secretly withdrawn to a country-seat, and being immediately betrayed by his own people, he was killed by Oswiu.[3]   He was a man admirably calculated to gain the favour of his subjects by his pecuniary liberality, and, as they relate, demonstrated his care for his soul by his fervent devotion.   Oswiu, thus sovereign of the entire kingdom, did everything in his power whereby to wipe out this foul stain, and to increase his dignity ; extenuating the enormity of that atrocious deed by the rectitude of his conduct for the future. Indeed, the first and highest point of his glory is, that, nobly avenging his brother and his uncle, he slew Penda,[4] king of the Mercians, that destroyer of his neighbours, that seed-plot of hostility, and from that period he either governed the Mercians, as well as almost all the Angles, himself, or was supreme over those who did so. Turning from this time altogether to offices of piety, that he might

---

[1] " Inhabited by monks, but at the present time by canons," A.C.L.
[2] See § 49.
[3] Oswine, king of Deira, was slain by Oswiu of Bernicia on the 20th of August, A.D. 651.
[4] Penda of Mercia was vanquished and slain by Oswiu, 15th Nov. A.D. 655. (Beda, E. H. § 221.)

be truly grateful for the favours of God which were perpetually
flowing down upon him, he proceeded to raise up and animate with
all his power the infancy of the christian faith, fainting through his
brother's death.   This faith, brought shortly after to maturity by
the learning of the Scots, but wavering in many ecclesiastical ob-
servances, he settled on canonical foundations;[1] first by Angilbert[2]
and Wilfrid, and next by archbishop Theodore, for whose arrival
in Britain[3] (although Egbert, king of Kent, as far as his province
is concerned, takes much from his glory) the chief thanks are due
to Oswiu.[4]   Moreover, building numerous habitations for the servants of God, he left not his country destitute of this advantage
also.   The principal of these monasteries, at that time for females,
but now for males, was situated about thirty miles north of York, and
was anciently called Streneshalh, but now Witebi: it was begun by
Hilda,[5] a woman of singular piety, and was augmented with large
revenues by Ethelfleda,[6] daughter of this same king, who succeeded
her in the government of it; in which place, also, she buried her
father with all due solemnity, after he had reigned twenty-eight
years.[7]   This monastery, like all others of the same locality, being
destroyed in the times of the Danish invasion (as will be related
hereafter), was bereaved of the bodies of many saints; for the bones[8]
of the blessed Aidan the bishop, of Cheolfrid the abbot, and of that
truly holy virgin Hilda, together with those of many others, were,
as I have related in the book which I lately published on the
"Antiquity of the Church of Glastonbury," at that time removed to
Glastonbury, and those of other saints to different places.   Now the
monastery, under another name, and somewhat restored as circumstances permitted, hardly presents a vestige of its former opulence.

§ 51. To Oswiu, who had two sons[9] (the elder, who was illegitimate, being rejected), succeeded the younger, Egfrid, legitimately
born; more valued on account of the good qualities of his most
pious wife Etheldritha, than for his own.   Yet he was certainly to be
commended for two things which I have read in the history of the
Angles;[10] his allowing his queen to dedicate herself to God, and his
promoting the blessed Cuthbert to a bishopric, whose tears at the
same time burst out with pious assent.   But my mind shudders at
the bare recollection of his outrage against the most blessed Wilfrid,[11]

---

[1] The principal points in dispute were, the time of celebrating Easter, confirmation, and the form of the tonsure. See Beda, E. H. § 228.
[2] Bishop of Dorchester. See § 29.   [3] See § 12.
[4] See Beda, E. H. § 245.   [5] See ante, § 35.
[6] If Ethelfleda was abbess at the time of her father's death, in 670, that office
must have been vacated, in her favour, by Hilda, some time before her own death,
which did not occur until 680.   [7] Oswiu died on the 15th February, A.D. 670.
[8] This passage, in which allusion is made to the history of Glastonbury, is
omitted in A. S. C. L., but occurs in D. E. M.
[9] Oswiu left a legitimate son, Ecgfrith, and an illegitimate one named Ealdfrith,
who were successively kings of Bernicia.
[10] The two facts here alluded to by Malmesbury are found in Beda. Ecgfrith's permission to his queen to take the veil is alluded to by that writer (§ 310), and Cuthbert's promotion to a bishopric during this reign is also casually mentioned, § 340.
[11] Wilfrith was ordained bishop of York, A.D. 665, and expelled from his bishopric in 677; he returned to England in 679, and was again expelled in 681. He
was recalled to Northumberland in 687.   In 692 he was again expelled, and
retired to Aethilred, of Mercia, in which year he governed the vacant see of

when, loathing his virtues, he deprived the country of this shining light.   Overbearing towards the suppliant, a malady incident to all tyrants, he overwhelmed the Irish,[1] a race of men harmless in genuine simplicity and guiltless of every crime, with incredible slaughter.   On the other hand, inactive towards the rebellious, and not following up the triumphs of his father, he lost the dominion over the Mercians ; and moreover, being defeated in battle by Ethelred the son of Penda, their king, he lost his brother also.[2] Perhaps these last circumstances may be truly attributed to the unsteadiness of youth ; but his conduct towards Wilfrid must be referred to the instigation of his wife[3] and of the bishops, more especially as Beda, a man who knew not how to flatter, designates him, in his book of the Lives of his Abbots,[4] as a man most pious and most beloved by God.   At length, in the fifteenth year of his reign, leading an expedition against the Picts, and eagerly pursuing them, as they purposely retired to some secluded mountains, he perished with almost all his forces.[5]   The few who escaped by flight came home with the news.   And yet the divine Cuthbert, from his knowledge of future events, had both attempted to keep him back when departing ; and at the very moment of his death, enlightened by heavenly influence, declared, though at a distance, that he was slain.

§ 52.   While a more than common report everywhere noised the death of Egfrid, " an intimation of it, borne on the wings of haste,"[6] reached the ears of his brother Alfrid.   Though the elder brother, he had been deemed by the nobility unworthy of the government from his illegitimacy, as I have observed,[7] and had retired to Ireland, either through compulsion or indignation.   In this place, safe from the persecution of his brother, he had from his ample leisure become deeply versed in literature, and had enriched his mind with every kind of learning ; on which account the very persons who had formerly banished him, esteeming him the better qualified to manage the reins of government, now sent for him of their own accord, and fate rendered efficacious their intreaties.   He did not disappoint their expectations ; for during the space of nineteen years[8] he presided over the kingdom in the utmost tranquillity and joy, doing nothing at which even greedy calumny itself could justly carp, except the persecution of that great man Wilfrid. However, he held not the same extent of territory as his father

---

Lichfield.   He was expelled again in 703 ; and in the following year, his cause being decided in his favour at Rome, he returned to England.   He died A. D. 709. His life has been written by Heddius, and is printed in Gale, vol. iii.   It will form part of the present Collection.   See also Beda, E. H. § 413.

[1]   Consult Beda, E. H. § 340, and Sax. Chron. A. D. 684.   See also Ogygia, p. 230, where the time and place of the invasion are specified.

[2]   See Beda, E. H. § 316 ; Sax. Chron. A. D. 679.

[3]   Irmenburg, the second wife of Ecgfrith, is the person here alluded to.   His first wife, Etheldritha, was divorced from him, and became a nun.

[4]   The Lives of the Abbots of Wearmouth and Jarrow has appeared in this series of English Historians.   See i. 604.

[5]   Ecgfrith was slain on the 20th May, A. D. 685.   See Beda, E. H. § 340 ; Sax. Chron. A. D. 685.

[6]   " Anxia præcipiti venisset epistola pinna."—Juvenal, Sat. IV. i. 149

[7]   See § 51.   [8]   Allhfrith died at Driffield on the 14th May, A. D. 76.

and brother, because the Picts (insolently profiting by their recent
victory, and attacking the Angles, who had become more indolent
through a lengthened peace) had curtailed his boundaries on the
north.

§ 53. He had for his successor his son Osred,[1] a boy of eight
years old, who, disgracing the throne for eleven years, and spending
an ignominious life in the seducing of nuns, was ultimately taken
off by the hostility of his relations. Yet he poured out to them
a draught from the same cup; for Kenred,[2] after reigning two, and
Osric eleven years,[3] left only this to be recorded of them, that they
expiated by a violent death the blood of their master, whom they
supposed they had rightfully slain. Osric, indeed, deserved a
happier end; for, as a heathen says, " he was more dignified than
other shades,"[4] because, while yet living, he had adopted Chelwulf,[5]
Kenred's brother, as his successor. Then Chelwulf ascended the
giddy height of empire, the seventh in descent from Ida; a man
competent in other respects, and withal possessed of a depth of
literature, acquired by good abilities and indefatigable attention.
Beda vouches for the truth of my assertion, who, at the very
juncture when Britain most abounded with scholars, offered his
History of the Angles[6] for correction to this prince more especially; making choice of his authority, to confirm by his high
station what had been well written, and of his learning, to rectify
by his talents what might be carelessly expressed.

Concerning Beda.

§ 54. In the fourth year of his reign,[7] that historian, after having
written many books for the holy church, entered the heavenly
kingdom, for which he had so long languished, in the year of our
Lord's incarnation seven hundred and thirty-four,[8] and in the
fifty-ninth of his age:[9] a man whom it is easier to admire than
worthily to extol; who, though born in a remote corner of the
world, was able to dazzle the whole earth with the brilliancy of his
learning. For even Britain, which by some is called another
world, since, surrounded by the ocean, it was not known by

[1] This statement agrees with Beda's, E. H. § 409; but Heddius, in his Life of
Wilfrid, writes that the throne had been occupied for two months by Eaduulf
before Osraed ascended it. He was slain in the year 716.

[2] Coenred was the son of Cuthwin.

[3] Osric died on the 9th of May, A. D. 729. (Beda, E. H. § 452.) He was a son
of Alhfrith.   [4] Virg. Æn. vi. 815.

[5] According to Beda, (E. H. § 448,) Ceoluulf ascended the throne in 729; but
according to the Saxon Chronicle in 731, and according to Matth. Westm. in 730.

[6] See the Preface to the Ecclesiastical History of the English Nation, which
that author addressed to king Ceolwulf.

[7] Ceoluulf ascended the throne on the 9th May, 729, and Beda died 26th May,
735; consequently his death must have taken place in the seventh year of the
reign of that monarch.   [8] See the last note.

[9] Beda was born in the year 674, and died in 735; consequently he must
have been in his sixty-first year. It would seem that Malmesbury is here misled
by the statement made by Beda as to his age, at the period when he composed his
Historia Ecclesiastica, he being then in the fifty-ninth year of his age; for he
writes that " from the time of receiving the priesthood till the fifty-ninth year of
my age, I have been employed for the benefit of myself and my friends in making
these extracts," &c.

many geographers, possesses, in its remotest region,[1] bordering on Scotland, the place of his birth and education. This region, formerly redolent with the grateful odour of monasteries, or glittering with a multitude of cities built by the Romans, now desolate through the ancient devastations of the Danes, or the more recent of the Normans,[2] presents but little to allure the mind. Here is the river Wear, of considerable breadth and rapid tide, which, running into the sea, receives the vessels borne by gentle gales, on the calm bosom of its haven.   Both its banks have been made conspicuous by one Benedict,[3] who there built churches and monasteries ;[4] one dedicated to Peter and the other to Paul, united in the bond of brotherly love and of the same monastic rule. The industry and patience of this man every one must admire, who reads the book[5] which Beda composed concerning his life and those of the succeeding abbots : his industry in bringing over a multitude of books, and being the first person who introduced in England constructors of stone edifices, or makers of glass windows, in which pursuits he spent almost his whole life abroad : the love of his country and his taste for elegance beguiling his painful labours, in the earnest desire of conveying something hitherto unknown to his countrymen ; for very rarely before the time of Benedict, were buildings of stone[6] seen in Britain, or did the solar ray cast its light into houses through the transparent glass. Again, his patience : for when in possession of the monastery of Saint Augustine at Canterbury, he cheerfully resigned it to Adrian when he arrived, not as one fearing the severity of the blessed Theodore the archbishop, but bowing to his authority. And farther, while long absent abroad, he endured not only with temper, but I may say with magnanimity, the substitution of another abbot, without his knowledge, by the monks of Wearmouth ; and on his return, admitted him to equal honour with himself in rank and power. Moreover, when stricken so severely with the palsy that he could move none of his

[1] The Venerable Beda was born in the district which then belonged to the Benedictine monasteries of Wearmouth and Jarrow, now forming part of the county of Durham.

[2] The devastations of the Danes commenced in 793, and were subsequently carried to a great extent during the reigns of Alfred and Ethelred. In the year 1069 the whole region was laid waste by the Conqueror.

[3] Benedict, surnamed Biscop : he came to England with Archbishop Theodore, and was by him made abbot of the monastery of St. Augustine, Canterbury, which he soon resigned, and went back to Rome. He travelled to Rome five several times, occupying himself while there either in learning the Roman ritual, or in collecting books, pictures, and ornaments of various descriptions for the monasteries which he had founded at Wearmouth : he also brought over masons from France to build a church after the Roman manner, as well as glass-makers. He appears to have been a man of refined taste for the times in which he lived. On his return to England, he obtained a considerable quantity of land near the mouth of the Wear, where he built the two monasteries of which he was abbot. He died 12th January, 690.   [4] The monasteries of Wearmouth and Jarrow.

[5] Beda wrote the lives of Benedict Biscop and his successors, Ceolfrith and Huaetberht, abbots of Wearmouth and Jarrow, in two books. It is included in the first volume of this series, p. 604.

[6] "lapidei tabulatûs." This seems intended to designate buildings with courses of stone in a regular manner, which is also implied by Malmesbury. De Gestis Pontif. iii. 148. Beda, whom he here follows, affords no assistance as to the precise meaning ; he merely states that Benedict caused a church to be erected after the Roman model.

limbs, he appointed a third abbot, because the other of whom we have spoken was not less afflicted with the same disease. And when the disorder, increasing, was just about to seize his vitals, he bade adieu to his companion, who was brought into his presence, with an inclination of the head only ; nor was he better able to return the salutation, for he was hastening still more quickly to his end, and actually died before Benedict. Chelfrid succeeded, under whom the affairs of the monastery flourished beyond measure. When, through extreme old age, life ceased to be desirable to him, he purposed going to Rome, that he might pour out, as he hoped, his aged soul an offering to the apostles his masters ; but failing of the object of his desires, he paid the debt of nature at the city of Langres. The relics of his bones were in after-time conveyed to his monastery, and, at the period of the Danish devastation, were taken with those of St. Hilda to Glastonbury.[1] The merits of these abbots, sufficiently eminent in themselves, their celebrated pupil Beda crowns with superior splendour. It is written, indeed, " A wise son is the glory of his father ;"[2] for one of them made him a monk, the other educated him. And since Beda himself has given some slight notices of these facts, comprising his whole life in a kind of summary, it may be allowed to turn to his words, which the reader will recognise, lest any variation of the style should affect the relation. At the end, then, of the Ecclesiastical History of the Angles,[3] this man, as praiseworthy in other respects as in this, that he withheld nothing from posterity, though it might be only a trifling knowledge of himself, says thus :—

§ 55. " I, Beda, the servant of Christ, and priest of the monastery of the holy apostles Peter and Paul which is at Wearmouth, have, by God's assistance, arranged these materials for the history of Britain. I was born within the possessions of this monastery, and at seven years of age was committed, by the care of my relations, to the most reverend abbot Benedict, to be educated, and afterwards to Chelfrid. Passing the remainder of my life from that period in residence at the said monastery, I have given up my whole attention to the study of the Scriptures, and, amid the observance of my regular discipline and my daily duty of singing in the church, have ever delighted to learn, to teach, or to write. In the nineteenth year of my life I received deacon's, in the thirtieth, priest's orders ; both, at the instance of abbot Chelfrid, by the ministry of the most reverend bishop John ;[4] from which time of receiving the priesthood till the fifty-ninth year of my age, I have been employed, for the benefit of myself and of my friends,

[1] The monks of Glastonbury were apparently extremely diligent in procuring relics by every possible means. There remains a very curious account of a contention concerning the body of St. Dunstan, which those monks asserted they had stolen from Canterbury, after it had been burnt by the Danes in the time of Ethelred. V. Anglia Sacra, ii. 222. [2] Prov. x. 1; xv. 20.
[3] V. 24, § 453. There are a few verbal variations between the text of Malmesbury and Beda.
[4] John of Beverley, bishop of Hexham in 686. He was made bishop of York, A.D. 705, and died 7th May, in the year 722.

in making these extracts from the works of the venerable fathers, or in making additions, according to the form of their sense or interpretation."

§ 56. Then, enumerating thirty-six volumes which he published in seventy-eight books, he proceeds,—" And I pray most earnestly, O merciful Jesus, that thou wouldest mercifully grant me, whom Thou hast kindly permitted to feed with benefit on the word of Thy wisdom, finally to come to Thee, the Fountain of all wisdom, and to appear for ever in Thy presence. Moreover,[1] I humbly entreat all persons, whether readers or hearers, whom this History of our Nation shall reach, that they be mindful to intercede with the Divine clemency for my infirmities both of mind and of body ; and that, in their several provinces, they make me this grateful return, that I, who have diligently laboured to record, of every province or of more exalted places,[2] what appeared worthy of preservation or agreeable to the inhabitants, may receive from all the benefit of their pious intercessions."

§ 57. Here my abilities fail, here my eloquence falls short ; ignorant which to praise most, the number of his writings or the gravity of his style. No doubt he had imbibed a large portion of heavenly wisdom, to be able to compose so many volumes within the limits of so short a life. Nay, it is even reported that he went to Rome, for the purpose either of personally asserting that his writings were consistent with the doctrines of the church, or of correcting them by apostolical authority, should they be found repugnant thereto. That he was at Rome I do not, however, affirm for fact :[3] but I have no doubt in declaring that he had been invited

---

[1] This paragraph is not placed at the end of the history, but is made to conclude the prologue in the printed copy of Beda.

[2] In allusion to his account of the holy places at Jerusalem and in its neighbourhood. Beda, E. H. §§ 404—407.

[3] Beda's invitation to Rome has already been discussed in the Preface to the Ecclesiastical History of that writer, § 29. The following is Hardy's note upon Malmesbury's account of this incident in the life of Beda, which the reader will be glad to see entire :—" From what is here stated, the tradition that Beda visited Rome met probably with supporters in Malmesbury's time, though he does not seem to attach great weight to it. The letter of pope Sergius, however, affords the strongest presumption that Beda was invited over ; and the argument of the learned Wilkins assigns a probable reason why the journey was not undertaken ; he thinks that the letter was written in the last year of the pontificate of Sergius, (A. D. 701,) and conjectures that the subsequent arrival of messengers in England with tidings of the pontiff's decease occasioned Beda to relinquish his purposed journey. An opinion, however, has been lately expressed, that ' the story of Beda's summons to Rome is founded upon an error committed by Malmesbury, who, having met with a letter in which pope Sergius requested Ceolfrith, abbot of Jarrow, to send one of his monks to Rome, concluded that Beda was that individual, and most unjustifiably inserted his name therein.' In support of this charge, it has been alleged that there is still extant (of an earlier date than Malmesbury's work) a copy of this letter (Tiberius, A. xv.) in which the passage relating to Beda does not occur. In answer to this it may be urged, that Ussher, who had seen and copied the letter from the MS. above alluded to, arrives at no such conclusion. He had, moreover, in his possession, an ancient MS. containing the letter entire, from which Malmesbury gives but extracts ; and therein Beda's name does occur, though he is not described as presbyter. The only inference drawn by Ussher is, that the omission of Beda's description is not without reason, inasmuch as he had not at that time been ordained priest. Before it can be admitted as a just inference that Malmesbury interpolated the passage in question, it must be shown

thither, as the following epistle will certify; as well as that the
see of Rome so highly esteemed him as greatly to desire his
presence.

§ 58. "Sergius the bishop, servant of the servants of God, to
Cheolfrid the holy abbot, sendeth greeting. With what words, and
in what manner, can we declare the kindness and unspeakable
providence of our God, and return fit thanks for his boundless
benefits, who leads us, when placed in darkness and the shadow of
death, to the light of knowledge?" And further on,—"Know that
we received the favour of the offering which your devout piety hath
sent by the present bearer, with the same joy and good-will with
which it was transmitted. Assenting, therefore, to the timely and
becoming prayers of your laudable anxiety with the deepest regard,
we entreat of your pious goodness, so acceptable to God, that, since
there have occurred certain points of ecclesiastical discipline, not
to be promulgated without farther examination, which have made
it necessary for us to confer with a person skilled in literature, as
becomes an assistant of the holy universal mother-church devoted
to God, you would not delay paying ready obedience to this our
admonition; but would send, without any loss of time, to our lowly
presence, at the church of the chief apostles my lords Peter and
Paul, your friends and protectors, that religious servant of God,
Beda, the venerable priest of your monastery,[1] whom, (God favouring your holy prayers,) the necessary discussion of the above-
mentioned points being, by the assistance of God, solemnly completed, you may expect shortly to return prosperously to you: for
whatever may be added to the church at large, by his assistance,
will, we trust, be profitable to the things committed to your
immediate care."

§ 59. So extensive was his fame then, that even the majesty of
Rome itself solicited his assistance in solving abstruse questions,
nor did Gallic conceit ever find in this Angle anything justly to
blame. All the Latin Church yielded the palm to his faith and
authority: for indeed he was of sound and simple faith, and of
pleasing eloquence; in all elucidations of the Holy Scriptures,
discussing those points from which the reader might imbibe the

that Tiberius, A. xv. was the identical copy of the letter he used; a conclusion
which cannot be fairly drawn, as it is incredible but that other copies of the letter
must have been extant when he wrote; and it ought rather to be contended that
the one he saw must have contained the passage in dispute; for Malmesbury
(whose great integrity is admitted by all writers) several times expressly declares
that he declined inserting anything in his history for which he had not the best
authority. Moreover, had he been guilty of the interpolation attributed to him,
it is improbable that he would have used language so candid as that he has
employed."

[1] Upon these words Hardy remarks :—" In the Cottonian MS. (Tib. A. xv. fol. 6)
the passage occurs thus: 'Dei famulum N. venerabilis tui monasterii.' These
words have been read incorrectly, as it seems, 'Dei nostri famulum.' From the
fact of the letter N. being found in the Cotton MS. for the name of the person
summoned to Rome, it might be inferred that, in the transcript from which the
writer copied, the name had been accidentally omitted, and that the passage was
not clear: some word appears wanting to complete the construction of the
sentence as it stands in Tib. A. xv."

love of God and of his neighbour, rather than those which might charm by their wit, or polish a rugged style.   Moreover, the irrefragable truth of that sentence, which the majesty of Divine Wisdom[1] proclaimed to the world, forbids any one to doubt the sanctity of his life : " Wisdom will not enter the malevolent soul, nor dwell in the person of the sinful ;" which indeed is said, not of earthly wisdom, which is infused promiscuously into the hearts of men, and in which even the wicked, who continue their crimes until their last day, seem often to excel, according to the divine expression,[2] " The sons of this world are in their generation wiser than the children of light ;" but it rather describes that wisdom which needs not the assistance of learning, and which dismisses from its cogitations those things which are void of understanding, that is to say, of the understanding of acting and speaking properly. Hence Seneca, in his book " De Causis,"[3] appositely relates, that Cato, when defining the duty of an orator, said, " An orator is a good man, skilled in speaking."   This ecclesiastical orator, then, used to purify his mind, that so he might be able to unveil the meaning of mystic writings.   How, indeed, could that man be enslaved to vice, who gave his whole soul and spirit to elucidate the Scriptures ?   For, as he confesses in his third book on Samuel,[4] if his expositions were productive of no advantage to his readers, yet they were of considerable importance to himself, inasmuch as, while fully intent upon them, he escaped the vanity and empty imaginations of the times.   Purified from vice, therefore, he entered within the inner veil, divulging in pure diction the sentiments of his mind.

§ 60.   But the unspotted sanctity and holy purity of his heart were chiefly conspicuous on the approach of death ; for although for seven weeks successively, from the indisposition of his stomach, he nauseated all food, and was troubled with such a difficulty of breathing that his disorder confined him to his bed, yet he by no means abandoned his literary avocations.   During whole days he endeavoured to mitigate the pressure of his disorder, and to lose the recollection of it, by constant readings with his pupils, and by examining and solving abstruse questions, in addition to his usual task of psalmody.   Moreover, the Gospel of St. John, which from its difficulty exercises the talents of its readers even in the present day, was translated by him into the English language, and accommodated to those who did not perfectly understand Latin.   Occasionally, also, would he admonish his disciples, saying, " Learn, my children, while I am with you : for I know not how long I shall continue ; and, although my Maker should very shortly take me hence, and my spirit should return to Him that sent and granted it to come into this life, yet have I lived long.   God hath rightly appointed my portion of days : I now desire to be dissolved, and to be with Christ."

§ 61.   Often, too, when the balance was poised between hope and

---

[1] Book of Wisdom, i. 4.   [2] Luke xvi. 8.   [3] Seneca, Controvers. lib. i.
[4] The sentiment is expressed in the prologue to the first book " Expositionis Allegoricæ in Samuelem Prophetam," Opp. iv. 209, ed. Bas. 1563.

fear, he would remark, "It is a fearful thing to fall into the hands of the living God.[1] I have not passed my life among you in such manner as to be ashamed to live, neither do I fear to die, because we have a kind Master;" thus borrowing the expression of St. Ambrose when dying. Happy man! who could speak with so quiet a conscience, as neither being ashamed to live, nor yet afraid to die ; on the one hand, not fearing the judgment of men; on the other, waiting with composure the hidden will of God. Often, when urged by extremity of pain, he comforted himself with these remarks : "The furnace tries the gold, and the fire of temptation the just man." "The sufferings of this present time are not worthy to be compared to the future glory which shall be revealed in us."[2] Tears, and a difficulty of breathing, accompanied his words. At night, when there were none to be instructed, or to note down his remarks, he passed the whole season in giving thanks and singing psalms ; fulfilling the saying of that very wise man,[3] "that he was never less alone than when alone." If at any time a short and disturbed sleep stole upon his eyelids, immediately chasing and repelling it, he showed that his affections were always intent on God, by exclaiming, "Lift me up, O Lord, that the proud calumniate me not. Do with thy servant according to thy mercy."[4] These and similar expressions, which his shattered memory suggested, flowed spontaneously from his lips, whenever the pain of his agonizing disorder became mitigated. But on the Tuesday before our Lord's Ascension, his disease rapidly increasing, there appeared a small swelling in his feet, the sure and certain indication of approaching death. Then the congregation being called together, he was anointed and received the communion ; and kissing them all, and requesting from each, that they would bear him in remembrance, he gave a small present, which he had privately reserved, to some with whom he had been in closer bonds of friendship. On Ascension-day, when his soul, tired of the frail occupation of the body, panted to be free, lying down on a hair-cloth near the oratory, where he had used to pray, with sense unimpaired and joyful countenance, he invited the grace of the Holy Spirit, saying, "O King of glory, Lord of virtue, who didst ascend this day triumphant into the heavens, leave us not destitute, but send upon us the Spirit of truth, which was promised by the Father." This prayer being ended, he breathed his last ;[5] and immediately the senses of all were pervaded by an odour, such as neither cinnamon nor balm could give, but coming as it were from paradise, and fraught with all the joyous exhalations of spring. At that time he was buried in the same monastery; but at present, report asserts[6] that he lies at Durham with the blessed Cuthbert.

---

[1] Heb. x. 31.   [2] Rom. viii. 18.

[3] Scipio Africanus was accustomed to observe, that he was never less unoccupied than when unoccupied, nor ever less alone than when alone.—Cicero, De Offic. i. 3.   [4] Psalm cxix. 124, Vulg.

[5] A letter descriptive of the last moments of Beda, written by one of his pupils present at the historian's death, is printed in the Introduction to Beda, § 35, in the volume of this series.

[6] Alfrid, a priest, is reported to have stolen Beda's bones from Jarrow, and

§ 62. With this man was buried almost all knowledge of history down to our times, inasmuch as there has been no Englishman either emulous of his pursuits, or a follower of his graces, who could continue the thread of his discourse, now broken short.   Some few, indeed, " whom the mild Jesus loved,"[1] though well skilled in literature, have yet observed an ungracious silence throughout their whole lives ; others, scarcely tasting of the stream, have fostered a criminal indolence.   Thus, to slothful, others more slothful continually succeeding, the warmth of science for a long time decreased throughout the island.   The verses of his epitaph will afford sufficient specimen of this indolence; disgraceful, indeed, and unworthy the tomb of so great a man :—[2]

> " Presbyter hic Beda, requiescit carne sepultus ;
> Dona Christe animam in cœlis gaudere per ævum :
> Daque illi sophiæ debriari fonte, cui jam
> Suspiravit ovans, intento semper amore."

§ 63. Can this disgrace be extenuated by any excuse, that there was not to be found even in that monastery, where during his lifetime the school of all learning had flourished, a single person who could write his epitaph, except in this mean and miserable manner ? But enough of this : now to my subject.

§ 64. Chelwulf, thinking it beneath the dignity of a Christian to be immersed in earthly things, abdicated the throne, after a reign of eight years, and assumed the monastic habit at Lindisfarne,[3] in which place how meritoriously he lived, is amply testified by his distinguished interment[4] near St. Cuthbert, and by many miracles vouchsafed from on high.

§ 65. He had made provision against the state being endangered, by placing his cousin, Egbert,[5] on the throne, which he, running the race of a good man, filled for twenty years with singular moderation.   Egbert had a brother of the same name, archbishop of York, who, by his own prudence and the power of the king, restored that see to its original state.[6]   For, as is well known to any one conversant in the history of the Angles,[7] Paulinus,[8] the first prelate

deposited them in the cathedral church of Durham, in the early part of the eleventh century   .
[1] Adapted from Virgil, Æn. vi. 129.
[2] It has been thought proper to insert the Latin epitaph in the text, as the observations turn wholly on the meanness of the lines, and to give the translation (from Sharpe) below :—
> " Here in the flesh rests Bede the priest ; O give
> His soul with joy eternally to live ;
> And let him quaff, O Christ, of wisdom's stream :
> This was his wish, his fond, perpetual theme."
[3] Ceolwulf, having abdicated the throne in favour of his cousin Eadberht, became a monk in the year 737.
[4] Ceolwlf was buried at Lindisfarne, but the exact year of his death is not known.
[5] Simeon of Durham and other authorities more correctly call this king Eadberht. According to Malmesbury, he had a brother of the same name, archbishop of York, Ecgberht, who was ordained bishop of that see A.D. 732, and died in 766.
[6] York again became an archiepiscopal see A.D. 735, in consequence of Ecgberht's frequent appeals to Rome.   [7] See Beda, E. H. §§ 112, 148, 149.
[8] Paulinus, after his flight from Northumbria, became bishop of Rochester. See § 26. He died 10th October, A.D. 644.

of the church of York, had been forcibly driven away, and dying
at Rochester, had left there that honourable distinction of the pall
which he had received from pope Honorius. After him many
prelates of this august city, satisfied with the name of a simple
bishopric, aspired to nothing higher: but when Egbert was en-
throned, a man of loftier spirit, and one who thought that, as it is
overreaching to require what is not our due, so is it ignoble to
neglect our right, he recovered the pall by frequent appeals to the
pope. This personage was, if I may be allowed the expression,
the depository and receptacle of every liberal art, and built a most
noble library at York: for this statement I cite Alcuin[1] as a competent witness; who, having sent him from the kings of England to
the emperor Charles the Great, to treat of peace, and being hos-
pitably entertained by him, observes in a letter to Eanbald,[2] third
in succession from Egbert: "Praise[3] and glory be to God, who hath
preserved my days in full prosperity, that I should rejoice in the
exaltation of my dearest son, who laboured in my stead in the
church where I had been brought up and educated, and presided
over the treasures of wisdom to which my beloved master, archbishop Egbert, had left me heir." Thus too to Charles Augustus:[4]
"Give me the more polished volumes of scholastic learning, such
as I used to have in my own country, through the laudable and
ardent industry of my master, archbishop Egbert.[5] And, if it please
your wisdom, I will send some of our youths, who may obtain
thence whatever is necessary, and bring back into France the
flowers of Britain, that the garden of paradise be not confined
to York, but that some of its offshoots may be transplanted
to Tours."

§ 66. This is the same Alcwin, who, as I have said,[6] being sent
into France to treat of peace, during his abode with Charles,
either captivated with the pleasantness of the country or the
kindness of the king, settled there; and being held in high
estimation, he instructed the king's mind, during his leisure
from the cares of state, with a thorough knowledge of logic,
rhetoric, and even astronomy. Alcwin was, of all the Angles of
whom I have read, next to the blessed Aldelm and Beda, certainly

[1] Flaccus Alcuinus, or, as he is sometimes called, Albinus, was a native of
Northumbria. He went to France, and became the preceptor of Charlemagne,
who made him abbot of St. Martin's at Tours, where he died. Such portions of
his correspondence as illustrate the history of our nation will be given in a subsequent part of this Collection.

[2] This letter, written in the month of August, A.D. 796, must have been
addressed to Eanbald II., as Eanbald I. died 29th July in that year. Eanbald
II. was consecrated 14th August, 796, and received the pall in the following
year.

[3] See Alcuini Opera, fol. Ratisbonæ, 1777; i. 63, ep. l.

[4] Alc. Opp. i. 52, ep. xxxviii.

[5] There has been some doubt expressed as to which of Alcuin's masters reference
is made in this letter. Alcuin studied under both Ecgberht and his successor
Ethelberht, as the author of his life writes: "Ecgberto, aº 766, 13 cal. Dec.
mortuo, Alcuinus divino munere Elcbertum seu Aelbertum loco amissi magistrum
accepit." Malmesbury here and elsewhere calls him Egbertus, and identifies him
with the archbishop who obtained the restoration of the archiepiscopal see in 735.
The similarity of the names, often confounded by the Norman scribes, has probably given rise to the question.   [6] See § 65.

the most learned, and has given proof of his talents in a variety of compositions.[1]

§ 67. But since I am arrived at that point where the mention of Charles the Great naturally presents itself, I shall subjoin a true statement of the descent of the kings of France, of which antiquity has said much ; nor shall I depart widely from my design, because to be unacquainted with their race I hold as a defect in information, seeing that they are our near neighbours, and those to whom the Christian world chiefly looks up ; and, perhaps, to glance over this compendium may give pleasure to many who have not leisure to wade through voluminous works.

On the Succession of Kings of France.

§ 68. The Franks were so called, by a Greek appellative, from the ferocity of their manners,[2] when, by order of the emperor Valentinian the First, they ejected the Alani, who had retreated to the Mæotian marshes. It is scarcely possible to believe how much this people, few and mean at first, became increased by a ten years' exemption from taxes ; such, before the war, being the condition on which they engaged in it. Thus augmenting wonderfully by the acquisition of freedom, and first seizing the greatest part of Germany, and next the whole of Gaul, they compelled their inhabitants to list under their banners : hence the Lotharingi and Alamanni, and other nations beyond the Rhine, who are subject to the emperor of Germany, affirm that they ought more properly to be called Franks ; and those whom we suppose to be Franks, they call by an ancient appellative Galwalæ, that is to say, Gauls. To this opinion I assent ; knowing that Charles the Great, whom none can deny to have been king of the Franks, always used the same vernacular language with the Franks on the other side of the Rhine. Any one who shall read the life of Charles will readily admit the truth of my assertion.[3] In the year, then, of the Incarnate Word four hundred and twenty-five,[4] the Franks were governed by Faramund their first king.[5] The grandson of Faramund was

---

[1] The text of Saville, supported by two MSS., C. and M., and a marginal cotemporary addition to a fourth (D.), here add : "He lies buried in France, at the church of St. Paul of Cormarie, which monastery Charles the Great built at his suggestion ; on which account, even at the present day, the subsistence of four monks is distributed in alms, for the soul of the same Alcuin, in that church." Some authors affirm that Alcuin was buried in the abbey of St. Martin de Tours, where he died, 18th April, 804. St. Paul de Cormarico was a cell to that abbey.—Bouquet, v. 765.

[2] The sophist Libanius, a writer of the fourth century, states that in his time there was on the Rhine, near the ocean. a nation of Celts so warlike and valiant that they acquired the name of φρακτοὶ, a name that has been corrupted into φραγκοὶ (Franci).

[3] The life of Charlemagne, written by Eginhardt, who was secretary to that monarch. Script. Franc. Duchesne, tom. ii.

[4] The supposed establishment of a monarchy in France is usually ascribed to the commencement of the reign of Faramond, A.D. 418 ; but Clovis may be more justly considered the founder of the French monarchy, A.D. 481.

[5] The foundation of the French monarchy by Faramond, and even his existence, have been justly questioned. Except in a short and suspicious line of the Chronicle of Prosper, (i. 638,) the name of Faramond is never mentioned before the seventh century.

Meroveus,[1] from whom all the succeeding kings were called Merovingians.[2] In like manner the sons of the kings of the Angles took
patronymical appellations from their fathers. For instance, the
son of Edgar was called Eadgaring ; the son of Edmund, Edmund-
ing ; and the rest in like manner ; commonly, however, they are
called Ethelings.[3] The native language of the Franks therefore
partakes of that of the Angles, by reason of both nations originating
from Germany. The Merovingians reigned successfully and
powerfully till the year of our Lord's incarnation six hundred
and eighty-seven.[4] At that period, Pipin,[5] son of Ansegise, was
made mayor of the palace among the Franks on the other side of
the Rhine. Seizing opportunities for veiling his ambitious views,
he completely subjugated his master Theodoric, the dregs as it were
of the Merovingians ; and to lessen the obloquy excited by the
transaction, he indulged him with the empty title of king, while
himself managed everything, at home and abroad, according to his
own pleasure. The genealogy of this Pipin,[6] both to and from him,
is thus traced : Ansbert the senator, by Blithilde the daughter of
Lothaire, the father of Dagobert, begot Arnold : Arnold begot St.
Arnulf, bishop of Metz :[7] Arnulf begot Flodulf,[8] Waltchise, Anchise:
Flodulf begot duke Martin,[9] whom Ebroin[10] slew : Waltchise begot

---

[1] He is supposed to have been the son of Clodion, whom he succeeded in the
year 447. He died A.D. 456.

[2] Saville's text and C. read, "Kings of the Franks to the time of Pepin were,"
&c. An ingenious critic has deduced the Merovingians from the great Marabo-
duus, and has clearly proved that the prince who gave his name to the first race
was more ancient than Mérovée. See Mémoires de l'Académie des Inscriptions,
xx. 52—90 ; xxx. 557—587. Gregory of Tours does not mention the Merovingian
name ; which may be traced, however, to the beginning of the seventh century
as the distinctive appellation of the royal family, and even of the French monarchy
of the first line.

[3] This epithet seems merely to imply nobility.

[4] The mayors of the palace of the kings of France began first to usurp the royal
authority during the reign of Clovis II. king of Neustria, A.D. 638. Thierri II.
being restored to the throne A.D. 673, first obtained the appellation of Fainéant
(which attached to all the kings of France of that race, owing to their subjection
to the mayors of the palace) after he was defeated A.D. 687, by Pepin II. duke of
Austrasia, who then became mayor of the palace in Neustria and Bourgogne ;
Thierri and his successors retaining only the name of king. The final extinction
of the dominion of the Merovingians in France, and the commencement of a new
line, took place in the year 752.

[5] Pepin, son of duke Ansegise, having defeated Thierri II., continued to govern
the kingdom without assuming the title of king. He died 16th December,
714, and was succeeded by his natural son, Charles Martel, who also contented
himself with the title of duke until his death, 22d October, 741.

[6] The genealogy of Pepin, deduced from Ansbert the senator, and Blithildo,
daughter of Clothaire I., is mentioned in many of the French chronicles ; but it is
considered to be fictitious, and its authority cannot be traced higher than the
time of Charlemagne. Malmesbury further follows the anachronism of some of the
chronicles in making Blithilde the daughter of Clothaire II. and sister of Dagobert.

[7] St. Arnoul, considered by some authors as the ancestor of the second race of
the kings of France, was chosen bishop of Metz A.D. 614. He was prime minister
of Dagobert, king of Austrasia, and died in 641. His life is printed in Acta
SS. Ord. S. Bened. sæc. ii. p. 150.

[8] Clodulfus (St. Clou), son of St. Arnoul, was made bishop of Metz 13th April,
A.D. 654, and died in 694. His life was written about the ninth century, and is
printed in Acta SS. Ord. S. Bened. sæc. ii. p. 1044.

[9] Martin, duke of Austrasia, son of St. Clou, bishop of Metz, was slain by
Ebroin, A.D. 680.

[10] He was mayor of the palace, and was slain by Ermenfroi A.D. 681.

the most holy Wandregesil the abbot : duke Anschise[1] begot
Ansegise : Ansegise begot Pipin : the son of Pipin was Carolus
Tudites,[2] whom they also call Martel, because he beat down the
tyrants who were rising up in every part of France, and nobly
defeated the Saracens, at that time infesting Gaul.   Following the
practice of his father, himself satisfied with the title of earl, he
kept the kings in a state of pupilage : he left two sons, Pipin and
Carloman.[3]   Carloman, from some unknown cause, relinquishing
the world, took the tonsure at Monte Cassino.[4]   Pipin was crowned[5]
king of the Franks, and patrician of the Romans, in the church of
St. Denis, by pope Stephen, the successor of Zachary.   For the
Constantinopolitan emperors, already much degenerated from their
ancient valour, giving no assistance either to Italy or the church of
Rome, which had long groaned under the tyranny of the Lombards,
this pope bewailed the injuries to which they were exposed from
them to the ruler of the Franks ; wherefore Pipin, passing the
Alps, reduced Desiderius,[6] king of the Lombards, to such difficulties,
that he restored what he had plundered to the church of Rome,
and took an oath that he would not attempt to resume it.   Returning to France after some years, he died,[7] leaving Charles and
Carloman surviving him.   In two years Carloman departed this
life.[8]   Charles,[9] obtaining the name of " Great" from his exploits,
enlarged the kingdom to twice the limits which it had possessed in
his father's time : and being contented for more than thirty years
with the simple title of king, abstained from the appellation of
emperor, though repeatedly invited to assume it by pope Adrian.
But when, after the death of this pontiff, his relations maimed the
holy Leo, his successor, in the church of St. Peter, by cutting out

[1] Malmesbury has been betrayed into the error of introducing an additional
generation, under a suspicion that Anschisus and Ansegisus were distinct persons ; whereas duke Ansegisus, brother of St. Clou, and father of Pepin, was also
called Anschisus and Ansigilus.   He was slain A.D. 678.   See Bouquet, iii. 306.

[2] The epithet of Martel, which Tudites seems also to imply, was given to him
as expressive of his weighty and irresistible strokes in battle.

[3] Carloman, the eldest son of Charles Martel, succeeded him in Austrasia ; and
Pepin, his younger son, in Neustria, Bourgogne, and Provence.

[4] Carloman left his estates to his brother Pepin, and retired into Italy, where
he built a monastery.   In 747 he became a monk in the monastery of Monte
Cassino, and died in the year 754.

[5] In the year 752, Childeric III., last of the Merovingian race, having been
declared incapable of governing, Pepin was proclaimed king by an assembly of the
states of France, and was consecrated by Boniface, bishop of Mayence.   His second
consecration by pope Stephen took place A.D. 754.

[6] It was Aistolphe, king of the Lombards, and not Desiderius, whom Pepin
obliged to restore the towns he had usurped from the Holy See.   Upon the death
of Aistolphe in the year 756, Desiderius, or Didier, duke of Tuscany, was proclaimed king ; he was the last of the native princes of Lombardy, having surrendered his sceptre and his capital to Charlemagne, by whom he was defeated in the
year 774.

[7] Pepin, first of the second race of the kings of France, called Le Bref from the
lowness of his stature, and Le Gros from his shape, died 24th September, in the
year 768, and was succeeded by his sons Carloman and Charles, of whom the
former had for his portion Austrasia, and the latter Neustria, Bourgogne, and
Provence.

[8] Carloman died at Sam̃uci en Laonois on the 4th December, A.D. 771.

[9] Charles, afterwards called Charlemagne, upon the death of his brother Carloman, inherited the whole monarchy.

his tongue, and putting out his eyes,[1] Charles hastily proceeded to
Rome to settle the state of the church.   Justly punishing these
abandoned wretches, he stayed there the whole winter, and restored
the pontiff, now speaking plainly and seeing clearly by the miraculous
interposition of God, to his customary power.   At this time the
Roman people, with the privity of the pontiff, on the day of our
Lord's Nativity,[2] unexpectedly saluted him with the title of Augustus; which title, though, from its being unusual, he reluctantly
accepted, yet afterwards he defended it with proper spirit against
the Constantinopolitan emperors, and left it, as hereditary, to his
son Lewis.[3]   His descendants reigned in that country, which is now
properly called France, till the time of Hugh, surnamed Capet,[4]
from whom is descended the present Lewis.[5]   From the same stock
came the sovereigns of Germany and Italy, till the year of our Lord
nine hundred and twelve.   Then Conrad,[6] king of the Teutons,
seized that empire.   The grandson of this personage was Otho the
Great,[7] equal in every estimable quality to any of the emperors
who preceded him.   Thus admirable for his valour and goodness,
he left the empire in hereditary succession to his posterity:[8] for the
present Henry[9] derives his lineage from his blood.

§ 69.   To return to my narrative: Alcwin, though promoted by
Charles the Great to the monastery of St. Martin in France, was
not unmindful of his fellow-countrymen; but exerted himself to
retain the emperor in amity with them, and stimulated them to
virtue by frequent epistles.   I shall here subjoin many of his
observations, from which it will appear clearly, how extremely soon

---

[1] Upon the death of pope Adrian, 25th December, A.D. 795, Leo III. was chosen
as his successor, in preference to Adrian's nephew, who employed conspirators to
assault and slay the pope during a procession.   The assurance of the miraculous
restoration of his eyes and tongue, of which he had been twice deprived by the
knife of the assassin, as given by Anastasius (ap. Labb. Concil. vii. 1079), is
supported by the credulity of some French annalists; but Eginhard, and other
writers of the same age, are more rational and sincere.   The mutilation of Leo
took place 25th April, A.D. 799.

[2] Charlemagne was crowned emperor of the West by pope Leo III. on Christmas-
day, in the last year of the eighth century.

[3] Charlemagne died at Aix-la-Chapelle, on the 28th of January, A.D. 814.
Several ancient writers, commencing the year either on the 25th of March, or at
Easter, place his death in 813. He was succeeded by his son Louis le Débonnaire,
also called the Pious.

[4] The race of Charlemagne terminated with Louis V., who died on the 22d of
June, 987. Hugh Capet, son of Hugh le Grand, was then chosen king, and consecrated at Rheims on the 3d July. He died 24th October, A.D. 996.

[5] Louis VI., called Louis le Gros, succeeded his father Philippe I., and was
consecrated at Orleans 3d August, 1108. He died 1st August, 1137.

[6] The German branch of the family of Charlemagne became extinct on the
death of Louis IV., 21st January, 912; when the Germans, in a general assembly
of the nation, elected Conrad, count of Franconia, emperor. He died 23d
December, 918.

[7] Otho the Great was not grandson of Conrad. He was elected emperor in
937, upon the death of his father, Henri l'Oiseleur, who was the son of Otho duke
of Saxony.

[8] Upon the extinction of the line of Charlemagne, the empire of the West
became elective.

[9] Saville's text, following MS. C., here adds, "the son-in-law of Henry, king of
England." This Henry was crowned emperor of Germany, A.D. 1105. He
married Matilda, the daughter of Henry I. of England, 7th January, 1114, and
died at Utrecht, 23d May, 1125.

after the death of Beda the love of learning declined even in his own monastery, and how quickly after the decease of Egbert the kingdom of the Northumbrians came to ruin, through the prevalence of degenerate manners.

§ 70. He says thus to the monks of Wearmouth,[1] among whom Beda had both lived and died, obliquely accusing them of having done the very thing which he begs them not to do :[2] "Let the youths be accustomed to attend the praises of our heavenly King, not to dig up the burrows of foxes, or pursue the winding mazes of hares : let them now learn the holy Scriptures, that when they are grown up they may be able to instruct others. Remember the most noble teacher of our times, Beda the priest ; what thirst for learning he had in his youth, what praise he now has among men, and what a far greater reward of glory with God !" Again, to those of York he says : "The Searcher of my heart is witness, that it was not for lust of gold that I came to France, or continued there, but for the necessities of the church."[3] And thus he writes to Offa, king of the Mercians :[4] "I was prepared to come to you, with the presents of king Charles, and to return to my country: but it seemed more advisable to me, for the peace of my nation, to remain abroad, not knowing what I could have done among those persons, with whom no one can be secure, or able to proceed in any laudable pursuit. Lo ! the holy places are laid desolate by Pagans,[5] the altars polluted by perjury, the monasteries dishonoured by adultery, the earth itself stained with the blood of rulers and of princes." Again, to king Egelred, third in the sovereignty after Egbert : "Behold[5] the church of St. Cuthbert sprinkled with the blood of God's priests, despoiled of all its ornaments, and the holiest spot in Britain given up to pagan nations to be plundered ; and where, after the departure of St. Paulinus from York, the christian religion first took its rise in our own nation, there misery and calamity took their rise also. What portends that shower of blood, which in the time of Lent, in the city of York, the capital of the whole kingdom, in the church of the chief of the apostles,[6] we saw tremendously falling on the northern side of the building from the summit of the roof, though the weather was fair ? Must not blood be expected to come upon the land from the northern regions ?" Again, to Osbert,[7] prince of the Mercians : "Our kingdom of the Northumbrians has almost perished through internal dissensions and perjury." So also to Adalard, archbishop of Canterbury :[8] "I speak this on account of the scourge[9] which has lately fallen on that part of our island which has been inhabited by our forefathers for nearly three

---

[1] " ad Wiorenses."   [2] See Alcuini Opp. i. 22, ep. xiii.

[3] This passage does not occur in any of the letters known to Froben, the last editor of Alcuin's works ; but it in reality forms part of Ep. vi. (Opp. i. 9), which will be given (for the first time) in its entire state, in the edition which will be included in the present series.

[4] See Alc. Opp. i. 57, ep. xlii.   [5] See Id. i. 20, ep. xii.

[6] Saville here reads, " St. Peter, the chief," &c.

[7] Froben has not been able to recover the letter from which this is an extract. See Alc. Opp. i. 297.   [8] See Alc. Opp. i. 15, ep. ix.

[9] Alcuin most probably here alludes to the devastations of the Danes, which began A. D. 793.

hundred and forty years. It is recorded in the writings of Gildas,[1] the wisest of the Britons, that those very Britons ruined their country through the avarice and rapine of their princes, the iniquity and injustice of their judges, the bishops' neglect of preaching, the luxury and abandoned manners of the people. Let us be cautious that such vices become not prevalent in our times, in order that the Divine favour may preserve our country to us, in that happy prosperity for the future which hitherto, in his most merciful kindness, He has vouchsafed to us."

§ 71. It has been made evident, I think, what disgrace and what destruction the neglect of learning and the immoral manners of degenerate men brought upon England! These remarks obtain this place in my History merely for the purpose of cautioning my readers.

§ 72. Egbert,[2] then, rivalling his brother in piety, and receiving the tonsure, gave place to Osulph[3] his son, who being, without any offence on his part, slain by his subjects, was after a twelvemonth's reign succeeded by Mollo:[4] and he carrying on the government with commendable diligence for eleven years,[5] fell a victim to the treachery of Alcred. Alcred,[6] in his tenth year, was compelled by his countrymen to retire from the government which he had usurped. Ethelbert[7] too, the son of Mollo, being elected king by their consent, was expelled by them at the end of five years. Alfwold,[8] next hailed sovereign, lamented, after eleven years, the perfidy of the inhabitants; being assassinated, though guiltless, which his distinguished interment at Hexham and divine miracles sufficiently declare. His nephew, Osred,[9] the son of Alhred, succeeding him, was expelled after barely a year, and gave place to Ethelbert, who was also called Athelred. He was the son of Mollo, also called Athelwald; and, obtaining the kingdom after twelve years of exile, held it during four, at the end of which time, unable to escape the fate of his predecessors, he was cruelly murdered.[10] At this many of the bishops and nobles, greatly shocked, fled from the country. Some, indeed, affirm that he was punished deservedly, because he had assented to the unjust murder of Osred;[11] whereas he had it in his power to quit the sovereignty, and restore him to

---

[1] The precise words cited by Alcuin are not to be found in either the Historia or the Epistola Gildæ, as these works at present exist; but the expressions of Gildas, to which Alcuin seems to allude in showing whence resulted the misfortunes of the country, occur in §§ 27, 66 of the Epistola.

[2] Edberht abdicated in the year 758, and became a monk. He died A. D. 768.

[3] Osulf was murdered on the 24th of July, 759.

[4] Mull Athelwald, the paternal uncle of Osulf, was elected king on the 5th August, 759.

[5] Mull Athelwald was expelled from Northumberland 30th October, A. D. 765, having completed the sixth year of his reign in the August preceding. The Saxon Chronicle and Florence of Worcester assign only six years to his reign.

[6] Alhhred was driven from the throne A. D. 774.

[7] Athelberht, or Athelred, the son of Mull Athelwald, was banished by Alfwold in 779.

[8] Alfwald was slain on the 23d September, A. D. 789.

[9] Osred was expelled from his kingdom A. D. 790, and Athelberht was restored after an exile of twelve years.

[10] Athelberht was murdered on the 19th April, A. D. 796.

[11] Compare Simeon of Durham, A. D. 790—792.

his throne. Of the beginning of this reign Alcwin thus speaks :
" Blessed be God, the only worker of miracles : Ethelred, the son
of Adelwald, went lately from the dungeon to the throne, from
misery to grandeur ; by the recentness of whose accession we are
detained from coming to you."[1] Of his murder he writes thus
to Offa, king of the Mercians :[2] " Your esteemed kindness is to
understand that my lord, king Charles, often speaks to me of you
with affection and sincerity, and in him you have the firmest friend:
he therefore sends becoming presents to your grace, and to the
several episcopal sees of your kingdom. In like manner he had
appointed presents for king Ethelred, and for the sees of his bishops;
but oh, dreadful to think ! at the very moment of despatching these
gifts and letters, there came a sorrowful account by the ambassadors, who returned out of Scotland through your country, of
the faithlessness of the people, and the death of the king. So
that Charles, withholding his liberal gifts, is so highly incensed
against that nation, calling it perfidious and perverse, and the
murderer of its sovereigns, and esteeming it worse than pagan, that
had I not interceded, he would have already deprived them of
every advantage within his reach, and have done them all the
injury in his power."

§ 73. After Ethelred no one durst ascend the throne ;[3] each
dreading the fate of his predecessor, and preferring a life of safety in
inglorious ease to a tottering reign in anxious suspense; for most
of the Northumbrian kings had made their exit by a violent death,
which was now become almost habitual. Thus being without a
sovereign for thirty-three years, that province became an object of
plunder and contempt to its neighbours ; for when the Danes,
who (as I have before related from the words of Alcwin) laid
waste the holy places, on their return home represented to their
countrymen the fruitfulness of the island and the indolence of its
inhabitants, these barbarians, coming over hastily and in great
numbers, obtained forcible possession of that part of the country
till the time of which we are speaking. Indeed, they had a
king of their own for many years, though he was subordinate
to the authority of the king of the West Saxons : however, after
the lapse of these thirty-three years, king Egbert[4] obtained the
sovereignty of this province, as well as of the others, in the year of
our Lord's incarnation eight hundred and twenty-seven, and the
twenty-eighth of his reign. And since we have reached his times,
mindful of our engagement, we shall speak briefly of the kingdom
of the Mercians ; and this, as well because we admire brevity in
relation, as that there is no great abundance of materials.

[1] The editor of Alcuin's works (1777) had not discovered the letter from which
Malmesbury took this extract. See Alc. Opp. i. 5, epist. ii. note (c).
[2] Alc. Opp. i. 57, epist. xlii.
[3] Malmesbury is incorrect in his account of the circumstances which attended
the decline and fall of the once illustrious kingdom of Northumbria. The better
informed Simeon of Durham, and Hoveden, may here be consulted with advantage.
[4] This statement is incorrect, for Egbert's rule did not extend over Northumbria.

Of the Kingdom of the Mercians.

§ 74. In the year of our Lord's incarnation six hundred and twenty-six, and the hundred and thirty-ninth after the death of Hengist, Penda,[1] the son of Wibba, tenth in descent from Woden, of noble lineage, expert in war, but at the same time an irreligious heathen, assumed the title of king of the Mercians, when, now arrived at the age of fifty, he had fostered his presumption by frequent incursions on his neighbours. Seizing the sovereignty, therefore, with a mind loathing quiet, and unconscious how great an enormity it was even to be victorious in a contest against his own countrymen, he began to attack the neighbouring cities, to infest the confines of the surrounding kings, and to fill everything with terror and confusion. For what would not that man attempt, who, by his lawless daring, had extinguished those luminaries of Britain, Edwin[2] and Oswald,[3] kings of the Northumbrians, Sigebert,[4] Egric,[5] and Anna,[6] kings of the East Angles, men in whom nobility of race was equalled by sanctity of life? Chenwalch also, king of the West Saxons, after being frequently harassed by him, was driven into exile;[7] though he deservedly paid the penalty of his perfidy towards God in denying his faith, and towards Penda himself in repudiating his sister.[8] It is now irksome to relate, that eagerly watching opportunities of slaughter, and like a raven greedily flying at the scent of a carcase, he readily joined in assisting Chedwalla,[9] and was of infinite service to him in recovering his dominion. In this manner, for thirty years, attacking his countrymen, he did nothing worthy of record against strangers. His insatiable desires, however, at last found an end suitable to their deserts: for being routed with his allies by Oswiu, who had succeeded his brother Oswald, more through the assistance of God than his military powers, Penda[10] added to the number of infernal spirits. By his queen Kineswitha[11] his sons were Weda, Wulfer, Ethelred, Merewald, Mercelin: his daughters, Kineburga and Kineswitha, both distinguished for inviolable chastity. Thus the parent, though ever rebellious towards God, produced a most holy offspring for heaven.

§ 75. His son Weda[12] succeeded him in a portion of the kingdom, by the permission of Oswiu, advanced to the government of the

---

[1] Great obscurity prevails about the early history of Mercia. Henry of Huntingdon considers Crida to have been the founder of that kingdom, about the year 584. Crida died in the year 600, and was succeeded by Wibba, who died A.D. 610. Ceorl was the next in succession, and Penda succeeded him. Malmesbury here follows the Saxon Chronicle in dating Penda's reign from A.D. 626; but Beda says that he reigned for twenty-two years, and died in 655. His reign began, therefore, in 633, the year of his victory over Edwin. See the Eccl. Hist. § 148.

[2] See § 48.   [3] See § 49.   [4] See § 97.   [5] See § 97.
[6] See § 97.   [7] See § 19.   [8] See § 19, and Beda, E. H. § 169.

[9] Penda joined Ceadwalla, king of the Britons, and defeated Edwin of Northumberland, at Hatfield, on the 12th of October, A.D. 633. See § 48.

[10] Penda was killed A.D. 655.   [11] See Beda, E. H. § 221.

[12] Weda is a blundering of the scribe or author; the son and successor of Penda, in Beda, the Saxon Chronicle, and other authorities, being called Peada. He was advanced to the government of the South Mercians by his kinsman, Oswiu, A.D. 656, and slain in the spring of the following year.

South Mercians; a young man of talents, and even in his father's lifetime son-in-law[1] to Oswiu. For he had received his daughter on condition of renouncing his idols and embracing Christianity, in which faith he would soon have caused the province to participate, the peaceful state of the kingdom and his father-in-law's consent conspiring to such a purpose, had not his death, hastened as they say by the intrigues of his wife, intercepted these happy prospects. Then Oswiu resumed the government,[2] which seemed rightly to appertain to him from his victory over the father, and from his affinity to the son. The spirit, however, of the inhabitants could not brook his authority more than three years;[3] for, expelling his generals, and Wulfer,[4] the son of Penda, being hailed as successor, the province recovered its liberty.

§ 76. Wulfer, that he might not deceive the expectation of the people, began to act with energy, to show himself an efficient prince by great exertions both mental and bodily; and finally he gave to Christianity, which had been introduced by his brother, and yet hardly breathing in his kingdom, every possible assistance. In the early years of his reign, he was heavily oppressed by the king of the West Saxons; but in succeeding times,[5] repelling the injury by the energy of his measures, he deprived him of the sovereignty of the Isle of Wight; and turning it, yet panting after heathen rites, into the proper path, he soon after bestowed it on Ethelwalk, king of the South Saxons, for whom he had stood as sponsor in baptism, as a recompense for his faith. But these and all his other good qualities are stained and deteriorated by the dreadful brand of simony; because he, first of the kings of the Angles, sold the sacred bishopric of London to one Wina,[6] an ambitious man. His wife was Ermenhilda, the daughter of Ercombert, king of Kent, on whom he begat Kenred and Waraburga, a most holy virgin, who lies buried at Chester. His brother Merewald married Ermenburga, the daughter of Ermenred, brother of the same Ercombert; by her he had issue three daughters, Milburga, who lies at Weneloc; Mildritha in Kent, in the monastery of St. Augustine, and Mildritha,[7] and a son Merefin. Alfrid, king of the Northumbrians, married Kineburga, daughter of Penda, who after a time, disgusted with wedlock, took the habit of a nun in the monastery which her brothers Wulfer and Aethelred had founded.

---

[1] Peada married Alchfleda, natural daughter of Oswiu, and was by her intrigues betrayed A.D. 657.

[2] After Penda was vanquished by Oswiu, the kingdom of Mercia fell into his hands, a portion of which he bestowed upon Peada, after whose death it reverted to Oswiu.   [3] See Beda, E. H. § 224.

[4] Upon the expulsion of Oswiu from Mercia, Wulfher succeeded to that kingdom, A.D. 657.

[5] Wulfher succeeded in A.D. 657. He defeated Cynewealh, king of Wessex, A.D. 661; and bestowed the Isle of Wight upon Aethiluualh of Sussex, for whom he had stood in baptism.—Sax. Chron. A.D. 661.

[6] Wini, bishop of Winchester, was driven from his see A.D. 696, and in that year purchased the bishopric of London from king Wulfher.—See Beda, E. H. § 170.

[7] Such is the reading of the Latin text; but we should substitute "Mildgytha." See the Genealogy in Florence of Worcester. pp. 387, 396.

§ 77. Wulfer dying at the end of nineteen years,[1] his brother
Ethelred[2] ascended the throne, more famed for his pious disposition than his skill in war.   Moreover, satisfied, in a single but
illustrious expedition into Kent,[3] with the display of his valour, he
passed the remainder of his life in quiet; except that, attacking
Egfrid, king of the Northumbrians,[4] who had passed beyond the
limits of his kingdom, he induced him to return home by killing
his brother Elwin.   He atoned, however, for this slaughter, after
due deliberation, at the instance of the blessed Theodore the archbishop, by giving Egfrid a large sum of money.[5]   Subsequently to
this, in the thirtieth year of his reign, taking the cowl, he became
a monk at Bardney,[6] and was ultimately promoted to be abbot.
This is the same person, who, being contemporary with Ina, king
of the West Saxons, confirmed by his authority also the privilege
which St. Aldelm, as we have before mentioned, brought from
Rome.[7]   His wife was Ostgida, sister of Egfrid, king of the
Northumbrians, by whom she had issue a son, named Ceolred.

§ 78. He appointed Kenred,[8] the son of his brother Wulfer, to
be his successor, who, equally celebrated for piety to God and
uprightness towards his subjects, ran his mortal race with great
purity of manners; and proceeding to Rome in the fifth year of his
reign,[9] passed the remainder of his life there in the offices of
religion; chiefly instigated to this by the melancholy departure of
a soldier, who, as Beda relates,[10] disdaining to confess his crimes
when in health, saw manifestly, when at the point of death, those
very demons coming to punish him, to whose vicious allurements
he had surrendered his soul.

§ 79. After him reigned Chelred,[11] the son of Ethelred his
uncle, as conspicuous for his valour against Ina, as pitiable for an
early death; for not filling the throne more than eight[12] years, he
was buried at Lichfield, leaving Ethelbald, the grand-nephew of
Penda by his brother Alwi,[13] as his heir.   This king enjoying
the sovereignty in profound peace, and for a long time, that is,
for the space of forty-one years, was ultimately killed by his

---

[1] According to Beda, E. H. § 452, Wulfher died A. D. 675, after a reign of
seventeen years.   [2] Aethilred succeeded his brother A. D. 675.
   [3] Aethilred wasted Kent in the year 676. Beda, E. H. § 452, and Sax. Chron.
A. D. 676.   [4] See § 51.
   [5] That is, he paid the weregild, which was a pecuniary mulct for killing a man;
one moiety of which went to the public purse, and the other to the relations of
the deceased.   The were of every man, from the prince to the slave, was established by law.   The legal compensation paid to king Ini by the Kentish men for
the death of Mull was, according to the Saxon Chronicle, no less a sum than thirty
thousand pounds.   A king's weregild was fixed at thirty thousand thrysmas, according to the laws of the North people.—See Anglo-Saxon Laws by Thorpe, i.
186, ed. 8vo.   See note, § 35.
   [6] Aethilred abdicated, and entered into a monastic life at Bardney, A. D. 704,
and was succeeded by his nephew Cenred. See the Saxon Chron. ad an.
   [7] See the note appended to § 35.   [8] A. D. 704.
   [9] Cenred's abdication and journey to Rome took place A. D. 709.
   [10] Beda, E. H. § 397.
   [11] Ceolred, the son of Aethilred, succeeded his cousin A. D. 709. Beda, E. H.
§ 412.   [12] Ceolred died A. D. 716. Beda, E. H. § 452.
   [13] Aethilbald came to the throne A. D. 716. In the Saxon Chronicle he is called
the son of Alwy.

subjects,[1] and thus met with a reverse of fortune. Bernred,[2] the author of his death, left nothing worthy of record, except that after-wards, being himself put to death by Offa, he received the just reward of his treachery. To this Ethelbald, Boniface,[3] archbishop of Mentz, an Englishman, who was subsequently crowned with martyrdom, sent an epistle,[4] part of which I shall transcribe, that it may appear how freely he asserts that those very vices had already gained ground among the Angles, of which Alcwin in after times was apprehensive. It will also be a strong proof, by the remark-able deaths of certain kings, how severely God punishes those guilty persons for whom his long-suspended anger mercifully waits.

§ 80. " To Ethelbald, my dearest lord, and to be preferred to all other kings of the Angles in the love of Christ, Boniface the arch-bishop, the legate appointed for Germany by the church of Rome, wisheth perpetual health in Christ.

" We confess before God that when we hear of your prosperity, your faith, and good works, we rejoice ; and if at any time we hear of any adversity befalling you, either in the chance of war or the jeopardy of your soul, we are afflicted. We have heard that being devoted to almsgiving, you prohibit theft and rapine, that you are a lover of peace, a defender of widows and of the poor ; and for this we give God thanks. Your contempt for lawful matrimony, were it for chastity's sake, would be laudable ; but that you wallow in luxury, and in adultery even with nuns,—this is disgraceful and damna-ble ; it dims the brightness of your glory before God and man, and transforms you into an idolater because you have polluted the temple of God. Wherefore, my beloved son, repent, and remember how dishonourable it is that you, who by the grant of God are sovereign over many nations, should yourself be the slave of lust to his disservice. Moreover, we have heard that almost all the nobles of the nation of the Mercians, following your example, desert their lawful wives, and live in guilty intercourse with adulteresses and nuns. Let the custom of a foreign country teach you how far distant this is from rectitude : for in Old Saxony, where there is no knowledge of Christ, if a virgin in her father's house, or a married woman under the protection of her husband, should be guilty of adultery, they burn her, strangled by her own hand, and hang up her seducer over the grave where she is buried ; or else cutting off her garments to the waist, modest matrons whip her and pierce her with knives, and fresh tormentors punish her in the same manner, as she is driven from town to town, till they destroy her. Again the Winedi, the most depraved race of men, have this custom : the wife, on the death of her husband, casts

---

[1] Ethilbald was slain at Seckington, in Warwickshire, A.D. 757, by Beornred, who thereupon usurped the throne.

[2] Beornred was dethroned and slain by Offa A.D. 757.

[3] Boniface, whose original name was Winfrith, archbishop of Mayence, desig-nated as the Apostle of the Germans, suffered martyrdom in Frisia, 5th June, A.D. 755. He addressed his admonitory epistle to Ethilbald in the year 745.

[4] This, and such others of the epistles of Boniface as illustrate the ecclesiastical history of our nation, will be found in the present series.

herself on the same funeral pile to be consumed with him. If then the Gentiles, who know not God, have so zealous a regard for chastity, how much more does it befit you, my beloved son, who are both a Christian and a king? Spare therefore your own soul, spare a multitude of people, perishing by your example, for whose souls you must give account. Give heed to this too ; if the nation of th Angles, (and we are reproached in France and in Italy, and by the very Pagans for it,) despising lawful matrimony, give free indulgence to adultery, a race ignoble, and despising God, must necessarily proceed from such a mixture, which will destroy the country by their abandoned manners, as was the case with the Burgundians, Provençals, and Spaniards, whom the Saracens harassed for many years on account of their past transgressions.

" Moreover, it has been told us that you have taken away from the churches and monasteries many of their privileges, thereby exciting, by your example, your nobility to do the like. But recollect, I entreat you, what terrible vengeance God hath inflicted upon former kings who have been guilty of the crime which we lay to your charge. For Chelred, your predecessor, the debaucher of nuns, the infringer of ecclesiastical privileges, was seized, while splendidly regaling with his nobles, by a malignant spirit, who snatched away his soul without confession and without communion, while he was talking with the devil and despising the law of God. He drove Osred also, king of the Deiri and Bernicians, who was guilty of the same crimes, to such excess, that he lost his kingdom, and perished in early manhood by an ignominious death. Charles also, governor of the Franks, the subverter of many monasteries, and the appropriator of ecclesiastical revenues to his own use, perished by excruciating pain and a fearful death.

§ 81. " Wherefore, my beloved son, we entreat with paternal and fervent prayers, that you would not despise the counsel of your fathers, who, for the love of God, anxiously appeal to your highness. For nothing is more salutary to a good king than the willing correction of such crimes when they are pointed out to him, since Solomon says, ' Whoso loveth instruction, loveth wisdom.' [Prov. xii. 1.] Wherefore, my dearest son, showing you good counsel, we call you to witness, and entreat you by the living God, and his Son Jesus Christ, and by the Holy Spirit, that you would recollect how fleeting and how short is the present life, how momentary is the delight of the filthy flesh, and how ignominious it is for a person of transitory existence to leave a bad example to posterity. Begin, therefore, to regulate your life by better habits, and correct the past errors of your youth, that you may have praise before men here, and be blest with eternal glory hereafter. We wish your highness health and growth in virtue."

§ 82. I have inserted in my narrative portions of this epistle, to give sufficient knowledge of these circumstances, partly in the words of the author, and partly in my own, shortening the sentences as seemed proper ; for which I shall easily be excused, because there was need of brevity for the sake of those who were eager to resume the thread of the history. Moreover, Boniface transmitted an epistle of like import to archbishop Cuthbert, adding that he should remonstrate with the clergy and nuns on the fineness and vanity of their dress. Besides, that he might not wonder at his interfering in that matter in which he had no apparent concern—that is to say, how or with what manners the nation of the Angles conducted itself—he gave him to understand that he had bound himself by oath to pope Gregory the third, not to conceal the conduct of the nations near him from the knowledge of the apostolical see; wherefore, if mild measures failed of success, he should take care to act in such manner, that vices of this kind should not be kept secret from the pope. Indeed, on account of the fine texture of the clerical vestments, Alcwin[1] obliquely glances at Adelard the archbishop, Cuthbert's successor, reminding him that when he should come to Rome to visit the emperor Charles the Great, the grandson of Charles of whom Boniface was speaking above, he should not bring the clergy or monks, dressed in party-coloured or gaudy garments, because the French clergy used only ecclesiastical habits.

§ 83. Nor could the letters of so great a man, which he was accustomed to send from watchful regard to his legation and love of his country, be without effect; for both Cuthbert the archbishop, and king Ethelbald, summoned a council for the purpose of retrenching the superfluities which he had stigmatised. The acts of this synod,[2] veiled in a multiplicity of words, I shall forbear to add, as I think they will better accord with another part of my work,[3] when I come to the succession of the bishops; but as I am now on the subject of kingly affairs, I shall subjoin a charter of Ethelbald as a proof of his devotion, because it took place in the same council:—

§ 84. "'It often happens, through the uncertain change of times, that those things which have been confirmed by the testimony and advice of many faithful persons, have been made of none effect by the contumacy of others, or by the artifices of deceit, without any regard to justice, unless they have been committed to eternal memory by the authority of writing and the testimony of charters. Wherefore, I Ethelbald, king of the Mercians, out of love to heaven and regard for my own soul, have felt the necessity of considering how I may, by good works, set it free from every tie of sin : for since the omnipotent God, through the greatness of his clemency, without any previous merit on my part, hath bestowed on me the sceptre of government, therefore I willingly repay Him out of that which He hath given. On this account I grant, so long as I live, that all monasteries and churches of my kingdom shall be exempted from public taxes,

---

[1] See Alc. Opp. i. 84, ep. lxiii. note (b).
[2] See Wilkins' Concilia, i. 94.
[3] They are inserted by Malmesbury in his History of the English Bishops, of which a translation will be given hereafter.
[4] The whole of Ethelbald's charter, of which this is but an extract, is printed in Cod. Dip. Ævi Saxon. i. 119, No. xcix., where its genuineness is admitted.

works, and impositions, except the building of forts and bridges, from which none can be released. And, moreover, the servants of God shall have perfect liberty in the produce of their woods and lands, and the right of fishing, nor shall they bring presents either to king or princes except voluntarily, but they shall serve God without molestation," &c.

§ 85. Lullus[1] succeeded Boniface, an Englishman by birth also, of whose sanctity mention is made in the life of St. Goar;[2] and these verses bear witness, which I remember to have heard from my earliest childhood :

> "Lullus, than whom no holier prelate lives,
> By God's assistance healing medicine gives,
> Cures each disorder by his powerful hand,
> And with his glory overspreads the land."

§ 86. However, to return to my history.: Offa,[3] descended from Penda in the fifth degree, succeeded Ethelbald ; he was a man of a great mind, and one who would endeavour to effect whatever he had preconceived : he reigned thirty-nine years. When I consider the deeds of this person, I am doubtful whether I should commend or censure. At one time, in one and the same individual, vices were so palliated by virtues, and at another, virtues came in such quick succession upon vices, that it is difficult to determine " how to characterise the changing Proteus :"[4] my narrative shall give examples of each. Engaging in a pitched battle with Kinewulf, king of the West Saxons,[5] he easily gained the victory, though the other was a celebrated warrior. When he thought artifice would better suit his purpose, this same man beheaded king Ethelbert,[6] who had come to him through the allurement of great promises, and was at that very time within the walls of his palace, deluded into security by his perfidious attentions ; and then unjustly seized upon the kingdom of the East Angles which Ethelbert had held.

§ 87. The reliques of St. Alban,[7] at that time obscurely buried, he ordered to be reverently taken up and placed in a shrine, decorated to the fullest extent of royal munificence with gold and jewels ; a church of most beautiful workmanship was there erected, and a society of monks assembled. Yet, rebellious against God, he endeavoured to remove the archiepiscopal see, formerly settled at Canterbury, to Lichfield ;[8] envying, forsooth, the men of Kent

---

[1] Lullus was appointed his successor in the see of Mayence by Boniface, on setting out for Friezeland A. D. 755; he died A. D. 785. The chief incidents of his life have been collected and commented upon by Mabillon, Act. SS. ord. S. Bened. III. ii. 355.

[2] See the Life of St. Goar, Act. SS. ord. S. Bened. sæc. ii. 276.

[3] Offa, having expelled Beornred, succeeded by general consent of the kingdom, A. D. 757.   [4] Hor. Epist. I. i. 90.

[5] See § 42.

[6] Ethelberht, king of East Anglia, was put to death by Offa A. D. 793.

[7] In the year 793, a monastery was commenced by Offa in honour of St. Alban, whose relics he caused to be removed thither, five hundred and seven years after St. Alban's death. See the Life of Offa, p. 307, annexed to the edition of Matthew Paris, Lond. 1640.

[8] This is discussed more fully by Malmesbury, in his History of the Bishops.

the dignity of the archbishopric; on which account he at last deprived Lanbriht the archbishop, worn out with continual exertion, (and who produced many edicts of the apostolical see, both ancient and modern,) of all the possessions within his territories, as well as of the jurisdiction over the bishoprics. From pope Adrian, therefore, whom he had wearied with plausible assertions for a long time, (for many things which ought not to be granted may be gradually drawn and artfully wrested from minds intent on other occupations,) he obtained, that there should be an archbishopric of the Mercians at Lichfield, and that all the prelates of the Mercians should be subject to that province. Their names were as follow :—Denebert, bishop of Worcester, Werenbert of Leicester, Edulf of Sidnacester, Wulheard of Hereford : and the bishops of the East Angles, Alheard of Helmham, Tidfrid of Dunwich : the bishop of Lichfield was named Aldulf. Four bishops, however, remained suffragan to the archbishop of Canterbury: London, Winchester, Rochester, and Selsey. Some of these bishoprics are now in being ; some are removed to other places ; others consolidated by venal interest : for Leicester, Sidnacester, and Dunwich, from some unknown event, are no longer in existence. Nor did Offa's rapacity stop here : but this downright public pilferer converted to his own use the lands of many churches, of which Malmesbury was one. But this iniquity did not long deform canonical institutions ; for soon after, Kenulf, Offa's successor, inferior to no preceding king in power or in faith, transmitting a letter to Leo, the successor of Adrian, restored Aethelard, who had succeeded Lanbriht, to his former dignity. Hence Albinus, in an epistle to the same Aethelard, says :[1] " Having heard of the success of your journey, and your return to your country, and how you were received by the pope, I give thanks with all my heart to the Lord our God, who, by the precious gift of his mercy, directed your way with a prosperous progress ; gave you favour in the sight of the pope ; granted you to return home with the perfect accomplishment of your wishes ; and has condescended, through you, to restore the holiest seat of our first teacher [2] to its pristine dignity." I think it proper to subjoin part of the king's epistle and also of the pope's, though I may seem by so doing to anticipate the regular order of time ; but I shall do it on this account, that it is a task of greater difficulty for me to blend together disjointed facts than to despatch those which I had begun.

§ 88. [3] " To the most holy and truly loving lord Leo,[4] pontiff of the sacred and apostolical see, Kenulf, by the grace of God king of the Mercians, with the bishops, princes, and every degree of dignity under our authority, sendeth the salutation of the purest love in Christ.

[1] See Alc. Opp. i. 84, ep. lxiii.
[2] St. Augustine, archbishop of Canterbury.
[3] This letter is printed by Wilkins, Concilia, i. 163, from Malmesbury. See also Baron. Annal. 796, § 18; Alford, Annal. 797, § 3.
[4] Leo III, elected pope 26th Dec. 795, died 11th June, 816. See Jaffé, Regist. Pontiff. pp. 215, 220.

"We give thanks ever to God Almighty, who is wont by the means of new guides, the former being taken to the life eternal, to guide the church, purchased by his precious blood, amid the diverse storms of this world, to the haven of salvation, and to shed fresh light upon it, in order that it be led into no error of darkness, but may pursue the path of truth without stumbling.   Wherefore the universal church justly rejoices, that, when the true Rewarder of all good men took the most glorious pastor of his flock, Adrian,[1] to be eternally rewarded in heaven, still his kind providence gave a leader to his sheep, not less skilled, to conduct the flock of God into the fold of life.   We also, who live in the farthest confines of the world, justly boast, beyond all other things, that the church's exaltation is our safety, its prosperity our constant ground of joy ; since your apostolical dignity and our true faith originate from the same source.   Wherefore I deem it fitting to incline the ear of our obedience, with all due humility, to your holy commands, and to fulfil, with every possible endeavour, that which it shall seem just to your piety that we should accomplish; but to avoid, and utterly reject, all that shall be found inconsistent with right.   But now, I Kenulf, by the grace of God king, humbly entreat your excellence that I may address you, as I wish, without offence, on the subject of our progress, that you may receive me with peaceful tranquillity into the bosom of your regard, and that the liberal bounty of your benediction may qualify me, gifted with no stock of merit, to rule my people ; in order that God may deign through your interces- sion to defend the nation, which, together with me, your apostolical authority has instructed in the rudiments of the faith, against all attacks of adversaries, and to extend that kingdom which He has given.   All the Mercian kings before me were by your prede- cessors deemed worthy to obtain this benediction : this I humbly beg, and this, oh most holy man, I desire to receive, that you would more especially accept me as a son by adoption, as I love you as a father, and always honour you with all possible obedience. For among such great personages faith ever should be kept invio- late, as well as perfect love ; because paternal love is to be looked upon as filial happiness in God, according to the saying of Heze- kiah, [Isaiah xxxviiii. 19,] ' A father will make known thy truth to his sons, O Lord :' in which words I implore you, oh loved father, not to deny to your son, unworthy though he be, the knowledge of the Lord in your holy words, in order that by your sound in- struction I may be enabled, by the assistance of God, to come to a better course of life.   And moreover, oh most affectionate father, we beg, with all our bishops and every person of rank among us, that concerning the many inquiries on which we have thought it right to consult your wisdom, you would courteously reply, lest the traditions of the holy fathers and their instructions should, through ignorance, be misunderstood by us ; but let your reply reach us in charity and meekness, that, through the mercy of God, it may bring forth fruit in us to perfection.

[1] Adrian I. filled the papal see from 1st Feb. 772, till 25th Dec. 795.   Jaffé, pp. 203, 215.

" The first thing our bishops and learned men allege is, that, contrary to the canons and papal constitutions enacted for our use by the direction of the most holy father Gregory, as you know, the jurisdiction of the metropolitan of Canterbury is divided into two provinces; to whose power, by the same father's command, twelve bishops ought to be subject, as is read throughout our churches, in the letter which he directed to his brother and fellow-bishop, Augustine, concerning the two metropolitans of London and York, which letter I doubt not you also possess. But that pontifical dignity, which was at that time intended for London, with the honour and distinction of the pall, was for his sake removed and granted to Canterbury. For since Augustine, of blessed memory, who, at the command of St. Gregory, ministered the word of God to the nation of the Angles, and so gloriously presided over the church of the Saxons, died in that city, and his body was buried in the church of St. Peter the chief of the apostles, which his successor St. Laurence consecrated, it seemed proper to the sages of our nation, that the metropolitan dignity should reside in that city where rests the body of the man who planted the true faith in these parts. The honour of this pre-eminence, as you know, king Offa first attempted to take away, and to divide into two provinces, through enmity conceived against the venerable Lanbert[1] and the Kentish people; and your pious fellow-bishop and predecessor, Adrian, at the request of the aforesaid king, first did what no one had before presumed, and honoured the prelate of the Mercians with the pall. But yet we blame neither of these persons, whom, as we believe, Christ crowns with eternal glory. Nevertheless we humbly entreat your excellence, on whom God has deservedly conferred the key of wisdom, that you would consult with your counsellors on this subject, and condescend to transmit to us what you may think necessary for us to observe hereafter, so that the coat of Christ, woven throughout without seam, may not suffer any rent from dissensions among us, but may, as we desire, through your sound doctrine be guided into the unity of true peace. We have written these things to you, most holy father, with great humility and regard, earnestly entreating your clemency, that you would kindly and justly reply to those things which have been of necessity submitted to you by us. Moreover, we wish that you would examine with pious love that epistle, which, in the presence of all our bishops, Ethelard the archbishop wrote to you more fully on the subject of his own affairs and necessities, as well as on those of all Britain, that whatever the rule of faith requires in those matters which are contained therein, you would condescend truly to explain. Wherefore, during the last year, I sent my own embassy and that of the bishops by Wada the abbot, which embassy he receiving, executed idly, yea even foolishly. At this time I send you a small present as a token of regard, respected father, by Birin the priest, and Fildas and Cheolberth my servants, that is to say, one hundred and twenty mancuses[2] together with letters,

---

[1] See § 87.
[2] The value of the mancus is doubtful. Sometimes it appears to mean the same

begging that you would condescend to receive them kindly, and give us your blessing. May God Almighty long preserve you safe, to the glory of his holy church."

§ 89. "To the most excellent prince, my son, Kenulf king of the Mercians, of the province of Saxony, pope Leo sendeth greeting.

"Our most holy and reverend brother Ethelard, archbishop of Canterbury, arriving at the holy thresholds of the blessed apostles Peter and Paul, as well for the faithful performance of his vow of prayer, as to acquaint us of the apostolic see with the cause of his consecration, hath brought to us the writings of your royal excellence, wherein finding, in two epistles filled with true faith, your great humility, we return thanks to Almighty God, who hath taught and inclined your most prudent excellence to have due regard with us in all things towards St. Peter the chief of the apostles, and to submit with meekness to all apostolical constitutions. Moreover, in one of these epistles we find that, were it requisite, you would even lay down your life for us, for the sake of our apostolical office; yea, you rejoice much in the Lord at our prosperity, and profess that when our letters of kindest admonition reach the ears of your cordiality, you will receive them with all humility and spiritual joy of heart, as sons do the gift of a father. It is added, too, that you had ordered a small present out of your abundance to be offered to us, an hundred and twenty mancuses; which sum, with ardent desire for the salvation of your soul, we have accepted. The aforesaid archbishop, with his attendants, has been honourably and kindly received by us, and has been supplied with every necessary assistance. In the meantime, trusting to your most prudent excellence, (since you observe, even in your own royal letters, that no Christian can presume to run counter to our apostolical decisions,) we therefore endeavour, with all possible diligence, to transmit and ordain what shall be of service to your kingdom, that, as a canonical censure enjoins your royal excellence, and all the princes of your nation, and the whole people of God, to observe all things which the aforesaid archbishop Ethelard our brother, or the whole body of the evangelical and apostolical doctrine, and that of the holy fathers and of our predecessors the holy pontiffs, ordain, you ought by no means to resist their orthodox doctrine in any thing, as our Lord and Saviour says in the gospel, 'He who receiveth you receiveth me, and he who receives a prophet in the name of a prophet, shall receive a prophet's reward.' [Matt. x. 40, 41.] And how much more do we praise the Almighty, for this same lord archbishop, whom you have so highly commended to us, as being what he really is, most honourable and skilful, and that you know him to be prudent, of good morals, worthy before God and men. Oh, dearest and loving son, and excellent good king, at these your assertions we praise Almighty God, who hath pointed out to you a prelate who, like a true shepherd, is able to

---

with the mark; at others, it is supposed equal to thirty pence of the money of that time, or seven shillings and sixpence.

prescribe due penance according to the doctrine of the holy
Scriptures, and to rescue the souls of those who are under his
sacerdotal authority from the nethermost hell, snatching them from
inextinguishable fire, bringing them into the haven of salvation,
and offering for them to God Almighty a sacrifice fit and pure in
the sight of the Divine Majesty. And since the aforesaid archbishop hath pleased us extremely in every respect, in all holiness
and conversation of life, confiding much to him, we give him such
episcopal power, by the authority of St. Peter the chief of the
apostles, whose office, though unworthily, we fill, that if any in his
province, as well kings and princes as people, shall transgress the
commandments of the Lord, he shall excommunicate him until
he repent; and if he remain impenitent, let him be to you as a
heathen man and a publican. But with respect to the aforesaid
Ethelard, now made archbishop of the church of Canterbury, since
your excellent prelates have demanded from us that we do him
justice concerning the diocesan jurisdiction which he lately held,
as well over bishops as monasteries, and of which he has been
unjustly deprived as you know, and which have been taken from
his venerable see; we, making most diligent search, have found
in our sacred depository that St. Gregory, our predecessor, delivered that diocese to his deputed archbishop, St. Augustine, with
the right of consecrating bishops, to the full number of twelve.
Hence, we also (the truth being ascertained) have, by our apostolical authority, ordination and confirmation, decreed that these be
placed on their ancient footing, and do restore them to him
entire: and we deliver to him the grant of our confirmation,
to be duly observed by his church, according to the sacred
canons."

§ 90. In the meantime Offa, that the outrages against his
countrymen might not secretly tend to his disadvantage, seeking
the friendship and conciliating the favour of neighbouring kings,
gave his daughter Ethelburga in marriage to Brithric, king of the
West Saxons.[1] He obtained the amity of Charles the Great, king
of the Franks, by repeated embassies, though he could find little in
the disposition of Charles to second his views: they had disagreed
before, insomuch that violent feuds having arisen on both sides,
even the intercourse of merchants was prohibited. There is an
epistle of Alcuin to this effect, part of which I shall subjoin, as
it affords a strong proof of the magnanimity and valour of
Charles, who spent all his time in war against the Pagans, rebels
to God.

§ 91. He says,[2]—" The Old Saxons,[3] and all the nations of the
Frisons, were converted to the faith of Christ, through the exertions of king Charles, who urged some with threats and tempted
others with rewards. A year ago the king made an attack upon
the Sclavonians, and subjugated them to his power. The Avares,

---

[1] See § 43.
[2] This letter is printed by Ussher (Veterum Epistolarum Hibernicarum Sylloge,
4to. Paris, 1665), ep. xviii. p. 36, and Alc. Opp. i. 6, ep. iii.
[3] The Westphalians.

whom we call Huns, made a furious attempt upon Italy, and being
conquered by the Christian generals of the aforesaid king, returned
home with disgrace. In like manner they rushed against Baugaria
[Bavaria], and were again overcome and dispersed by the Christian
army. Moreover, the princes and commanders of the same most
Christian king took great part of Spain from the Saracens, to the
extent of three hundred miles along the sea-coast; but, oh shame!
these accursed Saracens (who are the Hagarens) have dominion
over the whole of Africa and the larger part of Asia Major. I know
not what will be our destination, for some ground of difference,
fomented by the devil, has arisen between king Charles and king
Offa, so that on both sides all navigation is prohibited to the merchants. Some say that we are to be sent into those parts to treat
of peace."

§ 92. In these words, in addition to what I have remarked
above, any curious person may determine how many years have
elapsed since the Saracens invaded Africa and Asia Major. And
indeed, had not the mercy of God animated the native spirit of
the emperors of the Franks, the Pagans had long since subjugated
Europe also. For, holding the Constantinopolitan emperors in
contempt, they possessed themselves of Sicily and Sardinia, the
Balearic isles, and almost all the countries surrounded by the sea,
with the exception of Rhodes, Crete, and Cyprus: in our time,
however, they have been compelled to relinquish Sicily by the
Northmen; Corsica and Sardinia by the Pisans; and great part of
Asia, and Jerusalem itself, by the Franks and other Christian
nations of Europe. But as I shall have a fitter place to treat
largely of these matters hereafter, I shall now subjoin, from the
words of Charles himself, the treaty which was ratified between
him and Offa, king of the Mercians :—

§ 93. [1] " Charles, by the grace of God king of the Franks and
Longobards, and patrician of the Romans, to his esteemed and
dearest brother Offa, king of the Mercians, sendeth greeting.

" First, we give thanks to God Almighty for the purity of the
Catholic faith which we find laudably expressed in your letters.
Concerning pilgrims, who for the love of God and the salvation of
their souls wish to visit the residence of the holy apostles, let them
go peaceably without any molestation; but if persons not seeking
the cause of religion but that of gain, be found amongst them, let
them pay the customary tolls in proper places. We will, too, that
traders have due protection within our kingdom, according to our
mandate; and if in any place they suffer wrongful oppression, let
them appeal to us, or to our judges, and we will see full justice
done. Let your kindness also be apprised that we have sent some
token of our regard, out of our dalmatics[2] and palls, to each episcopal

---

[1] This letter is printed in Wilkins' Concilia, i. 158, and in Alc. Opp. tom. ii.
App. p. 618.

[2] The dalmatic was a garment worn by the clergy, and sometimes by princes;
its name is said to have been derived from its invention in Dalmatia. The pall
here, apparently, signifies an upper vesture also, in form resembling a cloak without sleeves; but it has a variety of meanings. See Du Cange.

see of your kingdom, or of Ethelred's,[1] as an almsgiving on account of our apostolical lord Adrian;[2] earnestly begging that you would order him to be prayed for, not as though doubting that his blessed soul is at rest, but to show our esteem and regard to our dearest friend.[3] Moreover, we have sent somewhat out of the treasure of those earthly riches which the Lord Jesus hath granted to us of his unmerited bounty, for the metropolitan cities; and for yourself, beloved, a belt, a Hunnish sword,[4] and two silk palls."

§ 94. I have inserted these brief extracts from the epistle, that posterity may be clearly acquainted with the friendship which existed between Offa and Charles; confiding in which friendly intercourse, although assailed by the hatred of many, he passed the rest of his life in uninterrupted quiet, and left as his successor[5] Egfert his son, who had been anointed king in his lifetime.[6] Studiously avoiding the cruel path trod by his father, Egfert restored, with profound devotion, the privileges of all the churches which his father had in his time abridged. The possessions also which his father had taken from Malmesbury, he restored into the hands of Cuthbert, then abbot of that place, at the admonition of Ethelard archbishop of Canterbury, a man of energy and a worthy servant of God, and who is uniformly asserted to have been its abbot before Cuthbert.[7] But while the hopes of Egfert's noble qualities were ripening, in his early years, untimely death cropped the flower or his youthful prime; on which account Albinus, writing to the patrician Osbert,[8] says, " I do not think that the most noble youth Egfert died for his own sins, but because his father, in the establishment of his kingdom, shed much blood." Dying after a reign of four months, he appointed Kenulf, nephew of Penda in the fifth degree by his brother Kenwalk, to succeed him.[9]

§ 95. Kenulf was a man truly great, and surpassed his fame by his virtues, doing nothing at which malice could justly carp : religious at home, victorious in war, his praises will be deservedly extolled so long as an impartial judge can be found in England ; equally to be admired for the extent of his power and for the lowliness of his

---

[1] Ethelred, or Ethelberht, of Northumbria, died 19th April, 796. Sim. Dunelm. ad an.   [2] Pope Adrian had died 25th December, 795.

[3] On this passage, and on its bearing upon the question of purgatory, see Ussher's Answer to a Jesuit, p. 176, ed. 1835.

[4] "unum gladium Huniscum."

[5] Offa died 29th July, A.D. 796, and was succeeded by his son Ecgfrith, who died in the same year. Some copies of the Saxon Chronicle, Florence of Worcester, and others, incorrectly place the death of Offa in the year 794. The letter from Charlemagne to Offa, written before April 796, mentions the death of Adrian; consequently Offa must have been living after the death of that pope, which took place on the 25th Dec. 795. Jaffé, Regist. p. 215.

[6] Ecgfrith was consecrated king during his father's life-time, A.D. 787.

[7] Some MSS. (A. D. L. M. followed by Saville) add, "from the circumstance of his choosing to be buried there."

[8] The editor of Alcuin's works (i. 74, note c) observes, that the letter from which Malmesbury has extracted this passage is not known, save through the pages of our historian.

[9] Ecgfrith died after a few months' reign, and Cenuulf was appointed his successor.

mind, of which he gave an eminent proof in restoring, as we have
related,[1] its faltering dignity to Canterbury,[2] little regarding earthly
grandeur in his own kingdom at the expense of deviating from
anciently enjoined canons.   Taking up in succession Offa's hatred
against the Kentish people, he sorely afflicted that province, and
led away captive their king, Edbrith, surnamed Pren;[3] but not long
after, moved with feelings of pity, he released him: for at Winchel-
combe, where he had built a church to God, which yet remains, on
the day of its dedication he freed the captive king at the altar, and
consoled him with liberty,[4] thereby giving a memorable instance of
his clemency.   Cuthred,[5] whom he had made king over the Kentish
people, was present to applaud this act of royal munificence.   The
church resounded with acclamations, the street shook with crowds
of people; for in an assembly of thirteen bishops and ten dukes,
no one refused a largess; all[6] departed with full purses.   Moreover,
in addition to those presents of inestimable price and number, in
utensils, clothes, and select horses, which the chief nobility received,
he gave to all who did not possess landed property[7] a pound of
silver; to each presbyter a manca of gold; to every monk a
shilling; and lastly, he made many presents to the people at large.
After he had endowed the monastery with such ample revenues as
would seem incredible in the present time, he honoured it by his
sepulture, in the twenty-fourth year of his reign.[8]   His son Kenelm,
of tender age, and undeservedly murdered by his sister Quendrida,[9]
gained the title and distinction of martyrdom, and rests in the
same place.

§ 96. After him, the kingdom of the Mercians declining, and, if
I may use the expression, nearly lifeless, produced nothing worthy
of historical commemoration.   However, that no one may accuse
me of leaving the history imperfect, I shall glance over the names
of the kings in succession.   Cheolwulf,[10] the brother of Kenulf,
reigning one year, was expelled in the second by Bernulf; who in
the third year of his reign, being overcome and put to flight by
Egbirht, king of the West Saxons,[11] was afterwards slain by the
East Angles, because he had attempted to seize on East Anglia, as
a kingdom subject to the Mercians from the time of Offa.   Ludecan,[12] after two years' sovereignty, was dispatched by these Angles

---

[1] See ante, § 87.

[2] The see of Canterbury was restored to its pristine eminence A.D. 798, after
Ethelhard's first return from Rome.   [3] See § 15.

[4] This, it appears, could avail him little, as his eyes had been previously put
out, and his hands chopped off. See Sax. Chron. A.D. 796.

[5] He had been made king of Kent after the defeat of Edbyrht Præn in 798.

[6] See Monast. Anglic. i. 189.

[7] "qui agros non habebant." This expression seems to imply an inferior class
of nobles, as Malmesbury mentions the commonalty, "populus," afterwards.

[8] See the Sax. Chron. A.D. 819.

[9] The legend of S. Kenelm will be given hereafter.

[10] Ceolwulf, the paternal uncle of Cenelm, succeeded to the kingdom in the year
821, and was deposed by Beornwulf, a Mercian noble, A.D. 823.

[11] The battle between Beornwulf and Ecgberht was fought at Ellandune (supposed to be Wilton, near Salisbury) A.D. 824. Beornwulf was slain by the East
Angles in the same year.

[12] Ludeca was slain A.D. 825, and was succeeded by Wiglaf.

as he was preparing to avenge his predecessor. Withlac,[1] subjugated in the commencement of his reign by the before-mentioned Egbirht, governed thirteen years, paying tribute to him and to his son, both in his person and his property. Berthwulf,[2] reigning thirteen years on the same conditions, was at last driven by the Danish pirates beyond sea. Burhred,[3] marrying Ethelswida, the daughter of king Athulf the son of Egbirht, exonerated himself by this affinity from the payment of tribute and the depredations of the enemy; but after twenty-two years, driven by them from his country, he fled to Rome, and was there buried at the school of the Angles, in the church of St. Mary. His wife at that time continuing in this country, but afterwards following her husband, died at Pavia.[4] Then the kingdom was given by the Danes to one Chelwulf,[5] an attendant of Burhred, who bound himself by oath that he would retain it only at their pleasure; after a few years it fell under the dominion of Elfred, the grandson of Egbirht. Thus the sovereignty of the Mercians, which prematurely bloomed by the overweening ambition of a heathen, altogether withered away through the pitiable inactivity of a dead-alive king, in the year of our Lord's incarnation eight hundred and seventy-five.

Of the Kingdom of the East Angles.

§ 97. As my narrative has hitherto treated of the history of the four more powerful kingdoms, I trust in a copious manner, as far as the perusal of ancient writers has enabled me to do so, it will now, as last in point of order, run through the governments of the East Angles and the East Saxons, as suggested in my preface; for the kingdom of the East Angles arose before that of the West Saxons, though posterior to the kingdom of Kent. The first[6] and also the greatest king of the East Angles was Redwald, tenth in descent from Woden, as they affirm; for all the southern provinces of the Angles and Saxons on this side the river Humber, with their kings, were subject to his authority. This is the person whom I have formerly mentioned[7] as having, out of regard for Edwin, killed Ethelfrid, king of the Northumbrians. Through the persuasion of Edwin, too, he was baptized; and afterwards, at the instigation

[1] Wiglaf was expelled from the throne of Mercia by Ecgberht A.D. 827, but was restored the following year; he died A.D. 839.

[2] Beorthwulf ascended the throne on the death of Wiglaf, A.D. 839. He was defeated by the Danes in 851, and died A.D. 852.

[3] Burgred came to the throne A.D. 852. His marriage with Ethulswitha, daughter of Ethelwulf, king of Wessex, took place at Chippenham, after Easter, in the year 854. He was defeated and expelled by the Danes A.D. 874, and fled to Rome, where he soon after died.   [4] Ethelswitha died at Pavia A.D. 889.

[5] Ceoluulf was placed on the throne by the Danes upon the expulsion of Burgred, A.D. 874; and in Aug. 877, Mercia was apportioned by Halfdan, and part given to Ceoluulf.

[6] Pagi refers the commencement of this kingdom to about the year 526, when the Angles, having landed upon the eastern shores of Britain, established themselves under their twelve chiefs. Uffa, one of the twelve, and who survived the others, did not assume the title of king of the East Angles before the year 571. The dynasty which he founded acquired the name of Uffingas. Uffa died A.D. 578, and was succeeded by his son Titil, who is supposed to have died in the year 599, and to whom Redwald his son succeeded. See Beda, E H. § 134.

[7] See § 47.

of his wife, abjured the faith.[1] His son Eorpwald embraced pure
Christianity, and poured out his immaculate spirit to God, being
barbarously murdered by the heathen Ricbert. To him succeeded
Sigebert,[2] his brother by the mother's side, a worthy servant of the
Lord, polished from all barbarism by his education among the
Franks : for, being driven into banishment by Redwald, and for
a long time associating with them, he had received the rites of
Christianity, which, on his coming into power, he graciously communicated to the whole of his kingdom, and also instituted schools
of learning in different places.[3] This ought highly to be extolled,
as men, heretofore uncivilized and irreligious, were enabled by his
means to taste the sweets of literature. The promoter of his
studies, and the stimulator of his religion, was Felix the bishop,[4] a
Burgundian by birth, who now lies buried at Ramsey. Sigebert,
moreover, renouncing the world and taking the monastic vow, left
the throne to his relation Egric,[5] with whom, being attacked in
intestine war by Penda, king of the Mercians, he met his death at
the moment when, superior to his misfortunes, and mindful of his
religious profession, he held only a wand in his hand. The successor of Egric was Anna,[6] the son of Eni the brother of Redwald,
involved in similar destruction by the same furious Penda ; he was
blessed with a numerous and noble offspring, as the second book
will declare in its proper place.[7] To Anna succeeded his brother
Ethelhere, who was justly slain by Oswiu, king of the Northumbrians, together with Penda, because he was an ally to him, and
was actually supporting the very army which had destroyed his
brother and his kinsman. His brother Ethelwald[8] in due succession left the kingdom to Aldulph[9] and Elcwold,[10] the sons of
Ethelhere. Next came Beorna ; after him Ethelred. His son

---

[1] See Beda, E. H. § 135.

[2] Eorpwald, who succeeded his father Redwald about the year 624, was baptized A.D. 627 ; and being slain in the same year by Richberht, who thereupon
usurped the throne during three years, his brother Sigiberht's accession must be
placed in the year 631.   [3] See Beda, E. H. § 199.

[4] Felix, first bishop of Dunwich, consecrated in the year 630, died on the 8th
March, A.D. 646. He was sent by Honorius, archbishop of Canterbury, for the
conversion of Sigiberht.

[5] Sigiberht abdicated, and became a monk in Bury St. Edmond's, A.D. 634,
having left his throne to his kinsman Egric. They were both slain by Penda of
Mercia in the following year.

[6] The accession of Anna, nephew of Redwald, took place A.D. 635. He was
slain by Penda A.D. 654, when he was succeeded by his brother Ethelher, who was
slain in the following year.

[7] Malmesbury, § 68, gives an account of the three daughters of king Anna, Etheldrith, Ethelburh, and Sexburh, and their descendants. See Beda, E. H. § 201.

[8] Upon the death of his brother Ethelhere, in 655, Ethelwald ascended the
throne. He died in 664.

[9] Eadwulf, son of Ethelhere, succeeded upon the death of his uncle in 664.
His mother was Heresuitha, sister of Hilda, abbess of Streaneshalch. The time
of his death is uncertain ; it happened between the years 680 and 683.

[10] Elcwold succeeded his brother Eadwulf, and died, according to Hickes, in
690. He was succeeded by Selraed, who died in 747, to whom Aelfuuald succeeded
in that year, and died in 749. After. him it seems that Hunbeanna and Alberht
(called by Matthew of Westminster and others, Beorna and Aethelbert) conjointly
reigned in East Anglia. Hickes makes Beorna and Aethelred succeed Elcwold in
690, and states that Beorna died before Aethelred ; but the dates of both their
deaths are unknown. The succession of the kings of East Anglia is involved in
great obscurity.

was St. Ethelbert,[1] whom Offa, king of the Mercians, killed through treachery, as has already been said,[2] and will be repeated hereafter. After him, through the violence of the Mercians, few kings reigned in Eastern Anglia till the time of St. Edmund,[3] and he was dispatched in the sixteenth year of his reign, by Hinguar, a heathen ; from which time the Angles ceased to reign in East Anglia for fifty years. For the province was nine years without a king, owing to the continued devastations of the Pagans : afterwards, both in it and in East Saxony, Guthrum, a Danish king,[4] reigned for twelve years in the time of king Alfred. Guthrum had for successor a Dane also, by name Eohric, who, after he had reigned fourteen years, was slain by the Angles because he conducted himself with cruelty towards them. Still, however, liberty beamed not on this people, for the Danish earls continued to oppress them, or else to excite them against the kings of the West Saxons, till Edward, the son of Alfred, added both provinces to his own West-Saxon empire, expelling the Danes and freeing the Angles, in the fiftieth year after the murder of St. Edmund, king and martyr, and in the fifteenth[5] of his own reign.

Of the Kingdom of the East Saxons

§ 98. Nearly coeval with the kingdom of the East Angles was that of the East Saxons : which had many kings in succession, though subject to others, and principally to those of the Mercians. First, then, Sleda,[6] the tenth from Woden, reigned over them, whose son, Sebert,[7] nephew of Ethelbert king of Kent by his sister Ricula, embraced the faith of Christ at the preaching of Mellitus, first bishop of London ; for that city pertains to the East Saxons. On the death of Sebert, his sons, Sexred and Seward, drove Mellitus into banishment;[8] and soon after, being killed by the West Saxons,[9] they paid the penalty of their persecution against

[1] Ethelberht, the son of Ethelred, was slain by Offa A.D. 793. See Act. SS. Bolland. 20 Maii, p. 241.   [2] See § 86.

[3] Edmund, the direct descendant of the ancient kings of East Anglia, was crowned on Christmas-day, A.D. 854 ; and was slain by Inguar, a Danish prince, on the 20th of November in the year 870.

[4] Guthorm, or Godrum, took the title of king of East Anglia by permission of king Aelfred A.D. 879, and died in 891 ; when he was succeeded by Eohric, who was slain in 905.

[5] According to the Saxon Chronicle, the East Anglians submitted to king Eadweard in the year 921, which is the fifty-first from the murder of king Edmund ; and following this statement, as Edward succeeded his father Alfred A.D. 901, the year of the expulsion of the Danes would be the twentieth of his reign. In Florence of Worcester, the union of the kingdoms under Edward the Elder is assigned to the year 918.

[6] Henry of Huntingdon considers the first king of Essex to have been Ercenwini, called by Florence of Worcester, in his Genealogy of the Kings, Escwini. His son Sleda succeeded him in 587, and died in 597.

[7] Saeberht, the son and successor of Sleda, began his reign in 597, and was converted to Christianity in 604. He died A.D. 616, and left his sons Seaxred and Sigeweard his successors.

[8] Mellitus, ordained bishop of London A.D. 604, was driven into banishment in 617. He was afterwards made archbishop of Canterbury, and died 24th April, A.D. 624. See Beda, E. H. §§ 95, 107.

[9] Seaxred and Sigeweard were slain in the year 623, and were succeeded by Sigiberht, surnamed the Little, son of Sigeweard.

Christ. Sigebert, surnamed the Little, the son of Seward, succeeding, left the kingdom to Sigebert,[1] the son of Sigebald, who
was the brother of Sebert. This Sigebert, at the exhortation of
king Oswiu, was baptized in Northumbria by bishop Finan,[2] and
brought back to his nation, by the ministry of bishop Chedd,[3] the
faith which they had expelled together with Mellitus. After
gloriously governing the kingdom, he left it in a manner still more
glorious ; for he was murdered by his near relations, merely because,
in conformity to the gospel precept, he used kindly to spare his
enemies, nor regard with harsh and angry countenance, if they were
penitent, those who had offended him. His brother Swithelm,[4]
having been baptized by the same Chedd in East Anglia, succeeded.
On his death, Sigher, the son of Sigebert the Little, and Sebbi, the
son of Seward, held the sovereignty. Sebbi's associate dying before
himself, he himself voluntarily retired from the kingdom in his
thirtieth year, becoming a monk, as Beda relates.[5] His sons
Segehard and Seufred reigned after him. On their decease Offa,
the son of Sigher, governed the kingdom for a short time;[6] a youth
of engaging countenance and disposition, in the flower of his age,
and highly beloved by his subjects. He, through the persuasion of
Kineswida, daughter of king Penda, whom he had anxiously sought
in marriage, being taught to aspire after heavenly affections, went
to Rome with Kenred, king of the Mercians, and the blessed Egwin,
bishop of Wictians;[7] and there being shorn, in due time he entered
the heavenly mansions. To him succeeded Selred, son of Sigebert
the Good,[8] during thirty-eight years ; who being slain, Swithed
assumed the sovereignty of the East Saxons ; but in the same year
that Egbert king of the West Saxons subdued Kent, being expelled
by him, he vacated the kingdom.[9] Nevertheless London, with

---

[1] Sigiberht died in the year 653, and was succeeded by Sigiberht, surnamed the
Good, who restored Christianity in Essex; he was slain A.D. 660. See Beda,
E. H. § 215.

[2] Finan, bishop of Lindisfarne, succeeded to that see on the death of Aidan in 651.

[3] Cedd was ordained bishop of London about the year 656, and died A.D. 664.
See Beda, E. H. § 214.

[4] Swithhelm, son of Sexbald, or Sigebald, succeeded his brother in 660, and
died in 665 ; when Sigheri, son of Sigiberht the Little, and Sebbi, son of Sigeweard, obtained the kingdom. Respecting the parentage of Sebbi, compare Dr.
Smith's note in Beda, E. H. iv. 30, and the charter of Oethilred of Essex, Cod.
Dip. Æv. Saxon. No. xxxv. p. 39.

[5] Beda, E. H. §§ 250, 283. Sebbi resigned the crown, and became a monk,
A.D. 693, and died in the following year. His life has been written by Capgrave,
from early legends to be found in the Acta SS. August, vi. 516. He was succeeded by his sons Sigehard and Swebred.

[6] Suebred died after 13th June, A.D. 704, and was succeeded by Offa, who went
to Rome with Cenred of Mercia A.D. 709, where both received tonsure by the
hand of pope Constantine.

[7] Egwin, bishop of Worcester, was consecrated A.D. 692, and sat till A.D. 717.

[8] Selred, or Swbriht, succeeded Offa in 709, and died in 738. Selraed, son of
Sigiberht the Good, was king of East Anglia, and not of the East Saxons ; he died
in 747. See § 97. Both Malmesbury and Florence of Worcester are confused in
their histories of the succession of the kings of East Anglia and Essex.

[9] Here must be some defect in all the MSS., or some misconception in the mind
of our author; for if Swithred succeeded upon the death of Swebriht in 738, or
even after Selred of East Anglia was slain in 747, it is improbable that he was
reigning when the Kentish men submitted to Ecgberht in the year 824. See the
Appendix to Florence of Worcester, p. 395, upon a hasty inspection of which
Malmesbury would seem to have founded his present statement.

the adjacent country, continued subject to the kings of the Mercians as long as they held their sovereignty.

Concerning the partition of the Kingdoms, and of the districts and sees of England.

§ 99. [1]The kings of Kent, it is to be observed, had dominion peculiarly in Kent, in which are two sees; the archbishopric of Canterbury, and the bishopric of Rochester.

§ 100. The kings of the West Saxons ruled in Wiltshire, Berkshire, and Dorsetshire, in which there is one bishop, whose see is now at Salisbury; formerly it was at Ramesbury, or at Shireburn. They also ruled in Sussex, which for some little time possessed a king of its own.[2] The episcopal see of this country was anciently in the sea-girt island of Selsey, as Beda relates,[3] where also the blessed Wilfrid built a monastery; the bishop now dwells at Chichester. They ruled too in the counties of Southampton and Surrey, which have a bishop, whose see is at Winchester: also, in the county of Somerset, which formerly had a bishop at Wells, but now at Bath: and in Domnonia, now called Devonshire, and Cornubia, now Cornwall. At that time there were two bishoprics, one at Crediton, the other at St. Germans; now there is but one, and the see is at Exeter.

§ 101. The kings of the Mercians governed the counties of Gloucester, Worcester, and Warwick; in these is one bishop, whose residence is at Worcester: and in Cheshire, Derbyshire, and Staffordshire; these have one bishop, who has part of Warwickshire and Shropshire; his residence is at the city of Legions [that is, at Chester] or Coventry; formerly it was at Lichfelde: in Herefordshire; and there is a bishop, having half Shropshire and part of Warwickshire and Gloucestershire, whose residence is at Hereford: in Oxfordshire, Buckinghamshire, Hertfordshire, half of Huntingdonshire, Bedfordshire, Northamptonshire, Leicestershire, Lincolnshire; which counties are under the jurisdiction of a bishop, now resident at Lincoln, formerly at Dorchester: and in Leicestershire and Nottinghamshire, of which the care in spiritual things belongs to the diocese of York; formerly they had their own bishop, whose seat was at Leicester.

§ 102. The kings of the East Angles had dominion over the county of Cambridge; there is a bishop, whose seat is at Ely: and over Norfolk and Suffolk; and there is a bishop whose see is at Norwich, formerly at Elmam or Thetford.

§ 103. The kings of the East Saxons ruled in Essex and half of

---

[1] This passage may be compared with Malmesbury's other work upon the English Bishops, under the head of the Bishops of the East Saxons.

[2] The history of this kingdom is not well authenticated. It is supposed to have been founded about the year 490 by Aelli, who came over to Britain in 477 with his three sons, Cymen, Wlenking, and Cissi. Aelli was succeeded by his son Cissi. The South Saxons were converted to Christianity by Wilfrid, bishop of York, in the reign of Ethilwalh, A.D. 681. The kingdom of Sussex appears sometimes to have been tributary to Kent, and at others to Wessex, to which it was finally united by Ecgberht, A.D. 824   [3] E. H. iv. c. 13, § 289.

Hertfordshire, where there anciently was, and still remains, the
bishopric of London.

§ 104. The kings of the Northumbrians governed all the
country which is beyond the river Humber, as far as Scotland; and
there were the archbishop of York, the bishops of Hexham, of
Ripon, of Lindisfarne, and of Candida Casa.[1] Hexham and Ripon
are no more; that of Lindisfarne is translated to Durham.

§ 105. Such were the divisions of the kingdoms, although the
kings, according to the vicissitude of the times, now one, and then
the other, would exceed their boundaries through their courage, or
lose them by their indolence; but all these several kingdoms Egbirht
subjugated by his abilities, and consolidated them into one empire,
reserving to each their own laws. Wherefore since I have passed
beyond his times, fulfilling my promise in a review of the different
periods, I will here fix the limits of my first volume, that the
various separate tracks of the different kingdoms may unite in the
general path of the West Saxon empire.

PREFACE TO BOOK II.

HERE BEGINNETH THE PREFACE TO THE SECOND BOOK.

A LONG period has elapsed since, as well through the care of my
parents as my own industry, I became familiar with books. This
pleasure possessed me from my childhood; this source of delight
has grown with my years: indeed, I was so instructed by my father,
that had I turned aside from these to other pursuits, I should have
considered it as jeopardy to my soul and discredit to my character.
Wherefore, mindful of the adage, "Covet what is necessary," I
constrained my early age to desire eagerly that which it was disgraceful not to desire. I gave, indeed, my attention to various
branches of literature, but in different degrees. Logic, for instance,
which gives arms to eloquence, I contented myself with barely
hearing: medicine, which ministers to the health of the body, I
studied with somewhat more attention: but having scrupulously
examined the several branches of ethics, I bow down to its
majesty, because it spontaneously unveils itself to those who study
it, and directs their minds to moral practice: history more especially, which, by a certain agreeable recapitulation of past events,
excites its readers, by example, to frame their lives to the pursuit
of good, or to aversion from evil. When, therefore, at my own
personal expense, I had procured some historians of foreign nations,
I proceeded, during my domestic leisure, to inquire if anything
concerning our own country could be found worthy of handing
down to posterity. Hence it arose that, not content with the
writings of ancient times, I began myself to compose; not, indeed,
in order to display my learning, which is comparatively nothing,

---

[1] Whithern, in Galloway.

but to bring to light events lying concealed in the confused mass of antiquity. In consequence, rejecting vague opinions, I have studiously sought for chronicles far and near, though I confess I have scarcely profited anything by this industry; for, perusing them all, I still remained poor in information, though I ceased not my researches as long as I could find anything to read. However, what I have clearly ascertained concerning the four kingdoms, I have inserted in my First Book, in which I hope truth will find no cause to blush, though perhaps a degree of doubt may sometimes arise. I shall now trace the monarchy of the West Saxon kingdom, through the line of successive princes, down to the coming of the Normans: which, if any person will condescend to regard with complacency, let him in brotherly love observe the following rule: "If before, he knew only these things, let him not be disgusted because I have inserted them; if he shall know more, let him not be angry that I have not spoken of them;" but rather let him communicate his knowledge to me while I yet live, that, at least, those events may appear in the margin of my history, which do not occur in the text.

THE SECOND BOOK OF WILLIAM OF MALMESBURY'S HISTORY OF THE KINGS OF ENGLAND.

BOOK II.

§ 106. My former volume terminated where the four kingdoms of Britain were consolidated into one. Egberht, the founder of this sovereignty, grand-nephew of king Ina by his brother Inegild,[1] of high rank in his own nation, and liberally educated, had been conspicuous among the West Saxons from his childhood. His uninterrupted course of valour begat envy; and as it is almost naturally ordained that kings should regard with suspicion whomsoever they see growing up in expectation of the kingdom, Brihtric, as before related,[2] jealous of his rising character, was meditating how to destroy him. Egbirht, seeing this, escaped to Offa, king of the Mercians. While Offa concealed him with anxious care, the messengers of Brihtric arrived, demanding the fugitive for punishment and offering money for his surrender. In addition to this, they solicited his daughter in marriage for their king, in order that the nuptial tie might bind them in perpetual amity. In consequence Offa,[3] who would not give way to hostile threats, yielded to flattering allurements, and Egbirht, passing the sea, went into France;[4] a

---

[1] Ecgberht was the son of Ealhmund, king of Kent, who was the son of Eafa, son of Eoppa, son of Ingild, the brother of Ini, king of Wessex. See § 116.

[2] See § 43.

[3] Offa could have had no immediate influence upon the expulsion of Brihtric, he having died A.D. 794.

[4] The Saxon Chronicle states that, before Ecgberht was king, Offa of Mercia and Beorhtric of Wessex drove him into France for three years. Sax. Chron. A.D. 836.

circumstance which I attribute to the counsels of God, that a man destined to so great a kingdom might learn the art of government from the Franks; for this people has no competitor among all the western nations in military skill or polished manners. This ill-treatment Egbirht used as a whetstone with which to rub off the rust of indolence,[1] to quicken the energy of his mind, and to adopt foreign customs, far differing from his native barbarism. On the death therefore of Brihtric, having returned to Britain, invited by frequent messages from his friends, he ascended the throne, at the earnest wish of his country, in the year of our Lord's incarnation eight hundred, and in the thirty-fourth year of the reign of Charles the Great of France, who survived this event twelve years.[2] In the meantime Egbirht, when he had acquired the regard of his subjects by his affability and kindness, first manifested his power against those Britons who inhabit that part of the island which is called Cornwall;[3] and having subjugated them, he proceeded to make the Northern Britons,[4] who are separated from the others by an arm of the sea, tributary to him. While the fame of these victories struck terror into the rest, Bernulf king of the Mercians, aiming at something great, and supposing it would redound to his glory, if he could remove the terror of others by his own audacity, proclaimed war against Egbirt. Deeming it disgraceful to retreat, Egbirt met him with spirit, and coming into action, Bernulf fled, being completely overthrown. This battle took place at Hellendun, A.D. 826.[5] Elated with this success, the West Saxon extending his views, in

[1] Horace, Ars Poet. 304.

[2] Malmesbury has fallen into error (following however the Saxon Chronicle) in fixing the accession of Egbert to the year 800, whereas it did not occur until A.D. 802, in which year, as we know from undoubted authority, Brihtric died. The information here given respecting the reign of Charlemagne is, of itself, sufficient to detect the error, and at the same time to correct it. See Pagi, A.D. 802, §§ 19, 20. The commencement of the reign of Charlemagne is usually dated from the 24th September, A.D. 768, when he succeeded to a portion of the French monarchy; consequently the thirty-fourth year of his reign was completed in September 802, the year in which Ecgberht undoubtedly ascended the throne. He died on the 28th January, 814, having, as Malmesbury observes, survived Ecgberht's accession twelve years. See § 43.

[3] According to the Saxon Chronicle, Ecgberht spread devastation in West Wales from east to west, A.D. 813. Matthew of Westminster assigns the year 808 to the conquest of Cornwall by Ecgberht.

[4] The Saxon Chronicle, Florence of Worcester, and others, place this event in the year 828. He seems to have made a vigorous effort to bring into subjection the various Celtic inhabitants who still remained in Britain, and his efforts were probably extended over many successive years. Hence the variations in the chronology of the annalists.

[5] MSS. A. D. E. M. support the text; 824, L; 825, C; Saville (probably a misprint) 806. The battle of Ellandune was fought A.D. 824, as one MS. correctly reads. The MS. followed in the text not only dates this battle two years later than the best authorities, but makes it also subsequent to an event which, even according to the statement in the text, it must have preceded. The subjugation of Kent by Ecgberht in 824 is there stated to have taken place in the twenty-fourth year of his reign; but according to the more correct computation, which places the commencement of Ecgberht's reign in January 802, the defeat of Beornwulf of Mercia, and the expulsion of Baldred from the throne of Kent, must both have occurred in the twenty-second year of Ecgberht's reign, A.D. 824. Malmesbury, however, adopting the year 800 as the date of Ecgberht's accession, incorrectly, though consistently with his statement, probably wrote and considered 824 to be the twenty-fourth regnal year of Ecgberht.

the heat of victory, sent his son Ethelwulf, with Alstan bishop of Shireburn and a chosen band, into Kent, for the purpose of adding to the West Saxon dominions that province, either grown indolent through long repose, or terrified by the fame of his valour.

§ 107. These commanders observed their instructions effectually: passing through every part of the country, and driving Baldred its king, with very little difficulty, beyond the river Thames, they subjugated to his dominion, in the twenty-fourth year of his reign, Kent, Surrey, the South Saxons, and the East Saxons, who had formerly been under the jurisdiction of his predecessors. Not long after, the East Angles, animated by the support of Egbirht, killed, by successive stratagems, Bernulf and Ludecan, kings of the Mercians.[1] The cause of their destruction was the perpetual incursions which they made, with their usual insolence, on the territories of others. Withlaf their successor, first driven from his kingdom by Egbirt, and afterwards admitted as a tributary prince, augmented the West Saxon sovereignty.[2]   In the same year the Northumbrians perceiving that themselves only remained, and were a conspicuous object, and fearing lest he should pour out his long-cherished anger on them, at last, though late, gave hostages and yielded to his power.[3]   Thus possessed of all Britain,[4] the rest of his life, a space of nine years, passed quietly on, except that, nearly in his latter days, a piratical band of Danes making a descent, disturbed the peace of the kingdom.[5]   So changeable is the lot of human affairs, that he who first singly governed all the Angles, could derive but little satisfaction from the obedience of his countrymen, while a foreign enemy was perpetually harassing himself and his descendants. Against these invaders the forces of the Angles making a stand, Fortune no longer flattered the king with her customary favours, but deserted him in the contest; for when, during the greater part of the day, he had almost secured the victory, he lost the battle as the sun declined; however, by the favour of darkness, he escaped the disgrace of being conquered.   In the next action, with a small force, he totally routed an immense multitude.[6]   At length, after a reign of thirty-seven years and seven months,[7] he departed this

---

[1] Beornwulf was slain A. D. 825, and Ludeca in the same year.

[2] Wiglaf, being expelled by Ecgberht A. D 827, was restored in the following year, but held his kingdom only as tributary to the crown of Wessex.

[3] Ecgberht led an army to Dore against the Northumbrians, and they there offered him obedience and allegiance, A.D. 827. See the Saxon Chronicle and Florence of Worcester under this year. Some additional particulars are given by Matthew of Westminster, but whence derived, or how far entitled to acceptance, is doubtful.

[4] Ecgberht was crowned king of Britain, in a great council held at Winchester, A. D. 829, by general consent of the whole nation. The annals of Winchester (Dom. A. 13) state that he then ordered that Britain should thereafter be called England, and they who had been before denominated Jutes, or Saxons, should for the future be called Englishmen.   [5] See the Sax. Chron. A. D 833.

[6] At the battle of Hengston, in Cornwall, fought A D. 835. See the Sax. Chron. ad an.

[7] This is taken from the Saxon Chronicle, A. D. 836. See, however, the charter of king Ecgberht (Cod. Dip. Ævi Sax. No. ccxl. p. 318), dated A. D. 838, and confirmed by his son Ethelwulf A. D. 839, which year is described as the first of his reign after his father's death. If the length of Ecgberht's reign be correctly stated here and in the Saxon Chronicle, his death could not have happened before

life, and was buried at Winchester; leaving an ample field of glory
for his son, and declaring that he must be happy, if he was careful
not to destroy, by the indolence natural to his race, a kingdom
which he himself had consolidated with such consummate industry.

Of King Ethelwulf.

§ 108. In the year of our Lord's incarnation eight hundred and
thirty-seven,[1] Ethelwulf (whom some call Athulf), the son of Egbirht, came to the throne, and reigned twenty years and five
months.[2] He was mild by nature, and infinitely preferred a life of
tranquillity to dominion over many provinces; and finally, content
with his paternal kingdom of the West Saxons, he bestowed all the
rest which his father had subjugated on his son Ethelstan,[3] of whom
it is not known when[4] or in what manner he died. He assisted
Burhred,[5] king of the Mercians, with an army against the Britons, and
highly exalted him by giving him his daughter[6] in marriage. He
both personally and by his generals[7] frequently overcame the piratical Danes, who were traversing the whole island and infesting the
coast with sudden descents, although, according to the chance of
war, he himself experienced great and repeated calamities; London
and almost the whole of Kent being laid waste.[8] Yet these dis-
asters were ever checked by the alacrity of the king's advisers, who
suffered not the enemy to trespass with impunity, but fully avenged
themselves on them by the effect of their united counsels. For he
possessed at that time two most excellent prelates, the blessed
Swithun of Winchester,[9] and Alstan of Shireburn,[10] who perceiving
the king to be of a heavy and sluggish disposition, perpetually stimulated him by their admonitions to the knowledge of governing.

August, A. D. 839. Simeon of Durham assigns thirty-six years only to the reign
of Ecgberht, and Florence of Worcester states that he died in the thirty-seventh
year of his reign. It is probable that these fluctuations originate in the uncertainty which prevailed as to the year in which this monarch's reign had its beginning. See p. 84, note [2].

[1] The date of the accession of Ethelwulf depends of course upon that which
may be assigned to the decease of his predecessor.

[2] In this computation Malmesbury probably includes the period that Ethelwulf
reigned during his father's life. The Saxon Chronicle assigns only eighteen years
and a half to his reign (though here the MSS. vary in a remarkable manner); and
this period being reckoned from his accession in August 839, would place his
death rightly in the year 853. According to Florence of Worcester, he died upon
the 13th of January. See that authority, p. 213.

[3] Ethelstan was made king of Kent, Essex, Surrey, and Sussex, by his father,
in 839.

[4] He was certainly dead before the return of his father Ethelwulf from Rome,
as at that time the districts usually assigned to the king's eldest son passed into
the hands of Ethelbald.

[5] The incidents respecting Burhred occurred A. D. 853.

[6] The marriage of Ethelswitha occurred after Easter of this year; the nuptials
were celebrated at Chippenham. See Florence of Worcester, A. D. 853, and Asser,
p. 445.   [7] See the Sax. Chron. under the years 845 and 851.

[8] This happened, according to the Saxon Chronicle, in the year 851; but, after
the Danes had passed the Thames into Surrey, Ethelwulf with an army met and
defeated them at Ockley.

[9] St. Swithun was appointed by king Ecgberht preceptor to his son Ethelwulf He became bishop of Winchester in 838, and died on 2d July, 862. See
Florence ad an.

[10] Ealhstân was bishop of Sherborne in 817, and died in 867.

Swithun, disgusted with earthly, trained his master to heavenly pursuits; Alstan, knowing that the business of the kingdom ought not to be neglected, continually inspirited him against the Danes, himself furnishing the exchequer with money, as well as regulating the army.   Any peruser of the Annals[1] will find many affairs of this kind both entered on with courage, and terminated with success, through his means.   He held his bishopric fifty years, happy in living for so long a space in the practice of good works : I should readily commend him had he not been swayed by worldly avarice, and usurped what belonged to others, when by his intrigues he seized the monastery of Malmesbury to his own use.   We feel the mischief of this shameful conduct even to the present day, although the monastery has baffled all similar violence from the time of his death till now, when it has fallen again into like difficulty.[2]   Thus the accursed passion of avarice corrupts the human soul, and forces men, though great and illustrious in other respects, into hell.[3]

§ 109. Confiding in these two supporters for the good management of the foreign and domestic concerns of his kingdom, Ethelwulf, after the subjugation of his enemies, turned to the establishment of God's worship, and granted the tenth of every hide of land within his kingdom to the servants of Christ, free from all tribute, exempt from all services.[4]   But how small a portion is this of his glory !   Having settled his kingdom, he went to Rome, and there offered to St. Peter that tribute which England pays to this day,[5] before pope Leo the fourth,[6] who had also, formerly, honourably received, and anointed as king, Elfred[7] his son, whom Ethelwulf had sent to him.   Continuing there one whole year, he nobly repaired the school of the Angles,[8] which, according to report, was first founded by Offa, king of the Mercians, and had been burnt down some time back.   Returning home through France, he married Judith,[9] daughter of Charles king of the Franks.

---

[1] See Sax. Chron. A.D. 823—825.

[2] Roger, bishop of Salisbury, seized it in like manner to his own use A.D. 1118, and held it till his death, 1139.   [3] Virg. Æn. iii. 56.

[4] See the charter itself, § 114.

[5] The Rome-scot, or Peter's pence, is here evidently alluded to as the tribute yet paid to Rome by England. Its origin and application are obscure. The grant appears to have been made after Ethelwulf's return to England. See Asser, p. 448. This grant is supposed by Spelman to have been made in a general council of the nation.

[6] Pope Leo having died 17th July, Ethelwulf's visit to him and the grant here mentioned must have occurred before that date.

[7] This was probably towards the end of the year 854.

[8] Matthew of Westminster (A.D. 727) states that the English school at Rome was founded by Ini, king of Wessex, with the consent and approbation of pope Gregory. Of this institution it is believed there is no early authentic account. The Angle-School was a quarter near St. Peter's, where the English pilgrims at Rome resided; it was destroyed by fire, according to the Saxon Chronicle, in 816; but the conflagration here referred to is probably that mentioned by Anastasius (Ap. Labb. Concil. viii. 6) as having taken place in the Saxon street at Rome soon after the accession of Leo IV. It probably remained in an unfinished state until the arrival of Ethelwulf.

[9] Ethelwulf's marriage with Judith, daughter of Charles le Chauve, took place at the palace of Verberie on the 1st (or the 7th) of October, 856. See Limier's Hist. Genealog. de France, p. 25.

§ 110. 'For Lewis the Pious,' son of Charles the Great, had four
sons; Lothaire, Pippin, Lewis, and Charles, surnamed the Bald;
of these Lothaire, even in his father's life-time,' usurping the title
of emperor, reigned fifteen years' in that part of Germany situate
near the Alps, which is now called Lorraine, (that is, the kingdom
of Lothaire,) and in all Italy, together with Rome. In his latter
days, afflicted with sickness, he renounced the world. He was a
man far more inhuman than any of those who had preceded him;
so much so, as even frequently to load his own father with chains
in a dungeon.' Lewis indeed was of mild and simple manners, but
he was unmercifully persecuted by Lothaire, because Ermengarde,
by whom he had his first family, being dead, he was doatingly fond
of Charles, his son by his second wife Judith.' Pippin,' another
son of Lewis, had dominion in Aquitaine and Gascony. Lewis,'
the third son of Lewis, in addition to Norica, which he had already,
possessed the kingdoms which his father had given him, that is to
say, Alemannia, Turingia, Austrasia, Saxony, and the kingdom of
the Avars, that is the Huns. Charles' obtained the half of France
on the west, and all Neustria,[10] Brittany, and the greatest part of
Burgundy, Gothia, Gascony, and Aquitania; Pippin the son of
Pippin being ejected thence, and compelled to become shorn as a
monk in the monastery of St. Metard,[11] who afterwards escaping
by flight, and returning into Aquitania, remained there in concealment for a long time; but being again treacherously deceived by
Ranulf the governor, he was seized, brought to Charles at Senlis,

---

[1] Malmesbury (according to Hardy) appears to have copied great part of this
account from a contemporary chronicle (ex libro Monasterii S. Wandregisili)
brought down to the year 877; and also to have consulted the chronicle of Ado,
archbishop of Vienne (A. D. 865—875,) and that of Hariulfe, a monk of St. Riquier,
who wrote A. D. 1088. (Fragmentum ex lib. Mon. S. Wandreg. extans in Cod. MS.
Abbatiæ S. Victoris, Paris. Num. 419; Bouquet, vii. 44.—Chron. Adonis, edit.
Paris. 1522 et 1561; Lugdun. 1677, in Bibliotheca Patrum.—Chron. Hariulfi,
apud Acherium, tom. ii. Spicilegii; fol. Paris. 1723.)

[2] Louis the Pious succeeded as sole emperor and king of France, 28th Jan.
814; he died 20th June, 840.

[3] Lothaire, king of France, was made king of Italy in the year 820; and, on
Easter-day (5th April) 823, he received the imperial crown from the hands of the
pope.

[4] Lothaire died in the abbey of Pruim, in Ardennes, on the 29th Sept. 855,
having taken the monastic habit only six days before.

[5] The emperor Louis I. was twice confined by his sons in the monastery of St.
Médard de Soissons; first in the year 830, and again in 833.

[6] Lothaire, Louis, and Pepin were the sons of Louis le Débonnaire by his first
wife Hermengarde, daughter of count Ingram; after her death (3d Oct. 818) the
emperor espoused Judith, daughter of Guelphe, duke of Ravensperg. Charles,
called Le Chauve, was the issue of this marriage.

[7] Pepin I. governed the kingdom of Aquitaine from the year 814, and died 13th
December, A.D. 838.

[8] Louis, brother of the emperor Lothaire, was made king of Bavaria A. D. 817;
and died at Frankfort 28th of August 876.

[9] Charles le Chauve succeeded his father, Louis le Débonnaire, in the kingdom
of France, 20th June, 840. His brother Lothaire disputed with him the succession, but in 843 the crown of France fell to the share of Charles by agreement.

[10] Neustria included the country afterwards called Normandy.

[11] In 852 Pepin was made a monk in the monastery of St. Médard; but, having
thence escaped back to Aquitaine in 855, he was betrayed by Rainulf, earl of
Poitou, in 864, and brought to Charles le Chauve, who then confined him in the
prison of Senlis, where he shortly after died.

and doomed to perpetual exile.   Moreover, after the death of the most pious emperor Lewis, Lothaire, who had been anointed emperor eighteen years before his father's decease, being joined by Pippin with the people of Aquitaine, led an army against his brothers, that is, Lewis, the most pious king of the Bavarians, and Charles, into the county of Auxerre, to a place called Fontenai ;[1] where, when the Franks with all their subject nations had been overwhelmed by mutual slaughter, Lewis and Charles ultimately triumphed, Lothaire being put to flight.   After this most sanguinary conflict, however, peace was made between them, and they divided the sovereignty of the Franks, as has been mentioned above.   Lothaire had three sons by Ermengarde,[2] the daughter of Hugo : first, Lewis,[3] to whom he committed the government of the Romans and of Italy; next, Lothaire,[4] to whom he left the imperial crown ; lastly, Charles,[5] to whom he gave Provence. Lothaire died in the year of our Lord's incarnation eight hundred and fifty-five, and the thirty-third year of his reign.[6]   Charles, his son, who on his death succeeded to the government of Provence, died in the eighth year of his reign.[7]   Then Lewis, emperor of the Romans, and Lothaire his brother, shared his kingdom of Provence.[8] But Lewis, king of the Norici, (that is of the Bavarians,) the son of Lewis the emperor,[9] in the year of our Lord's incarnation eight hundred and sixty-five, after the feast of Easter, divided his kingdom between his sons:[10] to Carloman[11] he gave Norica, (that is Bavaria,) and the marches bordering on the Sclavonians and the Lombards ; to Lewis,[12] Thuringia, the Eastern Franks and Saxony; to Charles[13] he left Alemannia and Curwalla, that is the county of Cornwall.[14]   Lewis himself reigned happily over his sons in full power for ten years, and then died in the year of our Lord's incarnation eight hundred and seventy-six, when he had reigned fifty-

[1] The memorable battle of Fontenai was fought 25th June, A.D. 841, when the emperor Lothaire and his nephew, Pepin II. king of Aquitaine, were defeated by Charles le Chauve, assisted by his brother, Louis of Bavaria.

[2] Hermengarde, daughter of count Hugh, was married to the emperor Lothaire in October, A.D. 821, and died 20th March, 851.

[3] Louis II., crowned king of Italy by pope Sergius in 844, became sole emperor of the West in 855.   He died without male issue on the 6th of August, 875, and was succeeded by his uncle, Charles le Chauve.

[4] King Lothaire died at Plesaunce, on the 8th of August, A.D. 869.

[5] Charles, youngest son of the emperor Lothaire, king of Provence.

[6] Thirty-two years and six months, reckoned from his acceptance of the imperial crown from pope Pascal I.

[7] Charles commenced his reign in Provence, A.D. 855, and died in 863, without children.

[8] The emperor Louis II. and Lothaire king of Lorraine, divided their brother's estates between them.   [9] Louis the Pious.

[10] This division in the year 865 is not mentioned by any other ancient French writer, with the exception of Hariulfe, who probably derived his statement from the same source with Malmesbury, viz. the Chronicle of St. Wandregisile.   The three sons of Louis, king of Bavaria, upon his death in 876, succeeded severally to his estates.

[11] Carloman, king of Bavaria, who died 22d March, 880.

[12] Louis, king of Germany, Saxony, and Austrasia, succeeded his father, Louis of Germany, A.D. 876, and died 20th Jan. 882.

[13] Charles, king of Suabia, called Le Gros, subsequently became emperor of the West and king of France.

[14] Literally, the Horn of Gaul, from the projection of Brittany.

four years.[1] Charles, king of the West Franks,[2] in the thirty-sixth
year of his reign, entering Italy, came to offer up his prayers in the
church of the apostles, and was there elected emperor by all the
Roman people, and consecrated by pope John on the eighth of the
kalends of January [25th Dec.], in the year of our Lord's incarnation eight hundred and seventy-five. Thence he had a prosperous
return into Gaul.   But in the thirty-eighth year of his reign, and
the beginning of the third[3] of his imperial dignity, he went into
Italy again, and held a conference with pope John ; and returning
into Gaul, he died, after passing Mount Cenis,[4] on the third of the
nones of October [5th Oct.], in the tenth of the indiction, in the
year of our Lord eight hundred and seventy-seven, and was succeeded by his son Lewis.[5]   Before the second year of his reign was
completed, this Lewis died in the palace at Compeigne, on the
sixth of the ides of April[6] [8th April], in the twelfth indiction, in the year of our Lord eight hundred and seventy-nine.
After him his sons, Lewis and Carloman, divided his kingdom.[7]
Of these, Lewis gained a victory over the Normans[8] in the district
of Vimeu,[9] and died soon after, on the day before the nones of
August [4th Aug.], in the year of our Lord eight hundred and
eighty-one, the fifteenth of the indiction,[10] having reigned two years
three months and twenty-four days. He was succeeded in his
government by his brother Carloman, who, after reigning three
years and six days,[11] was wounded by a wild boar in the forest of
Iveline, in Mount Ericus.   He departed this life in the year of our
Lord eight hundred and eighty-four, the second of the indiction,
the eighth of the ides of December [6th Dec.].   Next, Charles
king of the Suevi,[12] the son of Lewis king of the Norici, assumed
the empire of the Franks and Romans in the year of the incarnate
Word eight hundred and eighty-five, the third of the indiction,
whose vision, as I think it worth preserving, I here subjoin.

    [1] Louis, king of Bavaria, had nearly completed the fifty-ninth year of his reign,
reckoned from his accession in 817.
    [2] Charles le Chauve, king of France, succeeded his nephew, Louis II. in the
empire of the West, and received the imperial crown from the hands of pope
John VIII. at Rome, on Christmas-day, A.D. 875.
    [3] Charles had not completed his second year.   On 25th Dec. 875 he was
crowned, and died 6th Oct. 877.
    [4] Charles is said to have been poisoned by his Jewish physician, Sédécias, 6th
Oct. 877, at Brios, a village situate to the west of Mount Cenis.
    [5] Louis II. of France, and third of the empire, called Balbus, or Le Bègue, was
crowned king at Compiègne, 8th Dec. 877, and emperor A.D. 878.
    [6] The best writers state that Louis le Bègue died at Compiègne on the 10th
of April (quarto idus Aprilis), A.D. 879.
    [7] The former had France and Neustria; the latter, Burgundy and Aquitaine.
Charles le Gros, son of Louis king of Bavaria, obtained the Imperial States.
    [8] Louis defeated the Northmen, or Normans, A.D. 881, at a place called Saul-
court, when Guorm, their chieftain, was slain.   [9] . . . in pago Vimuiaco.
    [10] Malmesbury follows Hariulfe in placing the death of Louis III. of France on
the 4th of August, A.D. 881; but it must be observed that the fifteenth indiction
did not begin until the 25th of December, 881.
    [11] All the MSS. read "days;" but it is probably a mistake for "months."
Hariulfe says that he reigned "three years and a half."
    [12] Charles le Gros was crowned emperor of the West on Christmas-day, A.D. 880,
and took possession of the kingdom of France on the death of Carloman, 6th Dec.
884, to the prejudice of Charles le Simple, posthumous son of Louis le Bègue. He
was recognised as king of France about the end of January 885.

The Vision of Charles.

§ 111. [1]" In the name of God most high, the King of kings! As I Charles, by the free gift of God emperor, king of the Germans, and patrician of the Romans, and emperor of the Franks, on the sacred night of the Lord's day, after duly performing the holy service of the nocturns, went to the bed of rest, and sought the sleep of quietude, there came a voice to me, tremendously saying, ' Charles, thy spirit shall shortly depart from thee for a considerable time.' Immediately I was rapt in the spirit, and he who carried me away in the spirit was most glorious to behold ; and in his hand he held a clue of thread emitting a beam of purest light, such as comets shed when they appear. And he began to unwind it, and said to me, ' Take the thread of this brilliant clue, and bind and tie it firmly on the thumb of thy right hand, for thou shalt be led by it through the inextricable punishments of the infernal regions.' Saying this, he went before me, quickly unrolling the thread of the brilliant clue, and led me into very deep and fiery valleys, which were full of pits boiling with pitch, and brimstone, and lead, and wax, and grease. There I found the bishops of my father and of my uncles : and when I had asked them, in my terror, why they were suffering such dreadful torments ? they replied, ' We were the bishops of your father and of your uncles ; and instead of preaching, and admonishing them and their people to cultivate peace and concord, as was our duty, we were the sowers of discord and the fomenters of evil. On this account we are now burning in these infernal torments, together with other lovers of slaughter and of rapine; and hither also will your bishops and ministers come, who now delight to act as we did.' While I was fearfully listening to this, behold the blackest demons came flying about me, with fiery claws endeavouring to snatch away the thread of light which I held in my hand, and to draw it to them ; but, repelled by the rays of the clue, they were unable to touch it. Next running behind me, they tried to gripe me in their claws, and cast me headlong into those sulphureous pits; but my conductor, who carried the clue, threw a thread of the clue over my shoulders, and doubling it, drew me strongly after him ; and in this manner we ascended lofty fiery mountains, from which arose lakes, and burning rivers, and all kinds of metals seething, wherein I found immersed innumerable souls of the vassals and princes of my father and brothers, some up to the hair, others to the chin, and others to the middle, who mournfully cried out to me, ' While we were living, we were, together with you and your father, and brothers and uncles, fond

---

[1] The vision of Charles le Gros is copied by Malmesbury, verbatim, from Hariulfe's Chronicle, iii. 21 (tom. ii. Spicilegii, p. 323, fol. Paris. 1723). Alberic de Trois Fontaines gives the substance of it, and refers to Malmesbury :— " Sequitur mirabilis visio quæ facta est hoc anno 889 (rectius 886) eidem Karolo, secundum Willelmum Malmesbiriensem." The Annals improperly ascribed to Asser, sub an. 886, also recite the vision of Charles le Gros. (Gale, iii. 169.) In the French chronicles of St. Denis, and in some Latin MSS. the vision is erroneously attributed to Charles le Chauve. (Bouquet, ix. 60.)

of battle, and slaughter, and plunder, through lust of earthly things: wherefore we now undergo punishment in these boiling rivers, and in various kinds of metal.' While I was with the greatest alarm attending to these, I heard some souls behind me crying out, 'The great will undergo still greater torment.' I looked back, and behold on the banks of the boiling river, furnaces of pitch and brimstone, filled with great dragons, and scorpions, and different kinds of serpents, where I also saw some of my father's nobles, some of my own, and of those of my brothers and of my uncles, who said, 'Alas, Charles, you see what dreadful torments we undergo on account of our malice and pride, and the evil counsel which we gave to our kings and to you, for lust's sake.' When I could not help groaning mournfully at this, the dragons ran at me with open jaws filled with fire, and brimstone, and pitch, and tried to swallow me up: but my conductor tripled the thread of the clue around me, which by the splendour of its rays overcame their fiery throats, and drew me along more firmly. And we descended into a valley, which was in one part dark and burning like a fiery furnace, but in another so extremely enchanting and glorious, that I cannot describe it. I turned myself to the dark part which emitted flames, and there I saw some kings of my race in extreme torture; whereupon being beyond measure distressed, I expected that I should be immediately thrown into these torments by some very black giants, who made the valley blaze with every kind of flame. Trembling very much, the thread of the clue of light assisting my eyes, I saw, on the side of the valley, the light somewhat brightening, and two fountains flowing out thence: one was extremely hot, the other clear and just warm; two large casks were there besides. When, guided by the thread of light, I proceeded thither, I looked into the vessel containing boiling water, and saw my father Lewis [1] standing therein up to his thighs. Dreadfully oppressed with pain and agony, he said to me, 'Fear not, my lord Charles, I know that your spirit will again return into your body; and God hath permitted you to come hither, that you might see for what crimes myself and all whom you have beheld, undergo these torments. One day I am bathed in the boiling cask; next I pass into that other delightful water; which is effected by the prayers of St. Peter and St. Remigius,[2] under whose patronage our royal race has hitherto reigned. But if you, and my faithful bishops and abbots, and the whole ecclesiastical order, will quickly assist me with masses, offerings, psalms, vigils, and alms, I shall shortly be released from this cask of boiling water: for my brother Lothaire and his son Lewis have had these punishments remitted by the prayers of St. Peter and St. Remigius, and have now entered into the joy of God's paradise.' He then said to me, 'Look on your left hand;' and when I had done so, I saw two very deep casks boiling. 'These,' said he, 'are being prepared for you, if you do not amend and

---

[1] This was Louis of Bavaria.

[2] St. Remigius, "the apostle of the Franks," archbishop of Rheims, is supposed to have baptized Clovis. The commencement of his episcopate is commonly referred to the year 459, and his death to A.D. 533. See Gall. Christ. ix 10.

repent of your atrocious crimes.' I then began to be dreadfully afraid. And when my conductor saw my spirit thus terrified, he said to me, ' Follow me to the right of that most resplendent valley of paradise.' As we proceeded, I beheld my uncle Lothaire sitting in excessive brightness, in company with glorious kings, on a topaz-stone of uncommon size, crowned with a precious diadem; and nigh him, his son Lewis crowned in like manner. Seeing me near at hand, he called me to him in a kind voice, saying, ' Come to me, Charles, now my third[1] successor in the empire of the Romans. I know that you have passed through the place of punishment where your father, my brother, is placed in the baths appointed for him; but, by the mercy of God he will be shortly liberated from those punishments, as we have been, by the merits of St. Peter and the prayers of St. Remigius, to whom God hath given a special charge over the kings and people of the Franks; and unless he shall continue to favour and assist the dregs of our family, our race must shortly cease both from reign and empire: know, moreover, that the rule of the empire will be shortly taken out of your hand, nor will you long survive.' Then Lewis, turning to me, said, ' The empire which you have hitherto held belongs by hereditary right to Lewis,[2] the son of my daughter.' So saying, there seemed immediately to appear before me a little child; and Lothaire his grandfather,[3] looking upon him, said to me, ' This infant seems to be such an one as that which the Lord set in the midst of the disciples, and said, ' Of such is the kingdom of God; I say unto you, that their angels do always behold the face of my Father who is in heaven.' [Matt. xviii. 10.] But do you bestow on him the empire by that thread of the clue which you hold in your hand.' Untying, then, the thread from the thumb of my right hand, I gave him the whole monarchy of the empire by that thread; and immediately the entire clue, like a brilliant sunbeam, became rolled up in his hand. Thus, after this wonderful transaction, my spirit, extremely wearied and affrighted, returned into my body. Therefore let all persons know, willingly or unwillingly, forasmuch as, according to the will of God, the whole empire of the Romans will revert into his hands, and that I cannot prevail against him, compelled by the conditions of this my calling, that God who is the Ruler of the living and the dead will both complete and establish this, whose eternal kingdom remains for ever and ever. Amen."

§ 112. The vision itself, and the partition of the kingdoms, I have here inserted in the very words in which I found them. This Charles, then, had scarcely discharged the united duties of the

---

[1] The emperor Lothaire was succeeded by his son Louis II. followed by Charles le Chauve, whom his son Louis III., called Le Bègue, succeeded; Charles le Gros was, therefore, fourth in succession from Lothaire.

[2] Louis, surnamed l'Aveugle, son of Boso, king of Provence, and Hermengarde, daughter of the emperor Louis II. Louis was living after the 6th of January, 923, having granted a diploma of that date in the 23d year of his empire. He died about the year 929.

[3] The emperor Lothaire was great-grandfather of Louis l'Aveugle.

empire and kingdom for two years,[1] when Charles, the son of Lewis
who died at Compeigne, succeeded him.[2] This is the Charles who
married the daughter of Edward king of England, and gave Normandy to Rollo[3] with his daughter Gisla, who was the surety
of peace and pledge of the treaty.[4] To this, Charles, in the empire,
succeeded king Arnulf,[5] of the imperial line, tutor of that young
Lewis of whom the vision above-recited speaks.[6] Arnulf dying
after fifteen years,[7] this Lewis[8] succeeded him, at whose death one
Conrad,[9] king of the Teutonians, obtained the sovereignty. His
son Henry,[10] who succeeded him, sent to Athelstan, king of the
Angles, for his two sisters, Aldgitha and Edgitha, the latter of
whom he married to his son Otho,[11] the former to a certain duke
near the Alps.[12] Thus the empire of the Romans and the kingdom of the Franks being then and now severed from their
ancient union, the one is governed by emperors, and the other
by kings. But as I have wandered wide from my purpose,
whilst indulging in tracing the descent of the illustrious kings of
the Franks, I will now return to the course I had begun, and to
Athelwulf.

§ 113. On his return after his year's peregrination, and his
marriage with the daughter of Charles the Bald,[13] he found the dispositions of some persons contrary to his expectations: for Ethel-

[1] Charles did not survive two years, and died on the 12th or 13th January, A.D. 888.
[2] Charles, called Le Simple, posthumous son of Louis le Bègue, was crowned king of France at Rheims, 27th Jan. 893. He married Eadgiva, daughter of Edward the Elder, king of England, A.D. 919; and had by her a son, afterwards Louis IV. king of France, called d'Outremer. He died in prison at Peronne, on the 7th Oct. A.D. 929.
[3] About the year 912, the Normans settled in Neustria, and Charles bestowed his daughter Gisle, or Giselle, upon Rollo, first duke of Normandy, upon condition of his embracing Christianity.
[4] In allusion seemingly to the name of Charles's daughter Gisle, i. e. "pledge."
[5] Arnoul, the natural son of Carloman, king of Bavaria, was consecrated emperor by pope Formosus before 4th April, A.D. 896.
[6] Louis received the imperial crown from the pope in the year 901.
[7] It is not apparent from what period these fifteen years are to be computed. The emperor Arnoul died 29th Nov. A.D. 899, in the fifth year of his empire, having just completed the twelfth of his reign.
[8] Louis IV. son of Arnoul, is here confounded with Louis, son of Boson; it was the former who was chosen emperor by the princes of Germany, upon his father's death in 899. Though he was never recognised as emperor, upon his death Conrad was elected, and reigned in Germany till his death, 23d Dec. A.D. 918. The emperor Louis, son of Boson, survived Conrad king of Germany several years.
[9] Upon the death of Louis IV., Conrad count of Franconia, son-in-law of the emperor Arnoul, was chosen emperor of Germany A.D. 912.
[10] Henry emperor of Germany, called L'Oiseleur, was son of Otho duke of Saxony, by Liutgarde, daughter of the emperor Arnoul. See § 68, where a similar mistake occurs in calling Otho the great-grandson of Conrad. Henry died 2d July, A.D. 936; and his son Otho succeeded by election.
[11] Eadgitha, daughter of Edward the Elder, was married A.D. 930 to Otho, afterwards king, and subsequently emperor of Germany. She died 26th Jan. A.D. 947. See the Preface to Ethelwerd, and the Pedigree which follows it.
[12] Consult the Preface to Ethelwerd upon this point.
[13] Judith was betrothed to Ethelwulf in the month of July, and married 1st Oct. 856. (Bouquet, vii. 72.) She must at that time have been scarce thirteen years of age, for Charles was not married to Hermengarde until 12th Dec. 842.

bald his son, and Alstan bishop of Shireburn, and Enulf earl of Somerset, conspiring against him,[1] endeavoured to eject him from the sovereignty; but through the intervention of maturer counsel, the kingdom was divided between the father and his son. This partition was an unjust one; for malignity was so far successful that the western portion, which was the better, was allotted to the son, the eastern, which was the worse, fell to the father. He, however, with incredible forbearance, dreading "a worse than civil war," calmly gave way to his son, restraining, by a conciliatory harangue, the people who had assembled for the purpose of asserting his dignity. And though all this quarrel arose on account of his foreign wife, yet he held her in the highest estimation, and used to place her on the throne near himself, contrary to the West Saxon custom; for that people never suffered the king's consort either to be seated by the king, or to be honoured with the appellation of queen, on account of the depravity of Edburga,[2] daughter of Offa, king of the Mercians. She, as we have before mentioned,[3] being married to Brihtric, king of the West Saxons, used to persuade him (a tender-hearted man, as they report) to the destruction of the innocent, and would herself take off by poison those against whom her accusations failed. This was exemplified in the case of a youth much beloved by the king, whom she poisoned in this manner; and immediately afterwards Brihtric fell sick and died, from having previously drank of the same potion, unknown to the the queen. The rumour of this crime getting abroad, drove the poisoner from the kingdom. Proceeding to Charles the Great, she happened to find him standing with one of his sons; and after offering him presents, the emperor in a playful, jocose manner, commanded her to choose whom she liked best, himself or his son. Edburga choosing the young man for his blooming beauty, Charles replied with some emotion, "Had you chosen me, you should have had my son; but since you have chosen him, you shall have neither." He then placed her in a monastery, where she might have passed her life in splendour; but soon after, finding her guilty of incontinence, he expelled her.[4] Struck with this instance of depravity, the Saxons framed the regulation I have alluded to, though Ethelwulf weakened it by his affectionate kindness. He made his will[5] a few months before he died, in which, after the division of the kingdom between his sons Ethelbald and Ethelbirht, he set out the dowry of his daughter, and ordered that, till the end of time, one poor person should be clothed and fed from every tenth hide of his inheritance, and that every year three hundred mancas of gold should be sent to Rome, of which one hundred should be given to St. Peter, another to St. Paul for lamps, and the other to the pope for distribution. Dying two years after he came from Rome,[6] he was buried at Winchester in the cathedral. But that I may return from my digression to my proposed series, I shall here

---

[1] See Asser, p. 446.   [2] Id. p. 447.   [3] See § 43.
[4] Eadburh died in a miserable state in Pavia, where she was seen by many with whom Asser had conversed, begging a daily subsistence. See that authority, p. 448.
[5] See antea, note [5], § 109.   [6] He died A.D. 857.

subjoin the charter of ecclesiastical immunities [1] which he granted to all England.

§ 114. " Our Lord Jesus Christ reigning for evermore. Since we perceive that perilous times are pressing on us, that there are in our days hostile burnings, and plunderings of our wealth, and most cruel depredations by devastating enemies, and many tribulations of barbarous and Pagan nations, threatening even our destruction : therefore I Ethelwulf, king of the West Saxons, with the advice of my bishops and nobility, have established a wholesome counsel and general remedy ; and I have decided that there be given unto the servants of God, whether male or female, or laymen,[2] a certain hereditary portion of the lands possessed by persons of every degree, that is to say, the tenth manse,[3] but where it is less than this, then the tenth part ; that it may be exonerated from all secular services, all royal tributes great and small, or those taxes which we call ' Witereden.'[4] And let it be free from all things, for the release of our souls, and the obtaining remission of our sins, that it may be applied to God's service alone, exempt from expeditions, the building of bridges, or of forts ; in order that they may the more diligently pour forth their prayers to God for us without ceasing, inasmuch as we have in some measure alleviated their service." Moreover it hath pleased Alstan bishop of Shireburn, and Swithun bishop of Winchester, with their abbots and the servants of God, to appoint that every congregation of brethren and sisters at each church, every week on the day of Mercury, that is to say, Wednesday, should sing fifty psalms, and every priest two masses, one for king Ethelwulf, and another for his nobility, consenting to this gift, for the pardon and alleviation of their sins ; for the king while living they shall say, " O God, who justifiest ;" for the nobility while living, " Stretch forth, O Lord :" after they are dead ; for the departed king, singly ; for the departed nobility, in common : and let this be firmly appointed for all the times of Christianity, in like manner as that immunity is appointed, so long as faith shall increase in the nation of the Angles. This charter of donation was written in the year of our Lord's incarnation eight hundred and fourteen,[5] the fourth of the indiction, the fifth day of the nones of November [1st Nov.], in the city of Winchester, in the church of St. Peter, before the high altar ; and they have done this for the honour of St. Michael the archangel, and of St. Mary the glorious queen, the mother of God, and also for the honour of St. Peter the chief of the apostles, and of our most holy father pope Gregory,

---

[1] This charter occurs also in Ingulf, p. 590, with some variations. There is a little uncertainty as to the period at which this grant was made ; for Asser and his followers appear to place the donation before the king's journey to Rome. See also § 109.   [2] " Poor laymen," in Ingulph.
[3] Manse implies generally a dwelling and a certain quantity of land annexed ; sometimes it is synonymous with a hyde, or plough-land.
[4] See the Glossary to Thorpe's Saxon Laws, v. Wite.
[5] 814, D. E. M. ; 844 ; A. C. L. and Saville's text. But the date is incorrect, as it seems, in all the MSS., and proves the spurious character of the document. In the copy which is found in Ingulph, Burgred king of Mercia, and Edmund of East Anglia, are named as witnesses. The former ascended the throne A.D. 852 ; the latter was crowned on Christmas-day 854.

and all saints. And then, for greater security, king Ethelwulf placed the charter on the altar of St. Peter; and the bishops received it in behalf of God's holy faith, and afterwards transmitted it to all churches in their dioceses according to the above-cited form.

§ 115. From this king the English Chronicles trace the line of the generation of their kings upwards, even to Adam, as we know Luke the evangelist has done with respect to our Lord Jesus; and which perhaps it will not be superfluous for me to do, though it is to be apprehended that the utterance of barbarous names may shock the ears of persons unused to them.

§ 116. ¹Ethelwulf was the son of Egbirht, Egbirht of Elmund, Elmund of Eafa, Eafa of Eoppa, Eoppa was the son of Ingild the brother of king Ina, who were both sons of Chenred; Chenred of Chelwald, Chelwald of Cuda, Cuda of Cudwin, Cudwin of Cheaulin, Cheaulin of Chinric, Chinric of Cherdic, who was the first king of the West Saxons; Cherdic of Elesa, Elesa of Esla, Esla of Giwis, Giwis of Wig, Wig of Frewin, Frewin of Fridegar, Fridegar of Brond, Brond of Beldeg, Beldeg of Woden; and from him, as we have often remarked, proceeded the kings of many nations. Woden was the son of Fridewald, Fridewald of Frelaf, Frelaf of Finn, Finn of Godulf, Godulf of Geat, Geat of Teti, Teti of Beowi, Beowi of Sceld, Sceld of ²Sceaf, who, as some affirm, was driven on a certain island in Germany called Scandza (of which Jornandes,³ the historian of the Goths, speaks), a little boy in a skiff without an attendant, asleep with an handful of corn at his head, whence he was called Sceaf; and, on account of his singular appearance, being well received by the men of that country, and carefully educated, in his riper age he reigned in a town which was called Slaswic, but at present Haitheby. That country, called Old Anglia, whence the Angles came into Britain, is situated between the Saxons and the Goths. Sceaf was the son of Heremod, Heremod of Stermon, Stermon of Hadra, Hadra of Gwala, Gwala of Bedweg, Bedweg of Streph, and he, as they say, was the son of Noah, born in the ark.

§ 117. In the year of our Lord eight hundred and fifty-seven, the two sons of Ethelwulf divided their paternal kingdom :⁴ Ethelbald reigned in West Saxony, and Ethelbirht in Kent. Ethelbald, base and perfidious, defiled the bed of his father by marrying, after his decease, Judith his step-mother.⁵ Dying, however, at the end

---

¹ This pedigree occurs in the Saxon Chronicle, A.D. 855; and in Ethelwerd, p. 426; Asser, p. 844. Some variations occur between these several copies, and Florence of Worcester, p. 208.   ² See Ethelwerd, Chronicle, p. 426.

³ Jordanes, or Jornandes, secretary to the kings of the Goths who were in Italy. He flourished about A.D. 552. See Cave, Hist. Lit. i. 526. He wrote two historical works, one entitled "De Rebus Gothicis," and the other, "De Regnorum ac Temporum Successione."

⁴ Upon their father's death in 857. Athelbald reigned in Wessex, and Athelbert in Kent, Surrey, and Sussex. The former died about the month of July, A.D. 860, when his brother succeeded to the whole of his father's kingdom.

⁵ It is stated in the Annals of Winchester (Angl. Sacra, i. 204), that, by the admonition of St. Swithun, Athelbald repented of his incest, and separated from his mother-in-law. Judith returned to France about the year 861, which was not, however, until after the death of Athelbald. See Annal. Bertin. an. 862. (Bouquet, vii. 77.) She married Baldwin, count of Flanders, surnamed Bras de Fer, in 863.

of five years,[1] and being interred at Shireburn, the whole government devolved upon his brother. In his time a band of pirates,[2] landing at Southampton, proceeded to plunder the populous city of Winchester; but soon after being spiritedly repulsed by the king's generals, and suffering considerable loss, they put to sea; and coasting round, chose the isle of Thanet, in Kent, for their winter quarters. The people of Kent giving hostages, and promising a sum of money, would have remained quiet, had not these pirates, breaking the treaty, laid waste the whole district by nightly predatory excursions; but for this reason they mustered a force, and drove out the truce-breakers. Moreover Ethelbirht, ruling the kingdom with vigour and with mildness, paid the debt of nature after five years, and was buried at Shireburn.[3]

§ 118. In the year of our Lord's incarnation eight hundred and sixty-seven, Ethelred,[4] the son of Ethelwulf, enjoyed his paternal kingdom for the same number of years as his brothers. Surely it was a pitiable and grievous destiny that all of them should perish by an early death; unless it be that, in such a tempest of evils, these royal youths should prefer an honourable end, rather than a painful government. Indeed, so bravely and so vigorously did they contend for their country, that the blame is not to be imputed to them that their valour did not succeed in its design. Finally, it is related that this king was personally engaged in hostile conflict against the enemy nine times in one year,[5] with various success indeed, but for the most part victor, besides sudden attacks in which, from his skill in warfare, he frequently defeated those straggling depredators. In these several actions the Danes lost nine earls and one king, besides common people innumerable.

§ 119. One battle memorable beyond all the rest, was that which took place at Escendun: for the Danes having collected an army at this place, and divided it into two bodies—their two kings commanding the one, all their earls the other—the king Ethelred with his brother Elfred came upon them. It fell to the lot of Ethelred to oppose the kings, while Elfred was to attack the earls. Both armies eagerly prepared for battle, but, night approaching, deferred the conflict till the ensuing day. Scarcely had the morning dawned ere Elfred was ready at his post, but his brother, intent on his devotions, had remained in his tent; and

[1] Athelbald reigned two years and a half during his father's life, namely, from the time of Athelwulf's departure for Rome in 855; the two and a half years, from the end of 857 to July 860, when he died, make up the five years assigned to his reign by Malmesbury and the Saxon Chronicle.

[2] The Danes plundered Winchester in the year 860.

[3] Athelbert reigned in all nearly eight years, i. e. two and a half years in Kent, before he succeeded to the throne of Wessex, and upwards of five years after his brother's death. He died A. D. 866, and was succeeded by his brother Athelred.

[4] Malmesbury, in placing the accession of Athelred in the year 867, is one year later than the Saxon Chronicle, Asser, and Florence of Worcester. Thorne adopts the same date as Malmesbury. If, however, the period assigned by Malmesbury to this reign, and that of Aethelberht his predecessor, be correct, Athelred must have ascended the throne about February 866, and died 23d April, 871.

[5] Athelred was engaged in nine battles against the Danes before Easter, A. D. 871. See Asser, p. 452, and the Saxon Chronicle, p. 45 from which authorities the whole of this portion of the narrative is derived.

when urged on by a message that the Pagans were rushing forward
with unbounded fury, he declared that ne would not move one
step till his religious services were ended. This piety of the king
was of infinite advantage to his brother, too impetuous from the
thoughtlessness of youth, and already far advanced: for the battalions of the Angles were even now giving way, and bordering on
flight, in consequence of their adversaries pressing upon them from
the higher ground, for the Christians were fighting in an unfavour-
able situation, when the king himself, signed with the cross of God,
unexpectedly hastened forward, dispersing the enemy and rallying his
subjects: the Danes, terrified equally by his courage and the Divine
manifestation, consulted their safety by flight. Here fell Osecg their
king,[1] five earls, and an innumerable multitude of common people.

§ 120. The reader will not have failed to observe, that during
this time the king of the Mercians and of the Northumbrians,
eagerly seizing the opportunity of the arrival of the Danes, in
contest with whom Ethelred was fully occupied, and recovering
somewhat from their bondage to the West Saxons, had nearly
regained their original power. All the provinces, therefore, were
laid waste by cruel depredations, because each king chose rather to
resist the enemy within his own territories, than to assist his neighbours in their difficulties; and thus preferring to avenge injury
rather than prevent it, they ruined their country by their senseless
conduct. The Danes acquired strength without impediment, whilst
the apprehensions of the inhabitants increased, and each successive
victory, from the addition of captives, became the means of obtaining another. The country of the East Angles, together with their
cities and villages, was possessed by these plunderers; its king, St.
Eadmund,[2] slain by them in the year of our Lord's incarnation
eight hundred and seventy,[3] purchased an eternal kingdom by
putting off this mortal life. The Mercians, often harassed, alleviated their afflictions by giving hostages. The Northumbrians,
long embroiled in civil dissensions, made up their differences on
the approach of the enemy. Replacing Osbirht their king, whom
they had expelled,[4] upon the throne, and collecting a powerful
force, they went out to meet the foe; but being easily repelled,
they shut themselves up in the city of York, which was presently
after set on fire by the victors; and when the flames were raging to
the utmost, and consuming the very walls, they perished for their
country in the conflagration. In this manner Northumbria, possessed by right of war for a considerable time after, bewailed,
through a sense of former liberty, the galling yoke of barbarians.
And now Ethelred,[5] worn down by numberless labours, died and
was buried at Winburn.

[1] In the Saxon Chronicle and Asser, this king is called Bachsecg and Bægsceg.
In Danish history he is called Ivar.
[2] Edmund, king of East Anglia, was beheaded by Inguar, a son of Ragnar Lod-
brok (or, according to some, a son of Ivar, and grandson of Ragnar), 20th Nov. 870.
[3] So C. D. E. L. M. But A, followed by Saville's text, adds, "on the 12th of the
kalends of December" [20th Nov.].
[4] See at this point the narrative of Simeon of Durham.
[5] He died 23d April, 871.

§ 121. In the year of our Lord's incarnation eight hundred and seventy-two,[1] Alfred, the youngest son of Ethelwulf, who had, as has been related,[2] before received the royal unction and crown from pope Leo the Fourth at Rome, succeeded to the sovereignty and retained it with the greatest difficulty, but with equal valour, for twenty-eight years and a half. To trace in detail the mazy labyrinth of his labours was never my design, because a recapitulation of his exploits in their exact order of time would occasion some confusion to the reader; for to relate how an hostile army, driven by himself or his generals from one part of a district, retreated to another, and, dislodged thence, sought a fresh scene of operation, and filled every place with rapine and slaughter; and to follow him, and if I may use the expression, to go round the whole island with him, might to some seem the height of folly: consequently I shall touch on all points summarily. For nine successive years battling with his enemies, sometimes deceived by false treaties, and sometimes wreaking his vengeance on the deceivers, he was at last reduced to such extreme distress—scarcely three counties, that is to say, Hampshire, Wiltshire, and Somersetshire, standing fast by their allegiance—that he was compelled to retreat to a certain island called Adelingia, which from its marshy situation was hardly accessible. He was accustomed afterwards, when in happier circumstances, to relate to his companions in a lively and agreeable manner his perils there, and how he escaped them by the merits of St. Cuthbert;[3] for it mostly happens that men are pleased with the recollection of those circumstances which formerly they dreaded to encounter. During his retreat in this island, as he was one day in the house alone, his companions being dispersed on the river side for the purpose of fishing, he endeavoured to refresh his weary frame with sleep: and behold! Cuthbert, formerly bishop of Lindisfarn, addressed him while sleeping in the following manner: —"I am Cuthbert, if ever you heard of me: God hath sent me to announce good fortune to you; and since England has already largely paid the penalty of her crimes, God now, through the merits of her native saints, looks upon her with an eye of mercy. You too, so pitiably banished from your kingdom, shall shortly be again seated with honour on your throne, of which I give you this extraordinary token: your fishers shall this day bring home a great quantity of large fish in baskets; which will be so much the more extraordinary because the river, at this time rugged with ice, could warrant no such expectation, especially as the air, now dripping with cold rain, mocks the art of the fisher. But when your fortune shall succeed to your wishes, you will act as becomes a king, if you conciliate God your helper, and me his messenger, with suitable devotion." Saying thus, the saint relieved the sleeping king of his

---

[1] Alfred succeeded to the throne A. D. 871, which he held for thirty years and six months. The twenty-eight years and a half, assigned to Alfred's reign by Malmesbury and the Saxon Chronicle, are insufficient to reach A. D. 901, the year to which Malmesbury correctly refers the death of Alfred, and the accession of Edward the Elder. Upon this portion of Malmesbury's History, the Life of Alfred by Asser should be consulted.   [2] See § 109.
[3] See the Book of Hyde, p. 509.

anxiety ; and comforted his mother also, who was lying near him and endeavouring to invite some gentle slumbers to her hard couch to relieve her cares, with the same joyful intelligence.   Both awaking, they repeatedly declared that each had had the self-same dream, when the fishermen entering, displayed such a multitude of fishes as would have been sufficient to satisfy the appetite of a numerous army.   Not long after, venturing from his concealment, he hazarded an experiment of consummate art.   Accompanied only by one of his most faithful adherents, he entered the tent of the Danish king under the disguise of a mimic ;[1] and being admitted, in his assumed capacity of jester, to every corner of the banqueting-room, there was no object of secrecy that he did not minutely attend to both with eyes and ears.   Remaining there several days, till he had satisfied his mind on every matter which he wished to know, he returned to Adelingai ; and assembling his companions, pointed out the indolence of the enemy, and the easiness of their defeat.   All were eager for the enterprise, and himself collecting forces from every side, and learning exactly the situation of the barbarians from scouts whom he had sent out for that purpose, he suddenly attacked and routed them with incredible slaughter :[2] the remainder, with their king, gave hostages that they would embrace Christianity and depart from England,[3] which they performed ; for their king, Gudram,[4] whom our people call Gurmund, with thirty nobles and almost all the commonalty, was baptized, Alfred standing sponsor for him.   The provinces of the East Angles and Northumbrians[5] were given up to him, in order that he might, under fealty to the king, foster with hereditary right what before he had overrun with predatory incursion.   However, as the Ethiopian cannot change his skin, domineering over these tributary provinces with the haughtiness of a tyrant for eleven years, he died in the twelfth,[6] transmitting to his posterity the inheritance of his disloyalty, until subdued by Ethelstan, the grandson of Elfred,[7] they were, though reluctantly, compelled to admit one common king of England, as we see at the present day.   Such of the Danes as had refused to become Christians, together with Hasteng,[8] went over sea, where the inhabitants are best able

[1] This story is not to be found in Asser's Life of Alfred.   A somewhat similar anecdote is related of Olaf, the Danish prince, entering the camp of Athelstan in the disguise of a minstrel, at § 131.

[2] At a place called Ethandun, A.D. 878.   [3] *I.e.* Wessex.

[4] Guthorm was baptized at Aller, near Athelney, A.D. 878, and his baptismal name was Athelstan.

[5] This seems a mistake, as far as relates to Northumbria. The Saxon Chronicle has "Northerna," and Florence of Worcester, "Rex Northmannicus," which at first glance might easily be converted into Northumbria. See § 97, note [4].

[6] Guthorm died A.D. 891.

[7] The Danes were expelled from East Anglia, and the kingdom annexed to Wessex, under Edward the Elder, A.D. 918.   Malmesbury seems here to refer to the period of the death of Sihtric, king of the Northumbrians, A.D. 926, when Athelstan obtained the kingdom of Northumbria upon the expulsion of Guthferth in 927.

[8] It has been doubted whether the chieftain, who at this time headed the Danes against Alfred, be the same Hasting who distinguished himself by the extent and cruelty of his ravages in France and the south of Europe during the reign of Charles le Chauve.   This has been considered by some to be a son of the first

to tell what cruelties they perpetrated ; for over-running the whole maritime coasts to the Tuscan sea, they depopulated Paris and Tours, as well as many other cities seated on the Seine and Loire, those noble rivers of France. At that time the bodies of many saints being taken up from the spot of their original interment, and conveyed to safer places, have ennobled foreign churches with their reliques even to this day. Then also the body of St. Martin,[1] " venerated," as Sidonius[2] says, " over the whole earth, in which virtue resides though life be at an end," was taken to Auxerre by the clergy of his church, and placed in that of St. German,[3] where it astonished the people of that district by unheard-of miracles. And when they who came thither, out of gratitude for cures performed, contributed many things to requite the labours of those who had borne him to this church, as is commonly the case, a dispute arose about the division of the money,—the inhabitants of Tours claiming the whole, because their patron saint had called the contributors together by his miracles ; the natives, on the other hand, alleging that St. German was not unequal in merit, and was of equal efficacy ; that both indeed had visibly the same power, but that the prerogative of their church preponderated. To solve this knotty doubt, a leprous person was sought, and placed, nearly at the last gasp, wasted throughout, and already dead as it were in a living carcase, between the bodies of the two saints. All human watch was prohibited for the whole night—the glory of Martin alone was vigilant ; for the next day the skin of the man on his side appeared clear, while on that of German it was discoloured with its customary deformity. And that they might not attribute this miracle to chance, they turn the yet diseased side to Martin : but soon as the morning began to dawn, the man was found by the hastening attendants with all his skin smooth, perfectly cured, declaring the kind condescension of the resident patron, who yielded the honour to such a welcome stranger. Thus the inhabitants of Tours, both at that time and afterwards, safely filled their common purse by the assistance of their patron saint, till a more favourable gale of peace restored them to their former residence ; for these marauders infesting France for thirteen years, and being at last overcome by the emperor Ernulf and the people of Brittany[4] in many encounters, retreated into England as a convenient receptacle for their tyranny. During this space of time, Elfred had reduced the whole island to his power, with the exception of what

adventurer. The elder Hasting, it is alleged, had been converted to Christianity, and, as a vassal of Charles le Simple, joined the royal army in the invasion by the Normans under Rollo in 898. The period of the departure of Hasting from England, after his final defeat by Alfred in 896, would not render this identity improbable.

[1] See Mabill. Annal. Bened. lib. xxxiv. §§ 61—63.

[2] Caius Sollius Sidonius Apollinaris, bishop of Clermont, in Auvergne, one of the most illustrious prelates of the fifth century. He is said to have died 23d of August, A.D. 482. See Cave, Hist. Lit. i. 453.

[3] St. Germain, bishop of Auxerre in the fifth century.

[4] The Northmen, having been beaten in two successive battles in Brittany, met and defeated the army of the emperor Arnoul near Liege, 26th of June, 891, but soon after suffered a signal defeat from the emperor himself. See Pagi, ad an. 891, § 3.

the Danes possessed.   The Angles had willingly surrendered to his dominion, rejoicing that they had produced a man capable of leading them to liberty.   He granted London,[1] the chief city of the Mercian kingdom, to a nobleman named Ethered, to hold in fealty, and gave him his daughter Ethelfleda in marriage.   Ethered conducted himself with equal valour and fidelity, defended his trust with activity, and kept the East Angles and Northumbrians, who were plotting rebellion against the king, within due bounds, compelling them to give hostages.   Of what infinite service this was, the following emergency proved:—For after England had rejoiced for fourteen[2] years in the tranquillity of peace and in the fertility of her soil, then returned that northern pest of barbarians;[3] again returned war and slaughter; again arose conspiracies among the Northumbrians and East Angles: but neither strangers nor natives experienced the same fortune as in former years.   The one party, diminished by foreign contests, was less alert in their invasions; while the other, now experienced in war and animated by the exhortations of the king, was not only more ready to resist, but also to attack.   The king himself, with his usual activity, was present in every emergency, daunting the invaders, and at the same time inspiriting his subjects with the signal display of his courage: he would oppose himself singly to the enemy; by his own personal exertions he would rally his declining forces.   The very places are yet pointed out by the inhabitants where he felt the full malevolence of misfortune, or was unbefriended by success. It was necessary to contend with Elfred even after he was overcome, after he was prostrate; insomuch that when he might be supposed altogether vanquished, "yet, like a slippery serpent, he would escape from the hand which held him," glide from his lurking-place, and, with undiminished courage, spring on his insulting enemies; generally insupportable after flight, as becoming more circumspect from the recollection of defeat, more bold from the thirst of vengeance.   His children by Egelsuitha,[4] the daughter of earl Egelred, were Ethelsuida,[5] Edward, who reigned after him; Ethelfleda,[6] who was married to Ethelred earl of the Mercians; Ethelward,[7] whom they celebrate as being extremely learned; Elfreda[8] and Elfgiva,[9] virgins.   His health was so bad that he was constantly disquieted either by the piles, or some disorder of the intestines: it is said,[10] however, that he entreated this from God in

[1] See Asser, p. 469.

[2] So D. E. M.; "thirteen." A. C. L., followed by Saville.

[3] The Danes returned to England in 893. See Florence of Worcester, p. 229.

[4] Alfred married Ealhswith, or Ethelswitha, daughter of earl Athelred and Eadburh, of the royal family of Mercia, A.D. 868. She died A.D. 905.

[5] I. e. Ethelfleda. Asser mentions no daughter of Alfred by the name of Athelswitha, and Malmesbury here is in error. Athelfled was married to Athered, earl of Mercia, and died 12th of June, 919.   [6] See the last note.

[7] He died A.D. 922. See Florence, ad an.

[8] Alfthryth was married to Baldwin II. count of Flanders; but the year of their marriage is not recorded. He died 2d of Jan. 918, leaving two sons by her, then grown up.

[9] Elgiva, or Ethelgeofu, was dedicated to a monastic life, and became abbess of Shaftesbury.   [10] See Asser, p. 472.

his supplications, in order that, by the admonition of pain, he might
be less anxious after earthly delights.

§ 122. Yet amid these circumstances, the more retired life of the
king is to be admired and celebrated with the highest praise. For
although, as a certain one [1] has said, " Laws must give way amid
the strife of arms," yet he, amid the din of war, enacted statutes
by which his people might equally familiarise themselves with
religious worship and military discipline. And since, from the
example of the barbarians, the natives themselves began to lust
after rapine, insomuch that there was no safe intercourse without a
military guard, he appointed centuries, which they call "hundreds," [2]
and decennaries, which they call "tythings;" so that every Englishman, living according to law, must be a member of both. If
any one was accused of a crime, he was obliged immediately to
produce persons from his hundred and tything to become his
surety ; and whosoever was unable to find such surety must dread
the severity of the laws. If any who had been impleaded made his
escape, either before or after he had found surety, all persons of the
hundred and tything paid a fine to the king. By this regulation he
diffused such peace throughout the country, that he ordered that
golden bracelets, which might mock the eager desires of the pas-
sengers while no one durst take them away, should be hung up on
the public causeways, where the roads crossed each other. Ever
intent on almsgiving, he confirmed the privileges of the churches
as appointed by his father, and sent many presents over sea to
Rome, and to St. Thomas [3] in India. Sigelin, bishop of Shireburn,
sent ambassador for this purpose, [4] prosperously penetrated into
India—a matter of astonishment even in the present time. Returning thence, he brought back many brilliant exotic gems and
aromatic juices with which that country abounds, and a present
besides, more precious than the finest gold,—part of our Saviour's
cross, sent by pope Marinus [5] to the king. He erected monasteries wherever he deemed it fitting ; one in Adelingia, [6] where he
lay concealed, as has been above related, and there he made John [7]
abbot, a native of old Saxony; another at Winchester, which is

[1] Cicero, pro Milone, iv.
[2] See Thorpe's Glossary to the Saxon Laws, under the word Hundred.
[3] See Nicephorus, ii. 40, and on this tradition generally, Basnage, Hist. de
l'Eglise, p. 1113.
[4] This mission occurred in the year 883. The persons who then carried the
king's alms to Rome and India are simply called in the Saxon Chronicle Sighelm
and Ethelstan. Malmesbury here follows Florence, who considers that the Sighelm
employed in this mission was a bishop of Sherborne, and that he succeeded to
that dignity upon the death of Asser (faultily ascribed to A.D. 883). If Sighelm
was bishop of Sherborne, he could not have been the successor of Asser, who died
in A.D. 908 or 910.
[5] Marinus, or Martinus I. became pope in December 882, and died in 884.
[6] The Benedictine monastery of Athelney, in Somersetshire, was founded by
Alfred in the year 888, and dedicated to the Saviour, St. Peter, and St. Paul.
The foundation charter is printed in Reyneri Apostol. Bened. ii. 132; Dugd.
Monast. i. 202.
[7] Much discussion has arisen respecting this individual. It is sufficient for our
present purpose to refer our readers to Wright's Biograph. Liter. (Saxon period),
p. 419; Hist. Lit. de France, v. 417; Lingard, Anglo-Saxon Church, ii. 246. It
appears from these authorities that Malmesbury's narrative is erroneous.

called the New Minster, where he appointed Grimbald[1] abbot, who at his invitation had been sent into England by Fulco, archbishop of Rheims,[2] known to him, as they say, by having kindly entertained him when a child on his way to Rome.   The cause of his being sent for was, that by his activity he might awaken the study of literature in England, which was now slumbering and almost expiring.   The monastery of Shaftesbury[3] also he filled with nuns, where he made his daughter Elfgiva abbess.   From St. David's he procured a person named Asser,[4] a man of skill in literature, whom he made bishop of Shireburn.   This man explained the meaning of the works of Boethius, on the Consolation of Philosophy, in clearer terms, and the king himself translated them into the English language;[5] and since there was no good scholar in his own kingdom, he sent for Werefrith, bishop of the Wiccians,[6] out of Mercia, who by command of the king rendered into the English tongue the Books of Dialogues.[7]

At this time Johannes Scottus[8] is supposed to have lived, a man of clear understanding and amazing eloquence.   He had long since, from the continued tumult of war around him, retired into France to Charles the Bald, at whose request he had translated the Hierarchia of Dionysius the Areopagite,[9] word for word, out of the Greek into Latin.   He composed a book also, which he entitled Περὶ φύσεων μερισμοῦ, or Of the Division of Nature,[10] extremely useful in solving the perplexity of certain indispensable inquiries, if he be pardoned for some things, in which he deviated from the opinions of the Latins through too close attention to the Greeks.   In after time, allured by the munificence of Alfred, he came into England, and at our monastery, as report says, being pierced with the iron styles of the boys whom he was instructing, he was even looked upon as a martyr; which hesitating phrase I have not made use of to the disparagement of his holy spirit, as though it were matter of doubt, especially as his tomb on the left side of the altar, and the verses of his epitaph, record his fame.   These, though rugged and deficient in the polish of our days, are not so uncouth for ancient times :—

> " Here lies a saint, the sophist John, whose days
>   On earth were graced with deepest learning's praise·
>   Deem'd meet at last by martyrdom to gain
>   Christ's kingdom, where the saints for ever reign."

§ 123. Confiding in these auxiliaries, the king gave his whole soul to the cultivation of the liberal arts, insomuch that no Englishman was quicker in comprehending, or more elegant in translating;

---

[1] Concerning Grimbald, see the writers cited in the last note.
[2] See the Book of Hyde, p. 499.   [3] Dugd. Monast. i. 213.
[4] See the present Collection of Historians, ii. 443.
[5] Printed by Rawlinson at Oxford, 8vo. 1698.
[6] See Wright, p. 415. He was consecrated 7th of June, 873 (Whitsunday), and died 915.
[7] It is much to be regretted that this version is still unprinted.
[8] Concerning this John the Scot, see the authorities cited in p. 104, note [7], above.
[9] See Mabill. Annal. xxix. § 59 ; Wright, p. 421.
[10] It has been printed by Gale, Oxon. 1681. It was condemned by pope Honorius III. A.D. 1226.

and this was the more remarkable, because until twelve years of age [1] he absolutely knew nothing of literature. At that time, lured by a kind mother [2] under the mask of amusement, promising that he should have a little book which she held in her hand for a present if he would learn it quickly, he entered upon learning, in sport indeed at first, but afterwards drank of the stream with unquenchable avidity. He translated into English the greater part of the Roman authors, bringing off the noblest spoil of foreign intercourse for the use of his subjects; of which the chief books were, Orosius, [3] Gregory's Pastoral, Beda's [4] History of the Angles, Boethius [5] Of the Consolation of Philosophy; his own book, which he called in his vernacular tongue "Handboc," that is, a hand-book. [6] Moreover, he infused a great regard for literature into his countrymen, stimulating them both by rewards and punishments, allowing no ignorant [7] person to aspire to any dignity in the court. He died just as he had begun a translation of the Psalms. [8] In the prologue [9] to "The Pastoral" he observes, "that he was in-cited to translate these books into English, because the churches which had formerly contained numerous libraries had, together with their books, been burnt by the Danes; and that the pursuit of literature had gone to decay almost over the whole island, because each person was more occupied in the preservation of his life than in the perusal of books: wherefore he so far consulted the good of his countrymen, that they might now hastily view, what hereafter, if peace should ever return, they might thoroughly com-prehend in the Latin language; that he designed to transmit this book, transcribed by his order, to every see, with a golden style, [10] in which was a mancus of gold; that there was nothing of his own opinions inserted in this or his other translations; but that every-thing was derived from those celebrated men Pleimund, archbishop of Canterbury, Asser the bishop, Grimbald and John the priests."
But finally, briefly to elucidate his whole life, he so divided [11] the twenty-four hours which are constantly revolving by day and by night, as to employ eight of them in writing, in reading, and in prayer; eight in the refreshment of his body; and eight in despatching the business of the realm. There was in his chapel a candle with twenty-four divisions, and an attendant, whose peculiar province it was to admonish the king of his several duties by its consumption. One half portion of all revenues, provided they were justly acquired, he gave to his monasteries; [12] all his other income he divided into two equal parts. The first was again subdivided into three, of which the

---

[1] See Asser, p. 450.   [2] Compare Asser, under the year 866.
[3] The Anglo-Saxon version of the Universal History of Orosius has been edited by Daines Barrington, with an English translation. (Lond. 1773.)
[4] Printed by Whelock and Smith with their respective editions of the works of Beda.   [5] Printed by Rawlinson at Oxford, 8vo. 1698.
[6] See Wright, p. 395.   [7] Asser, p. 478.
[8] We have no further information respecting this work.
[9] Printed in Wise's edition of Asser, p. 81, Oxon. 1722. See also Wright, p. 393.
[10] This is obscure. What is rendered a style also signifies a table-book. In Alfred's preface it is called "an æstel" of fifty mancuses; but what that was can only be conjectured, as the word is not known to occur elsewhere. See Asser, by Wise, 86, 175.   [11] Asser, p. 477.   [12] Id. p. 476.

first was given to the servants of his court; the second to artificers, whom he constantly employed in the erection of new edifices, in a manner surprising and hitherto unknown to the English; the third he gave to strangers. The second part of the revenue was divided in such a mode that the first portion should be given to the poor of his kingdom, the second to the monasteries, the third to scholars, the fourth to foreign churches. He was a strict inquirer into the sentences passed by his magistrates, and a severe corrector of such as were unjust.[1] He had one unusual and unheard-of custom, which was, that he always carried in his bosom[2] a book in which the daily order of the Psalms was contained, for the purpose of carefully perusing it, if at any time he had leisure. In this way he passed his life, much respected by neighbouring princes; and he gave his daughter Ethelswitha[3] in marriage to Baldwin, earl of Flanders, by whom he had Ernulf and Adulf. The latter received from his father the county of Boulogne; from the other are descended the present earls of Flanders.[4]

§ 124. Elfred paying the debt of nature,[5] was buried at Winchester, in the monastery which he had founded, to build the offices of which, Edward his son purchased a sufficient space of ground from the then bishop and canons, giving for every foot a mancus of gold of the statute weight. The endurance of the king was astonishing, in suffering such a sum to be extorted from him; but he did not choose to offer a sacrifice to God from the robbery of the poor. These two churches were so contiguous that, when singing, they heard each other's voices: on this and other accounts, an unhappy jealousy was daily stirring up causes of dissension, which produced frequent injuries on either side. For this reason that monastery was lately removed out of the city, and became a more healthy as well as a more conspicuous place of residence. They report that Elfred was first buried in the cathedral, because his monastery was unfinished; but that afterwards, on

---

[1] Asser, p. 473. In the Mirror of Justice, chap. ii., it is stated that Alfred, in one year, condemned to be hanged no less than forty-four inferior judges in the hundred and county courts, for false judgments, either in condemning or acquitting men without the verdict of a jury.   [2] Asser, p. 470.

[3] See § 121, where Alfred's daughter, married to Baldwin II. count of Flanders, is called Elfreda, or Elfthryth; in French history she is called Elstrude. Baldwin (named Le Chauve in memory of his maternal grandfather) left two sons by this marriage, Arnoul, and Adulphus or Adalolfus, from the former of whom (Arnoul the Great, count of Flanders, A.D. 918) descended Matilda, queen of William the Conqueror. Adolphe died without issue A.D. 933.

[4] Here two MSS. (A. and H.) add: "The panegyric and account of the death of king Alfred.—Famous, warlike, and a conqueror; the diligent protector of widows, wards, orphans, and the poor; the best of the Saxon poets; the idol of his nation; affable to all and most generous; endowed with prudence, fortitude, temperance, and justice; most patient under the disease which afflicted him; most discreet and persevering in carrying out judicial decrees; and most watchful and devout in the service of God,—Alfred, king of the Anglo-Saxons, son of the most pious king Atheluulf, having reigned nine years and six months, died in the fourth year of the indiction, the 5th day of the kalends of November [28th Oct.], on the fourth day of the week; and being buried at Winchester, in the new monastery, he there, together with the just, awaits the garment of immortality and the glory of the resurrection." This passage occurs verbatim in the Chronicle of Florence of Worcester, A.D. 901, p. 233.

[5] Alfred died on the 28th of Oct. A.D. 901.

account of the folly of the canons, asserting that the royal [1] spirit,
resuming its carcase, wandered nightly through the buildings,
Edward, his son and successor, removed the remains of his father,
and gave them a quiet resting-place in the New Minster.[2]   These
and similar superstitions, such as that the dead body of a wicked
man runs about after death by the agency of the devil, the English
hold with almost inbred credulity,[3] borrowing them from the
heathens, according to the expression of Virgil,[4]—

  " Forms such as flit, they say; when life is gone."

§ 125.   In the year of our Lord's incarnation nine hundred and
one, Edward the son of Elfred succeeded to the government, and
held it twenty-three years[5]—much inferior to his father in literature, but greatly excelling him in extent of power; for Elfred indeed
united the two kingdoms of the Mercians and West Saxons,
holding that of the Mercians only nominally, as he had assigned it
to prince Ethered.   But, at Ethered's death,[6] Edward first brought
the Mercians altogether under his power; next, the West[7] and
East Angles and Northumbrians, who had become one nation with
the Danes; the Scots, who inhabit the northern part of the island,
and all the Britons, whom we call Welsh, after perpetual battles;
nor did he suffer one defeat.   He devised a mode of frustrating the
incursions of the Danes: for, repairing many ancient cities, or
building new ones in places calculated for his purpose, he filled
them with a military force, sufficient to protect the inhabitants and
to repel the enemy.   Nor was his design unsuccessful; for the inhabitants became so extremely valorous in these contests, that if they
heard of an enemy approaching, they rushed out to give them battle,
even without consulting the king or his generals, and constantly
surpassed them both in number and in warlike skill.   Thus the
enemy became an object of contempt to the soldiery, and of derision
to the king.   At last some fresh assailants, who had come over
under the command of Aethelwold, the son of the king's uncle,[8]
were all, together with himself, cut off to a man; those who had
previously settled in the country being either destroyed, or spared
under the denomination of Angles.   Aethelwold, indeed, had attempted many things in the earlier days of this king, and disdained
subjection to him, declaring himself his inferior neither in birth nor
valour; but being driven into exile by the nobility, who had sworn
allegiance to Edward, he brought over the pirates; with whom

---

[1] See the Book of Hyde, p. 518.   [2] On its removal called Hyde Abbey.
[3] The popular notion was, that the devil reanimated the corpse, and played
a variety of pranks by its agency; and that the only remedy was to dig up and
consume the body with fire. See Will. Neubrig. v. 22.   [4] Æn. x. 641.
[5] Edward the Elder was not crowned till Whitsunday (16th May), A.D. 902; if,
therefore, the commencement of his reign be dated from that day, he was yet in
his twenty-third year when he died; but he had completed his twenty-third year,
computed from his father's death, on 26th of October, A.D. 924.   He died at
Faringdon, probably before the close of that year, but certainly before the 30th of
January, A.D. 925.   [6] Ethered, earl of Mercia, died A.D. 912.
[7] Meaning probably the people of Essex, or East Saxons.
[8] Ethelwold, son of Ethelbert, the elder brother of Ælfred, was slain A.D. 905.
See the Saxon Chronicle, ad an.

meeting his death, as I have related, he gave proof of the folly of resisting our superiors in power. Although Edward may be deservedly praised for these transactions, yet, in my opinion, the palm should be more especially given to his father, who certainly laid the foundation of this extent of dominion. And here, indeed, Ethelfleda,[1] sister of the king and widow of Ethered, ought not to be forgotten, as she was a powerful accession to his party, the delight of his subjects, the dread of his enemies; a woman of an enlarged soul, who, from the difficulty experienced in her first (or rather only) labour, ever after refused the embraces of her husband, protesting that it was unbecoming the daughter of a king to give way to a delight, which after a time produced such painful consequences. This spirited heroine assisted her brother greatly with her advice; she was of equal service in building cities, nor could you easily discern whether it were more owing to fortune or her own exertions, that a woman should be able to protect men at home, and to intimidate them abroad. She died five years before her brother,[2] and was buried in the monastery of St. Peter at Gloucester, which, in conjunction with her husband Ethered, she had erected with great solicitude: thither, too, she had transferred the bones of St. Oswald the king from Bardney; but this monastery being destroyed in succeeding time by the Danes, Aldred, archbishop of York,[3] founded another, which is now the chief in that city.

Concerning the Children of Edward the Elder.

§ 126. As the king had many daughters, he gave Edgifa to Charles[4] king of the Franks, the son of Louis,[5] son of Charles the Bald, whose daughter, as I have repeatedly observed,[6] Ethelwulf had married on his return from Rome; and, as the opportunity has now presented itself, the indulgent reader will not think it irrelevant if I state the names of his wives and children. By Egwinna, an illustrious lady, he had Ethelstan[7] his first-born, and a daughter of whose name I find no written record,[8] but her brother gave her in marriage to Sihtric, king of the Northumbrians. The second son of Edward was Ethelward,[9] by Elfleda, daughter of earl Ethelm;

---

[1] For notices of Ethelfled, Lady of the Mercians, consult the Saxon Chronicle, A.D. 912—919.

[2] Ethelfled died at Tamworth, 12th of June, A.D. 919. She left a daughter by earl Ethered, named Elfwyn.

[3] Aldred, bishop of Worcester in 1046, after the death of archbishop Kinsinus was appointed to York, A.D. 1061, to hold both sees together; but the pope refused him the pall until he had given up Worcester. (Malmes. in Vita S. Wulstani.) He died 11th of September, 1069.

[4] Charles the Simple. See § 112.

[5] So C. D. E. L.; A. (followed by Saville) calls him Louis the Stammerer.

[6] See § 109, and § 113.

[7] Egwina, the mother of king Ethelstan, is said to have been Edward's concubine; but Malmesbury speaks doubtingly of this alleged stain on Ethelstan's birth. See § 131.

[8] The name of Edward's daughter, who was given by her brother Athelstan in marriage to Sihtric, king of Northumbria (30th of Jan. 925), does not occur in any of the early English Chronicles. She is called Beatrix by the Scottish historians.

[9] Ethelwerd died at Oxford a few days after his father, and was buried at Winchester. See § 131.

deeply versed in literature, much resembling his grandfather Elfred
in features and disposition, but swept off by death soon after his
father. By the same wife he had Edwin, of whose fate what the
received opinion is I shall hereafter describe,[1] not with confidence,
but doubtingly.   By her, too, he had six daughters : Edfleda,
Edgiva, Ethelhilda, Ethilda, Edgitha, Elfgiva : the first and third,
vowing celibacy to God, renounced the pleasure of earthly nuptials—
Edfleda in a religious, and Ethelhilda in a lay habit ; they both lie
buried near their mother at Wilton. Her father gave Edgifa, as I
have mentioned, to king Charles :[2] and her brother Ethelstan gave
Ethilda to Hugh:[3] this same brother also sent Edgitha and Elfgiva
to Henry emperor of Germany, the second of whom he gave to his
son Otho, the other to a certain duke near the Alps.[4] Again, by
his third wife named Edgiva he had two sons, Edmund and Edred,
each of whom reigned after Ethelstan ; two daughters, Edburga
and Edgiva. Edburga, a virgin dedicated to Christ, lies buried at
Winchester; Edgiva, a lady of incomparable beauty, was united by
her brother Ethelstan to Lewis prince of Aquitaine.[5] Edward had
brought up his daughters in such wise that in childhood they
gave their whole attention to literature, and afterwards employed
themselves in the labours of the distaff and the needle, that thus
they might chastely pass their virgin age ; and his sons were so
educated as first to have the completest benefit of learning, that
afterwards they might succeed to govern the state, not like rustics,
but philosophers.

Of the Normans, how they infested France, and how Rollo took the Daughter of the King of the Franks.

§ 127. Charles, the son-in-law of Edward, constrained thereto
by Rollo through a succession of calamities, conceded to him that
part of Gaul which at present is called Normandy. It would be
tedious to relate, for how many years, and with what audacity, the
Normans disquieted every place from the British ocean, as I have
before mentioned,[6] to the Tuscan sea. First Hasteng, and then
Rollo, who, born of noble lineage among the Norwegians,[7] though
obsolete from its extreme antiquity, was banished by the king's
command from his own country,[8] and brought over with him
multitudes, who were in danger either from debt or consciousness

---

[1] See § 139.
[2] See § 112. After the death of Charles le Simple, queen Edgiva married
Herbert, comte de Troyes, son of Herbert, comte de Vermandois, A.D. 951.
(Bouquet, ix. 126.)
[3] Hugh, count of Paris, surnamed the Great, son of Robert I. king of France,
the brother of king Eudes. He died A.D. 956, but left no issue by Eadhild. He
was the father of Hugh Capet, king of France.   [4] See § 112.
[5] Edgiva was married to Louis l'Aveugle, emperor and king of Arles. She had
by him a son named Charles Constantine, count of Vienne. (Bouquet, viii. 186.)
[6] Ante, § 121.
[7] Rollo was the son of Rognvald, jarl of Mære (slain A.D. 893), who was
descended in the maternal line from the famous Sigurdr Ring, king of Denmark
and Sweden.
[8] Rollo was banished from his native land by command of king Harald Hár-
fager, A.D. 895. (Snorre, Haralds Saga ens Harfagra, chap. xxiv. tom. i. p. 100;
ed. Hauniæ, 1777.)

of guilt, and whom he had allured by great expectations of advantage. Betaking himself therefore to piracy, after his cruelty had ranged on every side at pleasure, he experienced a check at Chartres:[1] for the townspeople, relying neither on arms nor fortifications, piously implored the assistance of the blessed Virgin[2] Mary. The shift too of the Virgin, which Charles the Bald had brought with other reliques from Constantinople,[3] they displayed to the winds, on the ramparts thronged by the garrison, after the fashion of a banner. The enemy on seeing it began to laugh, and to direct their arrows at it through the air : this, however, was not done with impunity ; for presently their eyes becoming dim, they could neither retreat nor advance. The townsmen with joy perceiving this, indulged themselves in a plentiful slaughter of them as far as fortune permitted. Rollo, however, whom God reserved for the true faith, escaped, and soon after gained Rouen and the neighbouring cities by force of arms, in the year of our Lord eight hundred and seventy-six,[4] and one year before the death of Charles the Bald, whose grandson Lewis,[5] as is before mentioned,[6] vanquished the Normans, but did not expel them : but Charles,[7] the brother of that Lewis, grandson of Charles the Bald by his son Lewis, as I have said above,[8] repeatedly experiencing from unsuccessful conflicts, that fortune gave him nothing which she took from others, resolved, after consulting his nobility, that it was advisable to make a show of royal munificence, when he was unable to repel injury ; and, in a friendly manner, sent for Rollo. He was at this time far advanced in years, and consequently easily inclined to adopt pacific measures. It was therefore determined by treaty,[9] that he should be baptized, and hold that country of the king as his lord. The inbred and untameable ferocity of the man may well be imagined ; for, on receiving this gift, as the bye-standers suggested to him that he ought to kiss the foot of his benefactor,[10] disdaining to kneel down, he seized the king's foot, and dragged it to his mouth as he stood erect. The king falling on his back, the Normans began to laugh, and the Franks to reprobate the transaction ; but Rollo apologised for his shameful conduct, by saying that it was the custom of his country. Thus, the affair being settled, Rollo returned to Rouen, and there died.[11]

[1] Rollo besieged Chartres in the year 911.

[2] Bishop Waltelme is said to have borne in his hand the tunic of the Holy Virgin, by means of which the besiegers were put to flight.

[3] See Mabill. Annal. S. Bened. A. D. 911 ; Gall. Christ. viii. 1108.

[4] So A. C. L. (adopted by Saville) ; 806 (906 ?) D. E. M. ; but both dates are at least twenty years later than the northern writers place this occurrence, and are manifestly inconsistent with the siege of Chartres, which occurred A. D. 911. Two invasions of Normandy are here erroneously blended together.

[5] Louis III. the son of Louis le Bègue.   [6] See § 110.

[7] Charles the Simple.   [8] See § 110.

[9] The terms of this treaty, it is believed, nowhere exist in an authentic form, and it is even very questionable if it ever were reduced to writing.

[10] The discourteous act here laid to the charge of Rollo is attributed by William of Jumiéges to one of the Norman knights in the duke's attendance. (Bouquet, viii. 257.)   Robert Wace, however, likewise makes the Norman chief himself guilty of the disrespect offered to the French king. (Roman de Rou.)

[11] Rollo abdicated in favour of his son William in the year 927. He died A. D. 931. (Bouquet, ix. 12, note.)

Concerning Hugh Capet, how he was made King of France.

§ 128. The son of this Charles was Lewis :[1] he, being challenged
by one Isambard,[2] who, turning Pagan, had renounced his faith,
called upon his nobility for their assistance. They not even deigning
an answer, one Hugh, son of Robert earl of Mont Didier, a youth
of no great celebrity at the time, voluntarily entered the lists for
his lord, and killed the challenger.[3] Lewis with his whole army
pursuing to Ponthieu, gained there a glorious triumph, either
destroying or putting to flight all the barbarians whom Isambard
had brought with him. But not long after, weakened by extreme
sickness, the consequence of this laborious expedition, he appointed
this Hugh, a young man of noted faith and courage, heir to the
kingdom. Thus the lineage of Charles the Great ceased with him,
because either his wife was barren, or else did not live long enough
to have issue. Hugh married one of the daughters of Edward,[4]
and begot Rodbert ;[5] Rodbert, Henry ; Henry, Philip ; Philip,
Lewis, who now reigns in France.[6] But to return to our Edward ;
I think it will be pleasing to relate what in his time pope Formosus
commanded to be done with respect to filling up the bishoprics,
which I shall insert in the very words I found it.[7]

§ 129. In the year of our Lord's nativity nine hundred and
four, pope Formosus sent letters into England, by which he
denounced excommunication and malediction upon king Edward
and all his subjects, instead of the benediction which St. Gregory
had given to the English nation from the seat of St. Peter ; because
for seven whole years the entire district of the Gewisi, that is, of
the West Saxons, had been destitute of bishops. On hearing this,
king Edward assembled a council of the senators of the English,
over which presided archbishop Pleimund,[8] interpreting carefully
the words of the apostolic legation. Then the king and the bishops
chose for themselves and their followers a salutary counsel, and,
according to our Saviour's words, " The harvest truly is plenteous,

---

[1] Louis IV. surnamed D'Outremer, returned from England, accompanied by
William archbishop of Sens, in the year 936, and was crowned on the 19th of
June in that year. He died at Rheims by a fall from his horse, 10th of Sep-
tember, A.D. 954.

[2] The events detailed in this section are greatly confounded. What is here
related of Louis IV. appears to belong to the reign of his uncle, Louis III.

[3] This statement is unsupported by satisfactory authority.

[4] Malmesbury, as it seems, would here refer to Hugh Capet, whom he confounds
with his father, Hugh the Great, the husband of Eadhild, or Ethilda, daughter of
Edward the Elder. See § 126. Hugh Capet, king of France, was consecrated
at Rheims 3d of July, A.D. 987, and died 24th of October, A.D. 996.

[5] He died at Vitry, near Paris, on the 4th of August, A.D. 1060.

[6] Louis VI. surnamed Le Gros, was consecrated at Orleans, 3d of August, 1108,
by the archbishop of Sens ; and died at Paris, 1st of August, 1137.

[7] This account is copied from a MS. (Bodley, 579) which was given by bishop
Leofric, who died 1073, to Exeter cathedral. The whole is so replete with
anachronisms as to leave the presumption of forgery beyond a doubt. The instrument is dated in 904, and Formosus died in May, 896 (Jaffé, p. 302), upwards
of five years before Edward commenced his reign ; whilst Frithestan was not
bishop of Winchester before the year 910. On the subject of the seven vacant
sees, consult Anglia Sacra, i. 554; Spelman ; and Wilkins, Concilia, i. 201. See also
Ingulf, p. 617.

[8] Archbishop of Canterbury.

but the labourers are few," [Matt. ix. 37,] they elected and appointed one bishop to every province of the Gewisi ; and that district which two had formerly possessed, they now divided into five. The council being dissolved, the archbishop went to Rome with splendid presents, appeased the pope with much humility, and related the king's ordinance, which gave the pontiff great satisfaction. Returning home, in one day he ordained in the city of Canterbury seven bishops to seven churches ; Fridestan to the church of Winchester, Adelstan to that of Cornwall, Werstan to that of Shireburn, Adelelm to that of Wells, Edulf to that of Crediton. Also to other provinces he appointed two bishops ;. to the South Saxons, Bernegus, a very proper person, and to the Mercians, Chenulf, whose see was at the city of Dorchester. All this the pope established in such wise, that he who should invalidate this decree should be damned everlastingly.

§ 130. Edward going the way of all flesh, rested in the same monastery with his father, which he too had augmented with considerable revenues, and in which he had buried his brother Adelward four years before.[1]

Of Ethelstan, the son of Edward.

§ 131. In the year of our Lord's incarnation nine hundred and twenty-four, Ethelstan the son of Edward began to reign, and he reigned sixteen years.[2] His brother Elward dying a few days after his father, had been buried with him at Winchester. At this place, therefore, Ethelstan being elected king by the unanimous consent of the nobility, he was crowned at a royal town which is called Kingston ; though one Elvred, whose death we shall hereafter relate in the words of the king,[3] with his factious party, (as sedition never wants adherents,) attempted to prevent it. The ground of this opposition, as they affirm, was that Ethelstan was born of a concubine ; but having nothing ignoble in him except this stain, if after all it be true,[4] he cast all his predecessors into the shade by his piety, as well as the glory of all their triumphs by the splendour of his own. So much more excellent is it that the qualities for which we are renowned should be inherent, rather than derived from our ancestors ; because the former is exclusively our own—the latter may be imputed to others. I forbear relating how many new and magnificent monasteries he founded ; but I will not conceal that there was scarcely an old one in England which he did not embellish either with buildings, or ornaments, or books,[5] or

---

[1] Ethelward, youngest son of king Alfred, died 16th of October, A. D. 922, rather more than two years before the death of his brother Edward. ·

[2] Malmesbury, Florence of Worcester, and the Saxon Chronicle, place the death of Ethelstan in the year 940 ; but if, as also stated by Florence (p. 242), this event be referred to Wednesday, 27th of October, Indict. xiv., his death must have occurred A. D. 941, before he had completed the seventeeth year of his reign. Yet there occur many charters dated in 940, and attested by Edmund as king. See Cod. Dipl. Nos. 379, 384—388.   [3] See §§ 136, 137.

[4] Malmesbury here, and again at the close of § 138, seems to imply a disbelief in the reputed meanness of Ethelstan's birth.

[5] Of this we have an illustration in the Cotton MS. Tiberius A. ii., a copy of the Gospels presented by king Ethelstan to Christ Church, Canterbury.

possessions. Thus he ennobled the new ones expressly, but the
old as though they were only casual objects of his kindness. With
Sihctric, king of the Northumbrians, who married[1] one of his
sisters, he made a lasting covenant ; he dying after a year,[2] Ethelstan
took that province under his own government, expelling one Aldulf,[3]
who resisted him.   And as a noble mind, when once roused,
aspires to greater things, he compelled Judwal, king of the Welsh,
and Constantine, king of the Scots, to quit their kingdoms.[4]   But
not long after, moved with commiseration, he restored them to
their original state, that they might reign under him ; saying, " it
was more glorious to make a king than to be a king."   His last
contest was with Analaf, the son of Sihctric,[5] who, with the before-
named Constantine, again in a state of rebellion, had entered his
territories under the hope of gaining the kingdom.   Ethelstan
purposely retreating, that he might derive great honour from
vanquishing his furious assailant, this bold youth, meditating unlawful conquests, had now proceeded far into England, when he
was opposed at Brunefeld[6] by the most experienced generals and
most valiant forces.   Perceiving, at length, what danger overhung
him, he assumed the character of a spy, and laying aside the
badges of his royalty, and taking a harp in his hand, he proceeded
to our king's tent.   Singing before the entrance, and at times
touching the trembling strings in harmonious cadence, he was
readily admitted ; professing himself a minstrel who procured his
daily sustenance by such employment.   Here he entertained the
king and his companions for some time with his musical performance, carefully examining everything while he was occupied in
singing.   When satiety of eating had put an end to their sensual
enjoyments, and the business of war was resumed among the nobles,
he was ordered to depart, and received the recompense of his
song ; but disdaining to take it away, he hid it beneath him in the
earth.   This circumstance was remarked by a person who had
formerly served under him, and immediately related to Ethelstan.
The king blaming him extremely for not having detected his enemy
as he stood before them, received this answer, " The same oath
which I have lately sworn to you, O king, I formerly made to
Analaf : and had you seen me violate it towards him, you might
have expected that I would have been guilty of similar perfidy
towards yourself.   But condescend to listen to the advice of your
servant, which is that you should remove your tent hence ; and

---

[1] A. (followed by Saville), "who married, as I have before said." See antea,
§ 126.
[2] Sihtric, king of the Northumbrians, died A. D. 926, and was succeeded by his
son Guthferth, whom Athelstan expelled in the following year, and then he
annexed Northumbria to his own dominions.
[3] Aldred, son of Eadulf, of Bamborough. See the Saxon Chronicle and Florenc
of Worcester, A. D. 926.
[4] The submission of the kings to Athelstan took place at Eamot on the 12th of
July, A. D. 926.
[5] There are several chiefs named Anlaf mentioned at this period in the Anglo-
Saxon Annals ; and it is not always easy to identify the individual who may be
mentioned.
[6] Brunanburh in Northumbria ; the exact site is not known. The battle was
fought A. D. 938. Two MSS. read Bruneford.

remaining in another place till the residue of the army come up, you will destroy your ferocious enemy by a moderate delay." Approving this admonition, he removed to another place. In the night, Analaf advancing well prepared, put to death, together with the whole of his followers, a certain bishop[1] who had joined the army only the evening before, and, ignorant of what had passed, had pitched his tent there on account of the level turf. Proceeding further, he found the king himself equally unprepared; who, little expecting that his enemy was capable of such an attack, had fallen into profound repose. But, when roused from his couch by the excessive tumult, and urging his people, as much as the night season would permit, to the conflict, his sword fell by chance from the sheath; upon which, while all things were filled with dread and blind confusion, he invoked the protection of God, and of St. Aldelm, who was distinctly related to him; and replacing his hand upon the scabbard he there found the sword, which is kept to this day,[2] on account of the miracle, in the treasury of the kings. Moreover it is, as they say, chased in one part, but can never be inlaid either with gold or silver. Confiding in this divine present, and at the same time, as it began to dawn, attacking the Norwegian, he continued the battle unwearied until the evening, and put him to flight with his whole army. There fell Constantine, king of the Scots, a man of treacherous energy and vigorous old age, five other kings, twelve earls,[3] and almost the whole assemblage of barbarians: the few who escaped were preserved to embrace the faith of Christ.

§ 132. Concerning this king,[4] a strong persuasion is prevalent among the English, that one more just or learned never governed the kingdom. That he was versed in literature I discovered a few days since, in a certain old volume, wherein the writer struggles with the difficulty of his task, unable to express his meaning as he wished. Indeed, I would subjoin his words for brevity sake were they not extravagant beyond belief in the praises of the king, and just in that style of writing which Cicero, the prince of Roman eloquence, in his book on Rhetoric, denominates "bombast." The custom of that time excuses the diction, and the affection for Ethelstan, who was yet living, gave countenance to the excess of praise. I shall subjoin therefore, in familiar language,[5] some few circumstances which may tend to augment his reputation.

§ 133. King Edward, after many noble exploits both in war and peace, a few days before his death subdued the contumacy of the city of Chester,[6] which was rebelling in confederacy with the Britons; and placing a garrison there, he fell sick and died at

---

[1] This was Werstan, bishop of Sherborne.

[2] It appears by the Patent Roll, 9th of John, that the king had among his regalia two swords, viz. "ensis Tristami et alius ensis:" it is not improbable that the sword which was preserved in the king's treasury when Malmesbury wrote, may have been the "alius ensis" referred to in the letters patent above cited.

[3] The Annals mention only five earls.   [4] That is, Athelstan.

[5] Malmesbury seems to have derived this account of Athelstan from some source not at present known.   [6] Urbem Legionum.

Ferendun, and was buried, as I before related, at Winchester.
Ethelstan, as his father had commanded in his will, was then
hailed king—recommended by his years, for he was now thirty,
and the maturity of his wisdom.   For even his grandfather Elfred,
seeing and embracing him affectionately, when a boy of astonishing
beauty and graceful manners, had most devoutly prayed that his
government might be prosperous ; indeed, he had made him a
knight[1] unusually early, giving him a scarlet cloak, a belt studded
with jewels, and a Saxon sword with a golden scabbard.   Next he
had provided that he should be educated in the court of Ethelfleda
his daughter, and of his son-in-law Ethelred ; so that, having been
brought up in expectation of succeeding to the kingdom by the
tender care of his aunt and of this celebrated prince, he repressed
and destroyed all envy by the lustre of his good qualities ; and after
the death of his father and decease of his brother, he was crowned
at Kingeston.   Hence, to celebrate such splendid events and the
joy of that day, the poet justly exclaims,—

> " Of royal race, a noble stem
> Hath chased our darkness, like a gem :
> Great Adelstan, his country's pride,
> Whose virtue never turns aside.
> Sent by his father to the schools,
> Patient he bore their rigid rules ;
> And drinking deep of science mild,
> Pass'd his first years unlike a child.
> Next, clothed in youth's bewitching charms,
> Studied the harsher lore of arms,
> Which soon confess'd his knowledge keen,
> As next was in the sovereign seen.
> Soon as his father, good and great,
> Yielded, though ever famed, to fate,
> The youth was call'd the realm to guide,
> And, like his parent, well preside.
> The nobles meet, the crown present;
> On rebels, prelates curses vent :
> The people light the festive fires,
> And show by turns their kind desires,
> Their deeds, their loyalty declare,
> Though hopes and fears their bosoms share.
> With festive treat the court abounds,
> Foams the bright wine, the hall resounds
> The pages run, the servants haste,
> Song cheers the soul, and food the taste,
> The minstrel sings, the guests commend,
> Whilst all in praise to Christ contend.
> The king with pleasure all things sees,
> And all his kind attentions please."

§ 134.   The solemnity of the consecration being finished, Ethelstan, that he might not deceive the expectation of his subjects and
fall below their opinion, subdued the whole of England, except
Northumbria, by the single terror of his name.   One Sihctric, a
relation of that Gurmund[2] who is mentioned in the history of
Elfred, presided over this people, a barbarian both by race and

---

[1] Here Malmesbury expresses himself in the language which was current at his
own period.   Upon the disputed question of the knighthood of the Anglo-
Saxons, see Lingard's Anglo-Saxon Church, ii. 1.

[2] Guthorm died A. D. 891.   See antea, § 121.

disposition; who, though he ridiculed the power of preceding kings, humbly solicited affinity with Ethelstan, sending messengers expressly for the purpose; and he himself, shortly following, confirmed the proposals of the ambassadors. In consequence, honoured by a union with his sister, and by various presents, he laid the basis of a perpetual treaty. But, as I have before observed,[1] dying at the end of a year, he afforded Ethelstan an opportunity for uniting Northumbria, which belonged to him both by ancient right and recent affinity, to his sovereignty. Analaf the son of Sihctric then fled into Ireland,[2] and his brother Godefrid into Scotland.[3] Messengers from the king immediately followed to Constantine, king of the Scots, and Eugenius, king of the Cumbrians, claiming the fugitive under a denunciation of war. The barbarians had not courage to resist, but without delay coming to a place called Dacor, they surrendered themselves and their kingdoms to the sovereign of England.[4] Out of regard to this treaty, the king himself stood as sponsor for the son of Constantine, who was ordered to be baptized at the sacred font. Godefrid, however, amid the preparations for the journey, escaped by flight with one Turfrid, a leader of the opposite party; and afterwards laying siege to York, when he could not succeed in bringing the townsmen to surrender either by entreaties or by threats, he departed. Not long after, being both shut up in a castle, they eluded the vigilance of the guards and escaped. Turfrid, losing his life quickly after by shipwreck, became a prey to fishes; Godefrid suffering extremely both by sea and land, at last came a suppliant to court. Being amicably received by the king, and sumptuously entertained for four days, he resought his ships—an incorrigible pirate, and accustomed to live in the water like a fish. In the meantime Ethelstan levelled with the ground the castle which the Danes had formerly fortified in York, that there might be no place for disloyalty to shelter in; and the booty which had been found there, which was very considerable, he generously divided among the whole army man by man; for he had prescribed himself this rule of conduct, never to hoard up riches, but liberally to expend all his acquisitions either on monasteries, or on his faithful followers. On these, during the whole of his life, he expended his paternal treasures, as well as the produce of his victories. To the clergy he was humble and affable; to the laity mild and pleasant; to the nobility, rather reserved, from respect to his dignity; to the lower classes, laying aside the stateliness of power, out of regard to their poverty, he was kindly condescending. He was, as we have heard, of middle height, thin in person, his hair flaxen, as I have

---

[1] See § 131.

[2] The flight of Anlaf the son of Sihtric into Ireland, here mentioned, has led some to identify him with Olaf of Ireland, who fought against Ethelstan in 938. The Saxon Chronicle states that in 944 king Edmund expelled from Northumberland two kings, Anlaf son of Sihtric, and Regenald son of Guthferth.

[3] Guthferth was expelled from the kingdom of Northumbria A.D. 927.

[4] Florence of Worcester, under the year 934 (Sax. Chron. 933), relates that Ethelstan, because Constantine, king of the Scots, had broken his treaty with him, marched against Scotland, and Constantine gave his son as a hostage to the English king.

seen by his reliques, and beautifully wreathed with golden threads. Extremely beloved by his subjects from admiration of his fortitude and humility, and terrific to those who rebelled against him, through his invincible courage, he compelled the rulers of the Northern Welsh, that is, of the North Britons, to meet him at the city of Hereford, and after some opposition to surrender to his power: so that he actually brought to pass what no king before him had even presumed to think of, which was, that they should pay annually, by way of tribute, twenty pounds of gold, three hundred of silver, twenty-five thousand[1] oxen, besides as many dogs as he might choose, which from their sagacious scent could discover the retreats and hiding-places of wild beasts, and birds trained to make prey of others in the air. Departing thence he turned towards the Western Britons, who are called the Cornwallish, because, situated in the west of Britain, they are opposite to the extremity of Gaul.[2] Fiercely attacking, he obliged them to retreat from Exeter, which till that time they had inhabited with equal privileges with the Angles, fixing the boundary of their province on the other side the river Tamar, as he had appointed the river Wye to the North Britons. This city,[3] then, which he had cleansed by purging it of its contaminated race, he fortified with towers, and surrounded with a wall of squared stone: and, though the barren and unfruitful soil can scarcely produce indifferent oats, and frequently only the empty husk without the grain, yet, owing to the magnificence of the city, the opulence of its inhabitants, and the constant resort of strangers, every kind of merchandise is there so abundant that nothing is wanting which can conduce to human comfort. Many noble traces of him are to be seen in that city, as well as in the neighbouring district, which will be better described by the conversation of the natives than by my narrative.

§ 135. On this account all Europe resounded with his praises, and extolled his valour to the skies: foreign princes with justice esteemed themselves happy if they could purchase his friendship either by affinity or by presents. Harold, king of Norway,[4] sent him a ship with a golden beak and a purple sail, furnished within all round with a close-set row of gilded shields. The names of the persons sent with it were Helgrim and Osfrid, who being received with princely magnificence in the city of York, were amply compensated by rich presents for the labour of their journey. Henry the first, (for there were many of the name,) the son of Conrad,[5] king of the Teutons and emperor of the Romans, demanded his sister, as I have before related, for his son Otho;[6] passing over so

---

[1] Caradoc, with greater probability, fixes the amount at five thousand.. See Lappenberg, ii. 108.   [2] Cornu Galliæ. See p. 89, note [14].

[3] Ethelstan subdued Howell at Exeter in the year 926, and probably kept his Christmas there at that time, as some of his laws are said to have been enacted at that place. See Saxon Laws, i. 217, 221, 229.

[4] Harald I. surnamed Harfager, king of Norway. Compare the account of Harald's embassy to king Ethelstan in 931. Snorro, Haralds Saga ens Harfagra, 'c. xli.—xliii.; tom. i. pp. 119—121. (Hist. Reg. Norveg. operâ Gerhardi Schöning, Havniæ, 1777.) And the criticism of Lappenberg upon this portion of Malmesbury's narrative may be consulted with advantage, ii. 1?5.

[5] See antea, p. 94, note [10].   [6] See antea. §§ 112, 126.

many neighbouring kings, but contemplating from a distance Ethelstan's noble descent and greatness of mind. So completely, indeed, had these two qualities taken up their abode with him, that none could be more noble or illustrious in descent, none more bold or prompt in disposition. Maturely considering that he had four sisters who were all equally beautiful, except only as their ages made a difference, he sent two to the emperor at his request; and how he disposed of them in marriage has already been related. Lewis,[1] prince of Aquitaine, a descendant of Charles the Great, obtained the third in wedlock: the fourth, in whom the whole essence of beauty had centered, which the others only possessed in part, was demanded from her brother by Hugh, king of the Franks.[2] The chief of this embassy was Adulf, son of Baldewin, earl of Flanders, by Ethelswitha, daughter of king Edward.[3] When he had declared the request of the suitor in an assembly of the nobility at Abendon, he produced such liberal presents as might gratify the most boundless avarice: perfumes such as never had been seen in England before: jewels, but more especially emeralds, the green-ness of which, reflected by the sun, illumined the countenances of the by-standers with agreeable light: many fleet horses with their trappings, and, as Virgil says, " champing their golden bits:"[4] an onyx vase so exquisitely chased, that the corn-fields really seemed to wave, the vines to bud, the figures of men actually to move, and so clear and polished, that it reflected the features like a mirror: the sword of Constantine the Great, on which the name of its original possessor was read in golden letters; on the pommel, upon thick plates of gold, might be seen fixed an iron nail, one of the four which the Jewish faction used for the cruci-fixion of our Lord: the spear of Charles the Great, which when-ever that invincible emperor hurled in his expeditions against the Saracens, he always came off conqueror;—it was reported to be the same which, driven into the side of our Saviour by the hand of the centurion,[5] opened by that precious wound the joys of paradise to wretched mortals: the banner of the most blessed martyr Maurice, chief of the Theban legion,[6] with which the same king, in the Spanish war, used to break through the battalions of the enemy, however fierce and wedged together, and put them to flight; a diadem, precious from its quantity of gold, but more so for its jewels, the splendour of which threw the sparks of light so strongly

[1] Louis king of Arles, son of Boso, married Eadgiva, daughter of Edward the elder.

[2] Perhaps we should read here, "Hugo dux Francorum." Hugh the Great, count of Paris, and son of Robert I. king of France, is so designated in the French Chronicles. His marriage with Eadhild took place A.D. 926. (Bouquet, viii. 289.)

[3] Malmesbury's statement is inaccurate at this point. This Adalof was earl of Boulogne, and was son of Baldwin of Flanders, and Alfthryth, the daughter of king Alfred; he was, consequently, cousin to Ethelstan. See Bouquet, ix. 74; and Lappenberg, ii. 107.   [4] Æneid, vii. 279.

[5] The legend of St. Longinus makes the centurion mentioned in the Gospel the person who pierced the side of our Lord, with many other fabulous additions. See Baron. Annal. A.D. 34, § 131.

[6] On the history of the Theban Legion, see Basnage, Hist. de l'Eglise, p. 1223; Oudin, Comment. de Script. Eccles. i. 1216.

on the beholders, that the more stedfastly any person endeavoured
to gaze, so much the more was he dazzled, and compelled to avert
his eyes : part of the holy and adorable cross enclosed in crystal,
where the eye, piercing through the substance of the stone, might
discern the colour and size of the wood : a small portion of the
crown of thorns, enclosed in a similar manner, which, in derision
of his government, the madness of the soldiers placed on Christ's
sacred head. The noble king, delighted with such great and exquisite
presents, made an equal return of good offices, and gratified the
soul of the longing suitor by an union with his sister.   Some of
these presents he left to the kings who succeeded him ; but to
Malmesbury he gave part of the cross and crown, by the support
of which, I believe, that place even now flourishes, though it has
suffered so many shipwrecks of its liberty, so many attacks of its
enemies.[1]   In this place he ordered Elwin and Ethelwin, the sons
of his uncle Ethelwerd, whom he had lost in the battle against
Analaf,[2] to be honourably buried, expressing his design of resting
here himself ; of which battle it is now proper time to give the
account of that poet, from whom I have taken all these transactions.

> '" His subjects governing with justest sway,
> Tyrants o'erawed, twelve years had pass'd away,
> When Europe's noxious pestilence stalk'd forth,
> And pour'd the barbarous legions from the North.
> Then pirate Analaf the briny surge
> Forsakes, while deeds of desperation urge.
> Her king consenting, Scotia's land receives
> The frantic madman and his horde of thieves :
> Now flush'd with insolence, they shout and boast,
> And drive the harmless natives from the coast.
> Thus while the king, secure in youthful pride,
> Bade the soft hours in gentle pleasure glide,
> Though erst he stemm'd the battle's furious tide,
> With ceaseless plunder sped the daring horde,
> And wasted districts with their fire and sword.
> The verdant crops lay withering on the fields,
> The glebe no promise to the rustic yields.
> Immense the numbers of barbarian force,
> Countless the squadrons both of foot and horse.
> At length fame's rueful moan alarm'd the king,
> And bade him shun this ignominious sting,
> That arms like his to ruffian bands should bend:
> 'Tis done—delays and hesitations end.
> High in the air the threatening banners fly,
> And call his eager troops to victory,
> His hardy force, an hundred thousand strong,
> Whom standards hasten to the fight along.
> The martial clamour scares the plund'ring band,
> And drives them bootless tow'rds their native land.
> The vulgar mass a dreadful carnage share,
> And shed contagion on the ambient air ;
> While Analaf alone, of all the crew,
> Escapes the meed of death so justly due,
> Reserved by fortune's favour, once again
> When Ethelstan was dead, to claim our strain.'

§ 136. This place seems to require that I should relate the
death of Elfred in the words of the king, for which I before

---

[1] The author has, apparently, the oppressions of bishop Roger constantly
before him.   [2] The battle of Brunanburh, A.D. 938.

pledged the faith of my narrative;[1] for as he had commanded the bodies of his relations to be conveyed to Malmesbury, and interred at the head of the sepulchre of St. Aldelm, so he honoured the place afterwards to such a degree as to esteem none more holy. Bestowing many large estates upon it, he confirmed them by charters, in one of which, after the donation, he adds the words which follow :—

Of the Death of Elfred, the rival of Ethelstan.

§ 137. "[2] Be it known to the sages of our kingdom, that I have not unjustly seized the lands aforesaid, or dedicated plunder to God ; but that I have received them, as the English nobility, and even John,[3] the pope of the church of Rome himself, have judged fitting, on the death of Elfred.   He, the jealous rival both of my happiness and life, consenting to the wickedness of my enemies, who on my father's decease, had not God in his mercy delivered me, wished to put out my eyes in the city of Winchester; but, on the discovery of their infernal contrivances, he was sent to the church of Rome to defend himself by oath before pope John.   This he did at the altar of St. Peter ; but at the very instant he had sworn, he fell down before it, and was carried by his servants to the English school,[4] where he died the third night after. The pope immediately sent to consult with us as to the disposal of his body, and whether it should be placed among other Christians.   On receiving this account, the nobility of our kingdom, with the whole body of his relations, humbly entreated that we would grant our permission that his remains might be buried with those of other Christians. Consenting, therefore, to their urgent request, we sent back our compliance to Rome, and with the pope's permission he was buried, though unworthy, along with other Christians.   And so all his property of every description was adjudged to be mine.   More-over, we have recorded this in writing, that, so long as Christianity reigns, it may never be forgotten whence the aforesaid land, which I have given to God and St. Peter, was granted to me ; nor do I know anything more just than that I should bestow this gift on God and St. Peter, who caused my rival to fall in the sight of all persons, and conferred on me a prosperous reign."

§ 138. In these words of the king, we may equally venerate his wisdom and his piety in sacred matters : his wisdom, that so young a man should perceive that a sacrifice obtained by rapine could not be acceptable to God ; his piety, in so gratefully making a return to God, out of a benefit conferred on him by divine vengeance.   Moreover, it may be necessary to observe, that at that

---

[1] See § 131.

[2] Ethelstan's charter to the monastery of Malmesbury is to be found in the author's Life of Aldhelm, bishop of Sherborne, Angl. Sacr. ii. 31 ; and in Kemble's Saxon Charters, No. 354 (ii. 177).   It is a spurious document.

[3] John XI. was consecrated in March 931, and died January 936. Jaffé, pp. 313, 314.

[4] The school of the Saxons at Rome was situated near the church of St. Peter. See p. 87, note [8].

time the church of St. Peter was the chief of the monastery, which
now is deemed second only; the church of St. Mary, which the
monks at present frequent, was built afterwards in the time of
king Edgar, under abbot Elfric.[1]   Thus far relating to the king I
have written from authentic testimony : that which follows I have
learned more from old ballads,[2] popular through succeeding times,
than from books written expressly for the information of posterity.
I have subjoined them, not to defend their veracity, but to put my
reader in possession of all I know., First, then, to the relation of
his birth.

Of the Birth of Ethelstan, and of the Murder of Edwin his brother.

§ 139.   There was in a certain village a shepherd's daughter,
a girl of exquisite beauty, who gained through the elegance of her
person what her birth could never have bestowed.   In a vision she
beheld a prodigy: the moon shone from her womb, and all England was illuminated by the light.   When she sportively related this

[1] The MS. C. here inserts the following passage :—

" How great was his reputation among the French, not only for his courage
in war, but also for his Christian piety, is satisfactorily proved by the following
epistle :—

" ' I Rohbod, the provost of Samson the high-priest, wish to the celebrated and
munificent king Ethelstan, the glory of this world and the blessedness of eternity,
to the honour of the great and undivided Trinity, and by the most effectual intercession of all saints.

" ' Let it be known to your goodness and majesty, O king Adelstan, most excellent among all the sovereigns of this present time, that while our realm still
preserved its stability, your father Edmund recommended himself by his letters
for admission into the guild of the fraternity of St. Samson, the great confessor,
and of Levenanus the elder, the archbishop and my relative, and of his clerks.
Wherefore, even to the present day we offer up unceasing prayers to Christ the
King for the health of his soul and of yours; and we promise—I and my twelve
clerks—as if we were kneeling before you on our knees, that day and night we
will pray to the mercy of God for you in our psalms, and masses, and prayers ;
observing, as we do, how your kindness is manifested towards us. And now I send
you some relics, which we are persuaded are dearer to you than all earthly glory ;
that is, the bones of St. Senator, and St. Paternus, and St. Scubilion the master of
the said Paternus, who departed to Christ upon one and the same day and hour
as Paternus did.   Assuredly these two saints are laid on the right and left of
St. Paternus in his tomb ; and their festivals are celebrated upon the ninth of the
kalends of October [23d Sept.] along with that of St. Paternus.   Wherefore, O
glorious king, we pray and humbly entreat you, who art the exalter of the holy
church, the humbler of wicked heathendom, the mirror for your own nation, the
example of everything that is good, the disperser of the enemies, the father of
clerks, the assister of the poor, the lover of all the saints, the invoker of angels
—we who deservedly dwell in France in banishment and captivity for our sins—
entreat you that, in the greatness of your bounty, you would not forget us.'   So
far the epistle.   The king sent the relics of St. Paternus to Malmesbury, and those
of the other saints to Mideltune, where he had erected a monastery from its
foundations.   For at that time, as I have before said, while the Norman pirates
were infesting the whole sea-coast, as well as the towns which were situated upon
the Loire, the bodies of the saints of Lesser Britanny, and of that part of Gaul
which is now called Normandy, were translated and removed to safer places, and
so were easily sold to any one who wished to purchase them from the poverty of
their bearers, and more especially to Ethelstan, a king in good reputation, and one
who eagerly coveted such commodities."

Paternus, bishop of Avranches, died at Vannes about A. D. 555.   A copy of his
Life is in the Coll. MS. Vesp. A. xiv., and an abstract is contained in Capgrave.

[2] Malmesbury frequently refers to historical ballads as the source of his
information.

to her companions in the morning, it was not so lightly received, but it immediately reached the ears of the woman who used to nurse the sons of the king. Deliberating on this matter, she took her home and adopted her as a daughter, bringing up this young maiden with costlier attire, more delicate food, and more elegant demeanour. Soon after, Edward the son of king Elfred, travelling through the village, stopped at the house which had been the scene of his infantile education: indeed, he thought it would be a blemish on his reputation to omit paying his salutations to his nurse. Becoming deeply enamoured of the young woman from the instant he saw her, he passed the night with her. Pregnant from this single intercourse, she realized her dream when she brought forth her son Ethelstan; for at the expiration of his childish years, as he approached manhood, he proved by many noble actions what just expectations of royal aptitude might be entertained of him. King Edward therefore dying, was shortly followed by his legitimate son Elward. All hopes now centered in Ethelstan; Elfred alone,[1] a man of uncommon insolence, who disdained to be governed by a sovereign whom he had not voluntarily chosen, secretly opposing with his party to the utmost. But he being detected and punished, as the king has before related, there were some who even accused Edwin the king's brother of treachery. Base and dreadful crime! to embroil fraternal affection by sinister constructions. Edwin, though imploring both personally and by messengers the confidence of his brother, and though invalidating the accusation by an oath, was nevertheless driven into exile. So far, indeed, did the dark suggestions of some persons prevail on a mind distracted with various cares, that, forgetful of a brother's love, he expelled the youth, an object of pity even to strangers, and that, too, in a mode cruel in the extreme; for he was compelled to go on board a vessel with a single attendant, without a rower, without even an oar, and the bark was crazy with age. Fortune laboured for a long time to restore the innocent youth to land; but when at length, far out at sea, the sails could not endure the violence of the wind, the young man, delicate and weary of life under such circumstances, put an end to his existence by a voluntary plunge into the water.[2] The attendant, wisely determining to prolong his life, sometimes by shunning the hostile waves, and sometimes by urging the boat forward with his feet, brought his master's body to land, in the narrow sea which flows between Whitsand and Dover. Ethelstan, when his anger cooled and his mind became calm, shuddered at the deed; and submitting to a seven years' penance, he inflicted severe vengeance on the accuser of his brother. He was the king's cup-bearer, and on this account had opportunity of enforcing his insinuations. It so happened, on a festive day as he was serving wine, that slipping with one foot in the midst of the chamber, he recovered himself with the other. On this occasion he made use of an expression

---

[1] See §§ 136, 137.
[2] Edwin was drowned at sea A.D. 933; Simeon of Durham adds, by the command of Ethelstan.

which proved his destruction : " Thus brother," said he, " assists brother." The king, on hearing this, ordered the faithless wretch to be put to death, loudly reproaching him with the loss of that assistance he might have had from his brother, were he alive, and bewailing his death.

§ 140. These circumstances of Edwin's death, though extremely probable, I the less venture to affirm for truth, on account of the extraordinary affection he manifested towards the rest of his brothers : for, as his father had left them very young, he cherished them whilst children with much kindness, and when grown up made them partakers of his kingdom. It is before related to what dignity he exalted such of his sisters as his father had left unmarried and unprovided for. Completing his earthly course, and that a short one, Ethelstan died at Gloucester.[1] His noble remains were conveyed to Malmesbury, and buried under the altar. Many gifts both in gold and silver, as well as reliques of saints, purchased abroad in Brittany, were carried before the body; for in such things, admonished as they say in a dream, he expended the treasures of his father, which he himself had for a long time kept whole and untouched. His years, though few, were full of glory.

Of King Edmund the First.

§ 141. In the year of our Lord's incarnation nine hundred and forty,[2] Edmund the brother of Ethelstan, a youth of about eighteen, received and held the government for six years and a half. In his time the Northumbrians, meditating a renewal of hostilities, violated the treaty which they had made with Ethelstan, and created Analaf, whom they had recalled from Ireland, their king. Edmund, who thought it disgraceful not to complete his brother's victorious course, led his troops against the delinquents; who presently retreating, he subjugated all the cities on this side the river Humber.[3] Analaf, with a certain prince, Reinald,[4] the son of that Gurmund, of whom we have spoken in the history of Alfred, after having ascertained the disposition of the king, offered to surrender himself, proffering his conversion to Christianity[5] as a pledge of his fidelity. His savage nature, however, did not permit him to remain long in this resolution, for he violated his oath, and irritated his lord ; in consequence of which, the following year[6] he suffered for his crimes, being doomed to perpetual exile. The province which

---

[1] He died on Wednesday, 27th of Oct. 941.

[2] The year upon which Edmund succeeded to the throne has been questioned ; but the authority of the Saxon Chronicle, and of many charters (Cod. Dipl. Nos. 379, 384—387), satisfy us in deciding that he ascended the throne immediately upon the death of his brother, in the end of A. D. 940.

[3] In the year 942, Edmund recovered from the Danes the five burghs, Leicester, Lincoln, Nottingham, Stamford, and Derby, and reduced all Mercia to his dominion.

[4] Regenald was the son of Guthferth, whom Ethelstan had expelled from Northumberland in 927. See § 131.

[5] Anlaf first, and Regenald soon after, in the year 943, received baptism at the instigation of king Edmund.

[6] In the year 944, king Edmund expelled from Northumberland the two kings, Anlaf the son of Sihtric, and Regenald the son of Guthferth. See § 134.

is called Cumberland, Edmund assigned to Malcolm king of the Scots, under fealty of an oath.[1]

§ 142. [2]Among the many donations which the king conferred on different churches, he exalted that of Glastonbury, through his singular affection towards it, with great estates and honours; and granted it a charter, in these words :[3]—

§ 143. " In the name of our Lord Jesus Christ, I Edmund, king of the Angles, and governor and ruler of the other surrounding nations, with the advice and consent of my nobility, for the hope of eternal reward and remission of my transgressions, do grant to the church of the mother of God, Mary of Glastonbury, and the venerable Dunstan, whom I have there constituted abbot,[4] the franchise and jurisdiction, rights, customs, and all the forfeitures of all their possessions; that is to say, burgherihta and hundred-setena, athas and ordelas, and infangenetheofas, hamsocne, and frithbrice, and forestal and tol, and team, throughout my kingdom; and their lands shall be free to them, and released from all exactions, as my own are. But more especially shall the town of Glastonbury, in which is situated that most ancient church of the holy mother of God, together with its bounds, be more free than other places. The abbot of this place alone shall have power, as well in causes known as unknown, in small and in great, and even in those which are above and under the earth, on dry land and in the water, in woods and in plains, and he shall have the same authority of punishing or remitting the crimes of delinquents perpetrated within it as my court has, in the same manner as my predecessors have granted and confirmed by charter; to wit, Edward my father, and Elfred his father, and Chentwine, Ine, and Chuthred, and many others, who more peculiarly honoured and esteemed that noble place. And that any one, either bishop, or duke, or prince, or any of their servants, should dare to enter it for the purpose of holding courts, or distraining, or doing anything contrary to the will of the servants of God there, I inhibit under God's curse. Whosoever, therefore, shall benevolently augment my donation, may his life be prosperous in this present world and long may he enjoy his happiness; but whosoever shall presume to invade it through his own rashness, let him know for certain, that he shall be compelled, with fear and trembling, to give account before the tribunal of the rigorous Judge, unless he shall first atone for his offence by proper satisfaction."

The aforesaid donation was granted in the year of our Lord Jesus Christ's incarnation nine hundred and forty-four, in the second of the indiction, and was written in letters of gold, in the book of the Gospels which he presented to the same church, elegantly adorned.

---

[1] A.D. 945. The Saxon Chronicle states that king Edmund granted Cumberland to Malcolm, king of the Scots, on condition that he should be *his fellow-worker* as well by sea as by land.

[2] Some MSS. (A. C. 1. G. H. and L.) omit this and the following sections.

[3] See Malmesbury, De Antiquitate Glaston. Ecclesiæ, (Gale, iii. 318,) and Kemble, Cod. Dipl. No. 400. The charter is spurious.

[4] St. Dunstan was appointed abbot of Glastonbury A.D. 942 (Flor. Wigorn.); A.D. 943 (Sax. Chron.) Compare Bridferth, De Vita S. Dunstani, Act. SS. 19 Maii.

§ 114. Such great and prosperous successes, however, were obscured by a melancholy death; for a certain robber named Leof, whom he had banished for his robberies, returning after six years' absence, totally unexpected, was sitting, on the feast of St. Augustine, archbishop of Canterbury [26th May], among the royal guests at Pukelechirche;[1] for on this day the English were wont to regale in commemoration of their preacher; by chance, too, he was placed near a nobleman whom the king had condescended to make his guest. This, while the others were eagerly carousing, was perceived by the king alone; when, hurried with indignation and impelled by fate, he leaped from the table, caught the robber by the hair, and dragged him to the floor; but the other secretly drawing a dagger from its sheath, plunged it with all his force into the breast of the king as he lay upon him. Dying of the wound,[2] he gave rise, over the whole kingdom, to many fictions concerning his decease. The robber was shortly torn limb from limb by the attendants who rushed in, though he wounded some of them ere they could accomplish their purpose. St. Dunstan, at that time abbot of Glastonbury, had foreseen his ignoble end, being fully persuaded of it from the gesticulations and insolent mockery of a devil dancing before him; wherefore, hastening to court at full speed, he received intelligence of the transaction on the road. By common consent, then, it was determined that his body should be brought to Glastonbury, and there magnificently buried, in the northern part of the tower. That such had been his intention, through his singular regard for the abbot, was evident from particular circumstances: the village where he was murdered was made an offering for the dead, that the spot which had witnessed his fall might ever after minister aid to his soul.

§ 145. In his fourth year, that is, in the year of our Lord nine hundred and forty-four,[3] William the son of Rollo, duke of Normandy, was treacherously killed in France, which old writers relate as having been done with some degree of justice. Riulf, one of the Norman nobility, owing William a grudge from some unknown cause, harassed him with perpetual aggressions. His son Anschetil, who served under the earl, to gratify his lord, ventured to offer violence to nature; for taking his father in battle, he delivered him into the power of the earl, relying on the most solemn oath, that he should suffer nothing beyond imprisonment. As wickedness, however, constantly discovers pretences for crime, the earl shortly after, feigning an excuse, sends Anschetil to Pavia, bearing a letter to the duke of Italy, the purport of which was his own destruction. Completing his journey, he was received on his entrance into the city in the most respectful manner. On delivering the letter, the duke, astonished at the treachery, shuddered that a warrior of such

---

[1] Pucklechurch in Gloucestershire.

[2] Any doubts which might exist as to the year of Edmund's death, in consequence of the different copies of the Saxon Chronicle fluctuating between A. D. 946 and 948, are removed by the precision with which the event is fixed by Florence as having occurred upon Tuesday, 26th of May. 94... There is extant (Cod. Dipl. No. 411) a charter granted by Eadred in A. D. 94...

[3] The best authorities place the assassination of William duke of Normandy on the 17th of December, A. D. 943. See the narrative of William of Jumiéges, iii. 12, ap. Camden's Scriptt. p. 623.

singular address should be ordered to be slain ; but as he would not
oppose the request of so renowned a nobleman, he laid an ambush
of a thousand horsemen, as it is said, for Anschetil when he left
the city.   For a long time, with his companions whom he had
selected out of all Normandy, he resisted their attack ; but at last
he fell nobly, compensating his own death by slaying many of the
enemy.   The only survivor on either side was Balzo, a Norman,
a man of small size, but of incredible courage ; although some say
that he was ironically called Short : this man, I say, alone hovered
round the city, and by his single sword terrified the townspeople as
long as he thought proper.   No person will deem this incredible,
who considers what efforts the desperation of one courageous man
will produce, and how little military valour the people of that region
possess.   Returning thence to his own country, he laid his complaint of the perfidy of his lord before the king of France : for fame
reported too that Riulf, while in chains, had had his eyes put out.
In consequence the earl, being cited to his trial at Paris, was met,
under the pretence of a conference, as they assert, and killed by
Balzo in the middle of the river Seine ;[1] thus making atonement
for his own perfidy, and satisfying the rage of his antagonist.   His
death was the source of long discord between the French and Normans, till by the exertion of Richard his son it had a termination
worthy of such a personage.   Truer histories indeed relate, that,
being at enmity with Ernulf earl of Flanders, he had possessed
himself of one of his castles, and that being invited out by him to
a conference, on a pretended design of making a truce, he was
killed by Balzo, as they were conversing in a ship ; that a key was
found at his girdle, which, being applied to the lock of his private
cabinet, discovered certain monastic habiliments ; for he ever
designed, even amid his warlike pursuits, that he would one day
become a monk at Jumièges, which place, deserted from the time
of Hasteng, he cleared of the overspreading thorns, and with princely
magnificence exalted to its present state.

Concerning King Edred.

§ 146.   In the year of our Lord nine hundred and forty-six,[2]
Edred, Edward's third son, assuming the government, reigned nine
years and a half.   He gave proof that he had not degenerated in
greatness of soul from his father and his brothers ; for he nearly
exterminated the Northumbrians and the Scots, laying waste the
whole province with sword and famine ; because, having with little

---

[1] The Seine is here written incorrectly for the Somme.   William of Jumiéges
relates that Arnoul earl of Flanders appointed a conference between the duke and
Arnoul at Picquigny on the Somme, when the count's chamberlain, Balzo le Court,
effected the duke's assassination.   Malmesbury's first account, incorrect as we
have seen in some of its details, may possibly have been founded on some tradi-
tional legend, which retained a lingering memory of the old Scandinavian " holm-
gang," or duel in the midst of a river.

[2] According to Florence of Worcester, Eadred was consecrated at Kingston, by
Odo, archbishop of Canterbury, on Sunday, 16th of August, A. D. 946.   By some
authorities his accession is placed (but incorrectly) in the year 948.   See note [2],
§ 144.

difficulty compelled them to swear fidelity to him, they broke their
oath, and made Iric their king.[1] He for a long time kept Wulstan,
archbishop of York, who it was said connived at the revolt of his
countrymen, in chains ; but afterwards, out of respect to his ecclesiastical dignity, he released and pardoned him.   In the meantime
the king himself, prostrate at the feet of the saints, devoted his life to
God and to Dunstan, by whose admonition he endured with patience
his frequent bodily pains,[2] prolonged his prayers, and made his
palace altogether the school of virtue. He died,[3] accompanied with
the utmost grief of men, but joy of angels ; for Dunstan, learning
by a messenger that he was sick, while urging his horse in order to
see him, heard a voice thundering over his head, " Now, king
Edred sleeps in the Lord."   He lies buried in the cathedral at
Winchester.

§ 147. In the year of our Lord nine hundred and fifty-five,[4] Edwy
the son of Edmund[5] the former king, taking possession of the kingdom, retained it four years—a wanton youth, who abused the beauty
of his person in illicit intercourse. Finally, taking a woman nearly
related to him as his wife, and doting on her beauty, he despised
the advice of his counsellors. On the very day on which he had
been consecrated king, in full assembly of the nobility, when deliberating on affairs of importance and essential to the state, he burst
suddenly from amongst them, darted wantonly into his chamber,
and rioted in the embraces of the harlot.[6] All were indignant at
the shameless deed, and murmured among themselves. Dunstan
alone, with that firmness which his name implies,[7] regardless of the
royal indignation, violently dragged the lascivious boy from the
chamber ; and through the instrumentality of Odo the archbishop,

---

[1] Snorro relates that Erik Blodöxe, son of Harald (Blátand) king of Norway,
received Northumbria from king Ethelstan. (Saga Hanokar Goda, chap. iii. p. 127.)
There is no certainty as to the date of Erik's accession, or of his death.   The
northern historians place his expulsion from the throne of Norway in the year
938, his acceptance of the kingdom of Northumbria in 939, and his death in 952.
Compare Sax. Chron. A.D. 948—954. On the individuals and the incidents here
mentioned, the narrative of Lappenberg, ii. 124, 125, may be consulted with
advantage, as also Johnstone's Antiquitates Celto-Scandicæ, p. 64, 4to. Havn.
1786. From this period Northumbria was governed by earls, a catalogue of whom
may be found in Hoveden.

[2] Some interesting details respecting the sickness and death of Edred are found
in the Life of St. Dunstan, § 20, ap. Act. SS. Maii, iv. 353.

[3] Edred died at Frome on the 23d of November, A.D. 955, according to Florence
of Worcester.   Tyrrel, i. 352, observes that "this king did not, as many believe,
die without issue ; and that his two sons, Elfrid and Bertfrid, were witnesses to
certain ancient charters cited by Speed."

[4] The accession of Edwy, in some copies of the Saxon Chronicle, is referred to
the year 955, and in others to the year 956. All doubt is removed by the existence of a previous charter, which bears the date of 955. See Cod. Dipl. No.
436 (ii. 306), attested by Edwy as king.

[5] MS. A. (followed by Saville) here reads, "son of Edmund the brother of
Ethelstan."

[6] This story is related in all the lives of St. Dunstan. Bridferth alone mentions
the name of Elfgyfu ; Eadmer and a MS. Life of St. Dunstan (Cott. MS. Nero,
E. i.) state that she was "ex magna et alta progenie nata, filiam adultam secum
habens ;" but all agree that there were two women, mother and daughter. Malmesbury, in his Life of St. Dunstan, repeats the same account.

[7] A similar expression occurs in Osberne, in his Life of St. Dunstan. In Anglo-
Saxon, "dun" signifies a hill, and "stan" a stone.

compelling him to repudiate the strumpet,[1] he made him his enemy for ever.   Soon after, upheld by the most contemptible supporters, he afflicted with undeserved calamities all the members of the monastic order throughout England, who were first despoiled of their property, and then driven into exile.   He drove Dunstan himself, the chief of monks, into Flanders.[2]   At that time the appearance of the monasteries was sad and pitiable.   Even[3] the monastery of Malmesbury, which had been inhabited by monks for more than two hundred and seventy years, he made a stye for secular canons.   But thou, O Lord Jesu, our Creator and Redeemer, gracious Disposer, and abundantly able to remedy our defects by means of those irregular and vagabond men ; Thou didst bring to light thy treasure, hidden for so many years—I mean the body of St. Aldelm, which they took up and placed in a shrine.   The royal generosity increased the fame of the canons, for the king bestowed on the saint an estate,[4] very convenient both from its size and vicinity.   But my recollection shudders even at this time to think how cruel he was to other monasteries, equally on account of the giddiness of youth and the pernicious counsel of his concubine, who was perpetually poisoning his unformed mind.   But let his soul, long since placed in rest by the interposition of Dunstan,[5] pardon my grief ; grief, I say, compels me to condemn him, because private advantage is not to be preferred to public loss, but rather public loss should outweigh private advantage.   He paid the penalty of his rash attempt even in this life, being despoiled of the greatest part of his kingdom,[6] shocked with which calamity he died, and was buried in the New Minster at Winchester.

Of King Edgar.

§ 148.   In the year of our Lord's incarnation nine hundred and fifty-nine, Edgar, the honour and delight of the English, the son of Edmund, the brother of Edwi, a youth of sixteen years old, assuming the government, held it for about a similar period.   The transactions of his reign are celebrated with peculiar splendour even in our times.   The divine love, which he sedulously procured by his devotion and energy of counsel, shone propitious on his years. It is commonly reported, that at his birth[8] Dunstan heard an angelic voice saying, " Peace to England so long as this child shall

---

[1] The Saxon Chronicle states that in the year 958, Odo archbishop of Canterbury separated king Edwy and Elfgyfu, because they were too nearly related.— Compare Florence of Worcester, A. D. 958.

[2] Dunstan was banished A. D. 956, and was honourably received by Arnoul, count of Flanders.

[3] The paragraph from "Even" down to "vicinity" occurs almost word for word in Malmes. De Vita Aldhelmi. (Angl. Sacr. ii. 32.)

[4] The charter to which Malmesbury alludes, dated A. D. 956, may be seen in the Cod. Dipl. No. 460 (ii. 336.)   It is a forgery.

[5] The soul of the king, by the prayers of Dunstan, is said to have been released from the devils who were carrying it away. See Osbern De Vita S. Dunstani. (Angl. Sacr. ii. 107.)

[6] The rebellion of the Mercians occurred A. D. 957, and Edgar was chosen as their king.   [7] Edwy died on the 1st of October A. D. 959.

[8] A. D. 943.   Compare Bridferth's Life of St. Dunstan.

reign, and our Dunstan shall live." The succession of events was
in unison with the heavenly oracle—so much, while he lived, did
ecclesiastical glory flourish, and martial clamour decay : scarcely
does a year elapse in the Chronicles, in which he did not perform
something great and advantageous to his country, in which he
did not build some new monastery. He experienced no internal
treachery, no foreign attack. Kinad king of the Scots, Malcolm
of the Cumbrians, that prince of pirates Mascus, all the Welsh
kings,[1] whose names were Dufnal, Giferth, Huual, Jacob, Judethil,
being summoned to his court, were bound to him by one, and that
a lasting oath ; so that, meeting him at Chester, he exhibited them
on the river Dee in triumph :[2] for putting them all on board the
same vessel, he compelled them to row him as he sat at the prow,
thus displaying his regal magnificence, who held so many kings in
subjection. Indeed, he is reported to have said that henceforward
his successors might truly boast of being kings of England, since
they would enjoy so singular an honour. Hence his fame being
noised abroad, foreigners, Saxons, Flemings, and even Danes themselves, frequently sailed hither, and were on terms of intimacy with
Edgar, though their arrival was highly prejudicial to the natives ; for
from the Saxons they learnt an untameable ferocity of mind, from
the Flemings an unmanly delicacy of body, and from the Danes
drunkenness, though they were before free from such propensities,
and disposed to observe their own customs with native simplicity
rather than admire those of others. For this, history justly and
deservedly blames him ; for the other imputations, which I shall
mention hereafter, rest upon no higher authority than ballads.

§ 149. At this time the light of holy men was so resplendent in
England, that you would believe the very stars from heaven smiled
upon it. Among these was Dunstan,[3] whom I have mentioned so
frequently, first abbot of Glastonbury, next bishop of Worcester,
and lastly archbishop of Canterbury ; of great power in earthly
matters, in high favour with God—in the one representing Martha,
in the other Mary. Next to king Elfred, he was the most extraordinary patron of the liberal arts throughout the whole island ; the
munificent restorer of monasteries. Terrible were his denunciations
against transgressing kings and princes ;[4] kind was his support of
the middling and poorer classes. Indeed, so extremely anxious
was he to preserve peace even in trivial matters, that, as his
countrymen used to assemble in taverns, and when a little elevated
with drink, quarrel as to the sharing of their liquor, he ordered gold

---

[1] See the Annales Cambriæ, A. D. 968.

[2] The celebration of Edgar's triumph on the Dee occurred in the year 973.
Some of these personages are mentioned as having attested charters granted by
Edgar in 966 and 971. See Cod. Dipl. Nos. 519 and 567.

[3] The life of St. Dunstan appears to have been a favourite theme with the
monkish writers. See a list of his biographers in Lappenberg (ii. 129). Dunstan
was born A. D. 925, made abbot of Glastonbury in 942, bishop of Worcester in 957,
and in the next year he was translated to London ; he was appointed to the see of
Canterbury in 959, and in the following year went to Rome to receive the pall
from pope John XII. He died A. D. 988.

[4] The severity with which he visited the profligate conduct of the kings Edgar
and Edwy is here alluded to.

or silver pegs[1] to be fastened in the pots, that, whilst every man knew his just measure, shame should compel each neither to take more himself, nor oblige others to drink beyond their own proper share.   Osberne,[2] precentor of Canterbury, second to none of these times in composition, and indisputably the best skilled of all in music, who wrote his life with Roman eloquence, forbids me (though I wish so to do) to relate further praiseworthy anecdotes of him. Besides, in addition to this, if the divine grace shall accompany my design, I intend,[3] after the succession of the kings, at least to particularise the names of all the bishops of each province in England, and to offer them to the knowledge of my countrymen, if I shall be able to coin anything worth notice out of the mintage of antiquity.   How powerful indeed was his example, is shown by the sanctity and virtue of Dunstan's disciples.   Adelwold,[4] who was made abbot of Abingdon, from having been a monk of Glastonbury, and afterwards bishop of Winchester, built so many and such great monasteries, as to make it appear hardly credible how the bishop of one city should be able to effect what the king of England himself could scarcely undertake.   I am deceived, and err through hasty opinion, if what I assert be not evident.   How great are the monasteries of Ely, Peterborough, and Thorney, which he raised from the foundations, and completed by his industry, which, though repeatedly reduced by the wickedness of plunderers, are yet sufficient for their inhabitants.   His life was composed in a decent style by Wulstan,[5] precentor of Winchester, who had been his attendant and pupil.   He wrote also another very useful work[6] "On the Harmony of Sounds," a proof that he was a learned Englishman, a man of pious life and correct eloquence.   At that time, too, Oswald[7] nephew of Odo,[8] who had been archbishop before Dunstan, from a monk of Fleury, becoming bishop of Worcester and archbishop of York, claimed equal honours with the others;

---

[1] Hence the phrase, "to drink to the pin." In the council of London, A.D. 1102, (Can. ix.) it was decreed that priests should not go to public drinkings, "nec ad pinnas bibant." See Labb. Concil. x. 729. Malmesbury, however, is wrong in ascribing to the Danes the introduction of drunkenness into England, as there unfortunately remains evidence to show that this vice was prevalent at a period before the arrival of that nation.

[2] Osberne's Life of St. Dunstan is printed in the Angl. Sacr. ii. 88, from a MS. in Lambeth Library; another copy is in the British Museum (Cott. Tiber. D. iii. fol. 119), in which nearly the whole of the second book is wanting. See also Acta SS. Maii, iv. 359.

[3] Malmesbury here refers to his work upon the Bishops of England, which has been printed by Saville, and of which a translation will be given in this series.

[4] Ethelwold was educated under St. Dunstan, and was made bishop of Winchester A.D. 963. He died 1st of August, A.D. 984.

[5] Wulstan's Life of Ethelwold has been printed by Mabillon (Act. Bened.v. 596). It relates all that is contained in Alfric's Life of Ethelwold, and often in the same words, but adds some things which the earlier life has not.

[6] Nothing further concerning this work is known to us. See Wright's Biog. Brit. Anglo-Saxon Period, p. 471.

[7] Oswald was made bishop of Worcester A.D. 960, and translated to York A.D. 972. He died on the 29th of February, A.D. 992. His life was written by Eadmer, and is printed in the Angl. Sacr. ii. 191.

[8] Odo was translated from Winchester to the see of Canterbury A.D. 934; he died A.D. 958. A life of him by Eadmer is printed in the Angl. Sacra, ii. 78; and by Mabill. Act. SS. ad. S. Bened. v. 286.

for, treading the same paths,[1] he extended the monastic profession
by his authority, and built a monastery at Ramsey, in a marshy
situation.[2]   He filled the cathedral of Worcester with regular
monks ; the canons not being driven out by force, but circumvented
by pious fraud.[3]   Bishop Adelwold, by the royal command, had
before expelled the canons from Winchester,[4] who, upon being given
the option [5] either to live according to rule or depart the place, gave
the preference to an easy life, and were at that time without fixed
habitations, wandering over the whole island.   In this manner these
three persons, illuminating England as it were with a triple light,
chased away the thick darkness of error.   In consequence, Edgar
advanced the monastery of Glastonbury, which he ever loved beyond
all others, with great possessions, and was anxiously vigilant in all
things pertaining either to the beauty or convenience of the church,
whether internally or externally.   It may be proper here to subjoin
to our narrative the charter he granted to the said church, as I have
read it in their ancient chartulary.

§ 150. " [6] In the name of our Lord Jesus Christ : Although

[1] Some most important reforms in the church were effected during the reign
of Edgar by archbishops Dunstan and Oswald, and by Ethelwold, bishop of
Winchester.

[2] Ramsey abbey was built by Ailwin, the alderman duke of the East Angles, at
the instigation of Oswald. See the Ramsey Chronicle in Dugd. Monast. i. 231.

[3] Upon the reformation of ecclesiastical societies by king Eadgar, Oswald
founded a new cathedral in the old churchyard, in which he placed a prior and
monks ; the secular canons of the old church, finding the people desert it, soon
took the monastic habit. See Eadmer, De Vita S. Oswaldi, Angl. Sacr. ii. 202.
Compare Malmesb. De Gest. Pont. lib. iii.

[4] The secular priests were expelled from the old minster at Winchester in the
year 963, by command of king Eadgar. Thom. Rudborne, Historia Major Winton.
Angl. Sacr. i. 218.   [5] One MS. is here glossed, " to wit, by the king."

[6] See this charter of king Eadgar in Malmesb. De Antiquitate Glaston. Ecclesiæ, (Gale, iii. 320 ;) and in the Cod. Dipl. No. 567. The date as it there
occurs is A. D. 971, indict. xiv. Some MSS., instead of sections 150, 151, read,
" Edgar of glorious memory, king of the Angles, son of king Edmund, whose
inclinations were ever vigilantly bent on divine matters, often coming to the
monastery of the holy mother of God at Glastonbury, and studying to honour
this place with dignity superior to others, hath by the common consent of the
bishops, abbots, and nobility, conferred on it many and very splendid privileges.
The first of which is, that no person, unless a monk of that place, shall there be
abbot, either in name or in office, nor any other, except such as the common
consent of the meeting shall have chosen, according to the tenor of the rule.
But should necessity so require that an abbot or monk of another monastery be
made president of this place, then he deems it proper that none shall be appointed
but such as the congregation of the monastery may elect to preside over them in
the fear of the Lord ; nor shall this be done if any, even the lowest of the congregation, can be there found fit for the office. He hath appointed, too, that the
election of their abbot shall rest for ever in the monks, reserving only to himself
and his heirs the power of giving the pastoral staff to the elected brother. He
hath ordained also, that so often as the abbot or the monk of this place shall
appoint any of their society to be dignified with holy orders, they shall cause any
bishop canonically ordained, either in his own cathedral, or in the monastery of
St. Mary at Glastonbury, to ordain such monks and clerks as they deem fit, upon
the title of St. Mary. He hath granted, moreover, that as he himself decides in
his own dominions, so the abbot or the convent shall decide the causes of their
entire island in all matters ecclesiastical or secular, without the contradiction of
any one. Nor shall it be lawful for any person to enter that island, which bore
witness to his birth, whether he be bishop, duke, or prince, or person of whatever order, for the purpose of there doing anything prejudicial to the servants of
God : this he forbids altogether, in the same manner as his predecessors have
sanctioned and confirmed by their privileges ; that is to say, Cenwine, Ina,

the decrees of pontiffs and the decisions of priests be fixed by unshaken bonds, like the foundations of the mountains, yet never-

Athellard, Cuthred, Elfred, Edward, Ethelstan, and Aedmund. When, therefore, by the common consent, as has been said, of his prelates, abbots, and nobility, he determined to grant these privileges to the place aforesaid, he laid his own horn, beautifully formed of ivory and adorned with gold, upon the altar of the holy mother of God, and by that donation confirmed them to the same holy mother of God and her monks to be possessed for ever. Soon after he caused this horn to be cut in two in his presence, that no future abbot might give or sell it to any one, commanding part of it to be kept upon the spot for a perpetual testimony of the aforesaid donation. Recollecting, however, how great is the temerity of human inconstancy, and on whom it is likely to creep, and fearing lest any one hereafter should attempt to take away these privileges from this place, or to eject the monks, he sent this charter of his royal liberality to the renowned lord, pope John, who had succeeded Octavian in the honour of the pontificate, begging him to corroborate these grants by an apostolical bull. Kindly receiving the legation, the pope, with the assenting voice of the Roman council, confirmed what had been already ordained, by writing an apostolical injunction, terribly hurling on the violators of them, should any be so daring, the vengeance of a perpetual curse. This confirmation therefore of the aforesaid pope, directed to the same place, king Edgar, of worthy memory, laid upon the altar of the holy mother of God for a perpetual remembrance, commanding it to be carefully kept in future for the information of posterity." We have judged it proper to insert both these instruments, lest we should be supposed to invent such things against those persons who seek to enter into the fold of St. Mary, not like shepherds, by the door, but like thieves and robbers, by some other way.

" Be it known to all the faithful, that I John, through the mercy of God the unworthy pope of the holy Roman see, am entreated by the humble request of the noble Edgar, king of the Angles, and of Dunstan, archbishop of the holy church of Canterbury, for the monastery of St. Mary of Glastonbury, which, induced by the love of the heavenly King, they have endowed with many and great possessions, increasing in it the monastic order, and having confirmed it by royal grant, they pray me also so to do. Wherefore, assenting to their affectionate request, I take that place into the bosom of the Roman church and the protection of the holy apostles, and support and confirm its immunities as long as it shall remain in the same conventual order in which it now flourishes. The monks shall have power to elect their own superior; ordination, as well of monks as of clerks, shall be at the will of the abbot and convent; we ordain, moreover, that no person shall have liberty to enter this island, either to hold courts, to make inquiry, or to correct. And should any one attempt to oppose this, or to take away, retain, diminish, or harass with vexatious boldness, the possessions of the same church, he shall become liable to a perpetual curse, by the authority of God, the Father, Son, and Holy Spirit, the holy mother of God, the holy apostles Peter and Paul, and all saints, unless he recant. But the peace of our Lord Jesus Christ be with all who maintain the rights of the place aforesaid. Amen. And let this our deed remain unshaken. Done in the time of Aelfward, abbot of the said monastery."

The aforesaid king Edgar confirmed these things at London, by his solemn charter, in the twelfth year of his reign; and in the same year, that is, of our Lord 965, the pope aforesaid authorized them in a general synod at Rome, and commanded all members of superior dignity, who were present at the said general council, to confirm them likewise. Let the despisers, then, of so terrible a curse, consider well how severe a sentence of excommunication hangs over their heads; and, indeed, to St. Peter the apostle, the chief of apostles, Christ gave the office both of binding or loosing, as well as the keys of the kingdom of heaven. But to all it must be plain and evident, that the head of the Roman church must be the vicar of this apostle, and the immediate inheritor of his power. Over this church then, John of holy memory laudably presided in his lifetime, as he lives to this day in glorious recollection, promoted thereto by the choice of God and of all the people. If, then, the ordinance of St. Peter the apostle be binding, consequently that of John the pope must be so likewise; but not even a madman would deny the ordinance of Peter the apostle to be binding; consequently, no one in his sober senses can say that the ordinance of John the pope is invalid. Either, therefore, acknowledging the power conferred by Christ on St. Peter and his successors, they will abstain from transgressing against the authority of so dreadful an interdict; or else contemning it, they will, with the devil and his angels, bring upon themselves the eternal duration of the curse aforewritten.

In

theless, in the storms and tempests of secular matters, the institutions of the holy church of God are often convulsed and broken by the corruption of reprobate men. Wherefore we perceive that it will be advantageous to posterity to confirm by writing what has been determined by wholesome counsel and common consent. In consequence, it seems proper that the church of the most blessed mother of God, the ever virgin Mary of Glastonbury, inasmuch as it has always possessed the chief dignity in my kingdom, should by us be honoured with some very special and unusual privilege. Dunstan, therefore, and Oswald, archbishops of Canterbury and York, exhorting thereto, and Brihtelm,[1] bishop of Wells, and other bishops, abbots, and chiefs assenting and approving, I Edgar, by the grace of God king of the English, and ruler and governor of the adjacent nations, in the name of the blessed Trinity, for the soul of my father who reposes there, and of my predecessors, do by this present privilege decree, appoint, and establish, that the aforesaid monastery and all its possessions shall remain free and exonerated from all payments to the exchequer now and for ever; they[2] shall have soc and sac, on strand, on stream, on wood, on felde, on grithbrice, on burhbrice, hundred-setena, morthas, athas, and ordeles, ealle hordas bufan eorthan, and beneothan, infangenetheof, utfangenetheof, flemeneferthe, hamsochene, frithbriche, forsteal, tol and team, just as free and peaceably as I have in my kingdom. And let the same liberty and power also as I have in my own court, as well in forgiving as in punishing, and in every other matter, be possessed by the abbot and monks of the aforesaid monastery within their court. And should the abbot or any monk of that place, upon his journey, meet a thief going to the gallows, or to any other punishment of death, they shall have power of rescuing him from impending danger throughout my kingdom. Moreover I confirm and establish, what has hitherto been scrupulously observed by all my predecessors, that the bishop of Wells and his ministers shall have no power whatever over this monastery, or its parish churches, that is to say, Stret, Mirelinch, Budecalege, Sceapwic, Sowy, or their chapels; or even over those contained in the islands, that is to say, Beocherie, otherwise called

---

In consequence, it is manifest that no stranger ever seized this monastery for himself, who did not, as shall appear, disgracefully lose it again; and that this occurred not by any concerted plan of the monks, but by the judgment of God for the avenging of his holy authority. Wherefore let no man reading this despise it, nor make himself conspicuous by being angry at it; for, should he do so, perhaps he will confess that to be said of himself which was designed to be spoken of another.

[1] The exact date of Brihthelm's appointment to the bishopric of Wells is not known. He was translated to Canterbury upon the decease of Elfsine (who was frozen to death on the Alps, in his journey to Rome for his pall); but he held the primacy only a few days, and was removed back to Wells. He died on the 15th of May, A.D. 973.—See Angl. Sacr. i. 101, 556; ii. 109, 682.

[2] Such of these terms as are not explained in the note, § 143, are understood to imply as follows:—Sac and soc, a right to decide disputes within the franchise, and to levy amerciaments, to compel the attendance of the tenants whether the cause arise on wood, on strand, or on field; to take cognizance of breach of sureties, murders, all hoards, whether above the earth or under the earth (this seems to imply treasure trove), thieves apprehended without the jurisdiction, and effects of fugitives.

Little Ireland, Godenie, Mertinesie, Patheneberge, Edredeseie, and
Ferremere, except only when summoned by the abbot for dedi-
cations or ordinations ; nor shall they cite their priests to their
synods or chapters, or to any of their courts, nor shall they suspend
them from their holy office, or presume to exercise any right over
them whatever.   The abbot shall cause any bishop of the same
province he pleases, to ordain his monks and the clerks of the
aforesaid churches, according to the ancient custom of the church
of Glastonbury, and the apostolical authority of archbishop Dunstan,
and the consent of all the bishops of my kingdom ; but the dedica-
tions of the churches we consign to the bishop of Wells, if he be
required by the abbots.   At Easter, let him receive the chrism of
sanctification, and the oil from the bishop of Wells, according to
custom, and distribute them to his before-mentioned churches.
This, too, I command above all other things : On the curse of God
and by my authority, saving the right of the holy Roman church
and that of Canterbury, I inhibit all persons of whatever dignity,
be they king, or bishop, or earl, or prince, or any of my dependents,
from daring to enter the bounds of Glastonbury, or of the above-
named parishes, for the purpose of searching, seizing, holding
courts, or doing anything to the prejudice of the servants of God
there residing.   The abbot and convent shall alone have power, in
causes known and unknown, in small and in great, and in every
thing as we have before related.   And whosoever, upon any occasion, whatever be his dignity, whatever his order, whatever his profession, shall attempt to pervert or nullify the preeminency of this my
privilege by sacrilegious boldness, let him be aware that he must
doubtless, with fear and trembling, before the strict Judge, give
account of it, unless he first endeavour to make reparation by
proper satisfaction."   The charter of this privilege the aforesaid
king Edgar confirmed by a solemn writing at London, in the
twelfth year of his reign, with the common consent of his nobles.
And in the same year, which was the nine hundred and sixty-fifth[1]
of our Lord's incarnation, and the fourteenth of the indiction,
pope John,[2] in a general assembly, confirmed the said charter at
Rome, and made all the men of chief dignity who presided at that
council confirm it; and also, from motives of paternal regard, sent
a letter to the following effect to earl Aluric, then grievously per-
secuting the aforesaid church.

§ 151. "John the bishop, servant of the servants of God, to
Aluric the distinguished earl, and our dearly beloved son in the
Spirit, perpetual health and apostolical benediction.   We have
learned from the report of certain faithful people, that you commit
many enormities against the church of the holy mother of God,
which is called Mary of Glastonbury, the chief in all Britain,[3] and

---

[1] A.D. 971 corresponds with the fourteenth indiction, as also with the twelfth
year of Eadgar's reign.   The copy printed by Kemble gives the date as at
London, A.D. 971, fourteenth indiction, and in the twelfth year of Edgar's reign.
The charter, however, is a forgery.
[2] John XIII. presided from the year 965 to the 5th of September, A.D. 972.
[3] MS. D. reads, England.

which is acknowledged to belong solely to, and to be under the protection of, the Roman pontiff from the earliest times ; and that you have, with boundless greediness, seized upon its estates and possessions, and even the churches of Brente and Piltun,[1] which, by the instrumentality of king Ina, it legally possesses, together with other churches, that is to say, Sowie, Stret, Merlinc, Budecale, Sapewic ; and that, on account of your near residence, you are constantly hostile to its interests. It however would have been becoming, from your living so near, that by your assistance the holy church of God might have been much benefited and enriched ; but what is horrible, it is impoverished by your hostility, and injured by your oppression. And since we doubt not that we, though unworthily, have received from St. Peter the apostle the care of all churches, and solicitude for all things, we therefore admonish your affection to abstain from plundering it, for the love of the apostles Peter and Paul, and respect to us, invading none of its possessions, churches, chapels, vills, and estates ; but if you persist, remember that, by the authority of the chief of the apostles committed to us, you shall be excommunicated and banished from the company of the faithful, subjected to a perpetual curse, and doomed to eternal fire with the traitor Judas."

§ 152. The monastic order, for a long time depressed, now joyfully reared its head ; and hence it came to pass that our monastery also resumed its ancient liberties. But this, I think, will be more suitably related in the words of the king himself :—

§ 153. [2] " I Edgar, king of all Albion, and exalted, by the subjection of the surrounding kings maritime or insular, through the bountiful grace of God, to an eminence never enjoyed by any of my progenitors, have often, mindful of so high an honour, diligently considered what offering I should more especially make from my earthly kingdom to the King of kings. In aid of my pious devotion, heavenly love suddenly insinuated to my watchful solicitude, that I should rebuild all the holy monasteries throughout my kingdom, which, as they were visibly ruined, with mouldering shingles and worm-eaten boards, even to the rafters, so, what was still worse, they had become internally neglected, and almost destitute of the service of God. Wherefore, ejecting those illiterate clerks subject to the discipline of no regular order, in many places I have appointed pastors of a holier race, that is, of the monastic order, supplying them with ample means out of my royal revenues to repair their churches wherever ruined ; one of whom, by name Elvric, in all things a true priest, I have appointed guardian of that most celebrated monastery, which the Angles call by a twofold name Maldelmesburh ; to which, for the benefit of my soul, and in honour of our Saviour, and the holy mother of God the ever virgin Mary, and the apostles Peter and Paul, and the amiable prelate Aldelm, I have restored, with munificent liberality, a

---

[1] MS. D. reads Wilton.
[2] King Edgar's charter to the monastery of Malmesbury is likewise to be found in Ingulf, p. 633 ; and in Kemble's Cod. Dipl. No. 584.

portion of land [1] (and here he describes it) with meadows and woods. This, leased out by the aforesaid clerks, was unjustly held by the contentious Edelnoth; but his vain and subtle disputation being heard by my counsellors, and his false defence being, in my presence, nullified by them, I have restored it to the use of the monastery in the year of our Lord nine hundred and seventy-four, in the fourteenth of my reign, and the first of my royal consecration." [2]

§ 154. And here I deem it not irrelevant to commit to writing what was supernaturally shown to this king. He had entered a wood abounding with game, and, as usually happens, while his associates were dispersed in the thicket for the purpose of hunting, he was left alone; and so pursuing his course, he came to the outlet of the wood and stopped there, waiting for his companions. Shortly after, seized with an irresistible desire to sleep, he alighted from his horse, that the enjoyment of a wholesome repose might assuage the fatigue of the past day. He lay down, therefore, under a wild apple-tree, where the clustering branches had formed a shady canopy all around. A river flowing softly beside him, added to his fatigue, by its gentle murmurs soothed him to sleep, when a bitch of the hunting-breed, pregnant and lying down at his feet, terrified him while slumbering; for though the mother was silent, yet the whelps within her womb barked in various sonorous tones, incited, as it were, by a singular delight in the place of their confinement. Astonished at this prodigy, as he lifted up his eyes towards the summit of the tree, he saw first one apple, and then another, fall into the river, by the collision of which, the watery bubbles being put in commotion, a voice articulately sounded, " Well is thee." Soon after, driven by the rippling wave, a little pitcher appeared upon the stream, and after that a larger vessel overflowing with water (for the former was empty); and although, by the violence of the stream, the greater vessel pressed upon the lesser that it might discharge its waters into it, yet it ever happened that the pitcher escaped, still empty, and again, as in a haughty and insulting manner, attacked the larger. Returning home, as the Psalmist says, [3] " He thought upon what had been done, and sought out his spirit." His mother addressed him, however, that she might cheer both his countenance and his heart, saying it should be her care to entreat God, who knew how to explain mysteries by the light of his inspiration. With this admonition he dispelled his grief and dismissed his anxiety, conscious of his mother's sanctity, to whom God had vouchsafed many revelations. Her name was Elfgifa, a woman intent on good works, and gifted with such affection and kindness that she would even secretly discharge the penalties of those culprits whom the sad sentence of the judges had publicly condemned. That costly clothing, which to many women is the pander of vice, was to her the means of liberality, as she would give a garment of the

---

[1] See here the texts already cited.
[2] Edgar was not consecrated king until the 11th of May, A.D. 973; but he must have completed the fourteenth year of his reign before the year 974, as he ascended the throne A.D. 959. See § 158.　　　[3] Psalm lxxvii. 6.

most beautiful workmanship to the first poor person she saw. Even malice itself, as there was nothing to carp at, might praise the beauty of her person and the work of her hands. Thoroughly comprehending the presage, she said to her son next morning, "The barking of the whelps while the mother was sleeping implies, that after your death, those persons, who are now living and in power, dying also, miscreants yet unborn will bark against the church of God. And whereas one apple followed the other, so that the voice, 'Well is thee,' seemed to proceed from the dashing of the second against 'the first, this implies that from you, who are now like a tree shading all England, two sons will proceed. The favourers of the second will destroy the first; when the chiefs of the different parties will say to each of the boys, 'Well is thee,' because the dead one will reign in heaven, the living one on earth. Forasmuch as the greater pitcher could not fill the smaller, this signifies that the Northern nations, which are more numerous than the English, shall attack England after your death; and although they may supply their losses by perpetual reinforcements of their countrymen, yet they shall never be able to fill this corner of the world, but instead of that, our Angles, when they seem to be completely subjugated, shall drive them out, and it shall remain under its own and God's governance, even unto the time before appointed by Christ."[1]

§ 155. Further perusal will justify the truth of the presage. The manifest sanctity both of parent and child ought here to be considered; that the one should see a mystery when broad awake without impediment, and that the other should be able to solve the problem by the far discerning eye of prophecy. The rigour of Edgar's justice was equal to the sanctity of his manners, so that he permitted no person, be his dignity what it might, to elude the laws with impunity. In his time there was no private thief, no public freebooter, unless such as chose to venture the loss of life for their attacks upon the property of others.[2] How, indeed, can it be supposed that he would pass over the crimes of men, who designed to exterminate even every beast of prey from his kingdom; and commanded Judval, king of the Welsh, to pay him yearly a tribute of three hundred wolves? This he performed for three years, but omitted in the fourth, declaring that he could find no more.

§ 156. Although it is reported that he was extremely small, both

---

[1] After "Christ," A. (followed by Saville) reads "Amen." The following passage occurs in the margin of another MS. (C 2.):—"The same king Edgar having gone into a wood for the purpose of hunting, happened to hear a little child weeping. He caused strict search to be made. At length, in an eagle's nest at the top of a tree, there was found a little boy most elegantly formed, having a bracelet on each arm, and wearing other royal ornaments, as though in token of the highest extraction, whom the king caused to be most carefully brought up and instructed, and at length advanced to the dignity of an earl."

[2] Edgar's laws for the punishment of offenders were horribly severe. The eyes were put out, nostrils slit, ears torn off, hands and feet cut off, and finally, after the scalp had been torn off, the miserable wretches were left exposed to birds or beasts of prey. V. Acta, Sanct. Jul. 2. in Vita Swythuni. The Anglo-Saxon version of Edgar's laws is printed in Thorpe's Ancient Laws and Institutes of England, i. 259, 8vo. As far as now preserved, they are not very severe.

in stature and in bulk, yet nature had condescended to enclose such
strength in that diminutive body, that he would voluntarily chal-
lenge any person whom he knew to be bold and valiant to engage
with him, and his greatest apprehension was, lest they should
stand in awe of him in these encounters. Moreover, at a certain
banquet, where the prating of coxcombs generally shows itself very
freely, it is reported that Kinnad, king of the Scots, said in a sportive manner, that it seemed extraordinary to him how so many
provinces should be subject to such a sorry little fellow. This was
caught up with malignant ear by a certain mimic, and afterwards
cast in Edgar's teeth, with the customary raillery of such people.
But he, concealing the circumstance from his friends, sent for
Kinnad, as if to consult him on some secret matter of importance,
and leading him aside far into the recesses of a wood, he gave him
one of two swords, which he had brought with him. " And now,"
said he, " as we are alone, you shall have an opportunity of proving
your strength. I will now make it appear which of us two ought
deservedly to command the other ; nor shall you stir a foot till you
try the matter with me, for it is disgraceful for a king to prate at
a banquet, and not to be prompt in action." Confused, and not
daring to utter a word, he fell at the feet of his sovereign lord, and
asked pardon for what was merely a joke, which he immediately
obtained. But what of this? Every summer, as soon as the
festival of Easter was passed, he ordered his ships to be collected
on each coast, cruising to the western part of the island with the
eastern fleet ; and (having returned from that expedition) with the
western to the north, and then again with the northern squadron
towards the east, affectionately vigilant lest pirates should disturb
the country. During the winter and spring, riding through the
provinces, he made inquiry into the decisions of men in power,
severely avenging violated laws. By the latter proceeding, he
watched over the administration of justice ; by the former, military
strength ; and in both he consulted public utility.

§ 157. There are some persons, indeed, who endeavour to dim
his exceeding glory by saying, that in his earlier years he was
cruel to his subjects, and libidinous in respect of virgins. Their
first accusation they exemplify thus. There was in his time one
Athelwold, a nobleman of celebrity, and one of his confidants ; him
the king had commissioned to visit Elfrida, daughter of Orgar,
duke of Devonshire, (whose charms had so fascinated the eyes of
some persons that they commended her to the king,) and to offer
her marriage if her beauty were really equal to report. Hastening
on his embassy, and finding every thing consonant to general
estimation, he concealed his mission from her parents, and procured the damsel for himself. Returning to the king, he told a
tale which made for his own purpose, that she was a girl of vulgar
and common-place appearance, and by no means worthy of such
transcendant dignity. When Edgar's heart was disengaged from
this affair, and employed on other amours, some tattlers acquainted
him how completely Athelwold had duped him by his artifices.
Driving out one nail with another, that is, returning him deceit for

deceit, he showed the earl a fair countenance, and, as in a sportive manner, appointed a day when he would visit this far-famed lady. Terrified almost to death with this dreadful pleasantry, he hastened before to his wife, entreating that she would administer to his safety by attiring herself as unbecomingly as possible; then first disclosing the intention of such a proceeding. But what did not this woman dare? She was hardy enough to deceive the confidence of her miserable lover, her first husband, to adorn herself at the mirror, and to omit nothing which could stimulate the desire of a young and powerful man. Nor did events happen contrary to her design; for he fell so desperately in love with her the moment he saw her, that, dissembling his indignation, he sent for the earl into a wood at Warewelle,[1] under pretence of hunting, and ran him through with a javelin. When the illegitimate son of the murdered nobleman approached with his accustomed familiarity, and was asked by the king how he liked that kind of sport, he is reported to have said, " Well, my sovereign liege, I ought not to be displeased with that which gives you pleasure," with which answer he so assuaged the mind of the raging monarch, that for the remainder of his life he held no one in greater estimation than this young man, mitigating the offence of his tyrannical deed against the father by royal solicitude for the son. In expiation of this crime, a monastery, which was built on the spot by Elfrida, is inhabited by a large congregation of nuns.

§ 158. To this instance of cruelty they add a second of lust. Hearing of the beauty of a certain virgin who was dedicated to God, he carried her off from a monastery by force, ravished her, and repeatedly made her partner of his bed. When this circumstance reached the ears of St. Dunstan, he was vehemently reproved by him, and underwent a seven years' penance; though a king, submitting to fast and to forego the wearing of his crown for that period.[2]

§ 159. They add a third, in which both vices may be discovered. King Edgar coming to Andover, a town not far from Winchester, ordered the daughter of a certain nobleman, the fame of whose beauty had been loudly extolled, to be brought to him. The mother of the young lady, shocked at the proposed concubinage of her daughter, assisted by the darkness of night, placed an attendant in his bed—a maiden, indeed, neither deficient in elegance nor in understanding. The night having passed, when Aurora was hastening into day, the woman attempted to rise; and being asked why she was in such haste? she replied, to perform the daily labour of her mistress. Retained, though with difficulty, on her knees, she bewailed her wretched situation to the king, and entreated her freedom as the recompense of her connexion with him, saying that it became his greatness not to suffer one who had ministered to his royal pleasure any longer to groan under the commands of

---

[1] Werewelle, called Harewood. A. followed by Saville.
[2] This seems to have been founded on the singular circumstance of his not having been crowned till within two years of his death. Edgar was crowned A.D. 973. See p. 137, note [2].

cruel masters. His indignation being excited, and sternly smiling, while his mind was wavering between pity to the girl and displeasure to her mistress, he at last, as if treating the whole as a joke, released her from servitude, and dismissed his anger. Soon after he exalted her, with great honour, to be mistress of her former tyrants, whether they liked it or not; he loved her entirely, nor left her bed till he took Elfrida, the daughter of Orgar, to be his legitimate wife. Elfrida bore him Edmund,[1] who dying five years before his father, lies buried at Rumsey; and Egelred, who reigned after him. Besides, by Egelfleda, surnamed the Fair, the daughter of the most powerful duke Ordmer, he begat Edward; and St. Edgitha, of Wulfrida, who it is certain was not a nun at that time, but being a lay virgin, had assumed the veil through fear of the king, though she was immediately afterwards forced to the royal bed; on which St. Dunstan, offended that he should desire lustfully a person who had been even the semblance of a nun, exerted the pontifical power against him.

§ 160. But however these things may be, this is certain, that from the sixteenth year of his age,[2] when he was appointed king, till the thirtieth, he reigned without the insignia of royalty. But then, the princes and men of every order assembling from all parts, he was crowned with great pomp at Bath, on the day of Pentecost; he survived only three years, and was buried at Glastonbury. Nor is it to be forgotten, that when abbot Eilward opened his tomb in the year of our Lord ten hundred and fifty-two, he found the body unconscious of corruption. This circumstance, instead of inclining him to reverence, served only to increase his audacity; for when the receptacle which he had prepared seemed too small to admit the body, he profaned the royal corpse by cutting it; the blood immediately gushing out in torrents, struck terror into the hearts of the bystanders. In consequence, his royal remains were placed above the altar, in a shrine which he had himself given to this church, with the head of St. Apollinaris, and the reliques of Vincent the martyr, which, purchased at a great price, he had added to the beauty of the house of God. The violator of the sacred body presently became distracted, and not long after, going out of the church, met his death by a broken neck. Nor did the display of royal sanctity stop thus; it proceeded still further, a man, lunatic and blind, being there cured. Deservedly then does the report prevail among the English, that no king, either of his own or former times in England, could be justly and fairly compared to Edgar. Nothing could be more holy than his life, nothing more praiseworthy than his justice, those vices excepted which he afterwards obliterated by abundant virtues: a man who rendered his country illustrious through his distinguished courage, and the brilliancy of his actions, as well as by the increase of the servants of God. After his death,[3] the state and the hopes of the English met with a reverse.

---

[1] Edmund died in the year 971, according to Florence; but in 972, according to the Saxon Chronicle.   [2] See p. 137, note [2].
[3] King Edgar died on Thursday, 8th of July, A.D. 975.

Of Edward, second of that name, the Martyr.

§ 161. In the year of our Lord's incarnation nine hundred and seventy-five, Edward the son of Edgar began to reign, and enjoyed the sovereignty for three years and a half. Dunstan, in common consent with the other bishops, elevated him to the royal dignity, in opposition, as it is said, to the will of some of the nobility and of his stepmother, who was anxious to advance her son Egelred, a child scarcely seven years of age, in order that herself might govern under colour of his name. Then, from the increasing malice of men, the happiness of the kingdom was impaired. Then, too, a comet was seen, which was asserted surely to portend either pestilence to the inhabitants, or a change in the government. Nor was it long ere there followed a failure of the crops, famine among men, murrain among cattle. An extraordinary accident happened at a royal town called Calne. For as soon as Edgar was dead, the secular canons who had been formerly expelled from the churches, rekindled the former feuds, alleging that it was a great and serious disgrace for new-comers to drive the ancient inmates from their dwellings;[1] that it could not be esteemed grateful to God, who had granted them their ancient habitations; neither could it be so to any considerate man, who might dread that injustice as likely to befal himself which he had seen overtake others. Hence they proceeded to clamour and rage, and hastened to Dunstan; the principal people, as is the custom of the laity, exclaiming more especially, that the injury which the canons had wrongfully suffered ought to be redressed by gentler measures. Moreover one of them, Elferius, with more than common audacity, had even overturned almost all the monasteries which the most reverend Adelwold[2] had built throughout Mercia. On this account a full synod being convened, they first assembled at Winchester.[3] What was the issue of the contest at that place other writings declare;[4] relating that the image of our Saviour, speaking decidedly, confounded the canons and their party. But men's minds being not yet at rest on the subject, a council was called at Calne, where, when all the senators of England (the king being absent on account of his youth) had assembled in an upper chamber, and the business was agitated with much animosity and debate, while the weapons of harsh reproach were directing against that firmest bulwark of

[1] Virg. Eclog. ix. 4.
[2] Saville's text here reads, " monk and bishop of Winchester."
[3] The council of Winchester appears, from Florence and Matthew of Westminster, to have been holden between the death of Edgar and the consecration of his son Edward in 975; but the Chronicon Wintoniense, cited by Spelman (Concil. Angl. i. 491), places it in the year 968. (See Wharton's note in Angl. Sacr. ii. 112.) Osberne, in his Life of Dunstan, improperly states that the council of Winchester and the council of Calne were both holden during the lifetime of Edgar. There appears, however, to be no doubt that the council of Calne was holden in 978, during the life of Edward the Martyr. Florence assigns it to the year 977.
[4] When the question was agitated whether the monks should be supported, or the canons restored, the crucifix is said to have exclaimed, " Far be it from you; you have done well; to change again would be wrong." See Eadmer and Osberne, Angl. Sacr. ii. 112.

the church, I mean Dunstan, but could not shake it, and men of every rank were earnestly defending their several sides of the question, the floor with its beams and supporters gave way suddenly, and fell to the ground. All fell with it except Dunstan, who alone escaped unhurt, by standing on a single rafter which retained its position: the rest were either killed or maimed for life. This miracle procured the archbishop peace on the score of the canons, all the English, both at that time and afterwards, yielding to his sentiments.

§ 162. Meanwhile king Edward conducted himself with becoming affection to his infant brother and his stepmother; retained only the name of king, and gave them the power; followed the footsteps of his father's piety, and gave both his attention and his heart to good counsel. The woman, however, with a stepmother's hatred, began to meditate a subtle stratagem, in order that not even the title of king might be wanting to her child, and to lay a treacherous snare for her son-in-law, which she accomplished in the following manner. He was returning home, tired with the chase, and gasping with thirst from the exercise, while his companions were following the dogs in different directions as it happened, when hearing that they dwelt in a neighbouring mansion, the youth proceeded thither at full speed, unattended and unsuspecting, as he judged of others by his own feelings. On his arrival, alluring him to her with female blandishment, she made him fix his attention upon herself, and after saluting him, while he was eagerly drinking from the cup which had been presented, the dagger of an attendant pierced him through. Dreadfully wounded, with all his remaining strength he spurred his horse in order to join his companions; when one foot slipping, he was dragged by the other through the winding paths, while the streaming blood gave evidence of his death to his followers. Moreover, they then commanded him to be ingloriously interred at Wareham,[1] grudging him even holy ground when dead, as they had envied him his royal dignity while living. They now publicly manifested their extreme joy, as if they had buried his memory with his body; but God's all-seeing eye was there, who ennobled the innocent victim by the glory of miracles; so much is human outweighed by heavenly judgment, for lights were there shown from above. There the lame walked; there the dumb resumed his faculty of speech; there every malady gave way to health. The fame of this pervading all England, proclaimed the merits of the martyr. The murderess, excited by it, attempted a progress thither; and was already urging forward the horse she had mounted, when she perceived the manifest anger of God; for the same animal which she had heretofore constantly ridden, and which was used to outstrip the very winds in speed, now by the command of God stood motionless. The attendants, both with whips and clamours, urged him forward, that he might carry his noble mistress with his usual readiness. Their labour was vain; they changed the horse, and the same circumstance recurred. Her obdurate heart, though late, perceived the meaning of the miracle; wherefore, what she was not herself per-

---

[1] Edward was martyred on the 18th of March, A.D. 978.

mitted to do, she suffered to be performed by another: for that
Elferius, whom I before blamed for destroying the monasteries,
repenting of his rashness, and being deeply distressed in mind, took
up the sacred corpse from its unworthy burial-place, and paid it
just and distinguished funeral honours at Shaftesbury: he did not
however escape unpunished, for, within a year afterwards, he was
eaten of the vermin which we call lice.   Moreover, since a mind
unregulated is a torment to itself, and a restless spirit endures its
own peculiar punishment in this life, Elfrida declining from her
regal pride, became extremely penitent; so that at Werewell, for
many years, she clothed her pampered body in hair-cloth, slept at
night upon the ground without a pillow, and mortified her flesh
with every kind of penance.   She was a beautiful woman, singu-
larly faithful to her husband, but deserving punishment from the
commission of so great a crime.   It is believed and commonly
reported, that from her violence to Edward the country, for a long
time after, groaned under the yoke of barbarian servitude.

§ 163. At Shaftesbury truly shines a splendid proof of royal
sanctity; for to his merit must it be attributed, that there a numerous choir of women, dedicated to God, not only enlighten those
parts with the blaze of their religion, but even reach the very
heavens.   There reside sacred virgins wholly unconscious of con-
tamination; there continent widows, ignorant of a second flame
after the extinction of the first; in all whose manners graceful
modesty is so blended with chastened elegance that nothing can
exceed it.   Indeed, it is matter of doubt which to applaud most,
their assiduity in the service of God, or their affability in their
converse with men; hence assent is justly given to those persons
who say that the world, which has long tottered with the weight of
its sins, is entirely supported by their prayers.

Of King Ethelred.

§ 164. In the year of our Lord's incarnation nine hundred and
seventy nine,[1] Ethelred, son of Edgar and Elfrida, obtaining the
kingdom, occupied rather than governed it for thirty-seven years.
The career of his life is said to have been cruel in the beginning,
wretched in the middle, and disgraceful in the end; for, in the
murder to which he gave his concurrence, he was cruel, base in
his flight and effeminacy, miserable in his death. Dunstan, indeed,
had foretold his worthlessness, having discovered it by a very filthy
token: for, when quite an infant, the bishops standing round, as he
was immersed in the baptismal font, he defiled the sacraments by a
natural evacuation,[2] at which Dunstan, being extremely angered,
exclaimed, "By God and his mother, this will be a sorry fellow!"
I have read that when he was ten years of age, hearing it noised
abroad that his brother was killed, he so irritated his furious
mother by his weeping, that, not having a whip at hand, she beat

---

[1] Ethelred succeeded his brother A.D. 978, and was crowned on the 14th of
April following.   He died 23d of April, 1016.
[2] A similar story is related of the emperor Constantine the Fifth, who obtained
the surname of Copronymus from his pollution of the baptismal font.

the little innocent with some candles she had snatched up; nor did she desist till herself bedewed him, nearly lifeless, with her tears. On this account he dreaded candles, during the rest of his life, to such a degree that he would never suffer the light of them to be brought into his presence. The nobility being assembled by the contrivance of his mother, and the day appointed upon which Dunstan, in right of his see, should crown him, he, though he might be ill-affected to them, forbore to resist, being a prelate of mature age, and long versed in secular matters. But, when placing the crown on his head, he could not refrain from giving vent, with a loud voice, to that prophetic spirit which he had so deeply imbibed. "Since,"[1] said he, "thou hast aspired to the kingdom by the death of thy brother, hear the word of God: Thus saith the Lord God, the sin of thy abandoned mother, and of the accomplices of her base design, shall not be washed out but by much blood of the wretched inhabitants; and such evils shall come upon the English nation as it hath never suffered from the time it came to England till that time." Nor was it long after, that is, in his third year, that seven piratical vessels came to Southampton,[2] a port near Winchester, and depopulating the coast fled back to sea: this I have not passed over, because many reports are circulated among the English concerning these vessels.

Of the Sloth of Ethelred, and the Invasion by the Danes.

§ 165. A secret enmity between the king and the bishop of Rochester had arisen from some unknown cause, in consequence of which he led an army against that city. It was signified to him by the archbishop, that he should desist from his fury, and not irritate St. Andrew, under whose guardianship that bishopric was; for as he was ever ready to pardon, so was he equally formidable to avenge. The bare message being held in contempt, he graced the intimation with money, and sent him a hundred pounds, that thus bought off he would raise the siege and retire. Taking the money, he sounded a retreat, and dismissed his army. Dunstan, astonished at the avarice of the man, sent messengers to him with the following words: "Since you have preferred silver to God, money to the apostle, and covetousness to me, the evils which God hath pronounced will shortly come upon you; but they will not come while I live, for this also hath God spoken." Soon after the death of this holy man,[3] which was in the tenth year of his reign, the predictions speedily began to be fulfilled, and the prophecies to have their consummation. For the Danes infesting every port,[4] and making descents on all sides with piratical agility,

---

[1] Compare Osbern. De Vita S. Dunstani, in Wharton's Angl. Sacr. ii. 113.

[2] Southampton was burnt by the Danes in 980, according to the best copy of the Saxon Chronicle. Florence and others also fix that event in 980.

[3] Dunstan died on Saturday the 19th of May, 988, in the twenty-ninth year of his archprelacy, and sixty-first of his age.

[4] Southampton, the Isle of Thanet, and Cheshire, were ravaged by the Danes in 980; Cornwall in 981; the Isle of Portland in 982; Watchet in 988, where the Danes were defeated; and Ipswich in 991.

so that it was not known where they could be opposed, it was
advised by Siricius,[1] second archbishop after Dunstan, that money
should repel those whom the sword could not ; so a payment of
ten thousand pounds satisfied the avarice of the Danes. This was
an infamous precedent, and totally unworthy of men, to purchase
liberty, which no violence can ever extirpate from a noble mind, by
money. They now, indeed, abstained a short time from their incursions ; but as soon as their strength was recruited by rest, they
returned to their old practices. Such extreme apprehension had
then seized the English, that there was not a thought of resistance:
if any indeed, mindful of their ancient glory, made an attempt to
oppose or engage them, they were unsuccessful, from the multitude
of their enemies, and the desertion of their allies. The leader of
revolt was one Elfric, whom the king had appointed to command
the fleet. This base deserter, instead of trying his fortune as he
ought, in a naval conflict, went over to the enemy on the night
preceding the battle, having first apprised them by messengers
what to provide against ; and though the king, for this perfidious
crime, ordered his son's eyes to be put out,[2] yet he returned again,
and again deserted. All Northumbria being laid waste, the enemy
was met in battle and put to flight. London[3] was besieged, but
honourably defended by its citizens. In consequence, the besiegers,
severely suffering and in despair of taking the city, retired; and
devastating the whole province to the eastward, compelled the king
to pay a sum of money, amounting to sixteen thousand pounds :
moreover, hostages being given, he caused their king Analaf to
come to him, stood sponsor for him at the baptismal font, and
soothing him with royal munificence, bound him by an oath that
he should never return into England again. The evil, however, was
not thus put to rest; for they could never provide against their
enemies from Denmark, who sprang up afresh, like the heads of
the hydra. A western province which is called Devonshire was
laid waste, the monasteries destroyed, and the city of Exeter set
on fire,[4] Kent given up to plunder, the metropolitan city and seat
of the patriarchs burnt, the holy patriarch himself,[5] the most
reverend Elfeg, carried away and bound in chains; and at last,
when required to plunder his tenants in order to ransom himself,

[1] Sigeric, or Siric, succeeded Ethelgar in the see of Canterbury A.D. 990. Upon
Ipswich being sacked by the Danes in 991, and Brihtnoth the alderman slain, the
archbishop advised that ten thousand pounds should be paid to them to depart
from the country. See Sax. Chron.

[2] Elfgar, son of duke Elfric, was deprived of his sight by command of the
king in the year 993.

[3] The Saxon Chronicle states that Anlaf and Sweyn came to London on the
nativity of St. Mary, A.D. 994, with ninety-four ships, and assaulted the city very
sharply, endeavouring to burn it; but they were bravely repulsed by the citizens.

[4] The incursion of the Danes into Devonshire appears to have been in the year
997, and again in 1001, in which year Exeter was ravaged. Exeter was besieged
again by Sweyn in the year 1003.

[5] Canterbury was besieged by the Danes A.D. 1012, and archbishop Elfheah was
captured and murdered by them. His life was written by Osberne, and is printed
in the Anglia Sacra, ii. 122, from a MS. in Lambeth Library. MSS. Cott. Otho,
A. xii., Vitel. D. xvii., and Tiber. D. iii. (injured by fire), also contain the same
narrative.

and refusing to do so, he was stoned, struck with a hatchet, and glorified heaven with his soul. After he was murdered, God exalted him, insomuch that when the Danes, who had been instrumental to his death, saw that dead wood besmeared with his blood miraculously grew green again in one night, they ran eagerly to kiss his remains, and to bear them on their shoulders. Abating thus of their native pride, they suffered his sacred corpse to be carried to London. There it was honourably buried ; and when taken up ten years afterwards, free from every taint of corruption, it conferred honour on his own cathedral.[1] To the present moment both its blood remains fresh, and its soundness unimpaired ; and it is considered as a miracle, that a carcase should be divested of its vital spirit and yet not turn to decay. That I may not be tedious in mentioning severally all the provinces which the Danes laid waste, let it be summarily understood, that out of thirty-two counties which are reckoned in England, they had already overrun sixteen, the names of which I forbear to enumerate on account of the ruggedness of the language.

In the meantime the king, admirably calculated for sleeping, disregarding these important transactions, would only yawn ; and if ever he recovered his senses enough to raise himself upon his elbow, he quickly relapsed into his original wretchedness, either from the oppression of indolence, or the adverseness of fortune. His brother's ghost also, demanding dire expiation, tormented him. Who can tell how often he collected his army? how often he ordered ships to be built? how frequently he called out commanders from all quarters, and yet nothing was ever effected? For the army, destitute of a leader, and ignorant of military discipline, either retreated before it came into action, or else was easily overcome. The presence of the leader is of much avail in battle. Courage manifested by him avails also ; experience, and more especially discipline, avail much ; and as I have said, an army destitute of these must be an irreparable injury to its countrymen, as well as a pitiable object of contempt to an enemy : for soldiers are a class of men who, unless restrained before the battle, are eager to plunder ; and if not animated during it, prone to flight. When the ships, built for the defence of the sea-coast, were lying at anchor, a tempest suddenly arising dashed them together, and rendered them useless by the destruction of their tackle. A few, fitted from the wrecks of the others, were, by the attack of one Wulnod, whom the king had banished, either sunk or burnt, and consequently disappointed the expectations of all England. The commanders, if ever they met to confer, immediately chose different sides, and rarely or never united in one good plan ; for they gave more attention to private quarrels than to public exigencies. If, in the midst of pressing danger, they had resolved on any eligible secret design, it was immediately communicated to the Danes by traitors : for besides Elfric, the succes-

---

[1] The body of Elfheah was translated from London to Canterbury in the year 1023. Osberne wrote a history of this translation, which is printed in the Anglia Sacra, ii. 143, from the Cotton. MS. Tiber. D. iii.

sor of Elfere, who had murdered the late king, there was one
Edric, a man infamously skilled in such transactions, whom the
king had made governor of the Mercians, one of the refuse of
mankind, and the reproach of the English ; an abandoned glutton,
a cunning miscreant, whom noble birth had provided with wealth,
and who had increased it by specious language and impudence.
This artful dissembler, capable of feigning anything, was accustomed, by pretended fidelity, to trace out the king's designs, that
he might treacherously divulge them. Often, when despatched to
the enemy as the mediator of peace, he inflamed them to battle.
His perfidy was sufficiently conspicuous in this king's reign, but
much more so in the next, of which I shall have occasion to
speak hereafter. Ulkill, earl of the East Angles, was the only
person who at that time resisted the invaders with any degree of
spirit, insomuch that, although the enemy had nominally the
victory, yet the conquerors are thought to have suffered much
more than the conquered ;[1] nor did it shame the barbarians to
confess this truth, while they so frequently bewailed that victory.
The valour of the earl was more conspicuously eminent, after the
death of Edelred, in that battle which mowed down the whole
flower of the province ; where, when he was surrounded from the
rear, deeming it disgraceful to fly, he gave fresh confidence to the
king by his blood ; but this happened some time after.[2]

At this juncture, that the measure of king Ethelred's misery
might be full, a famine ravaged all England ; and those whom war
had spared, perished through want. The enemy overran the
country with such freedom, that they would carry off their booty
to their ships through a space of fifty miles, dreading no resistance
from the inhabitants. In the midst of these pressing evils, the
expedient of buying off hostilities by money was again debated, and
accordingly adopted ; for first twenty-four, and soon after thirty
thousand pounds, were given, with what advantage succeeding
times will show. To me indeed, deeply reflecting upon the subject,
it seems wonderful how a man, who, as we have been taught to suppose, was neither very foolish, nor excessively cowardly, should pass
his life in the wretched endurance of so many calamities. Should
any one ask me the reason of this, I could not easily answer,
except by saying that the revolt of the generals proceeded from
the haughtiness of the king. Their perfidy has been spoken of
before ; I now hasten to instances of his violence, which was so
intolerable that he spared not even his own relations. For besides
the English, whom he despoiled of their hereditary possessions
without any cause, or defrauded of their property for suppositious
crimes ; besides the Danes, whom upon light suspicion only he
ordered to be all butchered on the same day throughout England,[3]
where was a dreadful spectacle to behold, each one compelled to

---

[1] Ulfkill attacked the Danes near Thetford, A.D. 1004, and though compelled
to retreat, yet occasioned so severe a loss to the enemy, that they are said to have
acknowledged that they had never endured a more powerful attack.

[2] Probably at Ashingdon, in Essex, A.D. 1016, where Ulfcytel was slain.

[3] The massacre of the Danes took place on the 13th of November, in the
year 1002.

betray his dearest guests, now become dearer from the tenderest connexions of affinity, and to cut short their embraces with the sword : yet besides all this, I say, he was so inconstant towards his wife, that he scarcely deigned her his bed, and degraded the royal dignity by his libidinous intercourse with harlots.   She too, a woman conscious of her high descent, became indignant at her husband, as she found herself endeared to him neither by her blameless modesty nor her fruitfulness ; for she had borne him two children, Elfred[1] and Edward.   She was the daughter of Richard earl of Normandy,[2] the son of William, who, after his father, presided over that earldom for fifty-two years, and died in the eighteenth year of this king.[3]   He lies at the monastery of Fescamp, which he augmented with certain revenues, and which he adorned with a monastic order by means of William, formerly abbot of Dijon.   Richard was a distinguished character, and had also often harassed Edelred ; which, when it became known at Rome, the holy see, not enduring that two Christians should be at enmity, sent Leo bishop of Treves into England to effect a peace.   The epistle[4] describing this legation was as follows :—

The Epistle of John the Pope.

§ 166. [5] " John the fifteenth, pope of the holy Roman church, to all faithful people.

Be it known to all the faithful of holy mother church, and our children spiritual and secular dispersed through the several regions of the world, that inasmuch as we had been informed by many of the enmity between Edelred king of the West Saxons and Richard the marquis, and being sorely grieved at this on account of our spiritual children ; taking therefore wholesome counsel, I summoned one of our legates, Leo, bishop of the holy church of Treves, and sent him with our letters, admonishing them that they should return from their ungodliness.   He, passing vast spaces, at length crossed the sea, and on the day of the Lord's nativity came into the presence of the said king, whom having saluted on our part, he delivered to him the letters we had sent. And all the faithful people of his kingdom and the wiser persons of either order being summoned, he granted, for love and fear of God Almighty, and of St. Peter the chief of apostles, and on account of our paternal admonition, the firmest peace for all his sons and daughters present and future, and all his faithful people, without deceit.   On which account he sent Edelsin, prelate of the holy church of Shireburn, and Leofstan son of Alfwold, and Edelnod

---

[1] Alfred was afterwards slain by the treachery of earl Godwin.

[2] Emma Elfgiva. She married Ethelred in 1002 ; and after his death she became the wife of king Cnut, in July 1017. She died in 1052.

[3] Richard died on the 20th of November, A.D. 996.

[4] See Wilkins' Concil. i. 264 ; Mansi Concil. xix. 81.

[5] This is the epistle of pope John XV. sometimes called XVI. who presided from 985 to 996.   John, son of Robert, was elected after the death of John XIV. (in April 985) ; but, dying before he was consecrated, he is not usually reckoned among the popes, although his successor is sometimes styled John XVI. He died previously to the month of July in the year 985. See Jaffé, p. 339.

son of Wistan, who passed the boundaries, and came to Richard the said marquis. He, peaceably receiving our admonitions, and hearing the determination of the said king, readily confirmed the peace for his sons and daughters present and future, and for all his faithful people, with this reasonable condition, that if any of their subjects, or they themselves, should commit any injustice against each other, it should be duly redressed, and that peace should remain for ever unshaken and confirmed by the oath of both parties : on the part of klng Edelred, to wit, Edelsin, prelate of the holy church of Shireburn, Leofstan the son of Alfwold, and Edelnod the son of Wistan ; on the part of Richard, Roger the bishop, Rodolf son of Hugh, Turstenc the son of Turgis. Executed at Rouen, on the kalends of March [1st March], in the year of our Lord nine hundred and ninety-one, the fourth of the indiction. Moreover, of the king's subjects, or of his enemies, let Richard receive none, nor the king of his, without their respective seals."

Concerning Gerbert.

§ 167. On the death of this pope John, Gregory succeeded ; and to him succeeded John XVI. ; and to the latter succeeded Silvester, also called Gerbert :[1] and I conceive it will not be without its use if we commit to writing those circumstances which are related and universally spoken of him. Born in Gaul, from a lad he grew up to be a monk at Fleury; afterwards, when he arrived at the double path of Pythagoras,[2] either disgusted at a monastic life, or seized by lust of glory, he fled by night into Spain, chiefly designing to learn astrology and other sciences of that description from the Saracens. Spain, formerly for many years possessed by the Romans, in the time of the emperor Honorius fell under the power of the Goths. The Goths were Arians down to the days of St. Gregory, when that people were united to the catholic church by Leander bishop of Seville, and by king Ricared[3] brother of Hermingild, whom his father slew on Easter night for professing the true faith.[4] To Leander succeeded Isidore,[5] celebrated for learning and sanctity, whose body, purchased for its weight in gold, Aldefonsus, king of

---

[1] Several early and valuable MSS. read as in the text; but E., the manuscript usually followed, and some others, confound John XV. called XVI. with Silvester II. whose name was Gerbert, and to whom all the legends related of him by Malmesbury are clearly intended to refer. Gerbert was consecrated pope early in the month of April, A.D. 999, and died 12th of May, 1003.

[2] The double path of Pythagoras is represented by the Greek γ, or the letter y. "Pythagoræ bivium ramis patet ambiguis γ." (Ausonius, Idyll. de Litter. Monosyll. xii. 9.) And Lactantius, vi. 6, says, "Dicunt humanæ vitæ cursum y litteræ esse similem ; quia unusquisque hominum, cum primum adolescentiæ limen attigerit, et in eum locum venerit partes ubi se via findit in ambas (Virg. A. vi. 540,) hæreat nutabundus."

[3] Recared II. son of Leovigild, was the first Catholic king of Spain. He was converted to that faith between the years 586 and 589, and with him the whole of the Visigoths of Spain abjured the profession of Arianism.

[4] Hermenegild, the eldest son of Leovigild. The inflexible constancy with which he refused to accept the Arian communion, from which he had been converted by Leander as the price of his safety, procured for him the honour of being enrolled among the saints of the Romish church.

[5] Isidore, archbishop of Seville during the sixth century.

Gallicia, in our times conveyed to Toledo. The Saracens, who had subjugated the Goths, being conquered in their turn by Charles the Great, lost Gallicia and Lusitania, the largest provinces of Spain; but to this day they possess the southern parts. As the Christians esteem Toledo, so do they hold Hispalis, which they commonly call Seville, to be the capital of the kingdom, practising divinations and incantations after the usual mode of that nation. Gerbert then, as I have related, coming among these people, satisfied his desires. There he surpassed Ptolemy with the astrolabe, and Alandræus in astronomy, and Julius Firmicus[1] in judicial astrology. There he learnt what the singing and the flight of birds portended; there he acquired the art of calling up spirits from hell; in short, whatever, hurtful or salutary, human curiosity has discovered; for there is no necessity to speak of his progress in the lawful sciences of arithmetic, music, astronomy, and geometry, which he imbibed so thoroughly as to show they were beneath his talents, and which, with great perseverance, he revived in Gaul, where they had for a long time been wholly obsolete. Being certainly the first who adopted the use of the abacus[2] from the Saracens, he gave rules which are scarcely understood even by laborious arithmeticians. He resided with a certain philosopher of that sect, whose good will he had obtained, first by great liberality, and then by promises. The Saracen had no objection to sell his knowledge; he frequently associated with him, would talk of matters at times serious, at others trivial, and lend him books to transcribe. There was, however, one volume, containing the knowledge of his whole art, which he could never by any means entice him to lend. In consequence, Gerbert burnt with anxious desire to obtain this book at any cost; "for we ever press more eagerly towards what is forbidden, and that which is denied is always esteemed more valuable."[3] Trying therefore the effect of entreaty, he besought him for the love of God and by his friendship; he offered him many things, and promised him more. When this failed, he tried a nocturnal stratagem. Attacking him with wine, his daughter conniving at the attempt through the intimacy which Gerbert's attentions had procured, he stole the book from under his pillow, and fled. Waking suddenly, the Saracen pursued the fugitive by the direction of the stars, in which art he was well versed. The fugitive too, looking back and discovering his danger by means of the same art, hid himself under a wooden bridge which was near at hand, clinging to it and hanging in such a manner as neither to touch earth nor water. In this manner, the

---

[1] Julius Firmicus Maternus, bishop of Milan about the middle of the fourth century; he wrote eight books on astronomy.

[2] Mr. Sharpe observes that the abacus was a counting-table; here it seems used metaphorically for arithmetic, Gerbert having written a treatise on arithmetic with that title. The authors of the Hist. Litt. de la France understand him literally as stealing a book containing the principles of the science, and then confound this supposed book with the conjuring treatise mentioned below. They also seem very much displeased with Malmesbury for relating these tales of their countryman, and attribute them to cardinal Benno; but there is nothing of this kind in his work published by Goldastus, and in Brown's Fasciculus.

[3] Ovid. Amor. III. 4, 17.

eagerness of the pursuer being eluded, he returned home. Gerbert then quickening his pace, arrived at the sea-coast. Here, by his incantations, calling up the devil, he made an agreement with him to be under his dominion for ever, if he would defend him from the Saracen, who was again pursuing, and transport him to the opposite coast : this was accordingly done. Probably some person may regard all this as a fiction, because the vulgar are used to undermine the fame of scholars, saying that the man who excels in any admirable science holds converse with the devil. Of this Boethius, in his book On the Consolation of Philosophy,[1] complains ; and affirms that he had the discredit of such practices on account of his ardent love of literature, as if he had polluted his knowledge by detestable arts for the sake of ambition. " It was hardly likely," says he, " that I, whom you dress up with such excellence as almost to make me like God, should catch at the protection of the vilest spirits ; but it is in this point that we approach nearest to a connexion with them, in that we are instructed in your learning, and educated in your customs." So far Boethius. The singular choice of his death confirms me in the belief [2] of his league with the devil ; for why, when dying, as we shall relate hereafter,[3] should he, gladiator-like, maim his own person, unless conscious of some unusual crime ? Accordingly, in an old volume which accidentally fell into my hands, wherein the names and years of all the popes are entered, I found written to the following purport :—" Sylvester, who was also called Gerbert, four years, one month, ten days · this man made a shameful end."

Of Gerbert's Scholars.

§ 168. Gerbert returning into Gaul, became a public professor, and taught in the schools. His brother philosophers and companions of his studies were, Constantine, abbot of the monastery of St. Maximin, near Orleans, to whom he addressed The Rules of the Abacus,[4] and Adelbold, bishop, as they say, of Winteburg, who himself gave proof of ability, in a letter which he wrote to Gerbert on a question concerning the diameter in Macrobius,[5] and in some other points. He had pupils, of exquisite talents and noble origin, namely Robert, son of Hugh surnamed Capet ; and Otho, son of the emperor Otho. Robert, afterwards king of France, made a suitable return to his master, and appointed him archbishop of Rheims. In that church are still extant,[6] as proofs of his

---

[1] Boethius, de Cons. Philos. lib. i. p. 14. (Glasguæ, 8vo. 1751.)

[2] Attention has been called to this passage by a note in the Rec. des Hist. de la France (tom. x.) harshly censuring Malmesbury's want of judgment. The partiality, however, for pope Silvester (he having been the first Frenchman who attained the dignity of chief pontiff), which the editor of that volume acknowledges, may in some measure explain, and perhaps excuse, the severity of the comment.   [3] See § 172.   [4] See p. 151, note [2].

[5] Macrob. in Somn. Scip. i. 20.

[6] The editor of tom. x. of the Rec. des Hist. de la France assents to the truth of this statement.

science, a clock[1] constructed on mechanical principles; and a hydraulic organ, in which the air, escaping in a surprising manner by the force of heated water, fills the cavity of the instrument, and the brazen pipes emit modulated tones[2] through the numerous apertures. The king himself, too, was well skilled in sacred music, and in this and many other respects a liberal benefactor to the church. Moreover, he composed that beautiful sequence, "The grace of the Holy Spirit be with us;" and the response, "O Judah and Jerusalem;" together with more which I should have pleasure in relating, were it not irksome to others to hear. Otho, emperor of Italy after his father, made Gerbert archbishop of Ravenna, and finally pope of Rome. He followed up his fortune so successfully, by the assistance of the devil,[3] that he left nothing unexecuted which he had once conceived. The treasures formerly buried by the inhabitants, he discovered by the art of necromancy, and removing the rubbish, applied them to his own desires. Thus viciously disposed are the wicked towards God, and thus they abuse his patience, though He had rather that they repent than perish. At last he found where his master would stop, and as the proverb says, "in the same manner as one crow picks out another crow's eyes," while endeavouring to oppose his attempts with art like his own.

How Gerbert discovered the Treasures of Octovian.

§ 169. There was a statue in the Campus Martius near Rome, I know not whether of brass or iron, having the forefinger of the right hand extended, and on the head was written, "Strike here." The men of former times supposing this should be understood as if they might find a treasure there, had battered the harmless statue by repeated strokes of a hatchet; but Gerbert convicted them of error by solving the problem in a very different manner. Marking where the shadow of the finger fell at noonday, when the sun was at its height, he there placed a post; and at night proceeded thither, attended only by a servant carrying a lanthorn. The earth opening by means of his accustomed arts, displayed to them a spacious entrance. They saw before them a vast palace, with golden walls, golden roofs, everything of gold; golden soldiers amusing themselves, as it were, with golden dice; a king of the same metal, reclining with his queen; delicacies set before them, and servants waiting; vessels of great weight and value, in which the sculpture surpassed nature herself. In the inmost part of the mansion, a carbuncle of the first quality, though small in appearance, dispelled the darkness of night. In the opposite corner stood

---

[1] Gerbert is by some supposed to have been the inventor of clocks; but his claim to the honour of that invention has been denied by Ditmar of Merseburg, who states that the horologium which Gerbert placed in the cathedral was only a species of sun-dial.

[2] This seems to be an organ acting by the application of steam. It was perhaps a modification of the revolving æolipile, an instrument mentioned by Vitruvius, i. 6.

[3] Mabillon imagined that this fable originated with cardinal Benno, and was inconsiderately adopted by subsequent writers.

a boy, holding a bow bent, and the arrow drawn to the head.
While the exquisite art of everything ravished the eyes of the
spectators, there was nothing which it was lawful to handle, though
it might be seen; for immediately as one stretched forth his hand
to touch anything, all these figures appeared to rush forward and
repel such presumption. Alarmed at this, Gerbert repressed his
inclination; but the servant could not refrain from snatching off
from a table a knife of admirable workmanship, supposing that, in
a booty of such magnitude, so small a theft could hardly be discovered. In an instant, the figures all starting up with loud
clamour, the boy discharged his arrow at the carbuncle, and in a
moment clad all in darkness; and had he not, by the advice of his
master, quickly thrown back the knife, they would have both suffered severely. In this manner, their boundless avarice unsatiated,
they departed, the lanthorn directing their steps. That he performed such things by unlawful devices, is the generally received
opinion. Yet, however, if any one diligently investigate the truth,
he will see that even Solomon, to whom God himself had given
wisdom, was not ignorant of these arts: for, as Josephus relates,[1]
he, in conjunction with his father, buried vast treasures in coffers,
which were hidden, as he says, in a kind of necromantic manner
under ground; neither was Hircanus, celebrated for his skill in
prophecy and his valour, who, to ward off the distress of a siege,
dug up by the same art three thousand talents of gold from the
sepulchre of David, and gave part of them to the besiegers, with
the remainder building an hospital for the reception of strangers.
But Herod, who would make an attempt of the same kind, with
more presumption than knowledge, lost in consequence many of
his attendants by an irruption of internal fire. Besides, when I hear
the Lord Jesus saying, " My Father worketh hitherto, and I work,"
I believe that He who gave to Solomon power over demons to such
a degree, as the same historian declares, that he relates there were
men even in his time who could eject them from persons possessed,
by applying to the nostrils of the patient a ring having the im-
pression pointed out by Solomon,—I believe, I say, that He could
give also the same science to this man; but I do not affirm that
he did give it.

How certain Persons sought for the Treasures of Octovian.

§ 170. But leaving these matters to my readers, I shall relate
what I recollect having heard when I was a boy, from a certain
monk of our house, a native of Aquitaine, a man in years, and a
physician by profession. " When I was seven years old," said he,
" despising the mean circumstances of my father, a poor citizen of
Barcelona, I surmounted the snowy Alps and went into Italy.
There, as was to be expected in a boy of that age, seeking my
daily bread in great distress, I paid more attention to the food of
my mind than of my body. As I grew up, I eagerly viewed many

[1] Josephus, Antiq. Jud. vii. 15. and viii. 2.

of the wonders of that country, and impressed them on my memory: among others I saw a perforated mountain, beyond which the inhabitants had from early times supposed that the treasures of Octovian were hidden.   Many persons were reported to have entered into these caverns for the purpose of exploring them, and to have there perished, being bewildered by the intricacy of the ways.   But, as hardly any apprehension can restrain avaricious minds from their intent, I with my companions, about twelve in number, meditated an expedition of this nature, either for the sake of plunder, or through curiosity.   Imitating, therefore, the ingenuity of Dædalus, who brought Theseus out of the Labyrinth by a conducting clue, we also, carrying a large ball of thread, fixed a small post at the entrance.   Tying the end of the thread to it, and lighting lanthorns, lest darkness as well as intricacy should obstruct us, we unrolled the clue ; and fixing a post at every mile, we proceeded on our journey along the caverns of the mountain in the best manner we were able.   Everything was dark and big with horror ; the bats, flitting from holes, dashed against our eyes and faces ; the path was narrow, and made dreadful on the left hand by a precipice, and a river flowing beneath it.   We saw the way bestrewed with bare bones ; we wept over the carcases of men yet in a state of putrefaction, who, induced by hopes similar to our own, had in vain attempted, after their entrance, to return.   After some time, however, and many alarms, arriving at the further outlet, we beheld a lake of softly murmuring waters, where the wave came gently rolling to the shores.   A bridge of brass united the opposite banks : beyond the bridge were seen golden horses of great size, mounted by golden riders, and all those other things which are related by Gerbert : and the mid-day sun darting upon them with redoubled splendour, dazzled the eyes of the beholders.   Seeing these things at a distance, we should have been delighted with a nearer view, meaning, if fate would permit, to carry off some portion of the precious metal.   Animating each other in turn, we prepared to pass over the lake.   All our efforts, however, were vain ; for as soon as one of the company, more forward than the rest, had put his foot on the hither edge of the bridge, immediately (wonderful to hear) it became depressed, and the further edge was elevated, bringing forward a rustic of brass armed with a brazen club, with which, dashing the waters, he so clouded the air as completely to obscure both the day and the heavens.   The moment the foot was withdrawn, peace was restored : the like attempt was made by many of us, with exactly the same result.   Despairing, then, of getting over, we stood there some little time ; and, as long as we could, at least glutted our eyes with the gold.   Soon after, returning by the guidance of the thread, we found a silver dish, which being cut in pieces and distributed in morsels, only irritated the thirst of our avidity without allaying it.   Consulting together the next day, we went to a professor of that time, who was said to know the unutterable name of God.   When questioned, he did not deny his knowledge, adding that so great was the power of that name that no magic, no witchcraft, could resist it.   Hiring him at a great price, fasting and confessed, he led us, prepared in the same manner, to a fountain.   Taking up some water from it in a silver vessel, he silently traced the letters with his fingers, until we understood by our eyes what was unutterable with our tongues.   We then went confidently to the mountain, but we found the further outlet beset as I believe with devils, hating, forsooth, the name of God, which was able to destroy their inventions.   In the morning a Jew necromancer came to me, excited by the report of our attempt; and having inquired into the matter, when he heard of our want of enterprise, 'You shall see,' said he, venting his spleen with loud laughter, 'how far the power of my art can prevail.' And immediately entering the mountain, he soon after came out again, bringing, as a proof of his having passed the lake, many things which I had noted beyond it; indeed, some of that most precious dust, which turned everything touched by it into gold—not that it was really so, but only retained this appearance until washed with water; for nothing effected by necromancy can, when put into water, deceive the sight of the beholders.   The truth of my assertion is confirmed by a circumstance which happened about the same time.

§ 171.   " There were in a public street leading to Rome two old women, than whom nothing could be more drunken or filthy, both living in the same hut, and both practising witchcraft.   If any lone stranger happened to come in their way, they used to make him appear either a horse, or a sow, or some other animal, expose him for sale to dealers, and gluttonize with the money.   By chance, on a certain night, taking in a lad to lodge who got his livelihood by stage-dancing, they turned him into an ass; thus possessing a creature extremely advantageous to their interests, who caught the eyes of such as passed by the strangeness of his postures, for in whatever mode the old woman commanded, the ass began to dance.   He retained, however, his understanding, though he had lost the power of speech.   In this manner the women had accumulated much money, for there was daily a large concourse of people from all parts to see the tricks of the ass.   The report of this induced a rich neighbour to purchase the quadruped for a considerable sum; and he was warned that, would he have him as a constant dancer, he must keep him from water.   The person who had charge of him rigidly fulfilled his orders.   A long time elapsed; the ass sometimes gratified his master by his reeling motions, and sometimes entertained his friends with his tricks.   But, however, as in time all things surfeit, he began at length to be less cautiously observed.   In consequence of this negligence, breaking his halter, he got loose, plunged into a pool hard by, and rolling for a long time in the water, recovered his human form.   The keeper inquiring of all he met, and pursuing him by the track of his feet, asked him if he had seen an ass.   He replied that himself had been an ass, but was now a man, and related the whole transaction. The servant astonished told it to his master, and the master to pope Leo, the holiest man in our times.   The old women were convicted, and confessed the fact.   The pope doubting this, was assured by Peter Damian, a learned man, that it was not wonderful that such things should be done: and by instancing the example of Simon Magus,[1] who caused Faustinianus to assume the figure of Simon, and to become an object of terror to his sons, he rendered his holiness better skilled in such matters for the future."

Of the Statue with a Speaking Head.

§ 172. I have inserted this narrative of the Aquitanian to the intent that, what is reported of Gerbert should not seem wonderful to any person; which is, that he cast, for his own purposes, the head of a statue, by a certain inspection of the stars when all the planets were about to begin their courses, which spake not unless spoken to, but then pronounced the truth either in the affirmative or negative. For instance, when Gerbert would say, " Shall I be pope?" the statue would reply, " Yes;" " Am I to die, ere I sing mass at Jerusalem?" " No:" they relate, that he was so much deceived by this ambiguity, that he thought nothing of repentance; flattering himself with the prospect of a very long life: for when would he think of going to Jerusalem to accelerate his own death? Nor did he foresee that at Rome there is a church called Jerusalem, that is, " the vision of peace," because whoever flies thither finds safety, be he guilty of whatsoever crime. We have heard that this was called the Asylum in the very infancy of the city, because Romulus, to increase the number of his subjects, had appointed it to be a refuge for the guilty of every description. The pope sings mass there on three Sundays, which are called " The station at Jerusalem." Wherefore when upon one of those days Gerbert was preparing himself for mass, he suddenly complained of feeling ill; growing worse, he took to his bed: and consulting his statue, he became convinced of its delusion and of his own approaching death. Calling, therefore, the cardinals together, he lamented his crimes for a long space of time. They being struck with sudden fear and unable to make any reply, raving, and losing his reason through excess of pain, he commanded himself to be cut into pieces, and cast forth piecemeal, saying, " Let him have the service of my limbs, who before sought their homage; for my mind never consented to that oath, nay, that abomination."

§ 173. And since I have wandered from my subject, I think it may not be unpleasant were I to relate what took place in Saxony in the time of this king, in the year of our Lord one thousand and twelve, and which is not generally known. It is better to dilate on such matters than to dwell on Ethelred's indolence and calamities: and it will be more pleasing certainly, and nearer the truth, if I subjoin it in the original language of the person who was a sufferer, than if I had clothed it in my own words. Besides, I think it ornamental to a work, that the style be occasionally varied.

---

[1] In the fabulous Itinerary of St. Peter, attributed to Clemens Romanus, Simon is represented as causing Faustinianus to assume his countenance, by rubbing his face with a medicated unguent, to the great alarm of his sons, who mistook him for Simon, and fled, until recalled by St. Peter.

Of the Dancing Men and Women.

§ 174. " I Otbert, a sinner, were I desirous of concealing the divine judgment which overtook me, yet the tremor of my limbs would betray me; wherefore I shall relate circumstantially how this happened, that all may know the heavy punishment due to disobedience. We were, on the vigil of our Lord's Nativity, in a certain town of Saxony, in which was the church of Magnus the Martyr, where a priest named Rotbert had begun the first mass. I was in the churchyard with eighteen companions, fifteen men and three women, dancing, and singing profane songs to such a degree that I interrupted the priest, and our voices resounded amid the sacred solemnity of the mass. Wherefore, having commanded us to be silent, and not being attended to, he cursed us in the following words, ' May it please God and St. Magnus, that you may remain singing in that manner for a whole year.' His words had their effect. The son of John the priest seized his sister, who was singing with us, by the arm, and immediately tore it from her body; but not a drop of blood flowed out. She also remained a whole year with us, dancing and singing. The rain fell not upon us; nor did cold, nor heat, nor hunger, nor thirst, nor fatigue assail us: we neither wore out our clothes nor shoes, but we kept on singing as though we had been insane. First we sunk into the ground up to our knees, next to our thighs; a covering was at length, by the permission of God, built over us to keep off the rain. When a year had elapsed, Herbert, bishop of the city of Cologne, released us from the tie wherewith our hands were bound, and reconciled us before the altar of St. Magnus. The daughter of the priest, with the other two women, died immediately; the rest of us slept three whole days and nights: some died afterwards, and are famed for miracles: the remainder betray their punishment by the trembling of their limbs." This narrative was given to us by the Lord Peregrine, the successor of the blessed Herbert, in the year of our Lord one thousand and thirteen.

§ 175. In that city—which formerly was called Agrippina, from Agrippa, the son-in-law of Augustus, but afterwards named Colonia, by the emperor Trajan, because being there created emperor he founded in it a colony of Roman citizens;—in this city, I repeat, there was a certain bishop, famed for piety, though hideous in his person; of whom I shall relate one miracle, which he predicted when dying, after having first recorded what a singular chance elevated him to such an eminent station. The emperor of that country going to hunt on Quinquagesima Sunday, came alone, (for his companions were dispersed,) to the edge of a wood where this rural priest, deformed and almost a monster, had a church. The emperor feigning himself a soldier, humbly begs a mass, which he immediately begins. The other in the meantime was revolving in his mind, why God, from whom all beautiful things proceed, should suffer so deformed a man to administer his sacraments. Presently, when that verse in the Tract occurred, " Know ye that the Lord he is God," the priest, chiding the inattention of an assistant, looked behind him, and with a louder voice, replied, as it were, to the emperor lost in thought, saying, " It is He who hath made us; and not we ourselves."   Struck with this expression, the emperor, esteeming him a prophet, exalted him, though unwilling and reluctant, to the archbishopric ; which, when he had once assumed, he dignified by his exemplary conduct; kindly encouraging those who did well, and branding with the stigma of excommunication such as did otherwise, without respect of persons.   The inhabitants of that place proclaim a multitude of his impartial acts ; one of which the reader will peruse in that abbreviated form which my work requires.

In a monastery of nuns in that city, there was a certain virgin who had there grown up, more by the kindness of her parents than through any innate wish for an holy life: this girl, by the attraction of her beauty and her affable language to all, allured many lovers ; but while others, through fear of God or the censure of the world, restrained their desires, there was one, who, excited to wantonness by the extent of his wealth and the nobility of his descent, broke through the bounds of law and of justice, and despoiled her of her virginity; and carrying her off he kept her as his lawful wife. Much time elapsed while the abbess entreated, and his friends admonished him not to persevere in so dreadful a crime ; but he, turning a deaf ear however to his advisers, continued as immoveable as a rock.   By chance at this time the prelate was absent, occupied in business at Rome : but on his return the circumstance was related to him: he commands the sheep to be returned to the fold directly; and after much altercation the woman was restored to the monastery: but not long after, watching an opportunity when the bishop was absent, she was again carried away.   Excommunication was then denounced against the delinquent, so that no person could speak to, or associate with him.   Holding it in contempt, however, he retired to one of his estates afar off, not to submit to the sentence but to elude its power, and there, a turbulent and powerful man, he lived in company with his excommunicated paramour.   But when it pleased God to call the bishop to heaven, and he was lying in extreme bodily pain upon his bed, the neighbours flocked around him, that they might partake the final benediction of this holy man,   The offender alone not daring to appear, prevailed on some persons to speak for him.   The moment the bishop heard his name he groaned, and then, (I add his very words,) spoke to the following effect, " If that wretched man shall desert that accursed woman, let him be absolved; but if he persist, let him be ready to give account before God, next year, at the very day and hour on which I shall depart ; moreover, you will see me expire when the bell shall proclaim the sixth hour."   Nor were his words vain: as he departed at the time he had predicted: and the other, together with his mistress, at the expiration of the year, on the same day, and at the same hour, was killed by a stroke of lightning.

How Sweyn was invited to England.

§ 176. But king Ethelred, after the martyrdom of St. Elfeg, as
we have related,[1] gave his see to a bishop named Living.[2] Moreover, Turkill, the Dane, who had been the chief cause of the archbishop's murder, had settled in England, and held the East Angles
in subjection. For, the other Danes exacting from the English a
tribute of eight thousand pounds, had distributed themselves, as
best suited their convenience, in the towns, or in the country; and
fifteen of their ships, with the crews, had entered into the king's
service. In the meantime Turkill sent messengers to Suane, king
of Denmark, inviting him to come to England, telling him that the
land was rich and fertile, but the king a driveller; and that, wholly
given up to wine and women, his last thoughts were those of war;
that in consequence he was hateful to his own people and contemptible to foreigners; that the commanders were jealous of each
other, the people weak, and that they would fly from the field the
moment the onset was sounded.

§ 177. Suane[3] was naturally cruel, nor did he require much
persuasion; preparing his ships, therefore, he hastened his voyage.
Sandwich was the port he made, principally designing to avenge
his sister Gunhildis. This woman, who possessed considerable
beauty, had come over to England with her husband Palling, a
powerful nobleman, and embracing Christianity had made herself a
pledge of the Danish peace. In his ill-fated fury, Edric had commanded her to be beheaded with the other Danes, though she
declared that the shedding her blood would bring great evils on the
whole kingdom. She bore her death with fortitude, neither turning pale at the time of execution, nor, when dead and her blood
exhausted, did she lose her beauty; her husband was murdered
before her face, and her son, a youth of amiable disposition, was
transfixed with four spears. Suane then proceeding through East
Anglia against the Northumbrians, received their submission without resistance; not indeed that the native ardour of their minds,
which brooked no master, had grown cool; but because Uhtred,[4]
their prince, was the first to give example of desertion. On their
submission, all the other people who inhabit England on the north
gave him tribute and hostages. Coming southward, he compelled
those of Oxford and Winchester to obey his commands; the
Londoners[5] alone protecting their lawful sovereign within their
walls, shut their gates against him. The Danes, on the other
hand, assailing with greater ferocity, nurtured their fortitude with

---

[1] See § 165.

[2] Lyfing, formerly called Ethelstan, was translated from Wells to Canterbury
in the year 1013; he died 12th June, 1020.

[3] The massacre of the Danes on St. Brice's day, A. D. 1002, and the murder of
Gunhilda, the sister of Sweyn, were long remembered by the Danes as incentives
to their hatred of the Saxon name. The attack made on England by the Danish
king in the following year would scarcely be considered ample revenge for so
great an injury, and Sweyn continued to infest the English coast from that time
until his death. The landing at Sandwich was effected in July 1013.

[4] Uhtred and the Northumbrians submitted to Sweyn in 1013.

[5] Sweyn was repulsed from London by Ethelred and Turcytell in 1013.

the hope of fame.   The townsmen were ready to meet death for freedom's sake, thinking they would never be forgiven should they desert their king, who had committed his life to their charge. While the conflict was raging fiercely on either side, victory be-friended the juster cause; for the citizens made wonderful exer-tions, every one esteeming it glorious to show his unwearied alacrity to his prince, or even to die for him.   One part of the enemy was destroyed, and another part drowned in the river Thames, because in their headlong fury they had not a bridge.   With his shattered army Suane retreated to Bath, where Ethelmer, governor of the western district, with his followers, submitted to him.   And, although all England was already stooping to his dominion, yet not even now would the Londoners have yielded, had not Ethel-red withdrawn his presence from among them; for, being a man given up to indolence, and, through consciousness of his own mis-deeds, supposing none could be faithful to him, and at the same time wishing to escape the difficulties of a battle and a siege, he by his departure left them to their own exertions.   However, applying the best remedy they could to their exigencies, they surrendered after the example of their countrymen.   They were men laudable in the extreme, and such as Mars himself would not have disdained to encounter, had they possessed a competent leader; for even while they were supported by the mere shadow of one, they risked every chance of battle, nay, even a siege of several months' con-tinuance.   He, in the meantime, giving fresh instance of his con-stitutional indolence, fled from the city, and arriving by secret journeys at Southampton, he passed over to the Isle of Wight. Here he addressed those abbots and bishops, who, even in such difficulties, could not bring themselves to desert their master, to the following effect: That they must perceive in what dreadful state his affairs and those of his subjects were; that he was banished from his paternal throne by the treachery of his generals, and that he, in whose hands their safety was formerly vested, now required the assistance of others; that though lately a monarch and a potentate, he was now a fugitive and an outcast—a melancholy change for him, because it certainly is more tolerable never to have had power, than to have lost it when possessed; and more especially disgraceful to the English, as this instance of their desertion of their prince would be noised throughout the world; that, through mere regard to him, they had exposed their houses and property to plunderers, and, although unprovided, had taken a voluntary flight; food was matter of difficulty to all; many had not even clothing; he commended their fidelity indeed, but still could not insure their safety; the country was now so completely subdued, the coast so narrowly watched, that there was no escape unattended with danger; that they should, therefore, confer together what was to be done; were they to remain, greater peril was to be apprehended from their countrymen than from their enemies; for, perhaps, they might purchase the favour of their new master by joining to distress them; and certainly to be killed by an enemy was to be ascribed to chance—to be betrayed by a fellow-citizen was to be

attributed to want of exertion ; were they to fly to distant nations,
it would be with the loss of honour; if to those who knew them,
the dread would be, lest their dispositions should take a tinge
from their reverse of fortune, for many great and illustrious men
had been killed on similar occasions ; but, however, he must make
the experiment, and ascertain the inclinations of Richard duke of
Normandy, who, if he should kindly receive his sister and nephews,
might probably not unwillingly afford him his protection. " His
favour shown to my wife and children," continued he, " will be
the pledge of my own security. Should he oppose me, I am confident, nay fully confident, I shall not want spirit to die here with
honour, in preference to living there with ignominy. Wherefore
this very month of August, while milder gales are smoothing the
ocean, let Emma make a voyage to her brother, taking our
children, our common pledges, to be deposited with him. Let
their companions be the bishop of Durham[1] and the abbot of
Peterborough ; I myself will remain here till Christmas ; and should
they send back a favourable answer, I will follow directly."

§ 178. On the breaking up of the conference all obeyed ; they
set sail for Normandy, while he remained anxiously expecting a
favourable report. Shortly after he learned from abroad that
Richard had received his sister with great affection, and that
he invited the king also to condescend to become his inmate.
Ethelred, therefore, going into Normandy, in the month of
January,[2] felt his distresses soothed by the attentions of his host.
This Richard was son of Richard the First,[3] and equalled his
father in good fortune and good qualities, though he certainly
surpassed him in piety. He completed the monastery of Fescamp,[4]
which his father had begun. He was more intent on prayer and
temperance than you would require in any monk or hermit. He
was humble to excess, in order that he might subdue by his
patience the petulance of those who attacked him. Moreover, it
is reported that at night, secretly escaping the observation of his
servants, he was accustomed to go unattended to the matins of the
monks, and to continue in prayer till daylight. Intent on this
practice, one night[5] in particular, at Fescamp, he was earlier than
customary, and finding the door shut he forced it open with
unusual violence, and disturbed the sleep of the sacrist. He,
astonished at the noise of any person knocking in the dead of
night, got up, that he might see the author of so bold a deed ; and
finding only a countryman in appearance, clothed in rustic garb,
he could not refrain from laying hands on him ; so that, moved
with vehement indignation, he caught hold of his hair, and gave
this illustrious man a number of severe blows, which he bore with

---

[1] According to Florence of Worcester, it was Elfhun bishop of London, who,
with Elfsine, abbot of Peterborough, accompanied Emma and her two sons, Edward and Alfred, into Normandy. See also Sax. Chron. A.D. 1013.
[2] 1st Jan. A.D. 1014.
[3] Richard II. called Le Bon, succeeded his father in 996. Several authorities
state that he died on the 23d of August, 1027; but William of Jumiéges (v. 17)
places his death in 1026.   [4] See Gallia Christ. xi. 201.
[5] Matins were sometimes performed shortly after midnight.

incredible patience, nor uttered a syllable.　The next day Richard laid his complaint before the chapter,[1] and, with counterfeited anger summoned the monk to meet him at the town of Argens, threatening that he would take such vengeance for the injury as all France should talk of.　On the day appointed, while the monk stood by almost dead with fear, he detailed the matter to the nobility, largely exaggerating the enormity of the transaction, and keeping the culprit in suspense, by crafty objections to what he urged in mitigation.　Finally, after he had been sentenced by the nobility, he kindly pardoned him; and to make his forgiveness more acceptable, he annexed all that town with its appurtenances, reported to be abundant in the best wine, to the office of this sacrist, saying that he was an admirable monk, who properly observing his appointed charge, broke not silence, though roused with anger.[2]　Dying after having held the duchy for twenty-eight years,[3] he ordered his body to be buried at the door of the church,[4] where it might be subjected to the feet of such as passed by, and to the drippings of the lofty eaves: but in our time, however, William,[5] third abbot of that place, regarding this as disgraceful, removed the long-continued reproach, and taking up the body, placed it before the high altar.　He had a brother, Robert,[6] whom he made archbishop of Rouen, though by this he not a little tarnished his reputation; for he, cruelly abusing this honour, at first committed many crimes, many atrocious acts, but growing in years, he certainly wiped off some of them by his very liberal almsgiving.　After Richard, his son of the same name obtained the principality, but lived scarcely a year.[7]　A vague opinion,[8] indeed, has prevailed, that, by the connivance of his brother Robert,[9] whom Richard the Second begat on Judith, daughter of Conan, earl of Brittany, a certain woman skilled in poisons removed the young man.　Bewailing his privity to this transaction, he departed for Jerusalem, after the seventh year of his earldom; venturing on an undertaking very meritorious at that time, by commencing, with few followers, a journey, exposed to incursions of barbarians, and strange, by reason of the customs of the Saracens.　He persevered, nevertheless, nor did he stop, but safely completed the

---

[1] It was customary to hold a chapter immediately after prime.

[2] This anecdote of Richard II., duke of Normandy, has been cited as a singular example of the manners of the age.　(Prol. Rec. des Hist. de la France, tom. x.)

[3] Richard II. held the duchy of Normandy thirty years.

[4] The church of Fécamp.　Compare Dudo de S. Quintin's account of the death of Richard II.

[5] William de Ros, the third abbot of Fécamp, died on the 8th of the kalends of April, 1107 (25th March, 1108).　See Gall. Christ. ix. 208.

[6] Robert was the son of Richard I., duke of Normandy, by his second wife Gonnor, who had been his concubine.　He was made comte d'Evreux by his father in the year 989, who also made him archbishop of Rouen in the same year; he died before Easter, 1036.　Some authorities place his death in 1037.　Gall. Christ. xi. 26.

[7] According to Mabillon (Annal. Bened. lvi. § 38), Richard III. died A.D. 1028, in the first year of his reign.

[8] See William of Jumiéges, vi. 2.

[9] Robert comte d'Hiêmes succeeded his brother in the dukedom of Normandy as Robert I. surnamed Robert le Magnifique, and le Diable.

whole distance; and purchasing admission at a high price, with bare feet and tearful eyes he worshipped at that glory of the Christians, I mean the sepulchre of our Lord. Conciliating the favour of God, as we believe, by this labour, on his return homewards he ended his days at Nice,[1] a city of Bithynia, cut off, as it is said, by poison, administered by his servant Ralph, surnamed Mowin, who had wrought himself up to the commission of this crime from a hope of the dukedom: but on his return to Normandy, the matter becoming known to all, he was detested as a monster, and retired to perpetual exile. To Robert succeeded William his son, then a child,[2] of whom, as I shall have to speak hereafter, I shall now return to my narrative.

§ 179. In the meantime Suane, as I have before related,[3] oppressed England with rapine and with slaughter : the inhabitants were first plundered of their property, and then proscribed. In every city it was matter of doubt what should be done: if revolt were determined on, they had none to take the lead; if submission were made choice of, then a kind ruler was wanting. Thus their public and private property, together with their hostages, was carried to the fleet; as he was not a lawful sovereign, but a most cruel tyrant. The kindness of God, however, did not long permit England to fluctuate in such keen distress, for the invader died[4] shortly after, on the Purification of St. Mary, though it is uncertain by what death. It is reported, that while devastating the possessions[5] of St. Edmund, that martyr appeared to him in a vision, and gently addressed him on the misery of his people; that when Suane replied insolently, he struck him on the head; and that in consequence of the blow he died, as has been said, immediately after. The Danes then elect Cnut, the son of Suane, king : the English, on the other hand, declaring that their natural sovereign was dearer to them, if he could conduct himself more like a king than he had hitherto done, send for king Edelred out of Normandy. He despatched Edward his son, first, to sound the fidelity of the higher orders and the inclination of the people, on the spot; who, when he saw the wishes of all tending to the favourable side, went back in full confidence for his father. The king returned,[6] and being flattered by the joyful plaudits of the English, that he might appear to have shaken off his constitutional indolence, he hastened to collect an army against Cnut, who was at that time in Lindesey, where his father had left him with the ships and hostages, and was levying fresh troops and horses, in order that, mustering a sufficient force, he might make a vigorous attack upon his enemies before they were prepared for him, vowing most severe vengeance, as he used to say, on the deserters. But, circumvented by a contrivance

[1] On the 2d of July, A.D. 1035. William of Jumièges, vi. 13.
[2] William the Bastard, afterwards king of England. He was not more than eight years of age at his father's death.   [3] See § 176.
[4] Sweyn died on the 2d of February, A.D. 1014.
[5] See Florence of Worcester, p. 262; also Capgrave, fol. cviii.
[6] Ethelred returned from Normandy A.D. 1014. The editors of the Rec. des Hist. de la France, on the authority of some chronologists, place the death of Sweyn, as well as the return of Ethelred to England, in the year 1015.

similar to his own, he retreated. Escaping at that time with much difficulty, and putting to sea with his remaining forces, he coasted the British ocean from east to south, and landed at Sandwich. Here, setting all divine and human laws at defiance, he despoiled his hostages, who were young men of great nobility and elegance, of their ears and noses, and some he even castrated : and so, tyrannizing over the innocent, and boasting of the feat, he returned to his own country.[1]

In the same year the sea-flood, which the Greeks call Euripus, and we Ledo,[2] rose to so wonderful a height,[3] that none like it was recollected in the memory of man, and overflowed the villages, and destroyed their inhabitants, for many miles.

The year following, a grand council of Danes and English was assembled at Oxford,[4] where the king commanded two of the noblest Danes, Sigeferd and Morcard,[5] accused of treachery to him by the impeachment of the traitor Edric, to be put to death. He had lured them, when deceived by his soothing expressions, into a chamber, and murdered them, when drunk to excess, by his attendants prepared for the purpose. The cause of their murder was said to be, his unjustifiable desire for their property. Their dependents, attempting to revenge the death of their lords by arms, were defeated, and driven into the tower of St. Frideswide's church, where, as they could not be dislodged, they were consumed by fire: however, shortly after, the foul stain was wiped out by the king's penitence, and the chancel was repaired. I have read the history of this transaction, which is reposited in the archives of that church. The wife of Sigeferd, a woman remarkable for her rank and beauty, was carried prisoner to Malmesbury; on which account Edmund, the king's son, dissembling his intention, took a journey into those parts, and becoming enamoured of her as soon as he saw her, he made her his wife ; cautiously keeping their union secret from his father, who was as much an object of contempt to his family as to strangers. This Edmund was not born of Emma, but of some other person,[6] whom fame has lost in obscurity. In other respects he was unexceptionable ; a young man of noble disposition, of great strength both of mind and person ; and, on this account, by the English called " Ireneside :" he would have shrouded the indolence of his father, and the meanness of his mother, by his own conspicuous virtue, could the fates have spared him. Soon after, at the instigation of his wife, he asked of his father the possessions of Sigeferd, which were of large extent among the Northumbrians, but he could not obtain them ; by his own exertions, however, he procured them at last, the inhabitants of that province willingly submitting to his power.

---

[1] Cnut returned to Denmark in 1014. See Flor. of Worcester and Sax. Chron.

[2] " Euripus" seems to be the tide generally, and " Ledo" the neap or low tide, and not the spring tide, as Malmesbury here implies.

[3] This incident is mentioned both by the Saxon Chronicle and Florence of Worcester.

[4] The great "gemot" or council, at Oxford, was held in the year 1015.

[5] The sons of Earngrim.   (Flor. Wigorn.)

[6] Probably he was the son of Elfred the daughter of Thored ; such, at least, is the statement of Ailred of Rievaux, cols. 362, 372.

§ 180. The same summer Cnut having settled his affairs in
Denmark, and entered into alliance with the neighbouring kings,
came into England,[1] determined to conquer or perish in the
attempt. Proceeding from Sandwich into Kent, and thence into
West Saxony, he laid everything waste with fire and slaughter,
while the king was lying sick at Cosham.[2]   Edmund, indeed,
attempted to oppose him, but being thwarted by Edric, he placed
his forces in a secure situation.   Edric, however, thinking it unnecessary longer to dissemble, but that he might now openly throw
off the mask, deserted to Cnut with forty ships; and all West
Saxony likewise followed his example, both delivering hostages, and
giving up their arms.   Yet the Mercians repeatedly assembled,
and stood forward to resist; and would but the king come, and
command whither they were to march, and bring with him the
leading men of London, they were ready to shed their blood for
their country.   But he, accustomed to commit his safety to fortifications, and not to attack the enemy, remained in London, never
venturing out, for fear, as he said, of traitors.   In the meantime
Cnut was gaining towns and villages over to his party; was never
unemployed; held consultations by night, and fought by day.
Edmund, after long deliberation, esteeming it best in such an
emergency to recover, if possible, the revolted cities by arms,
brought over Uhtred, an earl on the other side of the Humber, to
the same sentiments : for they imagined that such cities as were
yet doubtful which side to take, would determine at once, were
they to inflict signal vengeance on those who had revolted.   But
Cnut, possessed of equal penetration, circumvented them by a
similar contrivance; for, giving over the West Saxons and that part
of Mercia which he had subjugated to the custody of his generals,
he himself proceeded against the Northumbrians ; and by depopulating the country, compelled Uhtred to retire for the defence of
his own possessions ; and although he surrendered himself, yet with
inhuman levity he ordered him to be put to death.   His earldom was
given to Iric, whom Cnut afterwards expelled from England, when
pretending to equal power with himself.   Thus all being subdued,
he ceased not from pursuing Edmund, who was retreating by
intervals, till he heard that he was at London with his father. Cnut
then remained quiet till after Easter, that he might attack the city
with all his forces.   But the death of Ethelred[3] preceded the
attempt ; for in the beginning of Lent, he, on St. Gregory's day,[4]
breathed out a life destined only to labours and misery: he lies
buried at St. Paul's in London.   The citizens immediately proclaimed Edmund king, who mustering an army, routed the Danes
at Penn[5] and Gillingham, about Rogation-day.   After the festival
of St. John [24th June], engaging them again at Seorstan,[6] he

[1] Cnut arrived in England early in January, A.D. 1016.
[2] Probably Cosham, in Wiltshire. See Camd. Brit. col. 106.
[3] According to the Saxon Chronicle and Florence, Ethelred died at London on
Monday, 23d of April (St. George's day), A.D. 1016.
[4] So in all the MSS., but we should probably read "Georgii."
[5] Penn, near Gillingham.
[6] Supposed by Camden to be a stone which divided the four counties of Oxford,

retired from a drawn battle. His English had begun to give way, at the instance of Edric, who being on the adversaries' side, and holding in his hand a sword stained with the blood of a rustic whom he had dexterously slain, exclaimed, "Fly, wretches! fly! behold, your king was killed by this sword!" The English would have fled immediately had not the king, apprised of this circumstance, proceeded to an eminence, and taking off his helmet, shown his face to his comrades. Then brandishing a dart with all his force, he launched it at Edric; but being seen and avoided, it missed him, and struck a soldier standing near; and so great was its violence that it even transfixed a second. Night put a stop to the battle, the hostile armies retreating as if by mutual consent, though the English had well nigh obtained the victory. After this the sentiments of the West Saxons changed, and they acknowledged their lawful sovereign. Edmund proceeded to London, that he might liberate those deserving citizens whom a party of the enemy had blocked up immediately after his departure; moreover they had surrounded the whole city, on the parts not washed by the river Thames, with a trench;[1] and many had lost their lives in their mutual conflicts. Hearing of the king's approach, they precipitately took to flight; while he pursuing directly, and passing the ford called Brentford, routed them with great slaughter. The remaining multitude which were with Cnut, while Edmund was relaxing a little, and getting his affairs in order, again laid siege to London both on the land and river side; but being nobly repulsed by the citizens, they wreaked their anger on adjacent Mercia, laying waste the towns and villages with plunder, fire, and slaughter. The richest of the spoil was conveyed to their ships assembled in the river Medway, which flowing by the city of Rochester, washes its fair walls with a strong and rapid current. They were attacked and driven hence also by the king in person; who suddenly seizing the ford, which I have before mentioned at Brentford, dispersed them with signal loss. While Edmund was preparing to pursue and utterly destroy the last remains of these plunderers, he was prevented by the crafty and abandoned Edric, who had again insinuated himself into his good graces; for he had come over to Edmund, at the instigation of Cnut, that he might betray his designs. Had the king only persevered, this would have been the last day for the Danes; but being misled (as I have stated) by the insinuations of a traitor, who affirmed that the enemy would make no further attempt, he brought swift destruction upon himself and the whole of England. Being allowed by this means to escape, they again assembled; they attacked the East Angles, and at Assandun compelled the king himself, who came to their assistance, to retreat. Here, again, the person I am ashamed to mention so frequently, designedly gave the first example of flight. A small number, who,

---

Gloucester, Worcester, and Warwick. See Camd. Brit. col. 103; but cf. the note in Lappenb. ii. 139.

[1] The trench appears to have been made on the south side of the river, and the ships drawn to the west side of the bridge to besiege the city. See Sax. Chron.

mindful of their former fame and encouraging each other, had
formed a compact body, were cut off to a man. Here Cnut gained
the kingdom; here the glory of England fell; here the whole
flower of the country withered, amongst whom was Ulkill, earl of
East Anglia, who had gained immortal honour in the time of
Suane, when, first attacking the pirates, he showed that they might
be overcome: here fell, too, the chief men of the day, both
bishops and abbots.[1] Edmund flying hence almost alone, came to
Gloucester, in order that there, reassembling his forces, he might
attack the enemy, indolent, as he supposed, after their recent
victory. Nor was Cnut wanting in courage to pursue the fugitive.
When everything was ready for battle, Edmund demanded a single
combat, that two individuals might not, for the lust of dominion,
be stained with the blood of so many subjects, when they might
try their fortune without the destruction of their faithful adherents;
and observing that it must redound greatly to the credit of either,
to have obtained so vast a dominion at his own personal peril. On
the proposal being made, Cnut refused it altogether; affirming that
his courage was surpassing, but that he was apprehensive of trusting
his diminutive person against so bulky an antagonist; but, however,
as both had equal pretensions to the kingdom, since the fathers of
both had possessed it, it was consistent with prudence that they
should lay aside their animosity and divide England.[2] This pro-
position was adopted by each army, and confirmed with much
applause, both for its equity and its beneficent regard to the repose
of persons who were worn out with continual suffering. In consequence, Edmund, overcome by the general clamour, yielded to
peace, entered into treaty with Cnut, retained West Saxony for
himself, and conceded Mercia to the other. Dying soon after, on
the festival of St. Andrew, though by what mischance is not known,[3]
he was buried at Glastonbury near his grandfather Eadgar. Fame
asperses Edric, as having, through regard for Cnut, compassed his
death by means of his servants; reporting that there were two
attendants on the king to whom he had committed the entire care
of his person, and that Edric, seducing them by promises, at length
made them his accomplices, though at first they were struck with
horror at the enormity of the crime; and that, at his suggestion,
they drove an iron hook into his posteriors, as he was sitting down
for a necessary purpose. Edwin, his brother on the mother's side,[4]

[1] Eadnoth bishop of Dorchester, abbot Wulsige, earls Elfric, Godwine, and
Ethelward, are also named among the slain.
[2] According to the Saxon Chronicle, the meeting between Cnut and Edmund
took place at Olanege, near Deerhurst, an island on the river Severn. Henry
Huntingdon says they actually engaged, and that Cnut finding himself likely to
be defeated, proposed the division. (H. Hunt. l. 6.)
[3] The true circumstances of Edmund's death are involved in obscurity; but
there seems little doubt that he was assassinated in the year 1017. Florence of
Worcester and the Saxon Chronicle place his death on the 30th of Nov. 1016.
Florence, however, adds the year of the indiction, which corresponds with A.D.
1017.
[4] Edwi the brother of Eadmund Ironside, and Edwi called Ceorla Cyning, (king
of the Clowns,) were outlawed A.D. 1017. The former was afterwards slain by
order of Cnut. See Sax. Chron. Flor. Wigorn.

a youth of amiable disposition, was driven from England by Edric, at the command of Cnut, and "suffering extremely for a considerable time both by sea and land," his body, as is often the case, became affected by the anxiety of his mind, and he died in England, where he lay concealed after a clandestine return, and lies buried at Tavistock. His sons,[1] Edwy[2] and Edward,[3] were sent to the king of Sweden to be put to death; but being preserved by his pity, they went to the king of Hungary, where, after being kindly treated for a time, the elder died; and the younger married Agatha, the sister of the queen. His brothers by Emma,[4] namely, Elfred and Edward, lay securely concealed in Normandy for the whole time that Cnut lived. I find that their uncle Richard took no steps to restore them to their country; on the contrary, he married his sister Emma to the enemy and invader; and it may be difficult to say, whether to the greater ignominy of him who bestowed her, or of the woman who consented to share the nuptial couch of that man who had so cruelly molested her husband, and had driven her children into exile. Robert, however, whom we before mentioned as having gone to Jerusalem,[5] assembling a fleet and embarking soldiers, made ready an expedition, boasting that he would set the crown on the heads of his grand-nephews; and doubtless he would have made good his assertion, had not, as we have heard from our ancestors, an adverse wind constantly opposed him: but assuredly this was by the hidden counsel of God, in whose disposal are the powers of all kingdoms. The remains of the vessels, decayed through length of time, were still to be seen at Rouen in our days.

§ 181. Cnut began to reign in the year of our Lord one thousand and seventeen, and governed during twenty years. Though he obtained the sovereignty unjustly, yet he conducted himself with great affability and firmness. At his entrance on the government, dividing the kingdom into four parts, he himself took the West Saxons, Edric the Mercians, Turkill the East Angles, Iric the Northumbrians. His first care was to punish the murderers of Edmund, who had, under expectation of great recompence, acknowledged of their own accord the whole fact. He concealed them for a time, and then brought them forward in a large assembly of the people, where they confessed the mode of their attack upon him, and were immediately ordered to execution. The same year Edric, whom I cannot sufficiently revile, being by the king's command entrapped in the same snare which he had so frequently laid for others, breathed out his abominable spirit to hell. For, some quarrel arising, while they were angrily discoursing, Edric relying on the credit of his services,[6] and amicably, as it were, reproaching the king, said, "I first deserted Edmund for your sake, and after-

---

[1] *I. e.* of Eadmund Ironside.

[2] We should probably read here "Edmund." Edmund and Edward, sons of Edmund Ironside, were sent by Cnut to the king of Sweden. Flor. Wigorn, A.D. 1017.

[3] Edward married Agatha, and by her had issue Edgar Atheling, Christiana a nun, and Margaret, who married Malcolm king of Scotland.

[4] See § 179.   [5] See § 178.

[6] The MSS. A. C. and D. read, of the Mercians.

wards even despatched him in consequence of my engagements to
you :" at which expression Cnut's face turned red with indignation ;
and instantly pronouncing sentence, "And you, therefore," said
he, "shall die, and justly, since you are guilty of treason both to
God and me, by having killed your own sovereign and my sworn
brother ; thy blood be upon thy head, because thy mouth hath
spoken against thee, in that thou hast lifted thy hand against
the Lord's anointed:" and immediately, that no tumult might be
excited, the traitor was strangled ih the chamber where they sate,
and thrown out of the window into the river Thames,[1] thus
meeting the just reward of his perfidy. In process of time, as
opportunities occurred, Turkill[2] and Iric were driven out of the
kingdom, and sought their native land. The first, who had been
the instigator of the murder of the blessed Elfeg, was killed by the
chiefs the moment he touched the Danish shore.[3] When all England by this means became subject to Cnut alone, he began to
conciliate the English with unceasing diligence ; allowing them
equal rights with the Danes, in their assemblies, councils, and
armies ; on which account, as I have before observed,[4] he sent for
the wife of the late king out of Normandy, so that while they were
paying obedience to their accustomed sovereign, they should the less
repine at the dominion of the Danes. Another design which he
had in view by this, was to acquire favour with Richard, who would
think little of his nephews so long as he supposed he might have
others by Cnut. He repaired the monasteries throughout England,
which had been partly injured and partly destroyed by the military
incursions of himself and of his father: he built churches in all the
places where he had fought, and more particularly at Ashdown,[5]
and appointed ministers to them, who through succeeding ages
might pray to God for the souls of the persons there slain. At the
consecration of this church he himself was present, and the English
and Danish nobility made their offerings : it is now, according to
report, an ordinary church, under the care of a parish priest. Over
the body of the most holy Edmund, whom the Danes of former
times had killed, he built a church with princely magnificence,[6]
appointed to it an abbot and monks ; and conferred on it many
large estates. The greatness of his donation, yet entire, stands
proudly eminent at the present day; for that place surpasses
almost all the monasteries of England. He took up with his own
hands the body of the blessed Elfeg, which had been buried at St.
Paul's in London, and sending it to Canterbury, honoured it with

---

[1] Edric Streona was put to death, and thrown into the Thames, A. D. 1017.

[2] Thurcil, with his wife Eadgitha, was banished from England by Cnut, 11th
Nov. A. D. 1021.

[3] Osbern, in his History of the Translation of the body of archbishop Elfheah,
states that Thurcil having fled into Denmark, the Danish chiefs, fearing that he
would incite the people to rebellion, put him to death.   [4] See § 180.

[5] See Sax. Chron. A. D. 1020.

[6] This monastery was not founded by Cnut : Sigibert, king of East Anglia,
having abdicated his throne, built the monastery, at that time called Beadariches-
worth, and became a monk there. When it became the depository of the remains
of king Edmund, the name of the place was changed to Edmundsburh. In the
year 1020, Cnut rebuilt the monastery, and expelled the secular clerks, placing
therein a convent of Benedictine monks from Hulm in Norfolk.

due regard.[1] Thus anxious to atone for the offences of himself and of his predecessors, perhaps he wiped away the foul stain of his former crimes in the sight of God—certainly he did so with man. At Winchester especially he displayed the magnificence of his liberality: here he gave so largely that the quantity of precious metals astonished the minds of strangers, and the glittering of jewels dazzled the eyes of the beholders. This was at Emma's suggestion,[2] who, with pious prodigality, exhausted his treasures in works of this kind, while he was meditating fierce attacks on foreign lands; for his valour, incapable of rest, and not contented with Denmark, which he held paternally, and England, which he possessed by right of conquest, transferred its rage against the Swedes.[3] These people are contiguous to the Danes, and had excited the displeasure of Cnut by their ceaseless hostility. At first he fell into an ambush, and lost many of his people, but afterwards recruiting his strength, he routed his opponents, and brought the kings of that nation, Ulf and Eiglaf, to terms of peace. The English, at the instance of earl Godwin, behaved nobly in this conflict: he exhorted them not to forget their ancient fame, but clearly to display their valour to their new lord; telling them that it must be imputed to fortune that they had formerly been conquered by him, but it would be ascribed to their courage, if they overcame those who had overcome him. In consequence, the English exerted all their strength, and gaining the victory, obtained an earldom for their commander, and honour for themselves. Thence, on his return home, he entirely subdued the kingdom of Norway, putting Olave their king to flight;[4] who, the year following, returning with a small party into his kingdom, to try the inclinations of the inhabitants, found them faithless, and was slain with his adherents.

§ 182. In the fifteenth year of his reign, Cnut[5] went to Rome, and after remaining there some time, and atoning for his crimes, by giving alms to the several churches, he sailed back to England.[6] Soon after, with little difficulty, he subdued Scotland, then in a state of rebellion, and Malcolm her king, by leading an army thither. I trust it will not appear useless, if, to show his reformed life and princely magnificence, I subjoin the epistle[7] which he transmitted to the English on his departure from Rome, by the hands of Living,[8] abbot of Tavistock, and afterwards bishop of Crediton.

---

[1] See § 165.   [2] See post, § 196.

[3] Cnut sailed for Denmark in 1025, and engaged Ulf and Eglaf with a powerful army from Sweden, at a plain near the Holy River. (Sax. Chron.)

[4] The defeat of king Olaf, and the subjugation of Norway by Cnut, took place in 1028. Olaf returned to Norway A.D. 1030, in which year he was slain.

[5] According to the Saxon Chronicle, Florence of Worcester, and other English writers, Cnut went to Rome in the year 1031: but this date does not agree with that assigned for the coronation of the emperor Conrad at Rome by pope John XIX. (Easter Sunday 1027,) at which ceremony Cnut is said to have been present. According to Wippo, (Pistorius, Rer. Germ. Script. III. 472, Ratisbon. 1726,) the journey to Rome took place in 1027. See notes [4] and [5], p. 72.

[6] He returned by the way of Denmark, according to Florence of Worcester.

[7] This epistle also occurs in Florence of Worcester, A.D. 1031.

[8] Lyfing became bishop of Crediton, A.D. 1032; and on the death of Brihtheah, bishop of Worcester, (20th Dec. 1038,) he was translated to that see: he died A.D. 1046.

§ 183. " Cnut, king of all England, Denmark, Norway,[1] and part
of the Swedes, to Alnoth,[2] metropolitan, and Alfric[3] [archbishop]
of York, and to all bishops and nobles, and to the whole nation of
the English, high and low, sends greeting :

I notify to you, that I have lately been to Rome, to pray for
the forgiveness of my sins, for the safety of my dominions, and of
the people under my government. I had long since vowed such
a journey to God, but, hitherto hindered by the affairs of my kingdom, and other causes preventing, I was unable to accomplish it
sooner. I now return thanks most humbly to my Almighty God,
for suffering me, in my lifetime, to approach the holy apostles Peter
and Paul, and every shrine within and without the city of Rome,
which I could discover, and there, in person, to worship and adore
according to my desire. I have been the more diligent in the performance of this, because I have learnt from the wise, that St. Peter
the apostle has received from God the great power of binding and
loosing, and that he carries the key of the kingdom of heaven ; and,
consequently, I have judged it matter of special importance to seek
his influence with God. Be it known to you, that at the solemnity
of Easter, a great assembly of nobles was present with pope John[4]
and the emperor Conrad,[5] that is to say, all the princes of the
nations from mount Garganus[6] to the neighbouring sea. All these
received me with honour, and presented me with magnificent gifts.
But more especially was I honoured by the emperor with various
gifts and offerings, in gold and silver vessels, and palls, and very
costly garments. Moreover, I spoke with the emperor himself, and
our lord the pope and the nobles who were there, concerning the
wants of all my people, English as well as Danes ; observing that
there ought to be granted to them more equitable regulations, and
greater security on their passage to Rome ; that they should not be
impeded by so many barriers[7] on the road, nor harassed with unjust
exactions. The emperor assented to my request, as did Rodulf[8]
the king, who has the chief control over those barriers ; and all the

---

[1] If Cnut went to Rome in 1027, as the Danish chronologists affirm, he could
not at that time properly have styled himself king of Norway.

[2] Egelnoth, surnamed the Good, was consecrated archbishop of Canterbury in
the year 1020 ; he died in 1038.

[3] Elfric was made archbishop of York A.D. 1023.

[4] John XIX., sometimes called XX., succeeded his brother Benedict VIII. in
1024. The emperor Conrad II. received the imperial crown from his hands on
Easter-day 1027, at which ceremony Cnut is said to have been present, with
Rodolfe king of Burgundy, and other princes. This date does not correspond
with the statements of the English chroniclers, who place Cnut's journey to Rome
in 1031. The letter of Cnut bears no date, though he therein refers to the fact of
the emperor being present with pope John, and a great assemblage of noble
persons, at a festival on Easter-day, who honourably received him, and made him
valuable presents.

[5] Conrad II., surnamed Le Salique, was crowned emperor by pope John XIX.,
called XX., on Easter-day (26th March), 1027, in the presence of Cnut, as it is
said, and Rodolfe king of Burgundy.

[6] St. Angelo in Calabria.

[7] The several princes, through whose territories their passage lay, exacted large
sums for permission to pass, apparently, the defiles of the Alps.

[8] Rodolfe III., called Le Fainéant, succeeded his father in the kingdom of Arles
or Burgundy, A.D. 993. He is said to have been present with Cnut at the coronation of the emperor Conrad at Rome, on Easter-day 1027.

princes confirmed by an edict, that my subjects—traders as well as those who went on a religious account—should peaceably go and return from Rome, without any forced contribution to be paid to these warders of barriers, or tax-gatherers. Again I complained before the pope, and expressed my high displeasure, that my arch-bishops were oppressed by the immense sum of money which is demanded from them when they went, according to custom, to the holy residence to receive the pall : and it was determined that it should be so no longer. Moreover, all things which I requested for the advantage of my kingdom, from our lord the pope, and the emperor, and king Rodulf, and the other princes, through whose territories our road to Rome is situated, they have freely granted and confirmed by oath, under the attestation of four archbishops, twenty bishops, and an innumerable multitude of dukes and nobles who were present. Wherefore I give most hearty thanks to God Almighty, for having successfully completed all that I had wished, in the manner I had designed, and fully satisfied my intentions. Be it known, then, that since I have vowed to God himself hence-forward to reform my life in all things, and justly and piously to govern the kingdoms and the people subject to me, and to main-tain equal justice in all things ; and have determined, through God's assistance, to rectify anything hitherto unjustly done, either through the intemperance of my youth, or through negligence ; therefore I adjure and command my counsellors, to whom I have entrusted the counsels of the kingdom, that they by no means, either through fear of myself, or favour to any powerful person, suffer henceforth any injustice, or give cause for the growth of such, in all my king-dom. Moreover, I command all sheriffs and governors throughout my whole kingdom, as they regard my affection or their own safety, not to commit injustice towards any man, be he rich or poor, but to allow all, noble and ignoble, alike to enjoy impartial law, from which they are never to deviate, either on account of royal favour, or the person of any powerful man, or for the sake of amassing money for myself : for I have no need to accumulate money by unjust exaction. Be it known to you, therefore, that returning by the same way that I went, I am now going to Denmark, through the advice of all the Danes, to make peace and firm treaty with those nations, who were desirous, had it been possible for them, to deprive me both of life and of sovereignty : this, however, they were not able to perform, since God, who by his kindness preserves me in my kingdom and in my honour, and destroys the power of all my adversaries, has brought their strength to nought. More-over, when I have established peace with the surrounding nations, and put all our sovereignty here in the east in tranquil order, so that there shall be no fear of war or enmity on any side, I intend coming to England, as early in the summer as I shall be able to get my fleet prepared. I have sent this epistle before me, in order that my people might rejoice at my prosperity; because, as yourselves know, I have never spared, nor will I spare, either myself or my pains, for the needful service of my whole people. I now, therefore, adjure all my bishops and the governors of my kingdom, by the fidelity which you owe to God and to me, that you take care that before I come to England, all dues owing by ancient custom be discharged : that is to say, plough-alms,[1] the tenth of animals[2] born in the current year, and the pence owing to Rome for St. Peter, whether from cities or villages ; and in the middle of August, the tenth of the produce of the earth ; and on the festival of St. Martin, the first-fruits of seeds, to the church of the parish where each one resides, which is called in English " chirchseet."[3] If these and such•like things be not paid ere I come to England, all who shall have offended will incur the penalty of a royal mulct, to be exacted without remission according to law."

Nor was the effect wanting to this profession ; for he commanded all the laws which had been enacted by ancient kings, and chiefly by his predecessor Ethelred, to be observed for ever, under the penalty of a royal mulct ; in the observance of which the custom, even at the present day, in the time of good kings, is to swear by the name of king Edward, not that the king enacted, but that he observed them.[4]

§ 184. At that time there were in England very great and learned men, the principal of whom was Ethelnoth,[5] archbishop after Living.[6] Appointed primate from being dean, he performed many works truly worthy of record ; encouraging even the king himself in his good actions by the authority of his sanctity, and restraining him in his excesses; he first exalted the archiepiscopal cathedral by the presence of the body of St. Elfeg, and afterwards personally, at Rome, restored it to its pristine dignity.[7] Returning home, he transmitted to Coventry the arm of St. Augustine,[8] the teacher, which he had purchased at Pavia, for a hundred talents of silver and a talent of gold.[9] Moreover, Cnut took a journey to the church of Glastonbury, that he might visit the remains of his brother Edmund, as he used to call him ; and having finished his prayers, he placed over his tomb a pall, interwoven, as it appeared, with parti-coloured figures of peacocks. Near the king stood the before-named Ethelnoth, who was the seventh monk of Glastonbury who had become archbishop of Canterbury : first, Brithwald ;[10]

---

[1] Plough-alms, one penny paid to the church for every ploughland. "De qualibet caruca juncta inter Pascha et Pentecostem un‌‌m denarium, qui dicitur Ploualmes." (Ex Regist. de Ramesey, in Arch. Scac. fol. 153.)

[2] Payable at Whitsuntide.

[3] See Thorpe's Glossary appended to the Saxon Laws. v. Ciric-sceat, "an ecclesiastical due payable on the day of St. Martin, consisting chiefly of corn."

[4] Mr. Sharpe suggests that Malmesbury probably had in view the practice of the early princes of the Norman line, who swore to observe the laws of king Edward.

[5] See note at commencement of § 183.   [6] See § 176.

[7] These two transactions are inverted : Egelnoth went to Rome in 1022, and translated Alfheah's body in 1023. See Osberne, " De Translatione S. Elfegi." (Angl. Sacr.)

[8] See Baronii Annal. A.D. 725, § 7 ; and 744, § 2.

[9] Some copies omit the text as far as the end of § 18.

[10] Berhtwald was elected archbishop of Canterbury 1s‌ July, A.D. 692, and died 9th Jan. A.D. 731.

second, Adthelm,[1] formerly bishop of Wells; third, his nephew
Dunstan;[2] fourth, Ethelgar,[3] first abbot of the Newminster at
Winchester, and then bishop of Chichester; fifth, Siric,[4] who when
made archbishop gave to this his nursing mother seven palls, with
which, upon his anniversary, the whole ancient church is orna-
mented; sixth, Elfeg,[5] who from prior of Glastonbury was first
made abbot of Bath, then bishop of Winchester; seventh, Ethelnoth,[6] who upon showing to the king the immunities of his predecessors, asked, and asking obtained, that they should be confirmed
by the king's own hand to the following effect :—

§ 185. [7]"The Lord reigning for evermore, who disposes and
governs all things by his unspeakable power, wonderfully determining the changes of times and of men, and justly bringing them to
an uncertain end, according to his pleasure; and who from the
secret mysteries of nature mercifully teaches us, how kingdoms
which are lasting, instead of those which are fleeting and transitory, are to be obtained by the assistance of God; wherefore, I
Cnut, king of England, and governor and ruler of the adjacent
nations, by the counsel and decree of our archbishop Ethelnoth,
and of all the priests of God, and by the advice of our nobility, do,
for the love of heaven, and the pardon of my sins, and the remission of the transgressions of my brother,[8] king Edmund, grant to
the church of the holy mother of God, the ever-Virgin Mary, at
Glastonbury, its rights and customs throughout my kingdom, and
all forfeitures throughout its possessions, and that its lands shall be
free from all claim and vexation as my own are possessed by myself.   Moreover, I inhibit more especially, by the authority of the
Almighty, Father, Son, and Holy Spirit, and the curse of the ever-
Virgin, and so command it to be observed by the judges and
primates of my kingdom, as they value their own safety, every
person, be they of whatever order or dignity they may, from
entering on any account that island; but that all causes, ecclesiastical as well as secular, shall await the sole judgment of the
abbot and convent, in like manner as my predecessors have ratified
and confirmed by charters; that is to say, Chentwine, Ine, Cuthred,
Elfred, Edward,[9] Athelstan, the most glorious Edmund, and the
incomparable Edgar.   And should any one hereafter endeavour, on

---

[1] Athelmus was the first bishop of Wells, and was translated from that see to
Canterbury in the year 911.   The fact of his having been a monk of Glastonbury
is, however, disputed.   See Wharton's note in the Anglia Sacra, i. 556.

[2] See § 149.

[3] Ethelgar was originally a monk of Glastonbury, and was made the first abbot
of the new monastery founded at Winchester, after the secular canons were expelled.   He was consecrated bishop of Selsey in the year 980, translated to Canterbury in 988, and died 3d of Dec. 989.

[4] Siric, from a monk of Glastonbury, was made bishop of Wilton in the year
986; translated to Canterbury A.D. 1000; and died in 1005.

[5] From prior of Glastonbury, he became abbot of Bath; and afterwards, in the
year 984, bishop of Winchester.   He was translated to Canterbury in 1005, and
was slain by the Danes in 1012.

[6] See note, § 183, ad init.

[7] This charter occurs in Malmes. Antiq. Glast. Eccl., and is printed in Gale, iii.
323; and in the Cod. Dipl. No. 747 (iv. 40).   [8] See § 184.

[9] Saville's text inserts the name of Ethelred after that of Edward.

any occasion, to break in upon or make void the enactment of this grant, let him be driven from the communion of the righteous by the winnowing-fan of the last judgment; but should any person endeavour diligently, with kind intention, to perform these things, to approve, and to defend them, may God increase his portion in the land of the living, through the intercession of the most holy mother of God, and the rest of the saints. The grant of this immunity was written and published in the wooden church, in the presence of king Cnut, in the year of our Lord one thousand and thirty-two, of the indiction the second."[1]

§ 186. By the advice of the said archbishop, also, the king sending money to foreign churches, very much enriched Chartres, where at that time flourished bishop Fulbert,[2] most renowned for sanctity and learning; who, among other proofs of his diligence, very magnificently completed the church of our lady St. Mary, the foundations of which he laid, and which moreover, doing every thing he could for its honour, he rendered celebrated by many musical modulations. The man who has heard his chants, breathing only celestial vows, is best able to conceive the love he manifested in honour of the Virgin. Among his other works, a volume of epistles is extant, in one of which[3] he thanks that most magnificent king, Cnut, for pouring out the bowels of his generosity in donations to the church of Chartres.

§ 187. In the fifteenth year of Cnut's reign, Robert king of France, of whom we have before briefly spoken,[4] departed this life; a man so much given to alms, that when, on festival days, he was either dressing or putting off the royal robes, if he had nothing else at hand, he would give even these to the poor, did not his attendants purposely drive away the needy who were importuning him. He had two sons, Odo and Henry; the elder, Odo,[5] was dull; the other crafty and impetuous. The parents were divided in their affections for their children. The father loved the first-born, often saying that he should succeed him; the mother regarded the younger, to whom the sovereignty was justly due, if not for his age, yet certainly for his ability. It happened, as women are persevering in their designs, that she did not cease until, by means of presents and large promises, she had gained over to her side all the chief nobility who are subject to the power of France. In consequence, Henry, chiefly through the assistance of Robert the Norman, was crowned ere his father had well breathed his last. Mindful of this kindness, when, as I before related,[6] Robert went to Jerusalem,

---

[1] D. reads, first.

[2] Fulbert bishop of Chartres, (A.D. 1007—1029,) was a disciple of Gerbert, afterwards Silvester II. See Gall. Christ. viii. col. 1113. His works, consisting of epistles, sermons, canons, hymns, and other metrical pieces, were first printed in 1608, under the care of Charles de Villiers. (Op. Var. 8vo. Paris, 1608.) See Cave, Hist. Lit. ii. 125. He died about the year 1029. Gall. Christ. viii. col. 1116.

[3] See the letter of Fulbert to king Cnut, (an. 1020 or 1021,) No. xliv. p. 466, tom. x. Rec. des Hist. de la France. Fulberti Carnot Episc. Op. Var. 8vo. Par. 1608, Epist. xcvii. p. 92.   [4] See antea, § 168.

[5] Malmesbury, in common with the Chronicle of St. Martin de Tours, (apud Chesn. tom. iii. Script. Hist. Franc. p. 360,) and some other French chroniclers, is here betrayed into error respecting the sons of Robert king of France.

[6] See §§ 178 and 180.

Henry most strenuously espoused the cause of William his son,
then a youth, against those who attempted to throw off his yoke.
In the meantime Cnut finishing his earthly career, died at Shaftesbury, and was buried at Winchester.[1]

Of Harold, the Son of Cnut.

§ 188. In the year of our Lord's incarnation one thousand and
thirty-six,[2] Harold, whom fame[3] reported to be the son of Cnut,
by the daughter of earl Elfelm, succeeded, and reigned four years
and as many months. He was elected by the Danes and the
citizens of London, who, from long intercourse with these barbarians, had almost entirely adopted their customs. The English
resisted for a long time, rather wishing to have for their king
one of the sons of Ethelred, who were then in Normandy, or
else Hardecnut, the son of Cnut by Emma, at that time in Denmark. The greatest champion for justice, at this juncture, was
earl Godwin, who professing himself the defender of the fatherless,
and having queen Emma and the royal treasures in his custody, for
some time restrained his opponents by the power of his name ; but
at last, overcome by numbers and by violence, he was obliged to
yield. Harold, secure in his sovereignty, drove his mother-in-law
into exile.[4] Not thinking she would be safe in Normandy, (where,
her brother and nephews being dead, hostility was evinced against
a deserted orphan,) she passed over into Flanders to earl Baldwin,[5]
a man of tried integrity; who afterwards, (when king Henry died,[6]
leaving a young son, Philip,[7]) for some years nobly governed the
kingdom of France, and faithfully restored it to him when he came
of age, for he had married his aunt. Emma passed three years
securely under the protection of this man; at the expiration of
which time, Harold dying at Oxford, in the month[8] of April, was
buried at Westminster. The Danes and English then uniting in one
common sentiment as to the expediency of sending for Hardecnut, he
came by way of Normandy into England in the month of August;[9]
for Ethelred's sons were held in contempt by nearly all, more from the

---

[1] Cnut died on the 11th November, in the year 1035. (Sax. Chron. and Flor.
of Worcester.)

[2] After the death of Cnut the kingdom was at first divided : the northern part
fell to the share of Harold, and Hardacnut obtained the southern division. In the
year 1037 Harold was chosen to reign over all England. (Flor.)

[3] "Some men said of Harold, that he was the son of Cnut and Elfgife the
daughter of Elfelm, ealdorman; but it was thought very incredible by many men."
(Sax. Chron.) Florence states that Elgife, not being able to bear the king a son,
passed upon him the child of a cobbler.

[4] Emma was exiled in the year 1037.

[5] Baldwin, surnamed De l'Isle, earl of Flanders, succeeded his father Baldwin
IV. A.D. 1036, or as some affirm, A.D. 1035. Emma was honourably received by
the earl and his wife Adela, daughter of Robert king of France. (See Encomium
Emmæ.)

[6] King Henry died in 1060, leaving Philippe his successor, then only seven
years old.

[7] Philippe died in 1108.

[8] According to the Saxon Chronicle, Harold died on the 17th of March (xvi. kl.
Apr.) 1039.

[9] The Saxon Chronicle makes Hardacnut arrive at Sandwich on the 17th of
June.

recollection of their father's indolence than the power of the Danes. Hardecnut reigning two years except ten days, lost his life[1] amid his cups at Lambeth, nigh London, and was buried near his father at Winchester. He was a young man who evinced great affection towards his brother and sister; for his brother, Edward, wearied with continual wandering, revisiting his native land in the hope of fraternal kindness, was received by him (they say) with open arms, and entertained most affectionately. Rash, however, in other respects, at the instigation of Alfric, bishop of York, and of others whom I am loth to name, he ordered the dead body of Harold to be dug up, the head to be cut off, and thrown into the Thames, a pitiable spectacle to men! but being dragged up in a fisherman's net, it was buried in the cemetery of the Danes at London.[2] He imposed a rigid and intolerable tribute upon England, in order that he might pay, according to his promise, twenty[3] marks to the soldiers of each of his vessels. While this was harshly levied throughout the kingdom, two of the collectors, discharging their office rather too rigorously, were killed by the citizens of Worcester; upon which, burning and depopulating the city by means of his commanders, and plundering the property of the citizens, he sullied his fame and diminished the love of his subjects. But here I will not pass over in silence what tattlers report of Elfred the firstborn of Ethelred. Doubtful what to do between Harold's[4] death and the arrival of Hardecnut, he came into the kingdom, and was deprived of his eyes by the treachery of his countrymen, and chiefly of Godwin, at Gillingeham; from thence being sent to the monastery of Ely, he supported, for a little time, a wretched existence upon homely food; nine-tenths of his companions being beheaded, for by lot every tenth man was saved. I have mentioned these circumstances because such is the report; but as the Chronicles[5] are silent, I do not assert them for fact. For this reason, Hardecnut, enraged against Living, bishop of Credition, whom public opinion pointed at as author of the transaction, expelled him from his see; but, soothed with a bribe, he restored him within the year. Looking angrily too upon Godwin, he obliged him to clear himself by oath. He, to recover his favour entirely, added to his plighted oath a present of the most rich and beautiful kind. It was a ship beaked with gold, having eighty soldiers on board, who had two bracelets on either arm, each weighing sixteen ounces of gold; on their heads were gilt helmets; on their left shoulder they carried a Danish axe, with an iron spear in their right hand; and, not to enumerate every thing, they were equipped with such

---

[1] Hardacnut died on the 8th of June, A.D. 1042.   [2] St. Clement Danes.

[3] In the year 1040 a tribute for sixty-two ships, at the rate of eight marks for each steersman, was imposed. (Sax. Chron.; see also the statement of Florence of Worcester.) And in the following year a tribute was paid to the army of 21,099*l.*; and afterwards 11,048*l.* to thirty-two ships. (Sax. Chron.)

[4] According to Florence, Alfred died A.D. 1036, consequently prior to the death of Harold. We should probably read Cnutonis for Haroldi.

[5] The earlier editions of the printed Saxon Chronicle have no mention of this transaction, but there are two manuscripts which relate it. The story appears true in the main, but it is told with so much variety of time, place, &c., that it is difficult to ascertain its real circumstances.

arms, as that splendour vying with terror, might conceal the steel beneath the gold. But farther, as I had begun to relate, his sister Gunhilda, the daughter of Cnut by Emma, a young woman of exquisite beauty, who was sought but not obtained by many lovers in her father's time, was by Hardecnut given in marriage to Henry,[1] emperor of the Germans. The splendour of the nuptial pageant was very striking, and is even in our times frequently sung in ballads about the streets; where while this renowned lady was being conducted to the ship, all the nobility of England were crowding around, and contributing to her charges whatever was contained in the general purse or royal treasury. Proceeding in this manner to her husband, she cherished for a long time the conjugal tie; at length being accused of adultery, she opposed in single combat to her accuser, who was a man of gigantic size,[2] a young lad who took care of her starling,[3] whom she had brought from England, while her other attendants held back in cowardly apprehension. When, therefore, they engaged, the impeacher, through the miraculous interposition of God, was defeated by being hamstrung. Gunhilda, exulting at her unexpected success, renounced the marriage contract with her husband; nor could she be induced either by threats or by endearments again to share his bed, but taking the veil of a nun, she calmly grew old in the service of God.

Concerning the Emperor Henry.

§ 189. This emperor possessed many and great virtues; and nearly surpassed in military skill all his predecessors; so much so that he subdued the Vindelici and the Leutici,[4] and the other nations bordering on the Suevi, who alone, even to the present day, crave after Pagan superstitions. For the Saracens and Turks worship God the Creator, looking upon Mahomet not as God, but as his prophet; but the Vindelici worship Fortune, and putting her idol in the most eminent situation, they place a horn in her right hand, filled with that beverage made of honey and water, which by a Greek term we call hydromel. St. Jerome proves, in his eighteenth book on Isaiah, that the Egyptians and almost all the eastern nations do the same. Wherefore, on the last day of November, sitting round in a circle, they taste it in common; and if they find the horn full, they applaud with loud clamours, because in the ensuing year, Plenty with her brimming horn will fulfil their wishes in every thing; but if it be otherwise, they lament. Henry made these nations in such wise tributary to him, that upon every solemnity on which he wore his crown, four of their kings were obliged to carry a cauldron in which flesh was boiled, upon their shoulders, to the kitchen, by means of bars passed through four rings.

---

[1] Henry III., son of Conrad II.
[2] His name was Rodingar, and the youth opposed to him is said to have been a dwarf named Mimicon.
[3] Saville's text here reads, "a young lad of her brother's establishment."
[4] These people inhabited the country on and near the southern coast of the Baltic.

*Concerning the Emperor's Sister, and a certain Priest who was her
Lover.*

§ 190. Frequently, when disengaged from the turmoils of his
empire, Henry gave himself up to good fellowship and merriment,
and was replete with humour; which may be sufficiently proved by
two instances. He was so extremely fond of his sister, who was a
nun, that he never suffered her to be from his side, and her
chamber was always next to his own. As he was on a certain time
(in consequence of a winter remarkable for severe frost and snow)
detained for a long while in the same place, a certain clerk [1] about
the court became too familiar with the girl, and often passed the
greatest part of the night in her chamber ; and although he
attempted to conceal his crime by numberless subterfuges, yet some
one perceived it, (for it is difficult not to betray guilt either by look
or action,) and the affair becoming notorious, the emperor was the
only person who remained in ignorance, and who still believed his
sister to be chaste. On one particular night, however, as they were
enjoying their fond embraces, and continuing their pleasures longer
than usual, the morning dawned upon them, and behold snow had
completely covered the ground ; and then the clerk fearing that
he should be discovered by his track in the snow, persuaded his
mistress to extricate him from his difficulty by carrying him on her
back. She, regardless of modesty so that she might escape shame,
took her paramour on her back, and carried him out of the palace.
It happened at that moment that the emperor had risen for a
necessary purpose, and looking through the window of his chamber,
beheld the clerk mounted : he was stupified at the first sight, but
observing still more narrowly, he became mute with shame and
indignation. While he was hesitating whether he should pass over
the crime unpunished, or openly reprehend the delinquents, there
happened an opportunity for him to give a vacant bishopric to the
clerk, which he did : but at the same time whispered in his ear,
" Take the bishopric, but be careful you do not let women carry
you any more." At the same time giving his sister the rule over a
company of nuns, " Be an abbess," said he, " but carry clerks no
longer." Both confused, and feeling themselves grievously stricken
by so grave an injunction, desisted from a crime which they thought
revealed by God.

Of the Clerk who would not read the Gospel for the Emperor.

§ 191. He had also a clergyman about his palace, who abused
the depth of his learning and the melody of his voice by the vicious
propensities of the flesh, by being extremely attached to a girl of bad
character in the town ; with whom having passed one festival night,
he stood next morning before the emperor at mass, with counte-

---

[1] Clerk was a general term, including every degree of orders, from the bishop
downwards to the chanter. A story nearly similar has been told of the celebrated Eginhard and the daughter of Charlemagne.

nance unabashed. The emperor concealing his knowledge of the transaction, commanded him to prepare himself to read the gospel, that he might be gratified with the melody of his voice ; for he was a deacon. Conscious of his crime, he made use of a multitude of subterfuges, while the emperor, to try his constancy, still pressed him with messages. Refusing, however, to the very last, the emperor said, " Since you will not obey me in so easy a command, I banish you from the whole of my territories." The deacon yielding to the sentence, departed directly. Servants were sent to follow him, and in case he should persist in going, to bring him back after he had left the city. Gathering, therefore, immediately all his effects together, and packing them up, he had already gone a considerable distance, when he was brought back, not without extreme violence, and placed in Henry's presence. Pleasantly smiling, " You have done well," said he, " and I applaud your integrity for valuing the fear of God more than your country, and regarding the displeasure of Heaven more than my threats : accept, therefore, the first bishopric which shall be vacant in my empire ; only renounce your dishonourable amour."

§ 192. As nothing, however, is lasting in human enjoyments, I shall not pass over in silence a certain dreadful portent which happened in his time. The monastery of Fulda, in Saxony, is celebrated for containing the body of St. Gall,[1] and is enriched with very ample territories. The abbot of this place furnishes the emperor with sixty thousand warriors against his enemies, and possesses from ancient times the privilege of sitting at his right hand on the most distinguished festivals. This Henry of whom we are speaking was celebrating Pentecost at Mentz. A little before mass, while the seats were being prepared in the church, a quarrel arose between the attendants of the abbot and those of the archbishop, which of their masters should sit next the sovereign ; one party alleging the dignity of the prelate, the other ancient usage. When words made but little for peace, (as the Germans and Teutonians possess untractable spirits,) they came to blows. Some snatched up staves, others threw stones, while the rest unsheathed their swords : finally each used the weapon that his anger first supplied. Thus furiously contending in the church, the pavement soon streamed with blood : but the bishops hastening forward, peace was restored amid the remains of the contending parties ; the church was cleansed, and mass performed with joyful sound. But now to the wonder ; when the sequence was chanted, and the choir paused at that verse, " Thou hast made this day glorious," a voice in the air far resounded, " I have made this day contentious." All the others were motionless with horror, but the emperor the more diligently attended to his occupation, and perceiving the satisfaction of the enemy—" You," said he, " the inventor and also the instigator of all wickedness, you have made this day contentious and sorrowful to the proud ; but we by the grace of God, who made it glorious, will

[1] St. Gall was born in Ireland about A. D. 564 ; he passed through England into France A. D. 589, and his death happened probably in the year 646. His name occurs in the calendar upon 16th of October.

make it gracious to the poor." And now, the sequence beginning afresh, he implored the grace of the Holy Spirit by solemn lamentation : and you might suppose that He had vouchsafed his presence, some singing, others weeping, and all beating their breasts. When mass was over, assembling the poor by means of his officers, he gave them the whole of the entertainment which had been prepared for himself and his courtiers ; the emperor placing the dishes before them, standing at a distance according to the custom of servants, and clearing away the fragments.

§ 193. In the time of his father Conrad, he had received a silver pipe, such as boys in sport spirt water with, from a certain clerk, covenanting to give him a bishopric, when he should become emperor. This, when he was of man's estate, on his application he readily gave to him. Soon after he was confined to his bed with severe sickness : his malady increasing, he lay for three days insensible and speechless, while the breath of life only palpitated in his breast ; nor was there any other sign of life than the perception of a small degree of breathing, on applying the hand to his nostrils. The bishops being present, enjoined a fast for three days, and entreated Heaven, with tears and vows, for the life of the king. Recovering by these remedies, as it is right to think, he sent for the bishop whom he had so improperly appointed, and deposed him by the judgment of a council ; confessing that throughout those three days, he saw malignant demons blowing fire upon him through a pipe—fire so furious that ours in comparison would be deemed a jest, and to have no heat ; that afterwards there came a young man half-scorched, bearing a golden cup of immense size, full of water ; and that being soothed by the sight of him, and bathed by the water, the flame was extinguished, and he recovered his health ; that this young man was St. Laurence, the roof of whose church he had restored when it had gone to decay ; and, among other presents, had honoured it with a golden chalice.

§ 194. Here many extraordinary things occur, which are reported of this man ; for instance, of a stag which took him on its back, when flying from his enemies, and carried him over an unfordable river ; and some others which I pass by, because I am unwilling to go beyond the reader's belief. He died when he had completed the eighteenth year of his empire,[1] and was buried at Spires, which he rebuilt and called by that name, on the site of the very ancient and ruinated Nemetum. His epitaph is as follows :—

> " Cæsar, as was the world once great,
>   Lies here, confin'd in compass straight ;
>   Hence let each mortal learn his doom—
>   No glory can escape the tomb.
>   The flower of empire, once so gay,
>   Falls with its Cæsar to decay,
>   And all the odours which it gave
>   Sink prematurely to the grave.

---

[1] Henry died at Bodfeld, on the confines of Saxony and Thuringia, in the seventeenth year of his reign, but in the fifteenth of his empire, on the 5th of October, A. D. 1056, and was interred at Spires.

The laws which sapient fathers made,
A listless race had dared evade,
But thou, reforming by the school
Of Rome, gave back the ancient rule.
Nations and regions, wide and far,
Whom none could subjugate by war,
Quell'd by thy sword's resistless strife,
Turn'd to the arts of civil life.
What grief severe must Rome engross,
Widow'd at first by Leo's loss,
And next by Cæsar's mournful night,
Reft of her other shining light.
Living, what region did not dread,
What country not lament thee, dead?
So kind to nations once subdued,
So fierce to the barbarians rude,
That those who feared not, must bewail,
And such as grieved not, fears assail.
Rome, thy departed glory moan,
And weep thy luminaries gone."

§ 195. This Leo,[1] of whom the epitaph speaks, had been Roman
pontiff, called to that eminence from being Bruno, bishop of Spires.[2]
He was a man of great and admirable sanctity; and the Romans
celebrate many of his miracles. He died before the emperor
Henry, after a pontificate of five years.

Of St. Edward the Third, King and Confessor.

§ 196. In the year of our Lord's incarnation one thousand and
forty-two, Edward the son of Ethelred assumed the sovereignty,[3]
and held it not quite twenty-four years—a man, from the simplicity
of his manners, little calculated to govern, but devoted to God, and
in consequence directed by Him; for while he continued to reign,
there arose no popular commotions which were not immediately
quelled. There was no foreign war; all was calm and peaceable, both
at home and abroad, which is the more an object of wonder,
because he conducted himself so mildly, that he would not even
utter a word of reproach against the meanest person; for when
upon one occasion he had gone out to hunt, and a countryman had
overturned the stakes by which the deer are driven into the toils,
struck with noble indignation, he exclaimed, " By God and his
mother, I will serve you just such another turn, if ever it come in
my way!" Here was a noble mind, who could forget that he was
a king, under such circumstances, and could not think himself
justified in injuring a man, even of the lowest condition. In the
meantime, the regard which his subjects entertained for him was
extreme, as was also the fear of foreigners; for God assisted his
simplicity, that he might be feared who knew not how to be angry.
But however indolent or unassuming he himself might be esteemed,
he had nobles capable of elevating him to the highest pitch: for

---

[1] Pope Leo IX. was consecrated at Rome on the 12th of February, 1049; and
died on the 19th of April 1054. See Jaffé, p. 379.

[2] The more correct reading would seem to be " Tullensi episcopo.".

[3] Hardacnut died in 1042, and Edward was elected king in the summer of
that year; but he was not crowned until Easter-day [April 3d] in the following
year.

instance, Siward [1] earl of the Northumbrians, who at his command, engaging with Macbeth, the Scottish king, deprived him both of his life and of his kingdom, and placed on the throne Malcolm, [2] who was the son of the king of Cumbria. Again, Leofric of Hereford ; he, with liberal regard, defended him against the enmity of Godwin, [3] who, trusting to the consciousness of his own merits, paid little reverence to the king. Leofric and his wife Godiva, munificent in matters of religion, built many monasteries, as Coventry, St. Mary's Stow, Wenelok, Leon, and some others ; to the rest he gave ornaments and estates ; to Coventry he consigned his body, with a very large donation of gold and silver. Harold, [4] too, of the West Saxons, the son of Godwin, who by his abilities slew two brothers, kings of the Welsh, Ris and Griffin, and reduced all that barbarous country to the state of a province under fealty to the king. Nevertheless, there were some things which obscured the glory of Edward's times : the monasteries were deprived of their monks ; unjust sentences were passed by depraved men ; his mother's property, at his command, was almost entirely taken from her. But the injustice of these transactions was extenuated by his favourers in the following manner : the ruin of the monasteries, and the iniquity of the judges, are said to have taken place without his knowledge, through the insolence of Godwin and his sons, who used to laugh at the easiness of the king ; but afterwards, on being apprised of this, he severely avenged it by their banishment. [5] His mother "had for a long time mocked at the needy state of her son," nor had she ever assisted him, transferring the hereditary hatred of the father to the child ; for she had both loved Cnut more when living, and more commended him when dead ; besides, accumulating money by every method, she had hoarded it, regardless of the poor, to whom she would give nothing, for fear of diminishing her heap. Wherefore, that which had been so unjustly gathered together, was not improperly taken away, that it might be of service to the poor, and replenish the king's exchequer. Though much credit is to be attached to those who relate these circumstances, yet I find her to have been a religiously disposed woman, and to have expended her property on ornaments for the church of Winchester, and probably upon others. [6]

But to return : Edward receiving the mournful intelligence of the death of Hardecnut, was lost in uncertainty what to do, or whither to betake himself. While he was revolving many things in his mind, it occurred as the better plan to submit his situation to the opinion of Godwin. To Godwin, therefore, he sent messengers, requesting that he might in security have a conference with him. Godwin, though for a long time hesitating and reflecting, at length assented ; and when Edward came to him, and endeavoured to fall at his feet, he raised him up ; and when relating the death of

---

[1] See the Saxon Chronicle.

[2] Malcolm III. See the Saxon Chronicle, A.D. 1067.

[3] For an account of Godwin's rebellion, &c., see the Saxon Chronicle, A.D. 1051, 1052.   [4] Afterwards king of England.

[5] Earl Godwin and his sons were exiled in the year 1051.

[6] See § 181.

Hardecnut, and begging his assistance to effect his return to Normandy, Godwin made him the greatest promises. He said it was better for him to live with credit in power, than to die ingloriously in exile; that he was the son of Ethelred, and the grandson of Edgar; that the kingdom was his by right; that he was come to mature age, disciplined by difficulties, conversant in the art of well-governing from his years, and knowing from his former poverty how to feel for the miseries of the people; that if he thought fit to rely on him, there could be no obstacle, for his authority so preponderated in England, that wherever he inclined, there fortune was sure to favour; if he assisted him, none would dare to murmur; and just so was the contrary side of the question. Let him, then, only promise a firm friendship with himself, undiminished honours for his sons, and a marriage with his daughter; and he who was now shipwrecked almost of life and hope, and imploring the assistance of another, should shortly see himself a king.

§ 197. There was nothing which Edward would not promise, from the exigency of the time; so, fidelity being pledged on both sides, he confirmed by oath everything which was demanded. Soon after, convening an assembly at Gillingham,[1] Godwin having unfolded his reasons, caused him to be received as king, while homage was paid by all. He was a man of ready wit, and spoke fluently in the vernacular tongue; powerful in speech, powerful in bringing over the people to whatever he desired. Some yielded to his authority; some were influenced by presents; others admitted the right of Edward; and the few who resisted in defiance of justice and equity, were carefully marked, and afterwards driven out of England. Edward was crowned with great pomp at Winchester,[2] on Easter-day, and was instructed by Edsi,[3] the archbishop, in the established rules of government: these, at the time, he treasured up with readiness in his memory, and afterwards displayed in the holiness of his conduct. The above-mentioned Edsi, in the following year, falling into an incurable disease, appointed as his successor Siward, abbot of Abingdon; communicating his design only to the king and the earl, lest any improper person should aspire to so great an eminence, either by solicitation or by purchase.[4] Shortly after, the king took Edgitha, the daughter of Godwin, to wife;[5] a woman whose bosom was the school of every liberal art, though little skilled in earthly matters: on seeing her, if you were amazed at her erudition,[6] you must admire also the purity of her mind, and the beauty of her person. Both in her husband's lifetime, and afterwards, she was not entirely free from suspicion of dishonour; but when dying,[7] in the time of king William, she voluntarily satisfied

---

[1] This is the reading of all the MSS. except one, C., which states that the meeting was held at London.   [2] MS. C. here reads London.
[3] Eadsige was translated from Winchester to Canterbury in 1038.
[4] See the Saxon Chronicle and Florence.   [5] On the 23d of January, 1045.
[6] Ingulphus, alluding to Edgithe, writes in terms of the highest commendation. The passage, although of doubtful character, is worth examination, and may be seen in the present series, ii. 655.
[7] Edgithe died at Winchester seven days before Christmas (Dec. 19), in the year 1075, and was buried with great pomp in the same grave as her husband, at Westminster, by command of William the Conqueror.

the bystanders as to her unimpaired chastity by an oath. When
she became his wife, the king so artfully managed, that he neither
removed her from his bed, nor knew her after the manner of men.
I have not been able to discover whether he acted thus from dislike
to her family, which he prudently dissembled from the exigency of
the times, or out of pure regard to chastity; yet it is most notoriously
affirmed, that he never violated his purity by connexion with any
woman.   But since I have gotten thus far, I wish to admonish my
reader, that the track of my history is here but dubious, because the
truth of the facts hangs in suspense.   It is to be observed, that the
king had sent for several Normans, who had formerly slightly
ministered to his wants when in exile : one of these was Robert,
whom from being a monk of Jumieges, he had appointed bishop of
London, and afterwards archbishop of Canterbury.[1]   The English
of our times vilify this person, together with the rest, as being the
impeacher of Godwin and his sons, as the sower of discord, as the
purchaser of the archbishopric ; they say, too, that Godwin and his
sons were men of liberal mind, the steadfast promoters and defenders
of the government of Edward, and that it was not to be wondered
at if they were indignant when they saw men of yesterday, and
strangers, preferred to themselves ; still, that they never uttered
even a harsh word against the king whom they had formerly exalted
to the throne.   On the opposite hand, the Normans thus defend
themselves : they allege that both Godwin and his sons acted with
the greatest want of respect, as well as fidelity, to the king and his
party, aiming at equal sovereignty with him, often ridiculing his
simplicity, often hurling the shafts of their wit against him ; that
the Normans could not endure this, but endeavoured to weaken
their power as much as possible.   They say, too, that God manifested
at last with what kind of purity Godwin had served him ; for, after
his piratical ravages, of which we shall speak hereafter, when he
had been reinstated in his original favour, and was sitting with
the king at table, the conversation turning on Elfred,[2] the king's
brother, " I perceive," said he, " O king, that on every recollection of your brother, you regard me with angry countenance ; but
God forbid that I should swallow this morsel, if I have done anything which might tend either to his danger or your disadvantage."
On saying this, he was choked with the piece he had put into his
mouth, and closed his eyes in death ;[3] and being dragged from
under the table by Harold his son, who stood near the king, he
was buried in the cathedral of Winchester.

§ 198. On account of these discrepancies, as I have observed,
my narrative labours under difficulties, for I cannot precisely
ascertain the truth, by reason either of the natural dislike of these
nations towards each other, or because the English disdainfully bear
with a superior, and the Normans cannot endure an equal. In the

---

[1] Robert was made archbishop of Canterbury in the year 1051, and expelled in
the following year.   [2] See § 188.
[3] The Saxon Chronicle gives a somewhat different account of the circumstances
connected with the death of earl Godwin. See also Florence of Worcester, A.D.
1053.

following Book, however, when the opportunity occurs for relating the arrival of the Normans in England, I shall proceed to speak of their habits : at present I shall relate as accurately as I can [1] the grudge of the king against Godwin and his sons.

§ 199. Eustace earl of Boulogne, the father of Godfrey and Baldwin, who in our times were kings of Jerusalem,[2] had married the king's sister Goda, who had borne a son, named Ralph,[3] to her former husband, Walter of Mantes. This son, at that time earl of Hereford, was both indolent and cowardly ; he had given way in battle to the Welsh, and left his country and the city, together with the bishop, to be consumed with fire by the enemy, the disgrace of which transaction was wiped off by the valour of Harold, who arrived opportunely. Eustace, therefore, crossing the channel from Whitsand to Dover, went to king Edward on some unknown business. When the conference was over, and he had obtained his request, he was returning through Dover, where one of his avant-couriers dealing too fiercely with a citizen, and demanding quarters with blows rather than by entreaty or remuneration, irritated him to such a degree that he put him to death. Eustace, on being informed of the fact, proceeded with all his retinue to revenge the murder of his servant, and kill the perpetrator of the crime, together with eighteen others ; but the citizens flying to arms, he lost twenty of his people, and had multitudes wounded, himself and one more with difficulty making their escape during the confusion. Thence returning to court and procuring a secret audience, he made the most of his own story, and excited the anger of the king against the English. Godwin being summoned by messengers, arrived at the palace. When the business was related, and the king was expatiating on the insolence of the citizens of Canterbury, the better informed discretion of this man perceived that sentence ought not to be pronounced, since the allegations had been heard on one side of the question only. In consequence, though the king ordered him directly to proceed with an army into Kent, to take signal vengeance on the people of Canterbury, still he refused, both because he saw with displeasure that all foreigners were gaining fast upon the favour of the king, and because he was desirous of evincing his regard towards his own countrymen. Besides, his opinion was more accordant with equity, as it should seem, which was that the principal people of that town should be mildly summoned to the king's court, on account of the tumult. If they could exculpate themselves, they should depart unhurt ; but if they could not, they must make atonement, either by money or by corporal punishment, to the king, whose peace they had broken, and to the earl whom they

[1] See the Saxon Chronicle, an. 1052 (1050-1).
[2] Eustace II. surnamed Aux Grenons. He succeeded his father, Eustace I., in 1049; and married, in 1150, Goda, daughter of king Athelbert, and widow of Gautier comte de Mantes, by whom he had no issue : but by his wife Ida he left three sons; Eustace, who succeeded him; Godefroi, created in 1076 marquis d'Anvers after the emperor Henry IV. and afterwards duc de Bouillon, was elected king of Jerusalem in 1099 (23d of July), and dying 18th of July, 1100, was succeeded by his brother Baudouin, comte d'Edesse.
[3] See Florence of Worcester, A. D. 1051.—Ralph earl of Hereford died 21st of Dec. 1057. See Dugd. Baronage, i. 21.

had injured : moreover, that it appeared unjust to pass sentence on those people unheard, who had a more especial right to protection. After this the conference broke up ; Godwin paying little attention to the indignation of the king, as merely momentary.　In consequence of this, the nobility of the whole kingdom were commanded to meet at Gloucester, that the business might there be discussed in full assembly. Thither came those, at that time, most renowned Northumbrian earls, Syward and Leofric, and all the nobility of England.　Godwin and his sons alone, who knew that they were suspected, not deeming it prudent to be present unarmed, halted with a strong force at Beverstane, giving out that he had assembled an army to restrain the Welsh, who, meditating a revolt from the king, had fortified a town in the county of Hereford, where Swane, one of the sons of Godwin, was at that time in command.　The Welsh, however, who had come beforehand to the conference, had accused them of a conspiracy, and rendered them odious to the whole court, so that a rumour prevailed that the king's army would attack them in that very place.　On hearing this, Godwin sounded the alarm to his party ; he told them that they should not purposely withstand their sovereign lord, but if it came to hostilities, they should not retreat without avenging themselves ; and, had not better counsels intervened, a dreadful scene of misery, and a worse than civil war, would have ensued.　Some small share of amity between them, however, being restored, it was ordered that the council should be again assembled at London, and that Swane the son of Godwin should appease the king's anger by withdrawing himself ; that Godwin and Harold should come as speedily as possible to the council, with this condition, that they should be unarmed, bringing with them only twelve men, and should deliver up to the king the command of the troops which they had throughout England.　This on the other hand they refused ; observing that they could not go to a meeting of people banded against them, without sureties and pledges; that they would obey their lord in the surrender of the soldiers, as well as in everything else, except the risk of life and of reputation : should they come unarmed, their lives might be in danger ; if attended with few followers, it would detract from their glory.　The king had made up his mind too firmly to listen to the entreaties of those who interceded with him; wherefore an edict was published, that they should depart from England within five days.　Godwin and Swane retired to Flanders, and Harold to Ireland.　His earldom was given to Elgar, the son of Leofric, a man of active habits, who governed what he had received with ability, and readily restored it to Harold on his return.　Afterwards, on the death of Godwin, when Harold had obtained the dukedom of his father, he boldly reclaimed it, though by the accusation of his enemies he was banished [1] for a time.　All the property of the queen to the last penny was seized, and she her-

---

[1] Elfgar was outlawed in 1055, and, joining Griffin prince of Wales, invaded England, and his outlawry was reversed.　Upon the death of his father, earl Leofric, on the 30th of Sept. 1057, he succeeded to the earldom of Mercia; and in the following year, 1058, he was banished, but shortly afterwards returned, through the aid of Griffin, king of North Wales.

self was delivered into the custody of the king's sister at Warewell,
lest she alone should be void of care, whilst all her relations were
sighing for their country.

The following year the exiles, each emerging from his station,
were now cruising off the British Sea, infesting the coast with
piracy, and carrying away rich booty from the substance of their
countrymen.   Against these, on the king's part, more than sixty
sail lay at anchor: earls Odo and Ralph, relations of the king, were
commanders of the fleet.   Nor did this emergency find Edward
himself inactive; since he would pass the night on ship-board, and
watch the sallies of the plunderers, diligently compensating, by the
wisdom of his counsel, for that personal service which age and
infirmity denied.   But when they had approached each other, and
the conflict was on the eve of commencing, a very thick mist
arising, in a moment obscured the sight of the opponents, and
repressed the pitiable audacity of men.   At last Godwin and his
companions were driven, by the impetuosity of the wind, to the
port which they had left; and not long after, returning to their own
country with pacific dispositions, they found the king at London,
and were received by him on soliciting pardon.   The old man,
skilled in leading the minds of his audience by his eloquence,
dexterously exculpated himself from everything laid to his charge;
and in a short time prevailed so far as to recover undiminished
the honours of himself and of his children; to drive all the Normans, branded with ignominy, from England; and to get sentence
passed on Robert the archbishop, and his accomplices, for disturbing the order of the kingdom, and stimulating the royal mind against
his subjects.   But he, not waiting for violent measures, had fled of
his own accord while the treaties for peace were in agitation, and
proceeding to Rome, and appealing to the apostolical see on his
case, as he was returning through Jumieges, he there died, and was
buried in the church of St. Mary, which he chiefly had built at vast
expense.   While he was yet living, Stigand,[1] who was bishop of
Winchester, forthwith invaded the archbishopric of Canterbury : a
prelate of notorious ambition, who sought after honours too keenly,
and who, through desire of a higher dignity, deserting the bishopric
of the South Saxons,[2] had occupied the see of Winchester, which
he held along with the archbishopric.   For this reason he was
never honoured with the pall by the papal see, except that one
Benedict,[3] the usurper as it were of the papacy, sent him one;
either corrupted by money to make this grant, or else because bad

[1] Stigand was consecrated bishop over the East Angles in 1046; but he, es-
pousing the cause of the king's mother, was in the same year deprived of his
bishopric: in the following year, however, he was restored to it. Upon the death
of Elfwine, bishop of Winchester, in 1047, Stigand succeeded to that see; whence,
upon the outlawry of archbishop Robert, in 1052, he was translated to Canterbury, and received a pall from pope Benedict X. in 1058.

[2] Such is the statement of all the MSS., but should probably read East-
Saxons.

[3] On the death of Stephen IX. John bishop of Veletri was placed (30th March
1058) in the holy see by a faction, and retained it nine months and twenty days.
Although he was only a usurper, his name, as Benedict X. is placed among the
sovereign pontiffs.

people are pleased to gratify others of the same description. But
he, through the zeal of the faithful, being expelled by Nicholas,[1]
who legally assumed the papacy after being bishop of Florence,
laid aside the title he so little deserved. Stigand, moreover, in
the time of king William, degraded [2] by the Roman cardinals and
condemned to perpetual imprisonment, could not fill up the
measure of his insatiable avidity even in death ; for, on his decease,
a small key was discovered among his secret recesses, which, on
being applied to the lock of a chamber-cabinet, gave evidence
of papers, describing immense treasures, and in which were noted
both the quality and the quantity of the precious metals which
this greedy pilferer had hidden on all his estates : but of this
hereafter : I shall now complete the history of Godwin which I had
begun.

§ 200. When a young man, he had taken Cnut's sister to wife,
by whom he had a son, who in his early youth, while proudly
curveting on a horse which his grandfather had given him, was
carried into the Thames, and perished in the stream. His mother,
too, paid the penalty of her cruelty, being killed by a stroke of
lightning; for it is reported that she was in the habit of purchasing
companies of slaves in England, and sending them into Denmark,
more especially girls, whose beauty and age rendered them more
valuable, that she might accumulate money by this horrid traffic.
After her death he married another wife, whose descent I have not
been able to trace ;[3] by her he had Harold, Swane, Tosti, Wulnod,
Girth, and Leofwin. Harold became king for a few months
after Edward ; and being overcome by William at Hastings, there
lost his life and kingdom, together with his two younger brothers.
Wulnod, given by his father as an hostage, was sent over to Normandy by king Edward, where he remained all that king's time in
inextricable captivity ; and being sent back into England during
William's reign, grew old in confinement at Salisbury. Swane
being of an obstinate disposition, and faithless to the king, frequently revolted from his father and his brother Harold, and
turning pirate, tarnished the virtues of his forefathers by his depredations on the coast. At last, struck with remorse for the murder
of Bruno,[4] a relation, or as some say, his brother, he went to
Jerusalem, and returning thence was surprised by the Saracens, and
put to death. Tosti, after the death of Siward, was preferred to
the earldom of Northumbria by king Edward, and presided over

---

[1] Gerard bishop of Florence was elected on the 28th December, 1058, and
crowned on the 18th of the month following, by the name of Nicholas II. He
died at Florence in July 1061.

[2] Stigand was degraded at a great council held at Winchester in the octaves of
Easter, A.D. 1070, in the presence of the king and three Roman cardinals, for three
causes : for unjustly holding the see of Winchester with his archbishopric ; for
wearing the pall of archbishop Robert while yet alive, who was unjustly expelled ;
and for receiving a pall from Benedict the antipope. (See Simeon of Durham.)

[3] Earl Godwin's second wife's name was Gytha.

[4] For an account of the murder of Beorn the son of Ulf, see the Saxon Chronicle and Florence of Worcester. The position which these two individuals, Beorn
and Swain, occupied in the pedigree, may be seen in the genealogical table in
Langeb. Scripp. Rerum Danic. iii. 282.

that province for nearly ten years,[1] at the end of which he drove
the Northumbrians into rebellion by his severity: for finding him
unattended, they drove him from the district, not deeming it proper
to kill him from respect to his dignity; but they put to death his
attendants both English and Danes, and appropriated to their own
use his horses, his army, and his effects. As soon as this rumour
and the distracted state of that district reached the king, Harold
set forward to avenge the outrage. The Northumbrians, though
not inferior in point of numbers, yet preferring peace, excused
themselves to him for the transaction; averring that they were a
people free born and freely educated, and unable to tolerate the
cruelty of any prince; that they had been taught by their ancestors
either to be free or to die: did the king wish them to be obedient,
he should appoint Marcher the son of Elgar to preside over them,
who would experience how cheerfully they could obey, provided
they were treated with gentleness. On hearing this, Harold, who
regarded the quiet of the country more than the advantage of his
brother, recalled his army, and, after waiting on the king, settled
the earldom on Marcher. Tosti, enraged against every one, retired
with his wife and children to Flanders, and continued there till
the death of Edward: but this I shall delay mentioning, while I
record what, as I have learnt from ancient men, happened in his
time at Rome.

§ 201. [2] Pope Gregory the Sixth, first called Gratian, was a man
of great piety and austerity. He found the power of the Roman
pontificate so reduced by the negligence of his predecessors, that,
with the exception of a few neighbouring towns, and the offerings
of the faithful, he had scarcely anything whereon to subsist. The
cities and possessions at a distance, which were the property of the
church, were forcibly seized by plunderers; the public roads and
highways throughout all Italy were thronged with robbers to such
a degree, that no pilgrim could pass in safety, unless strongly
guarded. Swarms of thieves beset every path, nor could the tra-
veller devise any method of escaping them: they robbed alike the
poor and the rich; entreaty or resistance were alike unavailing.
The journey to Rome was discontinued by every nation, as every
man would much rather contribute his money to the churches in
his own country, than feed a set of plunderers with the produce of
his labours. And what was the state of that city which of old was
the only dwelling-place of holiness? Of a truth, there assassins, a
crafty and abandoned set of men, were roaming in the very Forum.
Had any one by stratagem eluded the people who lay in wait for him
upon the road, anxious, even at the peril of destruction, to see the
church of the apostle; even then, encountering these robbers, he was
never able to return home without the loss either of property or of
life. Even over the very bodies of the holy apostles and martyrs,

---

[1] Tosti succeeded to the earldom of Northumberland upon the death of earl
Siward, A. D. 1055, and was outlawed by his thanes in 1065.

[2] This character of Gregory must be accepted with considerable caution. The
duration of his pontificate extends from 1st May 1045, to 24th Dec. 1046, when
he was deposed, and his successor, Clement II., appointed.

even on the sacred altars, were swords unsheathed, and the offerings
of pilgrims, ere well laid out of their hands, were snatched away,
and consumed in drunkenness and fornication.   The papacy of
Gregory was greeted by this storm of evils.   At first he began to
deal gently with his subjects, and, as became a pontiff, rather by
love than by terror : he repressed the delinquents more by words
than by blows ; he entreated the townsmen to abstain from the
molestation of pilgrims, and the plunder of sacred offerings.   The
one, he said, was contrary to nature, that the man who breathed
the common air, could not enjoy the common peace; that Christians surely ought to have liberty of proceeding whither they pleased
among Christians, since they were all of the same household, all
united by the tie of the same blood, all redeemed by the same
price ; the other, he said, was contrary to the command of God,
who had ordained, that " they who wait at the altar are partakers
with the altar."[1]   Moreover, that the house of God ought to be
the house of prayer, not a den of thieves,[2] nor an assembly of
gladiators ; that they should allow the offerings to go to the use of
the priests, or the support of the poor ; that he would provide for
those persons whom want had compelled to plunder, by giving
them some honest employment to procure their subsistence ; that
such as were instigated by avaricious desire, should desist immediately, for the love of God and the credit of the world.   He invited,
by mandates[3] and epistles, those who had invaded the patrimony of
the church to restore what did not belong to them, or else to prove
in the Roman senate that they held it justly : if they would do
neither, they must be told that they were no longer members of
the church, since they opposed St. Peter, the head of the church,
and his vicar.   Perpetually haranguing to this effect, and little or
nothing profiting by it, he endeavoured to cure the inveterate disorder by having recourse to harsher remedies.   He then separated
from the body of the church, by the brand of excommunication, all
who were guilty of such practices, and even those who associated
or conversed with the delinquents.   Though he acted strictly according to his duty, yet his diligence in this business had well-nigh
proved his destruction ; for as one says, " He that reproveth a
scorner, getteth to himself shame ;"[4] so the abandoned crew began
to kick against this gentle admonition, to utter their threats aloud,
to clash their arms around the walls of the city, so as nearly even
to kill the pope.   Finding it now absolutely necessary to cut short
the evil, he procured arms and horses from every side, and equipped
troops of horse and foot : taking possession, in the first place, of
the church of St. Peter, he either killed or put to flight the plunderers of the oblations.   As fortune appeared to favour his designs,
he proceeded farther, and dispatching all who dared to resist,
restored to their original jurisdiction all the estates and towns which
had been for a considerable time lost.   In this manner peace,

---

[1] 1 Cor. ix. 13.   [2] See Matt. x. 13.
[3] None of the bulls of Gregory which have been preserved contain any reference
to these transactions.   [4] Prov. ix. 7.

which had been long driven into banishment by the negligence of many, was restored to the country by the exertions of an individual. Pilgrims now began securely to travel on the public ways, which had been deserted ; they feasted their eyes with pleasure on the ancient wonders within the city ; and having made their offerings, they returned home with songs of joy.   In the meantime, the common people of Rome, who had been accustomed to live by theft, began to call him sanguinary, and not worthy to offer sacrifice to God, since he was stained by so many murders ; and as it generally happens that the contagion of slander spreads universally, even the cardinals themselves joined in the sentiments of the people ; so that when this holy man was confined with the sickness which proved his death, they, after consulting among themselves, with matchless insolence recommended him not to think of ordering himself to be buried in the church of St. Peter with the rest of the popes, since he had polluted his office, by being accessory to the death of so many men.   Resuming spirit, however, and sternly regarding them, he addressed them in the following manner :—

§ 202. " If you possessed either a single spark of human reason, or of the knowledge of divine truth, you would hardly have approached your pontiff with so inconsiderate an address ; for throughout my whole life, I have dissipated my own patrimony for your advantage, and, at last, have sacrificed the applause of the world for your rescue.   If any other persons were to allege what you urge in defamation of me, it would become you to silence them by explaining away the false opinions of fools.   For whom, I pray you, have I laid up treasure ? for myself, perhaps : and yet I already possessed the treasures of my predecessors, which were enough for any man's covetousness.   To whom have I restored safety and liberty ? you will reply, to myself, perhaps : and yet I was adored by the people, and did, without restraint, whatever I pleased ; every mouth was filled with my praises, every day resounded my applause. These praises and these applauses have been lost to me, through my concern for your poverty.   Towards you I turned my thoughts, and found that I must adopt severer measures.   A sacrilegious robber fattened on the produce of your property, while your subsistence was only from day to day: he, from the offerings belonging to you, was clad in costly silk ; while your mean and tattered clothing absolutely grieved my sight.   In consequence, when I could endure this no longer, I acted with hostility to others, that I might get credit for the clergy, though at the loss of the citizens.   However, I now find I have lavished my favours on the ungrateful ; for you publicly proclaim, what others mutter only in secret.   I approve, indeed, freedom of speech, but I look for respectful behaviour. A dying parent is persecuted by his sons concerning his burial. Will you deny me the common home of all ?   The harlot, the usurer, the robber, are not forbidden an entrance to the church ; and do you refuse it to the pope ?   What signifies it whether the dead or the living enter the sanctuary, except it be that the living is subject to many temptations, so that he cannot be free from stain, even in the church ; often finding matter of sin, in the very place where he had come to wash it away; whereas the dead knows not how; nay, he who wants only his last sad office, has not the power, to sin. What savage barbarity then is it to exclude from the house of God, him in whom both the inclination and the power of sinning have ceased. Repent then, my sons, of your precipitate boldness, if perchance God may forgive you this crime, for you have spoken both foolishly and bitterly even to this present hour. But that you may not suppose me to rest merely on my own authority, listen to ·reason: every act of man ought to be considered according to the intention of his heart, that the examination of the deed may proceed to that point whence the design originated. I am deceived if the Word of Truth does not say the same;[1] ' If thine eye be single, thy whole body shall be full of light; but if thine eye be evil, thy whole body shall be full of darkness.' A wretched pauper hath often come to me to relieve his distress; and as I knew not what was about to happen, I have presented him with divers pieces of money, and dismissed him. On his departure he has met with a thief on the public road, has incautiously fallen into conversation with him, proclaimed the kindness of the apostolical see, and, to prove the truth of his words, produced the purse. On their journey, the way has been beguiled with various discourse, until the dissembler, loitering somewhat behind, has felled the stranger with a club, and immediately dispatched him; and, after carrying off his money, has boasted of a murder, which his thirst for plunder had excited. Can you therefore justly accuse me for giving that to a stranger which was the cause of his death? for even the most cruel person would not murder a man unless he hoped to fill his pockets with his money. What shall I say of civil and ecclesiastical laws? By these is not the self-same fact both punished and approved, under different circumstances? The thief is punished for murdering a man in secret; whereas the soldier is applauded, who destroys his enemy in battle; the homicide, then, is ignominious in the one and laudable in the other, as the latter slew the man for the safety of his country, the former for the gratification of his desire for plunder. My predecessor Adrian the First, of renowned memory, was applauded for giving up the investiture of the churches to Charles the Great; so that no person elected could be consecrated by the bishop till the king had first dignified him with the ring and staff; on the other hand, the pontiffs of our time have gotten credit for taking away these appointments from the princes. What at that time, then, might reasonably be granted, may at the present be reasonably taken away. But why so? because the mind of Charles the Great was not assailable by avarice, nor could any person easily find access, unless he entered by the door: besides, at so vast a distance it could not be required of the papal see to grant its consent to each person elected, so long as there was a king at hand who disposed of nothing through avarice, but always appointed religious persons to the churches, according to the sacred ordinances of the canons. At the present time, luxury and ambi-

[1] Matt. vi. 22, 23.

tion have beset every king's palace; wherefore the spouse of Christ deservedly asserts her liberty, lest a tyrant should prostitute her to an ambitious usurper. Thus, on either side, may my cause be denied or affirmed; it is not the office of a bishop to authorize war;[1] but it belongs to a bishop's function, if he see innocence made shipwreck of, to oppose it both by deed and word. Ezechiel accuses the priests for not strongly opposing, and holding forth a shield for the house of Israel, in the day of the Lord. Now there are two persons in the church of God, appointed for the purpose of repressing crimes; one who can rebuke sharply, the other who can wield the sword. I, as you can witness for me, have not neglected my part; as far as I saw it could profit I did rebuke sharply: I sent a message to him whose business it was to bear the sword; he wrote me word back that he was occupied in his war with the Vandals, entreating me not to spare my labour, or his expense, in breaking up the meetings of the plunderers. If I had refused what excuse could I offer to God, after the emperor had delegated his office to me? Could I see the murder of the townspeople, the robbery of the pilgrims, and yet slumber on? But he who spares a thief kills the innocent. Yet it will be objected that it is not the part of a priest to defile himself with the blood of any one. I grant it: but he does not defile himself who frees the innocent by the destruction of the guilty. Blessed, truly blessed are they who always keep judgment and do justice. Phineas and Mattathias were priests most renowned in fame; both crowned with the sacred mitre, and both habited in sacerdotal garb, and yet they both punished the wicked with their own hands. The one transfixed the guilty couple with a javelin; the other mingled the blood of the sacrificer with the sacrifice.[2] If then those persons, regarding, as it were, the thick darkness of the law, were carried away by a divine zeal for those shadowy mysteries, shall we, who see the truth with perfect clearness, suffer our sacred things to be profaned? Azarias[3] the priest drove away king Ozias when offering incense, and no doubt would have killed him, had he not quickly departed; the Divine vengeance however anticipated the hand of the priest, for a leprosy preyed on the body of the man whose mind had coveted unlawful things. The devotion of a king was disturbed, and shall not the desires of a thief be so? It is not enough to excuse, I even applaud, this my conduct; indeed I have conferred a benefit on the very persons I seem to have destroyed: I have diminished their punishment in accelerating their deaths. The longer a wicked man lives, the more he will sin, unless he be one whom God hath graciously reserved for a singular example. Death in general is good for all; for by it the just man finds repose in heaven, the unjust ceases from his crimes, the bad man puts an end to his guilt; the good proceeds to his prize; the saint draws nigh to his reward; the sinner looks forward to pardon, because death has fixed a boundary to his transgressions. Surely

[1] The MSS. A. and L. followed by Saville, read; either himself to fight, or to authorize war.
[2] See Numb. xxv. 6; and 1 Macc. ii. 14.　　[3] See 2 Chron. xxvi. 16—21.

then I ought to be thanked on behalf of those who through my conduct have been exempted from so many sufferings. I have urged these matters in my own defence, and to invalidate your assertions. However, since both your reasoning and mine may be fallacious, let us commit all to the decision of God; place my body, laid out in the manner of my predecessors, before the gates of the church, and let them be secured with locks and bars: if God be willing that I should enter, you will hail a miracle; if not, do with my dead body according to your inclination."

§ 203. Struck by this address, when he had breathed his last, they carried out the remains of the departed prelate before the doors, which were strongly fastened; and presently a whirlwind, sent by God, broke every opposing bolt, and drove the very doors, with the utmost violence, against the walls. The surrounding people applaud with joy, and the body of the pontiff was interred, with all due respect, by the side of the other popes.

Of the Witch who was dragged out of a Church by Devils.

§ 204. At the same time something similar occurred in England, not by divine miracle, but by infernal craft; which when I shall have related, the credit of the narrative will not be shaken, though the minds of the hearers should be incredulous; for I have heard it from a man of such character that he would swear he had seen it, and I should be ashamed to disbelieve him. There resided at Berkeley a woman addicted to witchcraft, as it afterwards appeared, and skilled in ancient augury; she was excessively gluttonous, perfectly lascivious, setting no bounds to her debaucheries, as she was not old, though treading fast towards the confines of age. On a certain day, as she was regaling, a jack-daw, which was a very great favourite, chattered something more loudly than usual; on hearing which the woman's knife fell from her hand, her countenance grew pale,—and deeply groaning, "This day," said she, " my plough hath completed its last furrow; to-day I shall hear of, and suffer, some dreadful calamity." While yet speaking, the messenger of her misfortunes arrived; and being asked why he approached with so distressed an air; " I bring news," said he, " from that village," naming the place, " of the death of your son, and of the whole family, by a sudden accident." At this intelligence the woman, sorely afflicted, immediately took to her bed, and perceiving her disorder rapidly approaching the vitals, she summoned her surviving children, a monk and a nun, by hasty letters; and, when they arrived, with faltering voice, she thus addressed them:—
" Hitherto, my children, I have, to my own miserable destruction, devoted myself to demoniacal arts; I have been the sink of every vice, the teacher of every allurement. Yet, while practising these crimes, I was accustomed to soothe my hapless soul with the hope of your piety; despairing of myself, I rested my expectations on you; I advanced you as my defenders against evil spirits, my safeguards against my strongest foes. Now, since I have approached the end of my life, and shall have those eager to punish who lured

me to sin, I entreat you by your mother's breasts, if you have any regard, any affection, at least to endeavour to alleviate my torments; and, although you cannot revoke the sentence already passed upon my soul, yet you may, perhaps, rescue my body by these means. Sew up my corpse in the skin of a stag; lay it on its back in a stone coffin; fasten down the lid with lead and iron; on this lay a stone, bound round with three iron chains of enormous weight; let there be fifty psalms sung for me by night, and as many masses by day, to allay the ferocious attacks of my adversaries. If I lie thus secure for three nights, on the fourth day bury your mother in the ground; although I fear, least the earth, which has been so often burdened with my crimes, should refuse to receive and cherish me in her bosom." They did their utmost to comply with her injunctions; but, alas! vain were pious tears, vows, or entreaties; so great was the woman's guilt, so great the devil's violence. For on the first two nights, while the choir of priests was singing psalms around the body, the devils, one by one, with the utmost ease bursting open the door of the church, though closed with an immense bolt, broke asunder the two outer chains; the middle one being more laboriously wrought, remained entire. On the third night, about cock-crow, the whole monastery seemed to be overthrown from its very foundation, by the clamour of the approaching enemy. One devil, more terrible in appearance than the rest, and of loftier stature, broke the gates to shivers by the violence of his attack. The priests grew motionless with fear, their hair stood on end, and they became speechless.[1] He proceeded, as it appeared, with haughty step towards the coffin, and calling on the woman by name, commanded her to rise. She replying that she could not on account of the chains: "you shall be loosed," said he, "and to your cost;" and directly he broke the chain, which had mocked the ferocity of the others, with as little exertion as though it had been made of flax. He also beat down the cover of the coffin with his foot, and taking her by the hand, before them all, he dragged them out of the church. At the doors appeared a black horse, proudly neighing, with iron hooks projecting over his whole back; on which the wretched creature was placed, and, immediately, with the whole party, vanished from the eyes of the beholders; her pitiable cries, however, for assistance, were heard for nearly the space of four miles. No person will deem this incredible who has read St. Gregory's dialogues;[2] who tells, in his fourth book, of a wicked man who had been buried in a church, and was cast out of doors again by devils. Among the French also, what I am about to relate is frequently mentioned. Charles Martel, a man of renowned valour, who obliged the Saracens, when they had invaded France, to retire to Spain, was, at his death, buried in the church of St. Denys; but as he had seized much of the property of almost all the monasteries in France for the purpose of paying his soldiers, he was visibly taken away from his tomb by evil spirits, and has no where been seen to this day. At length

---

[1] Virgil. Æn. iii. 48.
[2] Greg. Dial. l. iv. cap. liii. Opp. ii. 311. fol. Lut. Par. 1675.

this was revealed to the bishop of Orleans, and by him publicly made known.

Of the Ring that was put on the Finger of a Statue.

§ 205. But to return to Rome : there was a citizen[1] of this place, youthful, rich, and of senatorial rank, who had recently married ; and who, calling together his companions, had made a plentiful entertainment.   After the repast, when by moderate drinking they had excited hilarity, they went out into the field to promote digestion, either by leaping, or hurling, or some other exercise.   The master of the banquet, who was leader of the game, called for a ball to play with, and in the meantime placed the wedding-ring on the outstretched finger of a brazen statue which stood close at hand. But when almost all the others had attacked him alone, tired with the violence of the exercise, he left off playing first, and going to resume his ring, he saw the finger of the statue clenched fast in the palm. Finding, after many attempts, that he was unable either to force it off, or to break the finger, he retired in silence ; concealing the matter from his companions, lest they should laugh at him at the moment, or carry off the ring when he was gone.   Returning thither with some servants in the dead of night, he was surprised to find the finger again extended, and the ring taken away.   Dissembling his loss, he was soothed by the blandishments of his bride.   When the hour of rest arrived, and he had placed himself by the side of his spouse, he was conscious of something dense and cloud-like rolling between them, which might be felt, though not seen, and by this means was impeded in his embraces ; he heard a voice too, saying, " Embrace me, since you wedded me to-day; I am Venus, on whose finger you put the ring ; I have it, nor will I restore it."   Terrified at such a prodigy, he had neither courage nor ability to reply, and passed a sleepless night in silent reflection upon the matter.   A considerable space of time elapsed in this way; as often as he was desirous of the embraces of his wife, the same circumstance ever occurred ; while in other respects, he was perfectly equal to any avocation, civil or military.   At length, urged by the complaints of his consort, he detailed the matter to her parents, who, after deliberating for a time, disclosed it to one Palumbus, a suburban priest. This man was skilled in necromancy, could raise up magical figures, terrify devils, and compel them to do anything he chose.   Having bargained for a liberal reward, provided he succeeded in rendering the lovers happy, he called up all the powers of his art, and gave the young man a letter which he had prepared, saying, " Go, at such an hour of the night, into the high road, where it divides into four several ways, and stand there in silent expectation.   There will pass by human figures of either sex, of every age, rank, and condition ; some on horseback, some on foot ; some with countenances dejected, others elated with full-swollen insolence ; in short, you will perceive in their looks and gestures every token both of joy and of grief ;

---

[1] The MS. A. 1 informs us, by a gloss, that the name of the citizen was Lucianus, and that of his wife Eugenia.

though these should address you, enter into conversation with
none of them. This company will be followed by a person taller, and
more corpulent than the rest, sitting in a chariot ; to him you will,
in silence, give the letter to read, and immediately your wish will
be accomplished, provided you act with resolution." The young
man took the road he was commanded ; and, at night, standing in
the open air, experienced the truth of the priest's assertion by
every thing which he saw ; there was nothing but what was completed to a tittle. Among other passing figures he beheld a woman,
in meretricious garb, riding on a mule ; her hair, which was bound
above in a golden fillet, floated unconfined on her shoulders ; in her
hand was a golden wand, with which she directed the progress of
her beast ; she was so thinly clad, as to be almost naked, and her
gestures were wonderfully indecent. But what need of more ? At
last came the chief, in appearance, who, from his chariot adorned
with emeralds and pearls, fixing his eyes most sternly on the young
man, demanded the cause of his presence. He made no reply, but
stretching out his hand, gave him the letter. The demon, not
daring to despise the well-known seal, read the epistle, and immediately, lifting up his hands to heaven, "Almighty God;"[1] said he,
"how long wilt Thou endure the crimes of the priest Palumbus ?"
The devil then directly sent some of those about him to take the
ring by force from Venus, who restored it at last, though with great
reluctance. The young man thus obtaining his object, became
possessed of his long-desired pleasures without farther obstacle ;
but Palumbus, on hearing of the devil's complaint to God concerning him, understood that the close of his days was predicted.
In consequence, making a pitiable atonement by voluntarily cutting off all his limbs, he confessed unheard-of crimes to the pope
in the presence of the Roman people.

Concerning the Body of Pallas, Son of Evander.

§ 206. At that time the body of Pallas, the son of Evander, of
whom Virgil[2] speaks, was found entire at Rome, to the great
astonishment of all, having escaped corruption for so many ages.
Such, however, is the nature of bodies embalmed, that when the
flesh decays, the skin preserves the nerves, and the nerves the
bones. The gash which Turnus had made in the middle of his
breast measured four feet and an half. His epitaph was found to
this effect :—

> "Pallas, Evander's son, whom Turnus' spear
> Slew, like all others whom it reached, lies here."

Which epitaph I should not think was made at the time, though
Carmentis, the mother of Evander, is reported to have invented the
Roman letters, but that it was composed by Ennius, or some other
ancient poet. There was a burning lamp at his head, constructed
by magical art, so that no violent blast, no dripping of water could

---

[1] In L. 2, and Saville, the following words are added :—" In whose sight every
transgression is as a noisome smell."   [2] Virg. Æn. x. 474—487.

extinguish it. While many were lost in admiration at this, one person, as there are also some people expert in mischief, made an aperture beneath the flame with an iron style, which introducing the air, the light vanished. The body, when set up against the wall, surpassed it in height, but some days afterwards, being drenched with the drip of the eaves, it acknowledged the corruption common to mortals ; the skin and the nerves dissolving.

Of a Woman who had two Bodies.

§ 207. At that time too, on the confines of Brittany and Normandy, a prodigy was seen in one, or more properly speaking, in two women : there were two heads, four arms, and every other part two-fold to the navel ; beneath, were two legs, two feet, and all other parts single. While one was laughing, eating, or speaking, the other would cry, fast, or remain silent : though both mouths ate, yet there was only one passage. At last, one dying, the other survived, and the living carried about the dead, for the space of three years, till she died also, through the fatigue of the weight, and the stench of the dead carcase.

Many were of opinion, and some even have written, that these women represented England and Normandy, which, though separated by position, are yet united under one master. Whatever wealth these countries greedily absorb, flows into one common receptacle, which is either the covetousness of their princes, or the ferocity of surrounding nations. England yet vigorous, supports with her wealth Normandy now dead and almost decayed, until she herself perhaps shall fall through the violence of spoilers. Happy if she shall ever again breathe that liberty the mere shadow of which she has long pursued ! She now mourns, borne down with calamity, and oppressed with exactions ; the causes of which misery I shall relate, after I have despatched some things pertaining to my subject. For since I have hitherto recorded the civil and military transactions of the kings of England, I may be allowed to expatiate somewhat on the sanctity of certain of them ; and at the same time to contemplate what splendour of divine love beamed on this people, from the first dawning of their faith : since I believe you can no where find the bodies of so many saints entire after death, typifying the state of final incorruption. I imagine this to have taken place by God's agency, in order that a nation, situated, as it were, almost out of the world, should more confidently embrace the hope of a resurrection, contemplating the incorruption of the saints. There are, altogether, five which I have known of, (though the residents in many places boast of more ;) Saint Etheldritha,[1] and Wiburga,[2] virgins ; king Edmund;[3] archbishop

---

[1] Etheldrith was the daughter of Anna, king of the East-Angles, and wife of Ecgfrith. Beda, § 309, seq. has celebrated this lady.

[2] Wihtburg was another daughter of Anna, king of East-Anglia ; see the Saxon Chronicle, A. D. 797. Her body was found at Deorham, all whole and uncorrupted, five-and-fifty years after she had departed from this life. But Florence assigns the following year to that event.

[3] King of East-Anglia ; he was martyred on the 20th of November in the year 870. See § 96.

Elfeg;[1] and Cuthbert[2] the ancient father: who with skin and flesh unwasted, and their joints flexile, the last-named also having a certain vital warmth about him, appear to be merely sleeping. Who can enumerate all the other saints, of different ranks and professions, whose names and lives I have neither intention nor leisure singly to describe? yet oh, that I might hereafter have leisure! But I will be silent, lest I should seem to promise more than I can perform. In consequence, it is not necessary to mention any of the commonalty, but merely, (not to go out of the path of the history which I have commenced,) to specify the male and female offshoots of the royal stock, most of them innocently murdered; and who have been consecrated martyrs, not by human conjecture, but by divine acknowledgment: whence may be known how little indulgence they gave to the lust of pleasure, who inherited eternal glory by means of so easy a death.

§ 208. In the former book,[3] my history dwelt for some time on the praises of the most holy Oswald, king and martyr; among whose other marks of sanctity was this, which, according to some copies,[4] is related in the History of the Angles.[5] In the monastery at Selsey, which Wilfrid,[5] of holy memory, had filled with Northumbrian monks, a dreadful malady broke out and destroyed numbers; the remainder endeavoured to avert the pestilence by a fast of three days. On the second day of the fast, the blessed apostles Peter and Paul appeared to a youth who was sick with the disorder, and animated him by observing that he should not fear approaching death, as it would be a termination of his present illness, and an entrance into eternal life; that no other person of that monastery would die of this disorder, because God had granted this to the merits of the noble king Oswald, who was that very day supplicating for his countrymen: for it was on this day that the king, murdered by the faithless, had in a moment ascended to the heavenly tribunal: that they should search therefore in the book, in which the names of the dead were written, and if they found it so, they should put an end to the fast, give loose to security and joy, and sing solemn masses to God, and to the holy king. This vision being quickly followed by the death of the boy, and the anniversary of the martyr being found in the martyrology, and at the same time the cessation of the disorder being attested by the whole province, the name of Oswald was from that period inserted among the martyrs, which before, on account of his recent death, had only been admitted into the list of the faithful. Deservedly, I say, then, deservedly is he to be celebrated, whose glory God's approbation so signally manifested, as to order him to be dignified

---

[1] See Malmesb. de Gestis Pont. fol. 116.

[2] St. Cuthbert, sixth bishop and patron-saint of Lindisfarne, concerning whom see the History of the Church of Durham, by Simeon, which will be given in a subsequent volume of this series. In the year 1827 Cuthbert's tomb was opened a third time; a full and interesting account of the robes and reliques therein found has been published by the Rev. Mr. Raine of Durham (4to. Durham, 1828.)

[3] See § 49.

[4] Upon the variation in the different MSS. of the Ecclesiastical History at this point, see the note to Beda, p. 461.

[5] Beda, § 292. [6] See § 50.

with masses, in a manner, as I think, not usual among men.   The
undoubted veracity of the historian precludes the possibility of supposing this matter to be false, as does also the blessed bishop Acca,[1]
who was the colleague of the author.

§ 209. Egbert, king of Kent, the son of Ercombert, whom I
have mentioned before,[2] had some very near relations, descended
from the royal line ; their names were Ethelred and Egelbirt,[3] the
sons of Ermenred his uncle. Apprehensive that they might grow up
with notions of succeeding to the kingdom, and fearful for his
safety, he kept them about him for some time, with very homely
entertainment; and, at last, grudging them his regards, he removed
them from his court : and soon after, when they had been secretly
dispatched by one of his servants, named Thunre, (which signifies
Thunder,) he buried them under heaps of rubbish, thinking that a
murder perpetrated in privacy would escape detection.   The eye
of God, however, which no secrets of the heart can deceive, brought
the innocents to light, vouchsafing many cures upon the spot; until
the neighbours, being roused, dug up the unsightly heaps of turf
and rubbish cast upon their bodies, and forming a trench after the
manner of a sepulchre, they erected a small church over it.   There
they remained till the time of king Edgar, when they were taken up
by the blessed Oswald, archbishop[4] of Worcester, and conveyed to
the monastery of Ramsey; from which period, granting the petitions of the suppliant, they have manifested themselves by many
miracles.

§ 210. Offa, king of the Mercians, murdered many persons of
consequence for the security, as he supposed, of his kingdom, without any distinction of friend or foe; among these was king Egelbirt;
thereby being guilty of an atrocious outrage against the suitor of his
daughter.   His unmerited death, however, is thought, as I have
before mentioned, to have been amply avenged by the short reign
of Offa's son.[5]   Indeed God signalized his sanctity by such evident
tokens, that at this very day the episcopal church of Hereford is
consecrated to his name.   Nor should anything appear idle or
irrelevant, which our pious and religious ancestors have either admitted by their silence, or confirmed by their authority.

§ 211. What shall my pen here trace worthy of St. Kenelm,[6] a
youth of tender age? Kenulf, king of the Mercians, his father, had
consigned him, when seven years old, to his sister Quendrida, for
the purpose of education: but she, falsely entertaining hopes of the
kingdom for herself, gave her little brother in charge to a servant
of her household, with an order to murder him.   Taking out the
innocent, under pretence of hunting for his amusement, he murdered him and hid him in a thicket. But strange to tell, the crime
which had been so secretly committed in England, gained publicity
in Rome, by God's agency; for a dove from heaven bore a parch-
ment scroll to the altar of St. Peter, containing an exact account

---

[1] Acca, Wilferth's priest, succeeded to the bishopric of Hexham in 710.   Beda,
§ 426.   [2] See § 12.   [3] See § 13.
[4] He was at the same time bishop of Worcester, and archbishop of York.
[5] See §§ 86, 97.   [6] See § 95.

both of his death, and place of burial : but as it was written in the English language, it was vainly attempted to be read by the Romans and men of other nations who were present. Fortunately, however, and opportunely, an Englishman was at hand, who, translating the writing to the Roman people into Latin, gave occasion to the pope to write a letter to the kings of England, acquainting them with the martyrdom of their countryman. In consequence, in presence of a numerous assembly, the body of the innocent was taken up and removed to Winchelcumbe. The murderous woman was so indignant at the vocal chant of the priests and loud applause of the laity, that she thrust out her head from the window of the chamber where she was standing, and, by chance, having in her hands a psalter, she came in course of reading to the psalm, " Oh God of my praise," which, for I know not what charm, reading backwards, she thereby endeavoured to drown the joy of the choristers. At that moment, the witch's eyes, torn by divine vengeance from their hollow sockets, scattered blood upon the verse which runs, " This is the work of them who defame me to the Lord, and who speak evil against my soul."[1] The marks of her blood are still extant, proving the cruelty of the woman, and the vengeance of God. The body of the little saint is very generally reverenced, and hardly is there any place in England more venerated, or where greater numbers of persons attend at the festival ; and this is due to the long-continued belief of his sanctity, and the constant exhibition of his miracles.

§ 212. Nor shall my history be wanting in thy praise, Wistan,[2] blessed youth, son of Wimund, son of Wihtlaf king of the Mercians, and of Elhfleda, daughter of Chelwulf, who was the uncle of Kenelm ; I will not, I say, pass thee over in silence, whom Berfert thy relation so atrociously murdered. And let posterity know, if they deem this history worthy of perusal, that there was nothing earthly more praiseworthy than your disposition ; at which a deadly assassin becoming irritated, dispatched you ; nor was there any thing more innocent than your purity towards God ; invited by which, the secret judge deemed it fitting to honour you ; for a column of light, sent down from heaven, piercing the sable robe of night, revealed the wickedness of the deep cavern, and brought to view the crime of the murderer. In consequence, Wistan's venerable remains were taken up, and by the care of his relations conveyed to Rapendun ;[3] at that time a famous monastery, now a vill belonging to the earl of Chester, and its glory grown obsolete with age ; but at present thou dwellest at Evesham, kindly favouring the petitions of such as regard thee.

§ 213. Beda has related many anecdotes of the sanctity of the kings of the East Saxons and East Angles, whose genealogy I have in the first book[4] of this work traced briefly, because I could no where find a complete history of the kings. I shall, however, dilate somewhat on St. Edmund,[5] who held dominion in East Anglia, and

---

[1] Ps. cix. 20.
[2] Concerning St. Wistan, consult MSS. Harl. 2253, De Martyrio S. Wistani.
[3] Now Repton, in Derbyshire.   [4] See §§ 97, 98.   [5] See § 97.

to whom the time of Beda did not extend. That province, on the
south and east, is surrounded by the ocean ; on the north by deep
lakes and stagnant pools, which, stretching out to a vast distance in
length, with a breadth of two or three miles, afford abundance of
fish for the use of the inhabitants ; on the west it is continuous
with the rest of the island, but defended by the earth being thrown
up in the form of a rampart. The soil is admirable for pasture and
for hunting ; it is full of monasteries, and large bodies of monks are
settled on the islands of these stagnant waters ; the people are a
merry, pleasant, jocund race, though apt to carry their jokes to
excess.   Here,[1] then, reigned Edmund, a man devoted to God,
ennobled by his descent from ancient kings, and though he presided over the province in peace for several years, yet never through
the effeminacy of the times did he relax his courage.   Hinguar and
Hubba, two leaders of the Danes, came over to depopulate the
provinces of the Northumbrians and East Angles.   The former of
these seized the unresisting king, who had cast away his arms and
was lying on the ground in prayer, and, after the infliction of tor-
tures,[2] beheaded him. On the death of this saintly man, the purity
of his past life was evidenced by unheard-of miracles.   The Danes
had cast away the head, when severed from the body by the cruelty
of the executioners, and it had been hidden in a thicket : while his
subjects, who had tracked the footsteps of the enemy as they
departed, were seeking it, intending to solemnize with due honour
the funeral rites of their king, they were struck with the pleasing
intervention of God ; for the lifeless head uttered a voice, inviting
all who were in search of it to approach.   A wolf, a beast accustomed to prey upon dead carcases, was holding it in its paws, and
guarding it untouched ; which animal also, after the manner of a
tame creature, gently followed the bearers to the tomb, and neither
did nor received any injury. The sacred body was then, for a time,
committed to the earth ; turf was placed over it, and a wooden
chapel, of trifling cost, was erected.   The negligent natives, however, were soon made sensible of the virtue of the martyr, which
excited their listless minds to reverence him by the miracles which
he performed : and though perhaps the first proof of his power may
appear weak and trivial, yet nevertheless I shall subjoin it.   He
bound, with invisible bands, some thieves who had endeavoured to
break into the church by night ; this was done in the very attempt ;
a pleasant spectacle enough, to see the object of plunder hold fast
the thieves, so that they could neither desist from their enterprise
nor complete their design.   In consequence, Theodred bishop of
London, who lies at St. Paul's, removed the lasting disgrace of so
mean a structure, by building a nobler edifice over those sacred
limbs, which evidenced the glory of his unspotted soul, by surprising
soundness, and a kind of milky whiteness.   The head, which was
formerly divided from the neck, is again united to the rest of the

---

[1] From these words to the end of § 213, occurs in Malmes. De Gestis Pontif.
fol. 136 ; ed. fol. Lond. 1596.
[2] He was tied to a tree, and shot to death with arrows. See Abbo, De Passione
S. Edmundi, Regis Orientalium Anglorum; MS. S. Joh. Bapt. Oxon. No. 199.

body, showing only the sign of martyrdom by a purple seam. One circumstance indeed surpasses human miracles, which is, that the hair and nails of the dead man continue to grow ; these, Oswen, an holy woman, used yearly to clip and cut, that they might be objects of veneration to posterity. Truly this was an holy temerity, for a woman to contemplate and handle limbs superior to the whole of this world. Not so Lefstan, a youth of bold and untamed insolence, who, with many impertinent threats, commanded the body of the martyr to be shown to him ; desirous, as he said, of settling the uncertainty of report by the testimony of his eyesight. He paid dearly, however, for his audacious experiment ; becoming insane, and, shortly after, dying, swarming with worms. He felt indeed that Edmund was now capable of doing what he before used to do ; that is,—

"To spare the suppliant, but confound the proud ;"

by which means he so completely engaged the inhabitants of all Britain to him, that every person looked upon himself as particularly happy, in contributing either money or other gifts to St. Edmund's monastery. Even kings themselves, the masters of others, used to boast of being his servants, and sent him their royal crown, redeeming it, if they wished to use it, at a great price. The exactors of taxes also, who, in other places, gave loose to injustice, making no distinction between right and wrong, were there suppliant, and ceased their cavilling at St. Edmund's boundary,[1] admonished thereto by the punishment of others who had presumed to overpass it.

§ 214. My commendations shall also glance at the names of some maidens of the royal race, though I must claim indulgence for being brief upon the subject, not through fastidiousness, but because I am unacquainted with their miracles. Anna king of the East Angles had three daughters, Etheldritha, Ethelburga, and Sexburga. Etheldritha, though married to two husbands, yet by means of saintly continence, so Beda relates,[2] without any diminution of modesty, without a single sensual inclination, triumphantly displayed to heaven the palm of perpetual virginity. Ethelburga, first a nun, and afterwards abbess, in a monastery in France called Brigæ,[3] was celebrated for unblemished chastity; and it is well worthy of remark, that as both sisters had subdued the lusts of the flesh while living, so, when dead, their bodies remained uncorrupt, the one in England and the other in France ; insomuch, that their sanctity, which is abundantly resplendent, " may suffice to irradiate both poles." Sexburga was married to Ercombert king of Kent, and after his death, taking the veil in the same monastery with her sister Etheldreda, was proclaimed a saint. She had two daughters by king Ercombert, Ercongota, and Ermenilda ; of Ercongota, such as wish for information will find it in Beda ;[4] Ermenilda married

---

[1] This boundary is said to have been formed by Cnut, in consequence of his father Swayne having been killed by St. Edmund in a vision, for attempting to plunder his territory. See Malm. de Gest. Pontif. lib. ii. fol. 136 b. Much more on this subject occurs there.   [2] Hist. Eccl. § 309, seq.
[3] Faremoustier en Brie.   [4] Hist. Eccl § 172; and see ante. § 11.

Wulfer, king of the Mercians, and had a daughter, Werburga, a most holy virgin.[1] Of these two saints, the mother, [that is to say, St. Ermenhilda,] rests at Ely, where she was abbess after her mother, Sexburga ; and the daughter lies at Chester, in the monastery of that city, which Hugh earl of Chester, ejecting a few clerks who resided there in a mean and irregular manner, has recently erected. The praises and miracles of both these women, and particularly of the younger, are there extolled and held in veneration ; and though they are favourable to all petitions without delay, yet are they more especially kind and assistant to the supplications of women and youths.

§ 215. Merewald the brother of Wulfer, by Ermenburga, the daughter of Ermenred brother of Ercombert, had two daughters, Mildritha and Milburga. Mildritha, dedicating herself to celibacy, ended her days in the Isle of Thanet in Kent, which king Egbert had given to her mother, to atone for the murder of her brothers, Ethelred and Egelbert.[2] In after times being transferred to St. Augustine's monastery at Canterbury, she is there honoured by the marked attention of the monks, and celebrated equally for her kindness and affability to all, as her name implies. And although almost every corner of that monastery be filled with the bodies of saints of great name or merit, any one of which would be of itself sufficient to irradiate all England, yet no one is there more revered, more loved, or more gratefully remembered ; and she, turning a deaf ear to none who love her, is present to such as have regard to the salvation of their souls.

§ 216. Milburga[3] reposes at Wenloc ; she was formerly much in estimation by the neighbouring inhabitants ; but for some time after the arrival of the Normans, through ignorance of the place of her burial, she was neglected : lately, however, a convent of Culniac monks being established there, while a new church was erecting, a certain boy running violently along the pavement, broke into the hollow of the vault, and discovered the body of the virgin ; when a balsamic odour pervading the whole church, she was taken up, and performed so many miracles that the people flocked thither in great multitudes, so that the large-spreading plains could hardly contain the troops of pilgrims, while rich and poor came side by side, one common faith impelling all. Nor did the event deceive their expectations : for no one departed, without either a perfect cure, or considerable abatement of his malady, and some were even healed of the king's evil, by the merits of this virgin, when medical assistance had been unavailing.

§ 217. Edward the Elder, of whom I have before spoken at large,[4] had by his wife Edgiva,[5] several daughters. Among these

---

[1] See § 75.

[2] In book i. c. 1, it is said the compensation for their murder was made to their mother ; but here she is called their sister, which is the general account. When it was left to her to estimate this compensation (i.e. their weregild), she asked as much land as her stag should compass, at one course, in the Isle of Thanet, where she founded the monastery of Minster. See Thorn, col. 1910 ; and Natale S. Mildrythæ (Saxonicè), MS. Cott. Calig. A. xiv. 4.

[3] See § 75.   [4] See § 125.

[5] A. followed by Saville reads, Elfgiva ; C. and D. give Edelswida.

was Edburga, who, when scarcely three years old, gave a singular indication of her future sanctity. Her father was inclined to try whether the little girl would lean to God or to the world, and had placed in a chamber the symbols of the different professions; on one side a chalice, and the gospels; on the other, bracelets and neck-laces. Hither the child was brought in the arms of her indulgent nurse, and placed on her father's knee; she being desired to choose which she pleased, she rejected the earthly ornaments with angry looks, and falling down before the chalice and the gospels, she adored them with infant adoration. The company present exclaimed aloud, and fondly hailed the omen of the child's future sanctity; her father embraced the infant in a manner still more endearing. " Go," said he, " whither God calls thee; follow with prosperous pace the Spouse whom thou hast chosen, and truly blessed shall my wife and myself be, if we are surpassed in holiness by our daughter." When clothed in the garb of a nun, she gained the affection of all her female companions in the city of Winchester by the marked attention she paid them; nor did the greatness of her birth elevate her; as she esteemed it noble to stoop to the service of Christ. Her sanctity increased with her years, her humility kept pace with her growth; so that she used secretly to steal away the socks of the several nuns at night, and, carefully washing and perfuming them, lay them again upon their beds. Wherefore, though God signalized her while living by many miracles, yet I more particularly bring forward this circumstance, to show that charity began all her works, and humility completed them: and finally, many miracles, both in her lifetime and after her death, confirm the devotion of her heart and the incorruptness of her body, which the attendants at her churches at Winchester and Pershore relate to such as are unacquainted with them.

§ 218. The blessed Edgitha, the daughter of king Edgar, ennobles with her reliques the monastery of Wilton, where she was buried, and cherishes that place with her regard, where, trained from her infancy in the school of the Lord, she gained his favour by unsullied virginity, and constant watchings: repressing the pride of her high birth by her humility. I have heard one circumstance respecting her, from persons of elder days, which greatly staggered the opinions of men: for she led them into false conclusions from the splendour of her costly dress; being always habited in richer garb than the sanctity of her profession seemed to require. On this account, being openly rebuked by St. Ethelwold, she is reported to have answered with equal point and wit, " The judgment of God is true and irrefragable, while that of man alone is fallible; for pride may exist under mean clothing: wherefore I think that a mind may be as pure beneath these vestments as under your tattered furs." The bishop was deeply struck by this speech, admitting its truth by his silence; and reddening with joy that he had been branded by the sparkling repartee of the lady, he held his peace. St. Dunstan had observed her at the consecration of the church of St. Denys, (which she had built out of affection to that martyr,) frequently stretching out her right thumb, and making the sign of

the cross upon her forehead ; and being extremely delighted at it,
" May this finger," he exclaimed, "never see corruption :" and
immediately, while celebrating mass, he burst into such a flood of
tears, that he alarmed with his faltering voice an assistant standing
near him ; who inquiring the reason of it, " Soon," said he, " shall
this blooming rose wither ; soon shall this beloved bird take its
flight to God, after the expiration of six weeks from this time."
The truth of the prelate's prophecy was very shortly fulfilled ; for
on the appointed day, this noble, firm-minded lady expired in her
prime, at the age of twenty-three years. Soon after, the same saint
saw, in a dream, St. Denys kindly taking the virgin by the hand,
and strictly enjoining by divine command, that she should be
honoured by her servants on earth, in the same manner as she was
venerated by her Spouse and Master in heaven. Miracles multi-
plying at her tomb, it was ordered that her virgin body should be
taken up, and placed in a most lofty situation ; when the whole of
it was found resolved into dust, except the finger, with the abdomen
and parts adjacent : in consequence of which, some debate arising,
the virgin herself appeared in a dream to one of those who had seen
her remains, saying, " It was no wonder if the other parts of the
body had decayed, since it was customary for dead bodies to
moulder to their native dust, and she, perhaps, as a girl, had sinned
with those members ; but it was also highly just, that the abdomen
should see no corruption which had never felt the sting of lust ; as
she had been entirely free from gluttony or carnal copulation."

§ 219. Truly both these virgins support their respective monasteries by their merits ; each of them being filled with large assemblies of nuns, who answer obediently to the call of their mistresses
and patronesses, inviting them to virtue. Happy the man who
becomes partaker of those virgin prayers which the Lord Jesus
favours with kind regard. For, as I have remarked [1] of the nuns
of Shaftesbury, all virtues have long since quitted the earth, and
retired to heaven ; or, if any where, (but this I must say with the
permission of holy men,) are to be found only in the hearts of
nuns ; and surely those women are highly to be praised, who,
regardless of the weakness of their sex, vie with each other in the
preservation of their continence, and by such means ascend triumphant into heaven.

§ 220. To have been made acquainted with many of the royal
family of either sex is, I think, of importance ; as hence may be
gathered that king Edward, concerning whom I was speaking before
I digressed, had by no means degenerated from the virtues of his
ancestors. In fact, he was famed both for miracles and for the
spirit of prophecy, as I shall hereafter relate. In the exaction of
taxes he was sparing, as he abominated the insolence of collectors :
in eating and drinking he was devoid of the addiction to pleasure
which his state allowed : on the more solemn festivals, though dressed
in robes interwoven with gold, which the queen had most splendidly
embroidered, yet still he had such forbearance as to be sufficiently
majestic, without being haughty ; considering in such matters

1 See § 163.

rather the bounty of God than the pomp of the world.   There was one secular enjoyment in which he chiefly delighted ; which was hunting with fleet hounds, whose baying in the woods he used with pleasure to encourage : and again, the flying those birds, whose nature it is to prey on their kindred species.   In these exercises, after hearing divine service in the morning, he employed himself whole days.   In other respects he was a man by choice devoted to God, and lived the life of an angel in the administration of his kingdom : to the poor and to the stranger, more especially foreigners, and men of religious order, he was kind in invitation, munificent in his presents, and constantly exciting the monks of his own country to imitate their holiness.   He was of middle height ; his beard and hair swan-white ; his countenance florid; fair throughout his whole person; and his form of admirable proportion.

§ 221. The felicity of his times had been revealed in a dream to Brihtwold bishop of Wilton, and he had made it public.   For in the time of Cnut, when at Glastonbury, he was once intent on heavenly watchings, and the thought of the near extinction of the royal race of the Angles, which frequently distressed him, came into his mind, sleep stole upon him while he was thus meditating; and behold ! rapt on high, he saw Peter, the chief of the apostles, consecrating king Edward, who was then an exile in Normandy; his chaste life too was pointed out, and the exact period of his reign, twenty-four years, determined ; and, when inquiring about his posterity, it was answered, " The kingdom of the English belongs to God ; after you He will provide a king according to his pleasure."

§ 222. But now to speak of his miracles.   A young woman had married an husband of her own age, but having no issue by the union, the humours collecting abundantly about her neck, she had contracted a sore disorder ; the glands swelling so that she became a frightful object. Admonished in a dream to have the part affected washed by the king's hands, she entered the palace.   The king himself fulfilling this labour of love, rubbed the woman's neck with his fingers dipped in water : a speedy recovery followed his healing hand : the lurid skin opened, so that worms flowing out with the purulent matter, the noxious tumour subsided.   But as the orifice of the ulcers was large and unsightly, he commanded her to be supported at the royal expense till she should be perfectly cured ; however, before a week was expired, a fair new skin returned, and hid the scars so completely, that nothing of the original wound could be discovered : and within a year becoming the mother of twins, she increased the admiration of Edward's holiness.   Those who knew him more intimately, affirm that he often cured this complaint in Normandy : whence appears how false is their notion, who in our times assert, that the cure of this disease does not proceed from personal sanctity, but from hereditary virtue in the royal line.[1]

§ 223. A certain man, blind from some unknown mischance, had persisted in asserting about the palace that he should be cured,

[1] See Petr. Bles. in Epist. 150.

if he could touch his eyes with the water in which the king's hands
had been washed. When this was frequently related to Edward, he
derided it, and looked angrily on the persons who mentioned it;
saying that he himself was a sinner, and that the works of holy men
did not belong to him. But the servants, thinking this a matter
not to be neglected, put the man's dream to the proof, unknown to
the king, and while he was praying in church. The instant the
blind man was washed with the water, the long-enduring darkness
fled from his eyes, and they were filled with joyful light, amid the
grateful clamour of the by-standers. The king inquiring the cause
of the noise was informed of the fact; and when, by thrusting his
fingers towards the eyes of the man he had cured, and, perceiving
him draw back his head to avoid them, he had made proof of his
sight, he, with uplifted hands, returned thanks to God. In the
same way he cured a blind man at Lincoln, who survived him many
years, a proof of the royal miracle.

§ 224. That you may know the perfect virtue of this prince, in
the power of healing more especially, I shall add something which
will excite your wonder. Wulfwin, surnamed Spillecorn, the son
of Wulmar of Nutgareshale, was one day cutting timber in the
wood of Bruelle, and indulging in a long sleep after his labour, lost
his sight for seventeen years, from the blood, as I imagine, stagnat-
ing about his eyes: at the end of this time, admonished thereto in
a dream, he went round to eighty-seven churches, and earnestly
entreated a cure of his blindness from the saints. At last coming
to the king's court, he remained for a long time, in vain, in opposition to the attendants, at the vestibule of his chamber. He still
continued importunate, however, without being deterred, till at
last, after much difficulty, he was admitted by order of the king.
When he had heard the dream, he mildly answered, " By my lady
St. Mary, I shall be truly grateful, if God, through my means,
shall choose to take pity upon a wretched creature." In consequence, though he had no confidence in himself with respect to
miracles, yet, at the instigation of his servants, he placed his hand,
dipped in water, on the blind man; and in a moment the blood
dripped plentifully from his eyes, and the man, restored to sight,
exclaimed with rapture, " I see you, oh king! I see you, oh king!"
Having thus recovered his sight, he had charge of the royal palace
at Windsor, (for there the cure had been performed,) for a long time;
surviving his restorer several years. On the same day, from the
same water, three blind men, and a man with one eye, who were
supported on the royal alms, received a cure; the servants admi-
nistering the healing water with perfect confidence.

§ 225. One holy Easter day, he was sitting at table at Westminster, with the crown on his head, and surrounded by a crowd
of nobles. While the rest were greedily eating, and making up for
the long fast of Lent by the newly provided viands, he, with mind
abstracted from earthly things, was absorbed in the contemplation
of some divine matter, when presently he excited the attention of
the guests, by bursting into profuse laughter: and as none presumed
to inquire into the cause of this joy, he remained silent, as before,

until satiety had put an end to the banquet. After the tables were removed, and as he was disrobing in his chamber, three persons of rank followed him ; of these earl Harold was one, the second an abbot, and the third a bishop; who presuming on their intimacy, asked the cause of his laughter : observing, that it seemed just matter of astonishment to see him in such perfect tranquillity both of time and occupation, burst into a vulgar laugh, while all others were silent.   " I saw something wonderful," said he, " and there-fore I did not laugh without a cause."   At this, as is the custom of mankind, they began to inquire and search into the matter more earnestly, entreating that he would condescend to disclose it. After much reluctance he yielded to their persevering solicitations, and related the following wonderful circumstance ; saying, that the Seven Sleepers in mount Cælius had now lain for two hundred years on their right side ; but that at the very hour of his laughter, they turned upon their left : that they would continue to lie in this manner for seventy-four years, which would be a dreadful omen to wretched mortals.   For everything would come to pass in these seventy-four years, which the Lord had foretold to his disciples, concerning the end of the world : since nation would rise against nation, and kingdom against kingdom ; earthquakes would be in divers places : pestilence and famine, terrors from heaven, and great signs : changes in kingdoms : wars of the Gentiles against the Christians, and also victories of the Christians over the Pagans. Relating these matters to his wondering audience, he descanted on the passion of these sleepers, and the make of their bodies, though totally unnoticed in history, as readily as though he had lived in daily intercourse with them. On hearing this the earl sent a knight; the bishop, a clergyman ; and the abbot, a monk, to Maniches, the Constantinopolitan emperor, to investigate the truth of his declaration ; adding letters and presents from the king. After being kindly entertained, Maniches sent them to the bishop of Ephesus, giving them, at the same time, what is called a holy letter, that the martyr-relics of the Seven Sleepers should be shown to the delegates of the king of England.[1]   It fell out that the presage of king Edward was proved by all the Greeks ; who could swear they had heard from their fathers, that the men were lying on their right side ; but after the entrance of the English into the vault, they published the truth of the foreign prophecy to their countrymen. Nor was it long ere the predicted evils came to pass ; for the Agarens, and Arabs, and Turks, nations aliens from Christ, making havoc of the Christians, overran Syria, and Lycia, and Asia Minor altogether ; many cities too of Asia Major, among which was Ephesus, and even Jerusalem itself. At the same time, on the death of Maniches, emperor of Constantinople, Diogenes and Michaelius, and Bucinacius, and Alexius, in turn hurled each other headlong from the throne ; the last of whom, continuing till our time, left for heir his son John,[2] more noted for cunning and deceit than worth. He contrived many hurtful plots against the

---

[1] See Capgrave, Legenda Nova.
[2] John Comnenus became emperor of Constantinople in 1118.

pilgrims on their sacred journey; but venerating the fidelity of the
English, he showed them every civility, and transmitted his regard
for them to his son.[1] In the next seven years three popes, namely,
Victor,[2] Stephen,[3] and Nicholas,[4] diminished the vigour of the
papacy by their successive deaths. Almost immediately afterwards,
too, died Henry, the pious emperor of the Romans,[5] and was succeeded by his son Henry, who brought many calamities on the
city of Rome by his folly and his wickedness. The same year
Henry king of France, a good and active warrior, died by poison.[6]
Soon after, a comet, denoting, as they say, change in kingdoms,
appeared trailing its extended and fiery train along the sky : wherefore a certain monk of our monastery, by name Eilmer, bowing
down with terror at the sight of the brilliant star, wisely exclaimed,
" Thou art come! a matter of lamentation to many a mother art
thou come ; I have seen thee long since ; but I now behold thee
much more terrible, threatening to hurl destruction on this country."
He was a man of good learning for those times ; of mature age ;
and, in his early youth, had hazarded an attempt of singular
temerity : he had by some contrivance fastened wings to his hands
and feet, in order that, looking upon the fable as true, he might fly
like Dædalus, and collecting the air, on the summit of a tower, had
flown for more than the distance of a furlong ; but agitated by the
violence of the wind and a current of air, as well by the consciousness of his rash attempt, he fell and broke his legs, and was lame
ever after. He used to relate as the cause of his failure that he had
forgotten to provide himself with a tail.

§ 226. Another prophecy, somewhat like the last, Edward uttered
when dying, which I shall here anticipate. When he had lain two
days speechless, on the third, sadly and deeply sighing as he awoke
from his sleep, " Almighty God," said he, " if this be a real vision,
and not a vain illusion which I have seen, grant, but if the contrary,
deny, me the power of explaining it to the by-standers." Soon
after, speaking fluently, " I saw just now," continued he, " two
monks near me, whom formerly, when a youth in Normandy, I
knew both to have lived in a most religious manner, and to have
died like perfect Christians. These men, announcing themselves
as the messengers of God, spake to the following effect: 'Since the
chiefs of England, the dukes, bishops, and abbots, are not the
ministers of God, but of the devil, God, after your death, has
delivered this kingdom for a year and a day into the hand of the
enemy, and devils shall wander over all the land.' And when I said
that I would show these things to my people, and promised that
they should liberate themselves by repentance, after the example of

[1] On the Norman conquest many English fled to Constantinople, where they
were eagerly received by Alexius, and opposed to the Normans under Robert
Guiscard. See Orderic. Vitalis, p. 508.

[2] Victor II. He succeeded Leo IX. in 1056, and died in 1057.

[3] Frederic, brother of duke Godefroi, succeeded Victor II. on the 2d of August
1057.   [4] He succeeded to the holy see in 1059.

[5] Henry III. died at Botfeld, on the confines of Saxony, in the autumn of the
year 1056.

[6] Henry died on the 4th of August, 1060. The details of his death occur in
Will. Gemet. Hist. c. xxviii., with which compare Orderic. Vitalis, p. 480.

the Ninevites; 'Neither of these,' said they, 'shall take place; for they will not repent, nor will God have mercy on them.' When then, said I, may cessation from such great calamities be hoped for? They reply, 'Whenever a green tree shall be cut through the middle, and the part cut off, being carried the space of three acres from the trunk, shall, without any assistance, become again united to its stem, bud out with flowers, and stretch forth its fruit, as before, from the sap again uniting; then may a cessation of such evils be at last expected.'"

§ 227. Though others were apprehensive of the truth of this prediction, yet Stigand, at that time archbishop, received it with laughter, saying that the old man doted through disease. We, however, find the truth of the presage experimentally; for England is become the residence of foreigners and the property of strangers; at the present time there is no Englishman who is either earl, bishop, or abbot; strangers all, they prey upon the riches and vitals of England; nor is there any hope of a termination to this misery. The cause of which evil, as I have long since promised to narrate, it is now high time that my narrative should endeavour briefly to disclose.

§ 228. King Edward declining into years, as he had no children himself, and saw the sons of Godwin growing in power, despatched messengers to the king of Hungary, to send over Edward, the son of his brother Edmund, with all his family; intending, as he declared, that either he or his sons should succeed to the hereditary kingdom of England, and that his own want of issue should be supplied by that of his kindred. Edward came[1] in consequence, but died almost immediately at St. Paul's in London: he was neither valiant, nor a man of abilities. He left three surviving children; that is to say, Edgar, who, after the death of Harold, was by some elected king; and who, after many revolutions of fortune, is now living wholly retired in the country, in extreme old age; Christina, who grew old at Romsey in the habit of a nun; and Margaret, whom Malcolm king of the Scots espoused. Blessed with a numerous offspring, her sons were Edgar and Alexander, who reigned in Scotland after their father in due succession; for the eldest, Edward,[2] had fallen in battle with his father; the youngest, David,[3] noted for his meekness and discretion, is at present king of Scotland. Her daughters were Matilda, whom in our time king Henry, and Maria, whom Eustace the younger, earl of Boulogne, respectively espoused. The king, in consequence of the death of his relation, losing his first hope of support, gave the succession of England to William earl of 'Normandy.'[4] He was well worthy of such a gift, being a young man of superior mind, who had raised himself to the highest eminence by his unwearied exertion; moreover, he was his nearest relation by consanguinity, as he was the son of Robert, the son of Richard the second, whom we have

---

[1] Edward returned to England in 1057, and died in the same year.
[2] King Malcolm and his son Edward were slain A.D. 1093.
[3] David I. began to reign 27th of April, 1124, and died 24th of May, 1153.
[4] Ingulfus makes the same statement; but his evidence, on this point, as in most others, must be received with caution.

repeatedly mentioned as the brother of Emma, Edward's mother. Some affirm[1] that Harold himself was sent into Normandy by the king for this purpose; others, who knew Harold's more secret intentions, say, that being driven thither against his will, by the violence of the wind, he imagined this device, in order to extricate himself. This, as it appears nearest the truth, I shall relate.[3] Harold being at his country seat at Boseham,[4] went for recreation on board a fishing-boat, and, for the purpose of prolonging his sport, put out to sea; when a sudden tempest arising, he was driven with his companions on the coast of Ponthieu. The people of that district, as was their native custom, immediately assembled from all quarters; and those who were unarmed and few in number, were, as it easily might be, quickly overpowered by an armed multitude, and bound hand and foot. Harold, craftily meditating a remedy for this mischance, sent a person, whom he had allured by very great promises, to William, to say that he had been sent into Normandy by the king, for the purpose of expressly confirming, in person, the message which had been imperfectly delivered by people of less authority; but that he was detained in fetters by Guy earl of Ponthieu, and could not execute his embassy; that it was the barbarous and untamed custom of the country, that such as had escaped destruction at sea, should meet with perils on shore; that it well became a man of his dignity not to let this pass unpunished; that to suffer those to be laden with chains, who appealed to his protection, detracted somewhat from his own greatness; and that if his captivity must be terminated by money, he would gladly give it to earl William, but not to the contemptible Guy. By this means, Harold was liberated at William's command, and conducted to Normandy by Guy in person. The earl entertained him with much respect, both in banqueting and in vesture, according to the custom of his country; and the better to learn his disposition, and at the same time to try his courage, he took him with himself in an expedition which he at that time led against Brittany. There, Harold well approved both in ability and courage, won the heart of the Norman; and, still more to ingratiate himself, he of his own accord, confirmed to him by oath the castle of Dover, which was under his jurisdiction, and the kingdom of England, after the death of Edward. Wherefore, honoured both by having his daughter, then a child, betrothed to him, and by the confirmation of his ample patrimony, he was received into the strictest intimacy. Not long after his return home, the king was crowned[5] at London on Christmas-day, and being there seized with the disorder of which he was sensible that he should die, he commanded the church of Westminster to be dedicated on Innocents-day.[6] Thus, full of years

---

[1] Guil. Pictaviensis and Guil. Gemeticensis are the authors more especially alluded to in this statement.

[2] This is the statement of Eadmer and his followers.

[3] Compare this statment with Chron. Roberti de Monte ad Sigebertum, apud D'Acherium, p. 72.   [4] Near Chichester.

[5] It was customary for the king to wear his crown on the solemn festivals of Easter, Whitsuntide, and Christmas: it being placed on his head in due form by the archbishop of Canterbury. (See Ailr. Riev. de Vita S. Edwardi.)

[6] Westminster Abbey was consecrated on the 28th Dec. 1065. Ailred of Rie-

and of glory, he surrendered his pure spirit to heaven,[1] and was buried on the day of the Epiphany, in the said church, which he, first in England, had erected after that kind of style which now almost all attempt to rival at enormous expense. The race of the West Saxons, which had reigned in Britain five hundred and seventy-one years, from the time of Cerdic, and two hundred and sixty-one from Egbert, in him ceased altogether to rule. For while the grief for the king's death was yet fresh, Harold, on the very day of the Epiphany, seized the diadem, extorting their consent from the nobles; though the English say, that it was granted him by the king; but I conceive it alleged, more through regard to Harold than through sound judgment, that Edward should transfer his inheritance to a man of whose power he had himself always been jealous: although, not to conceal the truth, Harold would have governed the kingdom with prudence and with courage, in the character he had assumed, had he assumed it lawfully. Indeed, during Edward's lifetime, he had quelled, by his valour, whatever wars were excited against him; wishing to signalize himself with his countrymen, and looking forward with anxious hope to the crown. He first vanquished Griffin king of the Welsh, as I have before related,[2] in battle; and, afterwards, when he was again making formidable efforts to recover his power, beheaded him, appointing as his successors, two of his own adherents, that is, the brothers of this Griffin, Blegent, and Riwallo, who had obtained his favour by their submission.

The same year Tosti arrived on the Humber, from Flanders, with a fleet of sixty ships, and infested, with piratical depredations, those parts which were adjacent to the mouth of the river; but being quickly driven from the province by the joint force of the brothers, Edwin and Morchar, he set sail towards Scotland; where meeting with Harold Harvagre[3] king of Norway, then meditating an attack on England with three hundred ships, he put himself under his command. Both, then, with united forces, laid waste the country beyond the Humber; and falling on the brothers, reposing after their recent victory, and suspecting no attack of the kind, they first routed, and then blockaded them in York. Harold, on hearing this, proceeded thither with all his forces, and, each nation making every possible exertion, a bloody encounter followed; but the English obtaining the advantage, put the Norwegians to flight. Yet, (however reluctantly posterity may believe it,) one single Norwegian for a long time delayed the triumph of so many, and such great men. For standing on the entrance of the bridge, which is called Stantford Brigge,[4] after having killed several

vaulx, in his life of Edward, mentions various particulars respecting the origin of this foundation.

[1] The same expression occurs in the Sax. Chron. an. 1065. King Edward died on Thursday the 5th of Jan. 1066, after a reign of twenty-three years, six months, and twenty-seven days.

[2] See § 196.

[3] Harald here (erroneously) named the Fair-haired, called Hardrade (Severus), to distinguish him from Harald Harfagra, who was contemporary with Alfred the Great.

[4] The battle of Stanford Bridge took place on the 25th of Sept. 1066.

of our party, he prevented the whole from passing over. Being
invited to surrender, with the assurance that a man of such
courage should experience the amplest clemency from the English,
he derided those who entreated him; and immediately, with a stern
countenance, reproached them as a set of cowards who were unable
to resist a single individual. No one approaching nearer, as they
thought it unadvisable to come to close-quarters with a man who
had desperately rejected every means of safety, one of the king's
followers aimed an iron javelin at him from a distance; transfixed
with which as he was boastfully flourishing about, and too incau-
tious from his security, he yielded the victory to the English. The
army immediately passing over without opposition, destroyed the
dispersed and flying Norwegians. King Harvagre and Tosti were
slain; the king's son,[1] with all the ships, was kindly sent back to
his own country. Harold, elated by his successful enterprise,
vouchsafed to give no part of the spoil to his soldiers; on which
account many, as they found opportunity, stealing away, deserted
the king, as he was proceeding to the battle of Hastings: for with
the exception of his stipendiary and mercenary soldiers, he had very
few of the people with him.[2] This was the reason why, circumvented by a stratagem of William's, he was routed, with the army
he headed, after possessing the kingdom nine months and some
days. The effect of war in this affair was trifling; it was brought
about by the secret and wonderful counsel of God; since the
Angles never again, in any general battle, made a struggle for
liberty, as if the whole strength of England had fallen in the person
of Harold, who certainly might and deserved to pay the penalty of
his perfidy, even though it were by the instrumentality of the most
unwarlike people. Nor in saying this, do I at all derogate from
the valour of the Normans, to whom I am strongly bound, both by
my descent and for the advantages I enjoy. Still[3] those persons
appear to me to err, who augment the numbers of the English, and
underrate their courage; for while they thus design to extol the
Normans, they in fact degrade them. A mighty commendation
indeed! that a very warlike nation should conquer a set of people
who were obstructed by their multitude, and fearful through
cowardice! On the contrary, they were few in number and brave
in the extreme; and who, throwing aside every regard for their
personal safety, laid down their lives for their country. But,
however, as these matters await a more detailed narrative, I
shall now put a period to my second book, that I may return to
my composition, and my readers to the perusal of it, with fresh
ardour.

[1] His name appears to have been Edmund. (See the Sax. Chron.)
[2] What Malmesbury here relates is highly probable, from the shortness of the
time which elapsed from William's landing, to the battle of Hastings; only
fifteen days. In this period, therefore, the intelligence was to be conveyed to
York, and Harold's march into Sussex to be completed; of course few could
accompany him, but such as were mounted.
[3] Will. Pictaviensis, to whom he seems here to allude, asserts that Harold had
collected immense forces from all parts of England; and that Denmark had supplied him with auxiliaries also. But the circumstances mentioned in the preceding
note shew the absurdity of this statement.

Also published by Llanerch:

A HISTORY OF THE NORMAN KINGS
by William of Malmesbury

A HISTORY OF THE KINGS OF ENGLAND
by Simeon of Durham

A HISTORY OF THE
CHURCH OF DURHAM
by Simeon of Durham

TWO CELTIC SAINTS:
THE LIVES OF NINIAN & KENTIGERN
by Ailred & Joceline

THE BLACK BOOK OF CARMARTHEN
translations by Meirion Pennar

TALIESIN POEMS
translated by Meirion Pennar

SYMBOLISM OF THE CELTIC CROSS
by Derek Bryce

From booksellers.
For a complete list,
write to:
LLANERCH ENTERPRISES,
Felinfach, Lampeter,
Dyfed. SA48 8PJ.

ever use "Britoma" / vs. "Britain"?
why not? what is the relship prop / territory
as efficient war machinery
~t of the church = factual, rather than sacred
                                    miracle
rhetoric as moral problem.
wrong as rhetoric.
geografy - the islaed; now: more intent in Suldarism
            during the 45 krieg. see end of Bk 1.
The writing of history ~ intertwined w/ formation,
    → see descr. of Bede & beginning of Bk 2 / rollwar
                                            himself
do we believe him (as we believe Bede) when
    he says hist extolls the good & condemns the evil?
    wh. is the good / is evil for him? is
    moral / cert god / evil (as in Bede) or pol.?
                                            =
textual culture
The memorable - History
                        → England & its
feuing direct quotation.   ramifications
giving almost equal attention to force and to style.
anxieties by - sexuality of kingself - church hist.
wh. is the role of direct quotations? - character?